A Black Man's Journey from Sharecropper to College President

The Life and Work of
William Johnson Trent,

1873-1963

JUDY SCALES-TRENT

MONROE STREET
PRESS

A Black Man's Journey from Sharecropper to College President:
The Life and Work of William Johnson Trent, 1873-1963

Hardcover Edition ISBN: 978-1942545-46-0
Softcover Edition ISBN: 978-1942545-38-5
eBook ISBN: 978-1942545-41-5

Library of Congress Control Number: 2015959343

F I R S T   E D I T I O N

Students, Huntington Hall (1903)
courtesy of General Research & Reference Division, Schomburg Center
for Research in Black Culture, The New York Public Library, Astor, Lenox
and Tilden Foundation

Teachers and Administrators, Livingstone College, Salisbury, N.C. (1903)
courtesy of General Research & Reference Division, Schomburg Center
for Research in Black Culture, The New York Public Library, Astor, Lenox
and Tilden Foundations

Brass Band of the Young Men's Institute (ca. 1905)
courtesy of Heritage of Black Highlanders Collection, D. H. Ramsey
Library Special Collections, University of North Carolina at Asheville

William J. Trent and Langston Hughes (1950)
courtesy of Livingstone College, Salisbury, N.C.

United Negro College Fund (1963)
courtesy of Linda Anderson Cook and Darian W. Swig; photo by Bill Anderson

Cover Photo ©Rob McElroy 2015

Published by Monroe Street Press,
An Imprint of Wyatt-MacKenzie

MONROE STREET
P R E S S

for my sisters

Kay Trent Holloway
and
Toni Trent Parker

gone too soon

CONTENTS

I care not how dark the night: I believe in the coming of the dawn.

Joseph Charles Price

Introduction

ON A WARM, SUNNY DAY in April 1950, at Livingstone College, a small black school in Salisbury, North Carolina, the entire campus was flowering, as if preparing for a party. The dogwood trees, the redbuds, provided a scaffolding of color; azaleas were everywhere, pink, deep rose, white. And just in time for the festivities, the peonies raised their heavy heads, and bloomed.

Thursday classes had been canceled, and the students were thrilled. The campus had been buzzing for days as everyone prepared for the celebration of William Johnson Trent's twenty-five years as president of the school. They loved their president, they understood his contribution to the school, and they wanted to do him proud.

Julia Battle and Lovelace C. Dillingham were reviewing notes for their orations. Nathaniel Morgan was rehearsing his solo. Parker Bailey was on his way to the flower shop downtown to make sure he would be able to pick up the orchid for Mrs. Trent on time. All the students were busy cleaning their dormitories, as there was going to be an open house of all the dorms. The women in Goler Hall were giving a tea in the afternoon, so they were especially anxious about how their parlor looked. Howard Lynch was going over and over the principal address, which he would give during the celebration program. Should he leave in Plato's quote about the life not examined, or take it out? If you were walking by the auditorium that week, you would have heard the College Choral Union rehearsing the program of spirituals they would present in concert that evening.[1] It gave the students great pleasure to do this, for they knew how much their president loved spirituals. And along with envisioning the students preparing their presentations and cleaning their dormitory, we can imagine the men polishing their shoes, making sure that they had a clean white shirt, and we can picture some of the women looking around frantically to find that other white glove, because a lady did not attend a tea without her hat and gloves, and Livingstone women were expected to be ladies.

As he watched all this activity around him, as he saw the students working so hard to honor him, President Trent, at the age of seventy-six, must have been thinking back—thinking back not only about his past twenty-five years as president, not only about the decades he had spent as a leader in what was then called the "Colored Men's Department" of the Young Men's Christian Association (YMCA, or Y), but thinking way back, back to the beginning, when he was a child being raised by his mother and grandmother, aunt and uncles, all former slaves. Most of those early years were spent on a farm outside of Charlotte where the family had almost nothing—no money, no land, no mules, no house, and not much by way of clothes or household goods. So they worked as sharecroppers, laboring under the burning sun in fields of cotton and corn, year after year, all the while giving three-fifths of their yield to the landowner. What a long journey that had been, from sharecropper to YMCA leader to college president. He must have marveled at a world where a black man could make this journey.

And we too must marvel at his journey and wonder how such a life was possible. William Johnson Trent was my paternal grandfather. When I knew him, he was a college president. It was only recently that I learned of his hard early life. I could not understand how he came such a long way in his life, and I began this research to find the answer.

He was born in Charlotte, North Carolina, in 1873. And what a time that was for black people in the South! Newly freed, they were participating in a social movement of revolutionary proportions. Almost 40 percent of people in the South at the beginning of the Civil War had been enslaved, and now they were free. How would they live? Where would they work? How would they build community? They needed land and houses. They needed churches and schools and social organizations—institutions that structure a society and hold it together. They needed everything.

One reason Trent was able to make the journey from sharecropper to college president was his family's encouragement to get an education and become a leader of his people. Another reason was his own drive and passion, his sense of discipline and hard work, and his determination to never give up. Finally, he was able to make this journey because the black community was rapidly building churches and schools and social organizations when Trent was young, institutions that aimed to teach and guide black youth, strengthen black society, and build leaders. Among these organizations three would be central to Trent's life, in particular, and important in the lives of black people, in general: the African Methodist Episcopal (AME) Zion Church, Livingstone College, and the Colored Men's Department of the YMCA. By the time Trent left the farm these three institutions were active in western North Carolina, ready to encourage, support, and guide him. He would spend his life helping keep these institutions alive. This book, then, although about one person, is also about institution building in the black community between the end of the Civil War and the middle of the twentieth century.

Black people created the AME Zion Church in New York City in 1796, as a response to the racism of their white co-religionists, who would not allow them to play a full role within the Methodist Episcopal Church. Toward the end of the Civil War, in 1863, AME Zion leaders sent a missionary, Rev. James Walker Hood, to North Carolina to develop the church there for freed men and women, who were hungry to finally have their own churches, hungry to be able to hear and be guided by black preachers.[2]

Freed people were also desperate for schools. In 1830, the North Carolina legislature made it a crime to teach slaves to read.[3] So, by the end of the Civil War, not only were these newly freed people without an education, but also there were not enough educated black people in North Carolina to teach them. This led the state to begin to create normal schools to train black teachers as early as 1877.[4] It also led to an important migration as black and white men and women in the North moved south to set up schools and teach the freed people.

Many churches built schools and provided financial support for these teachers. Between 1866 and 1873, white churches created five schools for black students in North Carolina, schools that went beyond the elementary school level: Shaw University (Baptist), Bennett College (Methodist Episcopal), Scotia Seminary and Biddle University (Presbyterian), and St. Augustine (Episcopalian).[5]

The AME Zion Church understood that it was education that would put black people on the path to full citizenship. And so it is not surprising that it began to create schools. In 1882 it became the first black church to build a school in North Carolina that provided instruction beyond the elementary school level, when it built Livingstone College—an institution that included a grammar school, a normal school, a school of theology, and a college. Because the AME Zion Church was independent, it was free to decide what kind of education to offer, and made bold decisions—the decision to have only black teachers and administrators, the decision to provide a classical liberal curriculum, and the decision to offer this classical education to women students, for Livingstone's goal was to develop the full potential of all its students. At a time when many schools for black people were offering only the most basic elementary and industrial classes, when most of the black colleges had only white teachers and administrators, and when women were excluded from classical education, these were audacious moves by an independent black church and its independent school.

A young minister in the church, Joseph C. Price, became the first president of Livingstone, at the age of twenty-eight.[6] It was a time when black organizations were creating leaders as fast as they could, and youth was no bar to leadership.

This was also a time when black communities were developing and financing their own YMCAs. The goal of the Ys during this period was to provide a healthy, inspiring place where young men moving from the countryside to the cities could gather for guidance, for Bible study, for literacy classes, for sports, for housing, even for baths. And people were moving to North Carolina cities in droves. In 1880 only one city in the state had more than 10,000 inhabitants; by 1900, there were six cities of that size.[7] The Colored Men's Department of the national YMCA was trying to find leaders for these city Ys at the black colleges. There was a student YMCA group at Livingstone as early as 1883.[8]

The YMCA was not black controlled at the top leadership level, as were the AME Zion Church and Livingstone, but on the ground the YMCA was a black space, controlled by black Y leaders. These men took their job seriously, understanding that they were working to develop strong young men of character, thus providing support for the black community.

All three of these spaces then—the black church, the black school, the black YMCA—provided islands of safety for members of the black community, a place to debate the issues of the day, and a place to learn and to grow. These institutions also built national networks of their members and alumni, networks that would provide both community and support far into the future.

The story of Trent's life is the story of his study and work within these institutions. He spent eight years at Livingstone as a student in the grammar and normal schools, then in college. He was a Y leader for the Third North Carolina Volunteer Infantry, a black unit with black officers, during the Spanish-American War. He then went to Asheville, North Carolina, where he led the Young Men's Institute (YMI), an organization created by white millionaire George Vanderbilt for the black men who were helping construct his home, the Biltmore Estate. The YMI, which was much like a YMCA, soon became part of the Colored Men's Department of the national Y. Trent then led the Asheville Y, after which he became director of the black YMCA in Atlanta. After spending twenty-six years as one of the most important pioneer black Y leaders, Trent returned to Livingstone College, a black church school and his alma mater, where he served as president for the next thirty-two years. At three times in his life—when the Young Men's Institute, the Atlanta YMCA, and Livingstone College were foundering—Trent was called in to take a leadership role and turn the organizations around. He succeeded all three times. Trent's life work was thus influenced both by the Social Gospel Movement, which pushed for an active Christianity promoting the teachings of Jesus in the larger society, and by the Progressive Movement, which aimed not only to reform American society, but also to transform Americans themselves.

This biography describes Trent's leadership role on the ground, as he develops programs and raises money to rebuild these institutions and keep them functioning and thriving. We will see him in Asheville, planning activities for black men and boys and renting out space in the YMI building to support those programs. We will see how he works with the churches in Atlanta to raise the money to construct the Butler Street Y in that city. At Livingstone College we will see him working with various constituencies— faculty and students, the board of trustees, bishops in the AME Zion Church, and the accrediting agencies. As we learn about his life, then, we will be reading about the development of several important black organizations of the time.

An examination of Trent's life as he moved within these institutions also shows us how a specific group of men in the black middle class at this time networked, both to build leaders and to maintain these black organizations. We will see this networking in Trent's generation, and we will also see second-generation networking in the life of his son, William Johnson Trent Jr., who would spend decades trying to raise money for black schools.

After the depression in the 1930s and 1940s, as black colleges and universities were struggling to keep their doors open, the president of Tuskegee Institute, Frederick D. Patterson, suggested that the schools try to raise money as a group instead of competing with each other for funding. This led twenty-seven presidents of black colleges—including Trent Sr.—to create the United Negro College Fund (UNCF, or Fund), a consortium of twenty-seven black schools and the first cooperative fundraising venture of educational institutions in the country. Thus, this biography shows Trent Sr. helping create a new black institution at the same time that he was working hard to maintain and develop Livingstone College.

The presidents of these schools selected Trent Jr. to be the first executive director of the Fund. This choice made sense: he had graduated from a black college, he had taught at black colleges, and he had a master's degree in business administration. But he was also selected for this position because he lived within a network of two generations of black men who knew both father and son: Trent Sr.'s president colleagues, some of whom had been Y leaders at the same time as he, and a few of Trent Jr.'s friends from his youth, who had since become presidents of black schools. This book thus spans intergenerational strategies.

Trent Sr. was one of the founders of the United Negro College Fund, and Livingstone College was one of the first schools to join the Fund. So in this book we see father and son working together—as college president and as director of the UNCF—to find financial support for both Livingstone and the other schools in the Fund. In an important sense, then, Trent Jr. was continuing his father's work—his love for, and his commitment to, this one black school, Livingstone College. The task of Bill Trent (as Trent Jr. was known) was to expand this commitment to all the black colleges in the Fund and to move the issue of their survival to the national stage.

Finally, this book is not only about building institutions and creating leaders in the black community. This biography of William Johnson Trent also provides an intimate portrait of the life of one black man—born in the first generation after emancipation—from 1873 to the middle of the twentieth century, from Reconstruction to the boycotts and sit-ins of the 1950s and 1960s. It describes his journey from the farm to a leadership position in the black middle class, and describes, as well, this world he came to inhabit. The eight years he spent as a student at Livingstone were transformative years. The book therefore spends some time on this period, describing his studies, his friends and activities, the work he did to put himself through school, and the faculty members who inspired him. Through correspondence and business records, as well as through interviews with family, family friends, and former Livingstone students and teachers, we will also come to know him through his marriages and his losses, his friends and his children, his love of music and his love of books.

This work thus contributes to our understanding of how some in the postslavery generation of black people lived their lives, using education to move from the farm to the middle class and working to improve the lives of other African Americans. It also adds to our understanding of the day-to-day work of the head of black organizations like Asheville's Young Men's Institute, the black sections of the Young Men's Christian Association, and small black colleges. Finally, this book helps us understand how Trent's generation of black leaders raised the following generation for positions of national leadership.

William Johnson Trent Sr.'s generation moved through many changes—from the struggle for survival immediately after emancipation, to the struggle for the right to vote, to segregation and the loss of the vote, then to the nonviolent protest movement of the 1950s and 1960s. All this took place within the continuing threat, and the reality, of white violence. But during this dangerous time the black community was building important institutions that helped black people, in general—and helped Trent, in particular, move out into the world as a young man. He anchored himself in these institutions—the AME Zion Church, Livingstone College, the YMI and the black YMCA—and through them was able to build a useful life guiding and supporting black youth, thus developing a stronger black society.

Throughout his life, as he worked for black youth and the black community, William Johnson Trent was always hopeful. Like Livingstone's first president, Joseph Charles Price, he believed "in the coming of the dawn." His deep belief in racial "uplift" through the Y, in the Christian faith, and in education might well have seemed out of date to the young civil rights protesters of the 1950s and 1960s. But the men and women of Trent's generation had used the best tools available to them at the time, and this constellation of beliefs, held by so many in that group, had itself formed a long civil rights movement.

Chapter 1

Freedom's New Generation:
The Early Years

PEOPLE SAID THE WAR WAS OVER. People said they were free. They heard the news from black people walking down the road, from Union soldiers riding by on their horses, perhaps from the slave master himself. And so they left. Thousands and thousands of freedmen, freedwomen, and their children, they left those farms and plantations where they had planted and thinned the corn, where they had weeded and picked the cotton. They walked out of the sheds where they were hanging tobacco, dropping leaves along the way; they walked out of the watery rice fields where they had been building dikes. Men who were tapping pine trees for gum walked out of the forest and kept on walking.

Some left on horses or mules, others in wagons; some traveled in boats and canoes; others crowded the railroad stations. But many just walked. They packed clothing and blankets in cloth sacks, piled pots and pans and chickens on their backs, and they walked—a man over here with a hoe across his shoulder; a woman down the road with a baby strapped across her back, holding a small child by the hand. They walked to look for family members who had been sold away; they walked to find work—their own work this time—and a new home. And they walked away, and kept on walking, simply because they were free, finally free, and if freedom meant anything at all, it must have meant that they could go out into the world and leave the people who had said they could *not* leave.

But newly freed people were not the only ones traveling. It must have seemed like the whole world was on the move—wounded soldiers heading toward hospitals, Union soldiers heading north, Confederate soldiers wending their way back home, Freedman's Bureau agents moving into southern towns, white families returning to the homes they had abandoned at the approach of Union soldiers. Also on the move were black and white missionaries and educators from the North, traveling south to build churches and create schools. They were hoping to find a way to help 4 million Africans and African Americans, people who had been held in bondage for over 300 years.

This first chapter is about two groups of those travelers. We begin with Harriet Massey and her family, freed people who moved from rural North Carolina to Charlotte, North Carolina, then back to the countryside, as they tried to find a way to survive after emancipation. The second group includes those black ministers and educators in the North who moved to North Carolina after the war to develop the African Methodist Episcopal (AME) Zion Church and to create a new school for black people, Livingstone College.

It is when these two groups of travelers come together—when members of Harriet Massey's family meet ministers and educators from Livingstone College—that we begin to see what will ultimately become the transformation of both the family and the school itself. These meetings, repeated hundreds of times across the South in the first years of freedom, strengthened African American culture and helped sustain freed people.

After the war, when they finally understood that they were really free, many enslaved people left the people and places that marked their oppression. Some had already escaped long before the war was over: tens of thousands followed the Union army, where, they hoped, they would be safe.[1] But no matter when they left, they would have likely taken the time to talk it over with families and friends, to make plans, to gather provisions for the trip. They would have taken the time to think about what they might face if they left the world they knew, to start over in a new, unfathomable world. Where would they go? Would they be able to find work? to feed their families? Would the white people they met along the way be more dangerous than the white people they already knew? And indeed, all the newly freed men and women did not leave the places where they had been held in bondage. Some remained because of fear of the unknown, and some remained because of their ties to elderly family members who could no longer travel, ties to a community of support, ties to the land they had worked so many years, ties to the familiar, including sometimes even the slave-owner family.

For those who left, as they traveled, along the way they saw desolation: overturned wagons, burned houses, dead animals, bridges and fences destroyed, cotton gins and farm buildings burned to the ground, crops rotting in the fields. So many white men had been conscripted into the Confederate army, so many slaves had already left farms and plantations, that there had not been enough workers to tend the farms. And as Union forces traveled through the South during the final years of the war, they had destroyed anything white Southerners might use to keep a farm going and feed the Confederate army.

And this is where our story begins, with a woman and her children, who had lived and worked as slaves on a plantation in Union County, North Carolina, near the small town of Waxhaw, right on the South Carolina border—newly freed people who left that plantation behind them and headed north.[2] Harriet Massey, the mother, was born in the Carolinas, probably in the 1830s.[3] We know very little about her, but we do know that her parents were born in the United States.[4] And we know that, in 1870, she had four children, all of whom had been born in South Carolina: Ben

Miller, who was ten; Malinda Johnson, seven; George Johnson, age four; and Belle Miller, the baby, who was two.[5]

Black people in South Carolina grew cotton. In 1811, they produced half the cotton of the entire country. By the 1820s cotton production had spread north to southern North Carolina, where it was becoming an important crop.[6] Since Harriet Massey was living in South Carolina when she gave birth to her children, and since Union County, North Carolina, was on the border with South Carolina, we might imagine that she and her children worked in cotton fields on a plantation when they were slaves.

Compared with the rest of the South, there had not been many slaveholders in North Carolina. In 1860 only 28 percent of families in the state had any slaves at all, and, of those families, two-thirds had fewer than ten slaves.[7] But this does not mean that slavery was more benign in North Carolina than it was elsewhere. Slaveholders still beat, whipped, and killed enslaved men and women with impunity. One of the few facts we know about Harriet Massey is that she had large, ugly welts all over her back, scars made when a white overseer beat her with a whip.[8] It is the presence of an overseer that suggests that she had been enslaved on a plantation. And it is the presence of whip marks on her back that reminds us of the brutality of slavery.

Slave owners often manipulated the marriage choices of their slaves—sometimes for economic reasons, sometimes out of mere whim.[9] Harriet Massey, while enslaved, had been forced into "plural marriages," one relationship after the other.[10] Alexander Crummell, a leading black intellectual of the era, described the tragedy of such a system: "She [any black woman under slavery] and her husband and children were all the property of others. All these sacred ties were constantly snapped and cruelly sundered. This year she had one husband; and next year, through some auction sale, she might be separated from him and mated to another. There was no sanctity of family, no binding tie of marriage."[11]

This painful history may explain why we will see different surnames for Harriet and her children after emancipation—

Massey, Miller, and Johnson. The children might have chosen the surname of their birth father, or the father who raised them, and Harriet might have taken the name of the husband she chose for herself.

Whether right after emancipation or later, when Harriet and her children moved out into the world as free people, they headed northwest. By 1870 they were living in Charlotte, North Carolina, some twenty-four miles from Waxhaw. Like most newly freed men and women, they didn't travel far from the place where they had been held in bondage. Also, like many newly freed people, they moved to cities.

Having lost close ties with each other when they left plantations, black people hoped to re-create that community in cities. They also moved to cities to find work and, as well, to have easier access to black social institutions, like schools and churches.[12] As early as May 1865, the black community in Charlotte created the Clinton AME Zion Chapel, its first postwar institution. Freed people also moved to cities hoping to find protection through the Freedmen's Bureau. In Charlotte, the Bureau had established a camp and hospital for freed people and sometimes distributed clothing and rations to the poorest in that group.[13]

Charlotte had survived the war relatively unscathed. Because it had not lost all its rail lines during the war, it was able to maintain commercial links with both the interior of the state and the Atlantic coast. Cotton trade was the key to recovery, attracting merchants and stores. The city filled rapidly with white people impoverished by the war, wounded soldiers, federal agents from the Freedmen's Bureau, federal troops, and freed men and women.[14] In 1860, there were only 800 black people in Charlotte; ten years later that number had increased by 1,000.[15]

When Harriet Massey and her children arrived in Charlotte, they would have found a busy, noisy city, a city in the middle of a trade boom fueled by cotton. They would have seen the cotton district, with its warehouses and its buildings for cotton sales; farmers driving wagons loaded with cotton to the municipal cotton compress; railroad tracks and railroad cars that created a lot of noise and a lot of soot, bringing goods into the city and carrying cotton out. And there was "the Square," with shops and taverns crowding around it. The city also had hotels and a courthouse, as well as signs of development like gas lamps, a fire engine, and newspapers. Rich merchants and poor workers, black and white, all lived in the city alongside the shops: there was not yet a residential area. There was also not yet a black area.[16] Although there were some black settlements, blacks were not limited to living in those areas, as they would be later.[17] By the early 1870s, however, restaurants, saloons, the opera house, and public schools had been segregated.[18]

But black people had more choices than public schools. By 1870 there were at least 30 schools for black people in Charlotte, with approximately 700 students. Presbyterians and Quaker missionaries, and charitable institutions from the North, had created some of these schools, but freed people had created many on their own.[19]

In 1870, seven years after emancipation, black people in Charlotte were still doing traditional "black work." Over 86 percent worked in unskilled jobs. Eleven percent were skilled workers, and there were very few black professionals—only 3 teachers and 2 ministers. Of the 406 black women listed as employed in the 1870 census, only 5 were working in skilled jobs, and all of them were seamstresses. The rest were servants, farmworkers, laundresses, and cooks.[20]

So we are not surprised to learn that, in 1870, Harriet Massey and her family, coming out of slavery, were doing "black work." Harriet took in laundry and her daughter Malinda, at the age of fourteen, was a servant.[21] Ben, at seventeen, was a farmworker, and George, the younger brother, eleven years old, was a hostler, probably helping care for the horses at a local inn. And in a sign of the great hopes of the family, the 1870 Census also tells us that George had managed to attend school within the year, and that the youngest child, Belle, at the age of nine, was attending school.[22]

Harriet's work, doing laundry, was back-breaking and dangerous. It was dangerous because whether making soap from lye, building a fire, washing clothes in a tub of scalding hot water, or carrying bucket after bucket of water to and from the fire, she risked being burned by the lye, the hot water, and the fire. And it was back-breaking because just doing one load of wash with one boiling and one rinse took about 50 gallons of water. That meant that she had to carry 400 pounds of water from the pump or the well or the stream, to the tub, for each wash. And once the clothing and linens were in the tub, she had to scrub, lift, and wring out these items, which were weighed down by the water. It was hard enough to do this with clothing, but the wash would have also included large items like tablecloths and sheets. And she would do it over and over again: scrubbing, rinsing, scrubbing and rinsing again, wringing out, wringing dry; dipping clothes into starch, hanging them on the clothes line, taking them down; and then the ironing, with heavy irons heated over the fire, irons weighing eight to ten pounds, heavy irons preferred because they "made the work go faster."[23] It is not surprising to learn that washerwomen ended their day with "aching backs and hands too tender to sew."[24]

This was a terribly hard job. But it was a job that allowed women to work at home and care for children, one that provided some protection from sexual harassment and abuse—thus a job that held some attraction for poor women. Many women who preferred to work independently did laundry work.[25] This must have been even more important to freed women like Harriet, desperate to get away from constant white oversight and control.

And we shouldn't forget that at the same time that she was fetching water, boiling water, washing clothes, hanging up clothes, and ironing clothes for others, Harriet Massey was also doing the laundry for her own household, doing household chores, and watching over any young children in the family.

While Massey was taking in laundry, her fourteen-year old daughter, Malinda, worked as a servant, very likely for a white person or family. We don't know if she lived at home and went to work daily, or if she lived with the family she served, returning home perhaps one day a week. But if she had her choice, she would surely have wanted to work regular hours and live at home in order to have more control over her work, more independence, and more time with family. Her work would have likely included not only cleaning the house, but also doing the laundry and preparing three meals a day over an open hearth in the kitchen fireplace.[26] The fireplace was its own source of work, because the servant had to tend the fire all day to keep it hot, and sometimes even chop the firewood and carry it into the house.[27] Even if people were using coal in stoves in Charlotte in the 1870s to heat the home, she would have still had to tend the fire[28] and, as well, clean the soot and smoke from oil lamps.[29] Malinda would have been on her feet all day: cooking, cleaning, caring for children, tending the fire. Her tasks would have also included bringing fresh water into the house for cooking, bathing, cleaning, washing dishes, and doing laundry, and carrying out dirty bathwater, dirty dishwater, and the contents of chamber pots.[30]

If freed people in Charlotte had time and energy left over after work, they could have engaged in social activities centered on the church, fraternal and sororal organizations, and mutual aid societies: the Odd Fellows and the Prince Hall Masons were very popular groups in Charlotte in the 1870s.[31] Black men created these two fraternities as soon as the fraternal orders crossed the Atlantic from England in the late eighteenth and early nineteenth centuries.[32] Women had their own parallel organizations: the Household of Ruth was formed within the Odd Fellows in 1857, and the Order of the Eastern Star was formed within the Masons in 1874.[33]

These organizations provided funeral and death benefits as well as benefits when members were sick and couldn't work. But their benefits were more than monetary for they also provided safe spaces where members could experiment with leadership roles free of racism.[34] These organizations soon expanded to include social activities. Members organized parades, sponsored excursions to lodges in other towns, and welcomed guests from those lodges, thus creating a wider network of support.[35]

Harriet Massey's family might have also attended the special celebrations organized by the black community throughout the South, on the Fourth of July, as well as on January First, "Emancipation Day," to celebrate the day Lincoln signed the Emancipation Proclamation.[36] For this event, there was often a parade of the black organizations in the community. Those waiting for the parade to appear might have first heard a brass band, then, finally, might have seen the parade marching down the street, and behind it, people carrying the U.S. flag, a militia company, the fire company, and other black social organizations. Then the spectators would have followed the parade to the courthouse to hear speeches, sermons, and the reading of the Emancipation Proclamation.[37]

On December 30, 1873, when she was about seventeen years old, Malinda gave birth to a son, whom she named William Captain George Washington Trent.[38] The name seems strange to us today, but it was not uncommon at the time for black children born after Emancipation to be named after a white person who exemplified in some way the idea of freedom, and many African Americans considered George Washington the "ideal American."[39] Harriet Massey had great hopes for her grandson, who represented for her the hope of the Negro race.[40] Naming him "George Washington" was therefore an understandable choice.

The baby's father, Edward Lawrence Trant, was white. Born in 1847, he was raised in a wealthy slaveholding family in King William County, Virginia. In 1860 his widowed mother, Mildred, reported that she had forty-eight slaves, real estate with a value of $12,000, and a personal estate worth $25,000.[41] But during the first two years of the Civil War, in King William County, almost half the male slaves between the ages of eighteen and forty-five escaped, so Trant's family was surely becoming poor very quickly.[42] Edward joined the Confederate army in 1864, when he was seventeen.[43] Six years later, we find him in Charlotte working as a salesman and living with his older brother John, who had a candy store.[44]

It is not hard to imagine how Malinda and Edward might have met. They might have seen each other in a store; they might have passed each other on a street or on a road, out in the countryside; indeed, Malinda might have been a servant for the Trant brothers. The question that comes quickly to mind, however, is not so much how they met but the nature of their relationship. One immediately thinks of many white men who raped black women with impunity during the long years of slavery in this country. But when William was conceived, Malinda was not a slave. She and Edward were both free, and young, with all the beauty and hormonal energy of youth, and perhaps very attracted to each other.

North Carolina prohibited interracial marriage at this time.[45] But even as antimiscegenation laws tell us about the opposition to interracial unions, they also remind us that many white women and black men, black women and white men, were so attracted to each other that they wanted to marry and spend their lives together, despite the social opprobrium. So it is not impossible to think that at one point this young man and woman had some affection for each other.[46]

At a certain point Edward abandoned Malinda and their child. Before this disruption in their life, young William lived with his mother; afterward, he had to go live with his grandmother.[47] As a laundress working at home, Harriet would be able to work and take care of a growing child at the same time.

The fact that William had to go live with his grandmother after his father's desertion indicates that Malinda and the baby had been living elsewhere before they were abandoned. It also tells us that before this event Malinda had been able to take care of herself and her child, but that afterwards her life was so disrupted that she could no longer do that. This suggests, then, that Edward had provided some financial support to Malinda and the baby for a while and that after he withdrew it Malinda had to reconstruct her life. She very likely went to work as a live-in servant.

We don't know how long after William's birth Edward abandoned them. Was it long enough for the child to know his father, and miss him? Whatever the relationship between Edward and Malinda and their son, it is somehow telling that despite the abandonment, Malinda Johnson was willing to give the name "Trent" to her son, and that her son, even as he grew to be a man, was willing to keep it.[48]

There had been much confusion about the surnames of black people during slavery, and even after. Sometimes the slave owner refused to allow a slave to take a surname; sometimes the slave took one anyhow. Sometimes a slave owner refused to allow a slave to use the owner's family name, considering it a taint on his family honor. Others wanted their slaves to have their surname, as a way of marking their property.[49]

Freedom would cast a new light on this issue. Former slaves could now choose their own names, and changed them with ease. A free woman could now name her own child. And perhaps, after all the confusion surrounding names during slavery, it was a relief to have no confusion here. Despite the fact that the father abandoned his child, despite what must have been her anger at this act, by keeping the name Trent, Malinda could well have just been saying: "This man was your father; take his name."[50]

Malinda's family might well have been very excited about this birth, perhaps the first birth of a free child in the family. Certainly William's birth was of great importance to his grandmother. But it may have also reminded them of the dangerous times in which they lived: how could they raise this child safely to manhood? And well might they wonder, for immediately after emancipation there had been widespread violence—a wave of counterrevolutionary terror against black people. As one historian wrote: "How many black men and women were beaten, flogged, mutilated, and murdered in the first years of emancipation will never be known. Nor could any accurate body count [...] reveal the barbaric savagery and depravity that so frequently characterized the assaults made on freedmen [...] the severed ears and entrails, the mutilated sex organs, the burnings at the stake, the forced drownings, the open display of skulls and severed limbs as trophies."[51]

The Ku Klux Klan was very active in North Carolina in the early 1870s, and particularly active in the Piedmont area, where Charlotte is located.[52] Klan leaders were the most prominent white men in the state: state legislators, sheriffs and their deputies, wealthy farmers, and judges.[53] To maximize the terror, they generally rode at night, disguised, confronting freed people at their homes, often while they were asleep. They would then call for someone inside to come out, or simply drag the person outside, to be beaten, raped, or murdered.[54] This barbarism would last a long time in the collective memory of the black community.

In 1871, Congress enacted the Ku Klux Klan Act, which gave federal district attorneys the authority to prosecute certain civil rights violations if the states failed to protect black citizens. It also authorized the president to send federal troops into states to control the violence, and to suspend the writ of habeas corpus. After the law was passed, the federal government began the prosecution of Klansmen in earnest. President Grant sent federal troops into North Carolina, and hundreds of Klansmen were indicted. By 1872 federal intervention had led to a decline in violence in the South.[55]

But although violence may have declined, it did not stop. And no matter where the violence took place, reports of white cruelty and barbarism would resonate in black communities throughout the South. In North Carolina, Harriet Massey and her family would have certainly heard about what came to be known as "the Colfax massacre," which took place in Louisiana the year of William's birth. In early 1873, the black people who lived in Grant Parish, Louisiana, defending what they considered the lawful victory of the Republican Party for local office, and fearing that white Fusionists might take over, took up arms and took control of the town of Colfax. On Easter Sunday, three weeks later, they were overpowered by a much larger group of armed white men.[56] By the end of the day, many black people lay dead.[57] This event, called "the bloodiest single act of carnage in all of Reconstruction," would serve as a constant reminder to black people that the white reign of terror would not stop.[58]

At the same time that freed people in the South were moving out of slavery, traveling, testing the limits of freedom; at the same time that Harriet Massey and her family were moving to Charlotte, trying to figure out how to live in a city, how to earn enough money for food, shelter, and clothing, how to stay safe from the violence of the white community; at this very same time, hundreds of black ministers and educators from the North were traveling south, hoping to help their newly freed brothers and sisters. Among this group was a handful of educated black men, members of the AME Zion Church, whose lives, once they reached North Carolina, would intersect with the lives of members of Harriet Massey's family. As we will see, their work during these years would eventually have a great impact on young William's life.

The AME Zion Church was created in New York City in 1796, when black members of the city's Methodist churches were no longer willing to accept the limitations imposed on them by their white fellow church members.[59] This newly formed church sent out missionaries to spread its beliefs, and soon had churches throughout the North, and in Canada and the West Indies as well.[60] Church members were deeply concerned about their brothers and sisters held in bondage in the South. They were also deeply involved in the abolition movement, and helped hide slaves who had escaped. Thus the AME Zion Church was engaged in the social activism promoted by the Social Gospel Movement long before the Civil War.[61]

Toward the end of the Civil War, the church decided it was time to send missionaries south. Under the leadership of Eliza Ann Gardner, the New England Conference of the church raised enough money for this endeavor.[62] In 1864, the church sent Rev. James Walker Hood from his pastorate in Connecticut to North Carolina, to develop the AME Zion community in the Union-occupied part of that state. He soon arrived in New Bern, a small city in the eastern part of the state, only twenty-eight miles from the headquarters of the Confederate army. Two battles of the Civil

War were fought at New Bern while he was there. Thus, he literally began his work under fire.

Hood established the first AME Zion Church in the South, and the denomination spread rapidly throughout the state from east to west, attracting new members as it went.[63] For example, when Hood was appointed to the AME Zion church in Fayetteville in 1866, there were only 78 members. Three years later, there were 500 members.[64]

Freed men and women in the South were hungry for churches where they could practice their religion free from racism, and for black ministers to lead them. But it might be possible that their hunger for education was even greater.

In 1830, as whites in North Carolina began to get anxious about the ever-growing abolition movement, they enacted a statute "to prevent all persons from teaching slaves to read or write." A white person who violated the law could be fined or imprisoned; a slave who tried to teach a fellow slave to read or write would face "thirty-nine lashes on his or her bare back."[65] But slaves still learned. Sometimes white children taught them what they were learning in school; often a slave who knew how to read taught the others. Sundays were often important "school" days, for these were the days when the slave owner and his family left their home to go to church and socialize, and slaves were not required to work.[66] They could then teach each other and study without fear of retribution.

At the end of the war, the North Carolina State Board of Education appointed Rev. Hood assistant superintendent of public instruction, to supervise the public school education of black children.[67] The following year he reported that he had identified 152 black schools in the state, with 11,826 pupils. The Freedmen's Bureau and the American Missionary Association had created 19 of those schools; Quakers, Episcopalians, and Presbyterians had built another 51. There were also 82 other private schools.[68] We don't know who created these schools, but we do know that freed people often pooled their money to buy land and lumber to build schoolhouses, and built them with their unpaid labor. They paid a salary to the teacher, and often boarded them too.[69] When they didn't build schools, they created "schools" everywhere—in churches, in sheds, in stables, or in homes.[70] And no matter what the age, black people went to school. Grandparents sat next to their grandchildren; women came with their babies.[71]

Freed people's hunger for an education was real and great, but since so many southern states had prohibited teaching slaves to read and write, there were not enough teachers in the South for all the black people who wanted to learn. Many white educators came south to teach the freed people, but by and large black people were in charge of their own education. Thus we find not only black missionaries, but also black educators, heading south after the war. And they came in droves.

Although blacks in the North were only 2 percent of the northern population in 1870, they were twelve times as likely to travel south to teach in southern black schools as were whites from the North. This is striking data, made even more striking since black and white people in the North didn't have equal access to a good education: in 1870, the black illiteracy rate in the North was three to six times as great as the white illiteracy rate. Considering this, one historian concludes that "it would be more accurate to say that northern blacks were fifteen times more likely to have taught in the freed peoples' schools than were northern whites." Black teachers from the North also taught in southern schools longer than did white northern teachers.[72] By the early 1870s, most white northern teachers had returned home.[73]

Among this group of educated black men and women who traveled south to teach were the Harris brothers, Cicero and Robert, both graduates of the Cleveland High School.[74] In 1866, we find them in Fayetteville, in eastern North Carolina, the most highly populated area of the state and the area with the largest black population, where they taught at the Howard School, a Freedmen's Bureau school. The brothers were soon joined by their niece and nephew, also from Cleveland, brother and sister Alexander and Victoria Richardson.[75]

During this same period, the North Carolina Conference of the AME Zion Church was trying to develop its institution by creating schools; more specifically, a theological and collegiate institution. Church leaders had initially planned to build this school in Fayetteville.[76] But in 1877, almost as soon as they developed this plan, the North Carolina legislature took over the Howard School to create its first normal school for African Americans, and named Robert Harris principal.[77] In order to avoid competition with this school, then, the AME Zion Church decided to create its school in Concord, in the western part of the state. The school would be named Zion Wesley Institute. Rev. Hood was elected president of the board of trustees.[78]

Zion Wesley's first school session began in December 1879, in a church parsonage, with three students and four teachers. One of the teachers, and the new principal, was Cicero Harris.[79] Indeed, by this time Harris had become a minister in the AME Zion Church, and the church parsonage was his home.[80] The other teachers were Harris's niece and nephew, Victoria and Alexander Richardson; and his wife, Elizabeth Goin Harris.[81] The second session began in November 1880 with twenty-three students.[82] Unfortunately, despite great efforts to raise money for the school, the church was so unsuccessful that it suspended operation of the school in 1881.[83] But it did not give up its dream.

At the same time that the AME Zion Church was trying to create a school in western North Carolina, Joseph Charles Price, a member of that church and a student at Lincoln University in Pennsylvania, was dreaming of a new kind of school for black people. Price was born in 1854 in Elizabeth City, North Carolina, nine years before emancipation. He had never been a slave because, although his father was a slave, his mother was free.[84] As a child he attended Sunday school at an AME Zion Church in New Bern, North Carolina, where he met Rev. Hood. Hood immediately saw something remarkable in the boy. He followed Price's development over the years, and ultimately helped finance his education.[85]

At Lincoln, Price talked with fellow schoolmate and childhood friend Edward Moore about his dream of a new school for black people. He also discussed it with William Goler, who was a year ahead of him at Lincoln.[86] Goler, a Canadian, had started out in life as an apprentice bricklayer and plasterer, and worked in the building trades for three years in Boston until he had enough money to go to school.[87] Price asked Moore and Goler if they would join him in creating the school he envisioned.[88] It would be a new kind of school—a school created and controlled by black people. The classical education he received at Lincoln also influenced his vision. The curriculum at Lincoln University was patterned on the curriculum at Princeton, and the new school he wanted to create would be "a daughter of Lincoln University."[89] Thus, it would offer a classical curriculum too. As he later stated: "If we are men let us be educated as men. If thorough education is good for Whites, it is good for Blacks."[90]

Upon graduation, these three friends went their separate ways. Moore delivered the salutatory in Latin during his graduation ceremony in 1875, then became principal of Wilson Academy in Wilson, North Carolina.[91] Goler graduated as valedictorian of his class, and stayed on to receive a degree in theology at Lincoln University Seminary. After his studies he moved to Greensboro, then Winston, North Carolina, to pastor churches.[92]

In 1879, Price too graduated as valedictorian from Lincoln University's college, then continued his studies at that school's Theology Department. While still a student, he was ordained deacon and elder by Bishop Hood, and was licensed to preach: Price was rising rapidly in the church.[93]

In September 1881, after his graduation from the Department of Theology, he attended a Methodist ecumenical conference in London with Bishop Hood. At the conference, his superb oratory led the *London Times* to name him "The World Orator." Because of Price's skill as a speaker, Bishop Hood asked him to stay in England for a year and give speeches in order to raise at least $10,000 for the Zion Wesley Institute. Price agreed to stay.[94]

While Price was traveling around England, giving speeches about the dream of this school, church leaders in North Carolina continued trying to develop it. Cicero Harris proposed that Zion Wesley Institute be moved from Concord to Salisbury, some thirty miles away, for it was better situated with respect to railroad lines. This would make the school more accessible, thus more attractive, to teachers, students, and visitors.[95] The new principal of Zion Wesley, Alexander Richardson, then persuaded the white citizens of Salisbury that it would be to their advantage to have the school move to Salisbury. They were in such agreement that they donated $1,000 to the church for the move.[96] The first name on the list of donors was Moses Holmes, Salisbury's white mayor.[97]

Looking back, it seems quite surprising that the white leaders in this small southern town would be so interested in bringing a black school to town that they would offer money for the move. The first reason must have been economic: the school would have to buy provisions; faculty members would one day be building homes, setting up households, and buying furnishings; students would be looking to purchase school supplies, books, food, perhaps clothing. There was money to be made.[98] Another likely reason was the influence of blacks in the town. It took decades for whites in North Carolina to succeed in controlling newly franchised black voters after the Civil War. "As late as the mid-1890s, blacks in [...] North Carolina [...] were turning out for elections at rates at or above 50 percent."[99] And in the early 1880s, there were almost as many eligible black voters in Salisbury as there were adult white males. Indeed, in the election of 1883, when Republicans in Salisbury swept the vote, the main reason for their victory was the black vote.[100] So it was very likely a combination of factors—competition with neighboring cities, the desire for money, and the realities of the black vote—that led white leaders to want this black school in their town: money and power, an unbeatable combination.

But this is also a reminder that the white community in the South, like the black one, was not a monolith. Just as there were pockets of whites known to be so hostile to African Americans as to be dangerous, so too were there communities of whites who were not. The Quaker community, sixty miles from Salisbury in the Greensboro area, was one example.[101] There were surely more. We will understand the meaning behind this invitation and this gift better as we watch how the white community in Salisbury treats its black neighbors at Livingstone over the years.

Price returned from England a year later with about $10,000.[102] He persuaded church leaders to change the name of the school to Livingstone College.[103] The church paid $4,600 for thirty-eight acres of land right outside Salisbury, only a fifteen-minute walk to the business district. On the land there was a very big house, with ten large and several small rooms. There were, as well, outbuildings and a garden.[104] In 1882 the school moved to Salisbury, and Price was elected president of Livingstone College.[105] By this time there were already five private black schools in North Carolina that offered instruction beyond the public school level, but all had been created by white denominations.[106] Livingstone was the first college in the state to be created by a black church, and to have all black teachers, administrators, and trustees. This would give it a great deal of freedom in setting school policy and curriculum.

That first year Livingstone had ninety-four students.[107] The young women lived in the main building with the teachers, and the young men lived in a small building erected to house men students temporarily.[108] Price would be not only chief administrator and fundraiser of this new school: he would also teach oratory, mental and moral science, and theology.[109] He was twenty-eight years old.

This was a daunting task. So the new college president turned to former classmates Moore and Goler to help him. While pastoring his church in Winston, Goler received an "urgent request" from Price to come to Salisbury and help him at the college. Price explained to his friend that it was difficult for him to find teachers because "the institution was an experiment," and there was no money to pay teachers. "We can not promise you any pay for the first year," he wrote, "but after that some arrangements will be made for salaries." Goler agreed to come. During his first year there, he taught classes at Livingstone while still serving as pastor in Winston. In order to meet both obligations, after Sunday services in Winston, Goler left on horseback in the middle of the night and rode some thirty-six miles through the dark in order to get to Salisbury in time to meet with his students Monday morning.[110]

Price also called on his friend Edward Moore. In 1882, he sent Moore a telegram asking Moore to meet with him to discuss coming to Livingstone. After their meeting, Moore agreed to join him. He resigned from his position as head of Wilson Academy, even though the school offered to increase his salary if he would stay, and even though Price had told him there would be no pay the first year.[111] As Moore later said, undoubtedly with a smile: "Dr. Price kept his promise. I received not a cent of salary that first year."[112]

These three friends would form the core and the heart of the new AME Zion school. Working together, they would now have to figure out how to find money to construct school buildings, how to recruit students, how to find faculty, how to pay the faculty, and how to work with the bishops of the AME Zion Church. Zion Wesley Institute had just failed: its doors were closed. Was it possible for Price to do something different so that Livingstone would succeed? And if so, what might that be?

The AME Zion Church had made a false start with Zion Wesley Institute, so it decided to move the school from Concord to Salisbury, hoping once more to build a school that would grow and thrive. In much the same way, despite all their hard work, Harriet Massey and her family were not finding success in Charlotte, and began to think that there must be a better way to work and live. Perhaps they too should move. Indeed, they were not the only freed people to have second thoughts about their move from the countryside to cities after emancipation. Life in cities was much harder than they had expected.

Freed people had flooded the labor market in cities after the war, making it hard to find good jobs. Thus they were crowded into shanty towns, where they lived in extreme poverty.[113] In these congested settings, they came in contact with Union and Confederate soldiers, workers from the Freedmen's Bureau, freed men and women—people who had moved from other regions of the South or the North, bringing new pathogens with them. The combination of these privations and pathogens led to the rapid spread of diseases.[114] Freed people in cities also had to deal with hostility and harassment by white people. Federal authorities, as well as black leaders like Frederick Douglass, encouraged them to return to the country.[115] So after the great migration of freed people to cities after the war, several years later there was another great movement, but this time, it was freed people returning to rural areas to resume agricultural work.[116]

Harriet Massey and her children were part of this second migration. By 1880 Harriet, then about fifty years old, had left Charlotte and was living in Sharon, just a few miles south, with her son Ben, her daughter Belle, and two grandchildren. There, all the adults worked as laborers.[117] Harriet's daughter Malinda had also moved from the city. When William was six, they left Charlotte and moved south to a farm in the Griffith community, seven miles from Charlotte.[118] About that same time, on April 8, 1880, Malinda married Mack Dunn. Dunn, a farmworker, was twenty-six, and Malinda, twenty-four.[119]

Before the Civil War, slaves and free black people made up almost 40 percent of the southern population.[120] This was a huge laboring class, and the liberation of these workers was absolutely revolutionary. Their newfound freedom in the labor market put the entire economic system of the South in disarray, as freed men and women either left their former places of work, refused to work for the people they had previously worked for, or tried to negotiate better working conditions. Former slave owners who held on to their land were wondering how they would survive. Who was going to do the work on their farms, their plantations? Who was going to fell the timber, till the soil, sow the seeds, clean out weeds, bring in the crops? Freed men and women were also wondering how they would survive. The Dunn family was moving to the countryside to farm, but like thousands of other freed people, they had no house, no land, no draught animals to help with plowing. Their only resource was their labor. How could they farm without land, without tools for farming?

The solution the two groups arrived at would satisfy neither party. As the historian Scott Giltner has explained: "By the close of the 1860s, the planter's dream of a return to a system much like bondage and the former slave's dream of widespread fee-simple land ownership had melded into a compromise: contract labor, tenancy, and sharecropping."[121] As participants in this compromise, the Dunn family worked as sharecroppers, growing cotton and corn. Their agreement with the white landowner was that he would provide the land to farm and mules to help with plowing.[122] It is very likely that the landowner also furnished a place to live and some land for a personal garden, as well as basic food rations, gardening tools, and feed for the work animals.[123] In return, when their crops came in, the Dunns had to give the owner three-fifths of their yield.[124] The usual share for the landowner in the South was one-half of the yield, and in eastern North Carolina, the usual share was only 40 percent.[125] So we can already see that within a system of agrarian exploitation, the Dunn family was exploited even more.

Farm life was a hard life. In the corn fields, the Dunns would have to replant several times during the growing season to ensure that the plants survived pests, deer, and bad weather. They would also have to thin the crop as it sprouted, hoe it at least twice, and then pull dirt around each stalk to provide extra support. Cotton had its own demands. There was constant weeding throughout the growing season.[126] Then when it was time to pick the cotton, the farmworker hooked a long cotton sack across his shoulder. He would then go down each row, picking cotton, trying not to cut his fingers and wrists with the dried bristles, putting the cotton bolls into the sack, and dragging the sack along behind him, as it got heavier and heavier. It would not take long before his back was aching from stooping over.

But work in cotton and corn fields was not the family's only work. They also had to tend their own garden for their food. They might well have grown sweet potatoes, string beans, tomatoes, cabbage, lima beans, and okra. They may have had apple trees and grape vines. They would very likely have had chickens, goats, hogs, perhaps milk cows. And after tending to their garden during the growing season, they would then have to salt the meat and preserve the fruits and vegetables.[127] And we haven't even started to talk about the cooking and cleaning, fetching water, cutting wood, the laundry, the sewing and darning—the regular everyday work in a nineteenth-century farm home.

Young William certainly had to do chores around the farm. Even at the age of six he would have been expected to carry water out to the field, milk the cows, pick up dried manure, feed the hogs, carry the slop buckets out of the house, plant seeds, pull weeds, and keep the crows out of the field.[128] Young children probably also gathered kindling early in the morning for fires to heat water for cooking and bathing. Bigger children knocked down corn stalks in preparation for plowing, then stripped the corn leaves and tied them into bundles for fodder.[129] William also worked in the corn and cotton fields with the rest of his family. By the time he was ten, he was considered a plow hand, and sometimes did extra work off the family farm to earn money.[130]

The Dunn family would have supplemented their diet and their earnings from sharecropping, not only with their vegetable garden and fruit trees but also by hunting and fishing. Deer, raccoons, squirrels, wild ducks, wild turkeys, partridges, nightingales, mockingbirds: whatever they caught, they would eat.[131] It was often the children's task to catch frogs for dinner, a task many considered fun. And sometimes they caught rabbits, later served boiled or fried.[132]

Children often used slingshots to hunt.[133] But when the men hunted deer, they would have needed a gun and hunting dogs. It is very likely that Mack Dunn had hunting dogs and taught William to shoot and hunt. Oddly enough, it was not difficult for black people to get guns at this time, as the federal government was eager to sell surplus firearms after the war. Friends and neighbors sometimes shared guns, as they were expensive. But powder and shot were also expensive, so farmers often relied on hunting methods that didn't require guns, like traps for birds and rabbits. For fishing, they might create small dams in streams or rivers. And if the farmer didn't have a gun, he could always climb trees and use a club to catch sleeping possums and raccoons.[134] The Dunns would have used the produce, fish, and game themselves, but they may have also sold or traded these items, as well as other animal parts, like rabbit fur, or raccoon skin for hats.[135]

The Dunn family must have worked very hard, because despite having to give three-fifths of their yield to the landowner year after year, they eventually saved enough money to buy their own mules. This was an important step in the life of the family. For, once they had mules, they could negotiate a new contract with the landowner, one more in their favor. In this new contract, the Dunn family would pay a fixed sum instead of three-fifths of the yield.[136] No longer sharecroppers, they became renters and, as such, moved up both financially and socially. They were moving one more step away from white supervision and control; they were gaining some economic independence. They were still, however, farmers with no land of their own.

They worked hard, but even farmers do not work all the time. The Dunn family would have gotten together with friends and neighbors just to visit, to travel into town on a Saturday afternoon, or perhaps simply to make work more pleasurable. Whether they were quilting, building a house, shucking corn, or killing a hog, working together would make tedious work fun and at the same time strengthen neighborly ties. And in the evening, the elders would tell stories about what life used to be like. In this way young William heard stories of his family's life under slavery.[137]

It is very likely that the young boy also had time for play. The woods could be a playground for small children: grapevines became swings, and sapling became horses. Children got water from the spring on hot summer days when they went looking for berries, and swam in a branch which dammed up long enough to provide a pool. They learned to imitate the call of the blue jay and the whippoorwill, to identify birds, trees, mosses, lichen, and smaller plants; they knew where to look for the early and late berries, hickory nuts, and chestnuts.[138]

Since black families living in the countryside were now scattered across the land, building community was of great importance, and the church was central to this effort. As one of Trent's friends later explained about that era, people went to church "to worship, to hear the choir sing, to listen to the preacher, and to hear and see the people shout. It was a place of worship and also a social center. There was no other place to go."[139] These churches provided black people with the public venues that were denied them in the larger society. Serving as the community's meeting place, they were the site of meetings of all kinds: fraternal orders, political gatherings, temperance rallies, celebrations, and speeches.[140]

It was a place where children played, where young people went to socialize, and where, for a few hours, black people could escape the work of the week and the oppression of white Americans. Church was often several miles away, and since pastors were rare, sometimes there would be church services only every other Sunday, or once a month.[141] There would have also been other events at the church: not only Sunday school and Sunday services, but also quarterly church conference meetings, outdoor revivals in the summer when the crops were in, and weddings and funerals. In many households, when they returned home from church, no one worked: everything was quiet, and everyone rested.[142]

One church would come to have great importance to William's family. In 1867, on the outskirts of Charlotte, a group of freed men and women began to meet regularly in a grove of "chaney berry" trees, to sing praise songs to their Creator who had fashioned this beautiful world and carried them through to freedom. This spiritual community would become the foundation of the China Grove AME Zion Church, in Pineville.[143] Malinda and young William—perhaps Mack too—attended this church. Church records tell us that of the thirteen most important leaders during the early years of this church, only one of them was a woman, and that woman was Malinda Dunn.[144] Her role in the early days of this church gives us a sense of her character, her energy, her faith, and her devotion to the AME Zion Church. It is not surprising, therefore, that in his later years, Trent said that one of the greatest inspirations of his life was his "Christian home."[145]

Malinda's ability to stand strong in a church where men held all the leadership positions is also very telling. William would have watched his mother in this position and seen not only the value of church in the life of his family, but also what women could, and should, be doing in the world.

While the family was living on the farm, the pastor of the China Grove AME Zion Church was Josiah Samuel Caldwell. He became a minister in 1883, when he was twenty-one, but, thinking that he needed to learn more in order to be a better minister, he entered Livingstone College that same year, supporting himself and his family by working on a farm.[146] The following year, in 1884, a church historian wrote that two of the Livingstone students who were "candidates for the ministry" walked twenty and forty-two miles, respectively, from Salisbury to their church, for the Sunday service.[147] Since Pineville is forty-one miles from Salisbury, one of those students must have been Caldwell. After that exhausting trip, then Sunday services, then visits to the parishioners, Caldwell stayed overnight with the Dunn family.[148] This emphasizes the family's standing in the church. But it also shows us both the spirit of generosity in that family and what they could offer a visitor in terms of space, comfort, and food.

When he wasn't working on the farm, William went to school. North Carolina established a system of segregated black and white public schools in 1875. By 1876 there were 529 black men and 288 black women teaching 152,998 students in the state's black schools.[149] There were also many private elementary schools.

William's family wanted him to get an education: indeed, his mother insisted on it.[150] By the time he was ten, he was attending a small school in the countryside for three months in winter and two in the summer, and was thus able to help on the farm when it was time for planting or the harvest. When he was twelve, his uncle Ben Miller gave him his first book, *Walking with God*.[151] So we know that other family members also encouraged him to read and learn and continue his education.

The name of his school, "Philadelphia," suggests that it was, or had been, a Quaker school. Indeed, this was likely. As early as 1863, Quakers in Philadelphia formed the Friends' Freedmen Association, and immediately raised money to buy farm tools, clothing, and school equipment for freed people in Virginia and North Carolina. In Greensboro, North Carolina—not far from Charlotte—they bought thirty-four acres of land, then provided ten-year mortgages for those freedmen who wanted to buy land to farm.[152] They also opened elementary schools as soon as they could find teachers. Between 1865 and 1876, Quakers provided more than 20 percent of the white teachers in North Carolina's black schools.[153]

By 1869, there were 25 Quaker schools in North Carolina, with 37 teachers and 2,475 black students. The student population was equally split between male and female students, but it is striking to note that if we look at how many of these students actually attended classes, the number of female students "always present" was 858, whereas the "average attendance" of male students was 122.[154] Clearly the boys felt the constant pressure of farm work, or any other work that would help them support their family. As one teacher later noted, somewhat sadly, "[L]arge boys [...] came in on rainy days."[155]

Rev. Hood, who was, by 1869, state superintendent in charge of black schools, couldn't say enough good things about the Quaker schools, which he considered "second to none in character": "Without expectation of fee or reward; without attempting to teach the peculiar tenets of their faith; without any apparent desire to advance the interest of their own denomination, they are laboring to dispel the mist of ignorance which has so long hung over the colored people of the South."[156]

William's school was very likely a poor, wooden school.[157] Students and teachers of the day give us an idea of what William's school was like and what his school experience might have been. One student later wrote that his schoolhouse was made of "warped boards," with "benches arranged in a quadrangle around the old stove, the pile of wood in the corner, and the blackboard at the back. I see the teacher walking about the room, a huge switch in his hand" for students who didn't know their lesson, or who "fired the spit ball, which we stealthily wetted using our slates or geographies as screens."[158] When black writer Charles Chesnutt was teaching school in the South Carolina countryside in 1875, he had three classes with twenty-six students some days, some days twenty, mostly girls. There was great variety in their knowledge level. Over half of them were learning the alphabet, some could add and subtract, and only one could multiply "real well."[159]

At end of school year, students often put on a program for the community, where they sang, made speeches, perhaps put on a play.[160] William participated in these events, and probably enjoyed the singing most of all. On the evening of August 31, 1886, when he was twelve, while he and his classmates were practicing for their closing program, they felt the tremors of an earthquake that had just struck Charleston, South Carolina, some 175 miles away.[161] He never forgot that event: his fear kept this memory alive.

It was about this same time, in late summer or early fall—the season for revival services in his community—that William was overwhelmed by an impression of the Divine Presence and made a formal confession of faith in Christ. But he couldn't go through a formal conversion at the time because the church was so crowded with adults terrified by the earthquake. So it was during the next revival season the following year that he formally professed religion. He was thirteen years old.[162]

Conversion, "the new birth, or regeneration," is considered "the most essential experience of Methodism."[163] As an AME Zion bishop has explained: "Those who truly repent and believe on the

Lord Jesus Christ, and have the experience of the presence of the Holy Spirit in their hearts, are acknowledged to be born anew."[164]

Conversion is based on the experience of John Wesley, founder of the Methodist evangelical movement. Wesley initially thought that conversion involved a long process of thought and prayer, as a person changed slowly over time. But, Wesley tells us, on May 24, 1738, "the clear light of the gospel" broke through all the rules and philosophy that had framed his spiritual beliefs, and he simply accepted salvation without completely understanding what had happened to him. For Wesley, this "evangelical conversion" was a mystical experience which opened a new world before him.[165] There are many Methodists today who have not had this conversion experience; there are even Methodist ministers who have not had it. Those who have had it are considered very special in the Methodist Church.[166] So when William told his family and church members that he had experienced a conversion, many would have thought that there was something remarkable about this young man.

That same year another important event marked William's life. Years later he described the incident this way: "Rev. J. S. Caldwell, a student from Livingstone College was our Pastor, and he had to stay over and would spend the night at our home. One day after [the] meal, he put his hand on my hand and stated to my mother: 'When your son gets through school down here, send him to Livingstone.'"[167]

These two sentences appear on the first page of William's autobiography, a document so short that his life from birth to college graduation is compressed on one page. And on this page, there are only two events that seem to him to be worth a description. The first was the earthquake in 1886 that took place during the rehearsal for closing ceremonies at school. He remembered the shock of the tremors and the shock of fear: the ground was literally moving under his feet. The second event must have caused the same kind of shock and had the same weight as an earthquake in his mind. It was a brief interaction between him, his mother, and his pastor, but one so powerful that over fifty years later, he could still see the family seated around the table with the pastor; he could see the dishes, the remains of the meal; he could almost feel the pastor's hand on his. And he could still hear the words Rev. Caldwell said to his mother: "Send him to Livingstone." A lifetime later, when he was almost eighty, he said: "That thought remained with me through the years."[168]

Thus, we can see that by time he was thirteen, young Trent was already marked by influences that would carry him through the rest of his life: from his family, Christian faith, the importance of hard work, and the value of education; and from his pastor, the idea that life offered more for him than work on a farm. He should continue his education at Livingstone.

Livingstone would have been ready for him. For at the same time that the Dunn family was developing into a stronger economic unit, leaving the status of sharecroppers and becoming renters; at the same time that young Trent was beginning to think that he might be able to leave the farm to attend school; at that same time, the three friends from Lincoln University— Price, Goler, and Moore—were busy developing Livingstone.

Price had four goals for education at Livingstone: "developing the intellectual capacities of the race, long suppressed and hindered in its desire for knowledge; teaching moral concepts and ethical discipline through academic and religious training; promoting the economic opportunity and industrial skill of all elements of the population to guarantee the prosperity and perpetuity of the nation; and proclaiming and applying the religion of Jesus for better human relations and promoting all the ministries of good." He understood the task of the school, then, to be to train the "head, heart, and hand."[169] He also understood that Livingstone's graduates would play an important role in the creation of postslavery society in the South. As one of the church bishops later explained, their aim was to "make leaders."[170] And the school's alumni would spread around the country, forming networks of the black middle class that would strengthen black communities.

Livingstone was visionary in several ways. It was modern for its time because it was coeducational. Also, women could not only come to Livingstone as students: they could also study the classical course—Latin, Greek, mathematics, and the sciences. The opportunity to follow a classical course of studies was an opportunity that white women students in the South would not gain for twenty more years.[171] But the founders of Livingstone had a different understanding of what black women wanted, needed, and were entitled to. There was some grumbling in the AME Zion community that the school was going too far: women and men should not be at the same school. But the school stood firm. In 1888, the first class graduated from Livingstone's Classical Department with eight men and two women. The top student was Esther Carthey, who gave the valedictory in Latin.[172]

Livingstone would also be unique because it would be black-created, black-owned, and black-controlled. The board of trustees, the president, the administrative staff, the professors—all were black. It was the first North Carolina school created by a black church, thus, the first black school in the state backed by a large organization. For this reason, Livingstone had a certain stability. It had, as well, great independence in comparison with schools for black people created earlier by the Freedmen's Bureau, the state of North Carolina, and white civic and religious organizations.[173] All of those schools were funded and controlled by white groups, as were other black colleges in the South. For example, when the white president of Hampton University hired Booker T. Washington in 1879, Washington was one of the first black faculty members.[174] And Morehouse College in Atlanta did not have a black president until 1906.[175] The plan for Livingstone was that funds for the school were to come from black people—the students themselves, alumni, and members of the AME Zion Church. But this would prove to be difficult, as most black people were in a financially precarious position.

The school operated on a shoestring. Students would not be a large source of income, as they did not have to pay for either tuition or their room: both were free. Day students had to pay 50 cents a month for incidental expenses. Boarders had to pay $6 a month for food, laundry, fuel, and incidental expenses.[176] Even then, poor students had little access to cash. The school did provide some scholarships for those boarders who could not pay $60 for the ten-month school year. However, because the school was interested in fostering self-reliance, students who received scholarships were still required to provide half the money themselves.[177] There was never enough scholarship money for students, and many had to leave school for lack of a few dollars.

Livingstone received some financial sustenance from members of the AME Zion Church, mainly freed men and women, people who had little for themselves and even less to contribute to an organization. But contribute they did, even though the sums were often not large. In the 1887–1888 college catalog, we find a record of heartbreakingly small donations made the previous year, along with the name and hometown of the person making the donation. We read, for example:

Rev. A. J. McDonald, from Rush Chapel Ct.	$3.75
S. L. Wyatt, Clemmonsville	0.80
T. B. McCain, Troy	0.89
H. W. Richardson, Tillman Station	0.53

There were 207 individual donations that year, yielding $1,538.52. But the largest group of donations by far during this period came from President Price's fundraising trips to the North, where he received twenty-six donations, and returned with $1,464.48. His donors included attorneys in New York and Boston; churches and Sunday schools in Hartford, Connecticut; Brookline, Boston, and Wakefield, Massachusetts; the Young Men's Missionary Club in Woburn, Massachusetts; and the Christian Endeavor Society of the First Congregational Church, also in Woburn.[178] Thus, the school's 1887–1888 fundraising effort yielded $3,003, and Price obtained almost half of this in the North. Traveling to raise money for the school would remain one of his most pressing obligations.

The AME Zion leadership knew that if they wanted to create a collegiate and theological institution, they would also have to create elementary and secondary grades as feeder classes. Putting secondary schools on college campuses was common in white schools as well as black, in the North as in the South, until public high schools became common. What was unique about the black colleges was the inclusion of primary grades on college campuses, very likely due to the scarcity of public elementary schools for blacks.[179] North Carolina did not provide any public high schools for black youth until 1917; before that, the only high schools available to them in the state were the private schools provided by the black community.[180] It is therefore not surprising that, in 1890, less than 1 percent of black youth in North Carolina between the ages of fifteen and nineteen were enrolled in a secondary school.[181] As a result, Livingstone would have not only a college and a school of theology, but also a grammar school and a normal school. It would also have, from time to time, an industrial department.

The black Methodist churches "established nearly all the major colleges controlled by black organizations." These schools considered intellectual education more important than industrial education.[182] Joseph Price was very clear about what he called "necessity" for "intellectual culture." In 1879, as Zion Wesley Institute was holding its first session, he stated: "This is the day of battle for the man (especially the [N]egro), who aspires to a higher cultivation of that faculty which is the master-touch of his Maker. The untrained mind says that the time consumed in the pursuit of high intellectual attainments is wasted; the partially cultivated intellect decries the effort. And, we regret to say, that a few among the cultivated ones declare that it is untimely for the [N]egro, and go so far as to disparage his efforts in this direction."[183]

Samuel Chapman Armstrong, the white general who created Hampton Normal and Agricultural Institute in 1868, was in this group. Under his leadership, there would be no classical curriculum at that school, no study of classical languages or ancient civilizations.[184] He once fired two white teachers when he learned that they had been teaching algebra and Latin to a Hampton student.[185] In his view, an industrial education was needed to address the "shiftlessness, extravagance, and immorality" of black people.[186]

Livingstone lost white donors when they learned that industrial education was not a priority there. Railroad baron Collis P. Huntington donated money to the school until he learned of the industrial program at Tuskegee, then shifted his donations to that school, explaining that Booker T. Washington was "educating Negroes in the only sensible way."[187] We know now that this understanding of Washington's work at Tuskegee is incorrect. Industrial education was never the most important part of the school's educational program: it was predominantly a teacher-training school whose graduates went out and created even more schools for black people.[188] But sometimes the donors saw what they wanted to see, and sometimes they saw what President Washington wanted them to see. And showing donors a school that emphasized industrial education often paid off.[189]

In the 1887–1888 academic year, Livingstone had four departments. The first level was grammar school, the "Preparatory Department," which lasted five years. It was followed by three years of teacher training, in the "Normal Department." Interestingly enough, this is where we find what the school called "Industries." During the three-year normal studies sequence, along with classes like English, algebra, history, and Latin, boys were to study carpentry, cabinet making, and printing; and the girls, cooking, "plain sewing," then dress making and "fancy needle work."[190] It is interesting that these subjects were part of the normal school requirement. Perhaps these "industries" were subjects that would be taught by the new teachers. Or perhaps Livingstone thought that these skills might be important for teachers during those periods when teaching positions were not available, or as a way to supplement their meager salaries. As we will see, the size and importance of these industrial classes would wax and wane over the life of the school.

After successfully completing Normal Department studies, a student could then continue on for four years of college in the Classical Department, which led to the A.B. degree. Livingstone also had two theology departments. The English Theological Department was a two-year course for graduates from the normal school; the Classico-Theological Department provided a three-year course for graduates with the A.B. degree.[191] It is clear that the school was trying to develop more AME Zion ministers, and had decided to make that possible by giving students the choice of a shortened course of study—a five-year sequence after grammar school, instead of a ten-year sequence. School administrators must have understood that many students of theology would not be able to succeed in a rigorous program of classical study, would not be able to afford ten years of study, or would simply not be interested in spending so many years in school before beginning their ministry.

In 1887 the school broke ground for the construction of Dodge Hall, the second building on campus, which would be the boys' dormitory. To celebrate this important event, the administration canceled classes and suspended the routine work of the school. After a prayer service in the Huntington Hall chapel, President Price picked up a pickaxe, put it on his shoulder, and headed toward the exit. Professor Cicero Harris followed him carrying a shovel, and Professor Goler came behind with a spade, all three leading the assembled group—faculty, then students—out of Huntington Hall, toward the building site. When they arrived, they all threw dirt onto the site of the new building, then turned it over to the brick masons.[192] It was a joyful moment for the Livingstone family. Students, faculty, administration—all joined in to build their school, and they built community at the same time.

While Livingstone was growing and changing, change was coming to the Dunn family once more. In 1888 they faced an important question: what should they do with William? He wanted very much to get an education, and he surely wasn't getting one while working on the farm. Should they send him away to school? Could they afford to let him go? His mother especially wanted him to get an education. Classes in the local public school lasted only four months of the year, and, even then, there were many times when he had to miss classes in order to work on the farm. But at the age of fifteen, he was doing a man's work on the farm and was playing an important role in the economic security of the family. Losing his help on the farm would mean a loss of income right away. But they all knew what his future would be if he remained.

This must have been a difficult decision for the family. Teachers and ministers had undoubtedly told them that William was very smart. They all wanted him to improve his lot in life, and they knew that education could open doors. Not only would William's life be better, but his increased opportunities would likely redound to the benefit of the family. They were thinking in the short term, but in the long term too. Sending him away to school was a gamble, but it might also be an opportunity.

Also, like all black parents of this era, they also might have wondered about his safety. Would he be safer on the farm with them, or out in the world on his own? They had surely been worried about this for a long time. In a sense, their life on the farm was exactly like that of poor white farm families of the time: farming and hunting and fishing, making quilts with neighbors, a little schooling, going to church. But it was not the same, for there was a ground note of terror lying underneath the life of freed men and women: the South was, and always had been, a dangerous place for black people.

The Ku Klux Klan, Klan-like groups, and white individuals attacked every sign of black autonomy: schools, students, teachers, churches, black public officials. And there was a specific focus on those blacks who had managed to achieve some economic success, like black farmworkers who rented land, and those who owned their own farm animals.[193] As renters who owned their own mules, the Dunn family would have been very vulnerable.

Lynching had become an important tool of social control. In 1888, white people in the United States lynched 69 black people; the next year, they lynched 94; by 1892, that number had risen to 161. North Carolina was not the worst of the states. That record would have to go to Texas—352 black people lynched between 1882 and 1968; Georgia, 492, and Mississippi, 539. White people in North Carolina lynched "only" 86 black people during that same period, but it is hard to imagine that that comparatively low number could have diminished the fear felt by black North Carolinians.[194]

Convict leasing was another danger for black men in North Carolina. White farmers and owners of mines and factories, having lost their slaves, still needed workers. And so they found a way to create a new form of slavery by using the legal system. In 1866 North Carolina enacted a vagrancy law, facially neutral in order to appease federal officials, but interpreted in such a discriminatory fashion that there was no difficulty picking up and jailing any black man walking along the road. If found guilty of vagrancy, he might be released if he could pay court costs and bond; if he could not, the court could fine him, imprison him, or both, or, as the statute states, "sentence him to the workhouse for such time as the court might think fit."[195] In 1872 the state began to lease out its convicts to farms, mines, and factories.[196] Between 1880 and 1891, two-thirds of North Carolina's convict labor was working on the construction of railroads, where camps were notoriously bad with respect to food, sanitation, and overcrowding.[197] At least 10,000 black men were working at forced labor in the South by the end of the 1880s.[198]

William's safety was perhaps not the only family concern. We know that his mother supported his dream of education, as did his uncle George Johnson.[199] But did his stepfather offer support or resistance? Sometimes parents didn't want their child to leave the farm for school. Benjamin Mays's greatest opposition to his education was his father, who thought his son had learned enough in the local one-room schoolhouse and had no need for further schooling. In his view, "'[T]he more education, the bigger the fool and crook!'"[200] We don't know if William's entire family encouraged him to leave for school: perhaps some did, and others did not. But we do know that in 1888 he left his family, left the farm, and moved to Charlotte to study at St. Michael and All Angels, a school affiliated with that city's black Episcopal Church. He would live with his uncle George.[201]

Although the Dunn family had moved from Charlotte in 1879 when William was six, they had very likely visited the city many times after that. So for him to see Charlotte again might not have been as new and exciting as we might think. But to get the opportunity at the age of fifteen to stop living on a farm, to stop working in the fields, and truly live in a city and go to school whenever there were classes—that must have been remarkable.

In 1880 Charlotte had a population of over 7,000. Eight years later, when William moved there to go to school, there were several thousand more. The city already had a flourishing commercial center. The black community was flourishing, too, with its own newspaper, grocery stores, and artisans, as well as ministers and teachers.[202] It also had its own schools.

In 1882 the rector of the white Episcopal Church in Charlotte created a mission chapel for the black community, St. Michael and All Angels.[203] When black priest Primus Alston came to take charge of the parish, he opened a day school in a little wooden building connected to the church. This is where William attended school. Alston, born into slavery in 1851, had attended St. Augustine's College in Raleigh, and was ordained when he was forty-one. After his move to Charlotte he played such an important role in the city that he was called "the Booker T. Washington of Charlotte."[204] As head of the school and a leader in the black community, Alston would have been an important influence in young Trent's life.

William would surely have attended church in Charlotte, perhaps with his uncle. The first AME Zion Church in that city, Clinton Chapel, was near St. Michael's. This might have been his first choice of a church. But he might also have attended Charlotte's newer black church, Grace AME Zion, which grew out of the temperance movement.

In 1881, North Carolina held a statewide vote on prohibition, which failed. Although the ban on alcohol was voted down, the issue remained alive for those who had voted for prohibition. It was a time of great upset within the black community as its members struggled over this issue, and the disagreements sometimes played themselves out in church. In Charlotte's black community, this issue came to a head in December 1886, just two years before William returned to Charlotte, when forty members of Clinton Chapel left the church because they thought the minister was not exerting enough influence with respect to prohibition. They also thought that they were being persecuted within the church for their temperance beliefs. Those forty who left Clinton, considered "progressive [...] young people," formed a new church, Grace AME Zion.[205]

So perhaps William would have wanted to be with the "progressive young people." If so, he would have certainly met Thaddeus Lincoln Tate, one of the forty church founders and chairman of the board of trustees. Tate had opened a barber shop in Charlotte in 1882, the city's only "first class barber shop" at that time.[206] This was a barber shop for white men only, at a time when only blacks shaved and barbered whites.[207] In 1883, he was one of the founders of Charlotte's black Young Men's Christian Association (YMCA, or Y).[208] Three years later he married Mary Lincoln Butler: their first child, Margaret Hazel ("Maggie"), was born soon after.[209] So, by 1888, when fifteen-year old Trent arrived in Charlotte, Tate, at the age of twenty-three, was starting a family, had created a business, had helped found a church, and was one of the black movers and shakers in the city. Trent would have noticed Tate, and would have been impressed by Tate's role in the AME Zion Church and his growing stature in the wider black community. Over the years, these two men would become important in each other's lives.

Trent would have certainly had to work while attending school: the family was simply too poor to do without the money he could bring in. Perhaps he worked at the school or a nearby hospital; perhaps Alston helped students find jobs. Or perhaps Trent's uncle George had friends or neighbors who could have suggested places to find work. If William had any time at all to explore other activities in Charlotte, the city's new black YMCA would have been a welcoming and comfortable place for him.

The YMCA, which began in England in 1844, was created to provide supportive Christian fellowship groups for young men moving to cities from the countryside. As its founder, George Williams, explained, its goal was "to establish 'a work of sacrifice and service—a work for young men, improving their environment, giving them victory over their temptations, and above all, transforming character through allegiance to Jesus Christ.'"[210] Thus Y work promoted the goal of the Progressive Movement to "reconstruct the individual human being."[211] It also promoted the philosophy of the Social Gospel Movement, which maintained that "Christians could not be passive agents in the social order but should promote the teachings of Jesus."[212] Advocacy of the Social Gospel became an important part of student work within the Y.[213]

The YMCA arrived in the United States in 1851. Only two years later, Anthony Bowen, an African American, founded the first black Y in the United States, in Washington D.C.[214] By 1867, the black community had created YMCAs in Philadelphia; New York City; Charleston; and Harrisburg, Pennsylvania.[215] Howard University created the first Y for black students in 1869.[216] And, by 1883, there was a black YMCA in Charlotte.[217]

We can get a good idea of what the Charlotte YMCA was like by looking at the black Y that existed in Norfolk, Virginia, around the same time. In 1876, the International Committee of the YMCA decided to start Ys for black communities in the South. When, in 1887, it learned that black men in Norfolk had already created a prayer circle, it decided that this would be a good place to start. The YMCA sent Afro-Canadian William Alphaeus Hunton to Norfolk to transform this group into a Y.[218]

It began in a few rooms over a store. By 1888, it had literary and debating societies, educational classes, a choral club that sang throughout the region, and athletics, although it had no athletic equipment. In an effort to create a library, Y members sent a list of the books they wanted for a library out into the community, which donated hundreds of books. But the greatest interest at this YMCA was Bible study.[219]

Hunton, the group's general secretary, was the first black Y director in the South, and also director of the first black YMCA in the South.[220] Because of his success with the Norfolk Y, Hunton would go on to play a crucial role in the development of Ys in black communities for decades. And even though it is unlikely that Hunton would have met young William when he was living in Charlotte, Hunton too would soon play an important role in Trent's life.

Despite the support of his family, despite interest in his new school and classmates, the church, and other activities in Charlotte, William had never forgotten about the school Rev. Caldwell had mentioned years earlier: William should attend school at Livingstone. And so, in 1890, William left Charlotte to go to school in Salisbury.[221] We might imagine that he returned to the farm in Pineville to say goodbye to his family, neighbors, and friends before heading out. He was seventeen years old.

Chapter 2

Educating the First Generation of Free People:
Trent at Livingstone College

THERE IS A DRAWING OF THE Livingstone campus as it appeared in its early years. When you look at it, you see six college buildings spread out on the campus, all facing a walkway planted with trees. Next to the walkway lies a broad green, where the artist has drawn several dozen students. Beyond the green lies Monroe Street, a street planted with trees, one next to the other, on both sides of the street, and then, on Monroe Street itself, across from Livingstone, we see about a dozen small houses. If you sat and looked at this drawing for a while, you would get a feeling of spaciousness, order, and calm. It looks like a place where one could think and learn.

Will Trent arrived at Livingstone on January 10, 1890. Some of the many poor students at the school had walked hundreds of miles to get there. Trent, too, may well have walked to Salisbury from his uncle's home in Charlotte, some forty-two miles away.

When he arrived, he would have seen only four buildings on the campus. Huntington Hall, a large-frame three-story building, was the school's first building, the one that was on the land when the church bought it. Rooms in this building served as chapel, classrooms, and dining hall. In the school's early years, this was also where students and faculty roomed.[1] Just before Trent's arrival, the school had built two brick buildings: Dodge Hall, a boys' dormitory, and Hopkins Hall, a dormitory for girls.[2]

The school had also recently erected Ballard Hall, a two-and-a-half- story brick building created for the industrial training of men students. It had space and tools for teaching carpentry, cabinetmaking, shoemaking, and tailoring.[3] This is also where young men learned printing and where they published *Star of Zion,* the journal of the AME Zion Church, and *The Livingstone*, a monthly magazine edited and published by the students.[4]

Livingstone was a small school in those days. When Trent arrived, only 217 students were enrolled. There were 26 in the Classical Department (the college), 46 in the Normal Department, and 145 in the Preparatory Department (grammar school). Thirty-six students were in the Theological Department, and, of these, 6 were in "itinerant work"; that is, they were students who also were pastors at nearby churches.[5] It is very likely that all the students in the Theological Department and most of the students in the Collegiate Department were men; whereas, in the Normal and Preparatory Departments, the student body was split almost equally between young men and women.[6]

In such a small school, Trent would have met all the faculty and administrators fairly quickly. But there were five who would provide the most inspiration for him during his school years. Many years later, he told a reporter: "I received my greatest inspiration, apart from my Christian home, from Livingstone and those who served here during my student days—Dr. Price, Mrs. Tucker, Dr. Edward E. Moore, W. H. Goler, and F. H. Noble," considered "pioneers in the early history of the college."[7] Because of their importance in his life, it is of some value to describe the character and work of these five people and think about how they might have influenced him when he was a student.

Even before his arrival on campus he would very likely have heard of President Price, who, by 1890, was already an important activist for black rights and a nationally recognized leader of the black community. We can see his influence in the respect afforded him by his peers. In early 1890, 141 delegates from 23 states came together in Chicago to create the National Afro-American League as a permanent national organization. The League was created to address the crucial issues facing the black community: lynching and mob violence, the continued suppression of the right to vote, chain gangs and the convict lease program, segregation in public accommodations and on common carriers, unequal funding for black schools, and poor wages. The delegates elected Price president.[8] The following month, 445 men from 23 states gathered in Washington, DC, to create the Citizens' Equal Rights Association. They too chose Price as chairman of their convention.[9]

Price also had a reputation as a great speaker. W. E. B. Du Bois called him "the acknowledged orator of his day."[10] Booker T. Washington invited him to give the first commencement address at Tuskegee in 1885.[11] And at a talk in Nashville to promote a state temperance amendment, 4,000 people came to hear him speak.[12]

There were those who thought that had Price not died before Frederick Douglass, he would have taken on Douglass's role of spokesman for black Americans.[13] But despite his involvement with national matters, Price was devoted to Livingstone and its students. In 1888, President Grover Cleveland offered Price the position of minister-resident and consul general of the United States at Liberia. Price declined with these words: "I thank you for the honor you do me to offer me the Post of Minister to Liberia but I think I can do more good for my people here in Salisbury."[14] Although he received many other offers to leave the college for positions in government, the private sector, or the church, Price chose to stay at the school.[15]

Trent might well have sensed something in common with Price. As with Price, one of his parents had been a slave;[16] like Price, he "came up the hard way," in a deeply poor family.[17] And he admired Price's commitment to religion in his life. Many years later he described Price as "deeply spiritual," noting that when Price was a student at Lincoln University, he spent every Friday "in fasting and prayer."[18]

Goler, who came with Price early on to help create the school, had been of great help to Price during the early years. Because he had bricklaying experience, in addition to his teaching responsibilities, he was also in charge of the Industrial Department, and supervised the construction of the new buildings on campus.[19] Price used to say that "things would go all right 'if Goler is on the grounds.'" Goler was considered a "born teacher, a scholar, [...] a theologian of the first water, an impassioned speaker,[...] tender hearted and sympathizing as a woman, patient and forbearing almost to a fault [...] [but] when the occasion demands it, bold and stern as a lion. He leads."[20]

Trent later described him with some affection as "that rugged, thrifty, tender-hearted Goler."[21] Price was the visionary, the person who dreamed of the school. He was the orator, the national leader, the person who traveled around the country raising money. Goler was more pragmatic.[22] He was not the man who had the vision of this school, but he was on campus, and he would get things done.

The third in this group of college friends was Edward Moore. When Trent was a student, Moore was teaching Latin and Greek, and was also the college physician. After graduating from Lincoln University in 1879, he had studied medicine at the University of California, then received his medical degree at Illinois Medical College in Chicago.[23] He later went back to school and, in 1892, received a doctorate from Lincoln University in classical languages.[24]

The first faculty at Livingstone had only four professors in the Classical and Theological Departments: Price, Goler, and Moore were three of the four.[25] Thus, when Trent named the five people at Livingstone who most influenced him while he was there, three of them were truly pioneers. The other two on his list were Frank H. Noble, professor of mathematics and the natural sciences, and Mrs. Annie C. Tucker. Professor Noble was considered an "omnivorous reader, entertaining instructor [...] [and] a born teacher." He was not only a professor; he was also treasurer of the college.[26] In addition, after he arrived at Livingstone in 1884, he taught himself law and passed the North Carolina bar exam six years later.[27]

Among the five Livingstone figures whom Trent named as important influences, Annie Tucker was the only woman. She was also the only one who was not a faculty member. A student once wrote that she was a "matron," and had been "Lady Principal" of the college.[28] She was in charge of the girls, the girls' dormitory, and housekeeping throughout the college.[29] The precise scope of her tasks is not clear, but it probably also included "teaching morality and monitoring the sexual behavior" of both students and faculty, one of the tasks of the Lady Principal at Tuskegee.[30] A church bishop later wrote that, at Livingstone, Tucker "led Bible teaching and soul-saving in the college for her generation" and was considered a "builder of character of boys and girls." She also taught oratory, especially to the girls.[31] Tucker was considered the primary cause of the success of the Young Women's Christian Temperance Union (YWCTU) at Livingstone, an organization created by Livingstone teacher Mary Lynch in 1891.[32] So it appears that the young women students at Livingstone were in some sense in her charge and under her supervision, in both the physical and spiritual senses. She also undoubtedly touched the lives of the young men on campus. In an expression of some fondness, one of her former students called her the "Mother-Matron of Livingstone College."[33]

We should not be surprised that her name appeared on Trent's list for women had always been powerful influences in his life. In the interview where he named these great influences, he started the list with his "Christian home," which meant his mother and grandmother, and he ended it with the name "Annie C. Tucker."

We don't have the faculty listing for 1890, when Trent arrived on campus. But we do know that between 1884 and 1886, the Livingstone staff included eight faculty members, four teachers in the Industrial Department, a librarian, and a matron. Three of the faculty members had B.A. degrees, two had M.A. degrees, and three were ministers. In a pattern we will see repeating in later years, women taught within a very limited sphere. In the College Department, the men professors taught oratory, "mental and moral science," theology, Greek and Latin language and literature, "sacred geography," mathematics, biblical literature, rhetoric, history, Greek exegesis, homiletics, and natural sciences. Men also headed and taught classes in the grammar school. Miss Ellen Dade, the only woman on the faculty, taught music.[34]

Upon his arrival, Trent would also have met his fellow students. Many students in the Classical Department came from far away—from Pennsylvania; Washington, DC; Kentucky; and Alabama, as well as from North and South Carolina. In the Normal Department, most of the students were from North Carolina, but there were also students from South Carolina; Washington, DC; and Alabama. In the largest department, the grammar school, many were from Salisbury.[35] Since the Salisbury students did not have to pay board, and no students had to pay tuition, this was clearly a wonderful opportunity for black youth in that town.

Students came from other parts of the world—from Liberia and the West Indies. Thus, Trent would find himself in the midst of a diverse group of students. Some were fairly wealthy; some arrived at Livingstone already well read; others were accomplished musicians. One student who transferred from Howard University subscribed to the *Washington Post*.[36] Simon Fuller, born and raised in Liberia on his parents' coffee plantation, had been reading Latin since he was ten.[37] Many other students were very poor. One student walked 125 miles to get to Livingstone, and another, 255 miles. A young man wore threadbare clothes and suffered from the cold during the winter; another wore only rags for years. Some left school for a while due to poverty, and returned when they had earned some money. Others never returned. President Price tried to help as many students as he could. A student who had only one shirt washed it every night to wear clean the next day. When

President Price learned of this, he provided the young man with board and bought him clothes.[38] When another student could not meet his board bill, Price said: "Come and share with me at my table."[39] But the need was too great for one person to meet. Classmate W. A. Peggans, who rode to school in a freight car, suffered frostbite one winter because his clothes were so ragged.[40]

So when young Trent arrived at Livingstone, he would have found himself for the first time immersed day and night in a world of young men and women from varied backgrounds and from different parts of the world, who were living, working, and studying together in a Christian learning community. In such a place, it would not have been difficult for Trent to find a place where he felt comfortable. And his world would be getting larger.

When we learn about President Price buying clothes for one student and feeding another, it reminds us that the school was so small that the college president would notice this kind of detail. Indeed, faculty and students who lived on campus lived in the same building and ate together at the same dining-room tables.[41] It also shows us that the teachers and administrators were committed to their students and wanted to foster a sense of community. Students later said that at Livingstone they didn't feel like they were living at a boarding school: they felt like they were living in a family.[42]

As he was meeting the faculty and fellow students, Trent was also learning about the rules at Livingstone that would shape his life there—rules about work, about religious devotions, and about social life.

Livingstone required all students to work one hour a day for the school, with the proviso that such work was not to interfere with their studies.[43] The young women did all the household work in the dormitories, under the supervision of the matron.[44] Women in the sewing class also made commencement dresses for the young women, as well as the uniforms for the football team.[45] Men worked on the school's farm, which provided vegetables for student meals—garden peas, cabbages, turnips, white potatoes, sweet potatoes—and even strawberries for two of the students' favorite desserts, strawberry shortcake and strawberries with cream.[46] The men also cut the firewood and whitewashed the buildings. Some tasks, of course, were more disliked than others. Cutting firewood, for example, was not a popular task. One of the students later explained, with a certain sense of humor: "I met but one student there who really seemed to enjoy sawing wood, and his name was Harvey Higgins. The presumption is that he did not, at the time, know any better. I write, however, in the name of truthful history that he, too, learned to abhor the wood-yard."[47]

Because it was founded by a church, Livingstone also had requirements surrounding the spiritual life of the students. In order to be admitted to the school, applicants had to provide certificates of good moral character. Livingstone was clear that it was a school with religious instruction at its core. New students had to bring a Bible with them for Sunday school and their private studies. They were required to attend daily devotional services in the chapel, weekly prayer meetings, and Sunday school in the chapel every Sunday morning, as well as church later on in the day.[48] The school considered the development of the students' character an important goal.

Livingstone also exercised strict control over the personal lives of the students. They could not leave the campus without the permission of the president, nor could they speak with members of the other sex in classrooms or on the school grounds without special permission. They were not allowed to drink alcohol, smoke, curse, or deface the buildings. They could send or receive mail only through the president or matron. The school even controlled what they wore: they were to dress in plain and inexpensive style. On public occasions, the men were to wear blue suits, and the women, blue flannel or worsted dresses, except for Commencement Day, when the women had to wear white.[49]

But even though the school rule stated that men and women students could not speak with each other, they certainly still *noticed* each other. One of the young men composed a poem about his women classmates that begins like this:

You may talk of your velvets, your satins and silks,
They are pretty, we'll all confess;
But there's nothing so pretty, so school-like, so neat,
As the girl in the blue flannel dress.[50]

We also have good evidence that, like all rules, the rules to keep the men and women students apart did not always work. We know, for example, that even though men and women had to enter Huntington Hall through separate doors and use separate stairs on their way to chapel, there was a place on a landing where they could meet "accidentally" for a "hasty kiss." They named the place "the Rubicon," and would say to each other: "Meet me on the Rubicon."[51] One former student wrote about men graduates who had married women graduates: "It is a pleasure to note that they have lived happily together. None have ever separated nor been in the courts. Livingstone men make husbands; Livingstone women make wives."[52]

The school offered more than classes. Each student was required to be a member of one of the school's two literary societies—the Garrison Literary Society for students in the Normal Department, and the Hood Literary Society for the college students. The school also sponsored debates, speakers' contests, guest speakers, and student publications. And on their own, simply as creative and energetic young people, the students also formed athletic groups and clubs, organized get-togethers, wrote poems, and composed songs.[53]

When he arrived at Livingstone, Trent had only $40 in his pocket, but was going to have to pay $8.50 a month for board for the next five months.[54] This would have barely been enough money to last him until he could find work during the summer, so he would have very likely started thinking about how to earn money right away. He said later that once when he ran out of money a faculty member helped him out.[55] Perhaps it was during his first few months there. He also might have earned money right away by doing extra chores on campus. When black educator Benjamin Mays was beginning his studies at South Carolina State College, he had to pay six dollars a month. His brother promised him three dollars a month for a few months, but he had to earn the rest. The school gave him the job of cleaning out the outhouses in the middle of the night—work he called "nauseating," but work nonetheless that gave him enough money to stay in school.[56] So perhaps relatives sent Trent a little money during those first months, and perhaps Trent also found work on campus that allowed him to remain at school that first semester until the summer, when he could work full time.

I recall my father telling me that, in his later years, Trent liked to tell people that when he arrived at Livingstone, he had never seen a toothbrush before. He watched his roommate brush his teeth, then took up his roommate's brush to do the same, an act which must have greatly shocked that young man![57] This story reminds us that he was a poor and unsophisticated farm boy who had lived in a very limited world when he arrived at Livingstone, poor even in comparison with the other black youth at the school. An upperclassman who noticed Trent when he arrived later wrote: "Innocent in actions and appearances, he took his place where he belonged—with the poor of the school."[58]

What must Trent have thought as he first arrived on the campus, as he began to understand what was being offered there, as he began to experience life in an academic world? In an interview many years later he said that he had originally gone to Livingstone to learn how to make bricks.[59] Students had been making bricks there for years. By 1887, they had made over a million bricks, sold many of them for money for the school, and used the rest to build all the new buildings on campus.[60] Vocational training was available at Livingstone at this time and would have provided the means for Trent to learn a trade. He would have been able to earn money for his family fairly rapidly. But industrial classes were only available to students in the Normal Department.[61] And the school had placed him in Livingstone's grammar school. He would soon move up to the Normal Department and be able to learn brickmaking.

But at some point in his studies, he decided not to stop at the end of normal school. Did someone there at Livingstone—a faculty member? a classmate? the matron?—did someone see something in him that led them to push him toward college? Did he himself have the thought that he could, and wanted to, do more with his life? Or did these first months and years at Livingstone, this opportunity to study and read full time within a supportive and exciting learning community—did this make him want to learn more, and then more? In any event, no matter how the decision was made, at some point Trent decided to take the long view of making money and supporting his family. He loved learning, and was hoping that somewhere down the road his education would pay off in a better way.

Upon his arrival, the school administration conducted an assessment to see which class he should be in, and concluded that he should be in the Grammar Department. There were five grammar classes, starting with the E level and going up to A. Trent was assigned to the B class. We don't know how much schooling he had in the small rural school in Pineville, or in Rev. Alston's school in St. Michael and All Angels Episcopal Church in Charlotte. But this assessment tells us that it was not much, since he had only completed three years of grammar studies by time he was seventeen. In 1891, schoolchildren in North Carolina averaged only sixty-four school days a year.[62] And he had undoubtedly missed many of those days in order to work in the fields. Now that he was at Livingstone, he would have to work very hard to catch up. If he earned enough money to stay in school, and if he concentrated on his studies, he would graduate from grammar school in two years, at the age of nineteen.

We don't know what textbooks were used in the B class in 1890 when Trent arrived. But we do know that during academic year 1887–1888, students in Livingstone's B class studied history, geography, arithmetic "to power and roots," reading, grammar, and spelling. They also had lessons in writing and drawing.[63] The publishing houses and the authors of the textbooks for history, geography, and reading would try to shape how he viewed the world and his place in it. By 1890, Reconstruction was over, and white supremacy was on its way to being institutionalized. It is not surprising, then, that all three texts taught the lesson of white supremacy.

The geography textbook used in the B class, Maury's *Manual of Geography*, provides many well-done maps, descriptions of plateaus and rivers, animals and vegetation, summaries of agricultural and mineral wealth, and lists of major cities around the world. Had the author presented only this, the students would have learned a lot. But the author decided to present very early in the book a description of the various groups of humans, and the hierarchy of humankind.

The author divided humanity into "five great races." First in the list is Caucasian, called "the most enlightened and the most enterprising of the races." "Science and invention," Maury continues, "belong to them." Next, in order of "enlightenment," comes the Mongolian, "which includes [...] the Eskimos, who are savage," and "the progressive Japanese"; the Malay, who "are fond of the sea and given to piracy"; the American Indian, "mostly savages"; and finally, what he calls "the Ethiopian" race, "found chiefly in Africa where it is in a savage state." To illustrate this hierarchy, the book provides a drawing of five men, one from each race. In the middle is the white man, with representatives of the four "not-so-great" races arrayed in a circle around him. All the men are wearing clothes except the black person, who wears only beads.[64] This picture thus presents in a visual way the same lesson presented in the text: the white man is the most important, and the black man is the "savage." At the same time, the students would learn that the most important representatives of each "race"— indeed, the *only* representatives—are men. By the time the readers arrive at the section on Africa toward the end of the text, they will not be surprised to learn that in the "land of the blacks, [...] some of them till the soil and raise cattle, others have skill in tempering steel and working gold, but they are generally exceedingly ignorant and degraded."[65]

Swinton's history text takes the student from Christopher Columbus's travels to Lee's surrender at Appomattox. It is a book about exploration and conquest and war: the description of the battles of the Revolutionary War and "the Rebellion, or War of Secession," takes up fully a quarter of the book. Again, it is a book about men: women do not appear in this description of American history.[66] The first time the author refers to slavery, it is in the context of the Spanish conquest in the Americas, and seems very enlightened. The Spaniards, Swinton explains, "treated the poor natives with most unchristian cruelty; for they enslaved them, and wore out their lives in merciless toil in the mines and on the plantations."[67] But when the author moves from Spanish slavery in Florida and Mexico to English slavery in Virginia, the notion that people who enslave others are "unchristian" and cruel disappears. After explaining that it was the growing market for tobacco that led planters in Virginia to buy more and more slaves, the author explains: "In those days many of the people did not think it was right to hold slaves, but there were so many Negroes that the Virginians did not see what was to be done with them."[68] The lesson here, then, is that the English weren't cruel like the Spaniards. They weren't even responsible for slavery. They just didn't have many good ideas. Like Topsy in *Uncle Tom's Cabin*, slavery just "growed."

One wonders what these young black students thought when they read these books. They knew that black people were not "savages." They knew that their African schoolmate was not "ignorant and degraded." They must have realized, too, that they knew more about slavery than the author of the history book wanted to present. Many of them had parents who had been enslaved; probably all of them had relatives who had been. Like Trent's relatives, these freed men and women had told their children what life was like during slavery; like Trent, they had read the story of slavery in marks on their relatives' bodies before reading words about it in this book. One wonders if they even expected the textbooks to present something different. Perhaps, either in class or later on, they talked about the text's treatment of "Ethiopians" and slavery, so as to diffuse the power of these ignorant lessons on their lives.

This history book may well have provided Trent with his first formal lesson about his namesake, George Washington, called here "the greatest character of the war of Independence [...] great in every way, not only as a soldier, but as a statesman and a man."[69]According to Swinton, even as a youth Washington was noted for "his self-reliance, courage, and love of the right."[70] Although he was sometimes defeated, and often had to retreat, his most important character trait was "firmness in the worst times and places," for he "never for a moment lost faith in the cause."[71] Trent had probably dropped the middle names he had been given at birth—"Captain George Washington"—by time he went to Livingstone, and replaced them with Johnson, his mother's family name. But he might well have stopped for a moment when he read these lines about the man the author called "first in the hearts of his countrymen," as he thought about why his family gave him this name, and what they expected him to do with his life.[72] Perhaps he, too, was supposed to play an important role in his people's fight for "independence."

There are several possible reasons why he removed "Captain George Washington" from his name. Perhaps it sounded too clumsy. Perhaps he got tired of explaining why his family had given him this name. Or perhaps he replaced it with Johnson after learning that although George Washington had many wonderful character traits, he also built his wealth on the backs of his slaves.[73]

Students in grammar class B had a reader that made a serious effort to appeal to boys with a selection of short poems and morality lessons, as well as short excerpts from adventure stories and biographies. It is easy to see how a young man would want to keep reading stories about Daniel Boone, Robin Hood, or Robinson Crusoe. There was nothing in the reader, however, to encourage the young women at Livingstone to keep reading. Although Louisa May Alcott wrote five of the eighty-seven pieces in this reader, two of them, from her book *Little Men*, were about the adventures of a very energetic and brave young boy, who was able to persuade his teacher to save a poor child from a life on the streets, and who later played dangerous games out in a field with his friends.[74] The two excerpts from *Little Women*, in contrast, do not show the girls doing anything creative, energetic, or playful. They are not even outside. Instead, we see Meg and Jo inside the house sitting by the bed, waiting for their mother, as their sister Beth lies dying.[75]

Nothing in this book referred directly to the lives of the black children who read it. The book contains, however, two fairly strong negative references to the color black. The first comes in the excerpt from *Alice in Wonderland*, when Alice is talking to her "wicked" black kitten which needs to be punished, and comparing it to Snowdrop, her good white kitten. The second reference is in a poem about a man who, "taking a vomit, threw up three black crows." As the poem goes on, it turns out that he hadn't vomited "three black crows": he threw up "two black crows." And then, only one; until finally, we learn that he had vomited "something that was as black, sir, as a crow!"[76]

It is, of course, merely speculation that these editorial decisions were made to reflect and maintain a social system in which white boys are active, adventurous, and the most important players on the scene; white girls are barely visible and, even when seen, are passive players in their own life; and black boys and girls, even though they are invisible, are still "wicked," and as dirty and disgusting as vomit. But given the times, it would have been surprising if publishing companies presented a different picture of the world. And even if these editorial decisions were made in a subconscious way, they were still teaching young readers very important lessons about the world they lived in. For they showed them who existed center stage, and who did not; who was supposed to be in power, and who was not; who was clean and good, and who was not.

Trent immediately set out to master his schoolwork. He was considered "industrious, a hard student."[77] But he would not be able to spend all his time on his studies. He also had to fulfill his obligation to the school to work one hour a day on school maintenance. One of his chores was to saw wood for the girls' dormitory.[78] He also tried to find more food than was served at school. As one of his schoolmates later wrote: "W. J. Trent was the first to come to Livingstone and outrun rabbits. He used to average about two a week. When questioned by W. H. Davenport as to how he got them, he declared that he caught them by 'main force.' But when Bennie Brown of Montgomery, Ala., came, he changed this mode of procedure. He used to hide, and when the rabbit came hopping by he politely fell on him. These two ate rabbit for years."[79]

This story shows us once more that Livingstone was an impoverished school, that students were often hungry, and that Trent was a poor boy who had learned how to hunt for food while he was very young. The classmate who told this story thought catching rabbits to eat was strange and amusing, reminding us once more that Trent was one of the poorer students at the school.

At the end of Trent's first semester, in May 1890, he heard President Price's commencement speech. One observer described both the speech and the audience's response to his words:

> He came forward amid thunderous applause and began a speech which is remembered till now by all who heard it. It was the most subdued and pathetic speech I ever heard him deliver. Eloquent it was, and yet there was no attempt at oratory. It caught and held the audience in fond embrace and would not release it till the speaker had done. And when he had finished, when the last word had been said, there was a stillness like unto that which sometimes precedes a great storm. The great audience seemed lost in thought. Suddenly from the rear of the hall someone commenced to applaud, then others joined in.[80]

Young Trent was equally moved, and later described how the speech had affected him: "The master of the platform and of great assemblies took charge. I saw men and women under the spell of his oratory stand on the seats, and many of the men threw their hats in the air, yelling for joy. It so affected me, a student in the grades, that I left the campus and went down to the woods close by, there to spend several hours alone."[81] Still and always a farm boy, he continued to find comfort in the countryside.

That same month, all around campus—in the dormitories, in the library—Livingstone faculty and students would have likely been talking about the latest edition of *The Southland*, a political quarterly journal founded by President Price, and edited by Simon Atkins, who had come to Livingstone in 1884 to head the grammar school.[82] The journal stated as its object "the highest good of the race and hence the best interests of the nation and of the whole people."[83] The first item in the journal was an essay by "Mrs. A. J. Cooper, Editor," entitled "Prospectus to our Woman's Department."[84]

The author, Anna Julia Cooper, born in 1858 to a slave mother, studied at St. Augustine's Normal and Collegiate Institute in Raleigh, where, by the age of eight, she was already tutoring the older children. She received both a B.A. and an M.A. degree in mathematics from Oberlin College, then taught at Wilberforce University and at St. Augustine's. By 1890, when she wrote this essay, she was teaching at the M Street High School in Washington, DC.[85] When she had taught at St. Augustine's, one of her students had been Simon Atkins,[86] now head of Livingstone's grammar school and editor of *The Southland.* So it is not surprising that either Atkins or Price, perhaps both, asked her, as she puts it, to "take charge of the Woman's Department (whatever that means) for *The Southland.*" Her essay was a response to that request.

She began by noting that "fifty years ago, the woman's department [...] was a pretty clearly defined 'sphere,' including primarily the kitchen and nursery and graced by the pre-eminently 'womanly' avocation of darning, knitting, sewing on buttons and painting on every discoverable bit of china and canvas, forlorn looking cranes balanced idiotically on one foot."[87] But, she continued, the expansion of women's activities had made the definition of a "Woman's Department" very complicated. This is a "grave responsibility," she wrote, one that extends "through so many and such varied interests, acting and reacting upon such vital issues, with such multitudinous problems to solve, such momentous forces to shape and direct," that such a task seems

"Herculean" in nature. Given this new understanding, she asked the following questions:

> Will some one of the initiated then please rise and explain what *is* Woman's Department? or rather had I not better ask what *isn't* Woman's Department? What   is she to let scrupulously alone? Which one of the interests of this plodding, toiling, sinning, repenting, falling, aspiring humanity can afford to shut her out or dare deny the fact of her influence? What plan for renovating society, what scheme for purifying politics, what reform in church or in State, moral, social or economic, what movement upward or downward of the human plane, is lost on her? [...] *All* departments are hers [....] I am a Negro, and think nothing pertaining to the Negro foreign to me.[88]

It is to the credit of Price and Atkins that they chose Cooper to be an editor of their journal, albeit an editor of "the Woman's Department." But it is to their even greater credit that they not only decided to publish this essay, which criticizes their limited vision of women's role, but also put it on the first page of the journal. In so doing, Price and Atkins taught the students two valuable lessons: that the debate on women's rights was important, and that the words of black women who spoke out about their rights must be heard. No doubt this essay opened a lively discussion on campus about the role of black women in the larger society.

This edition of *The Southland* also included three essays by prominent African Americans, debating the division of the black vote. At their most basic level, these essays remind us that at this point in Reconstruction, black men were indeed voting, despite white efforts to limit the black vote through fraud, gerrymandering, poll taxes, threats of violence, and violence itself.[89] The narrow issue here, however, was the question of party loyalty: should African American men continue to vote solely for the Republican Party, the party of emancipation? The first response, by Livingstone's own Professor Goler, was clear: "Let no party be allowed to count definitely on the Negro vote to ride into power [....] That which is easily acquired is seldom much valued [....] Let the vote be divided: it will be appreciated by the party who succeeds to power. It will make them more faithful to *promises* when they see that a failure to keep the one will be followed by a loss of the other."[90]

The second essay was by John R. Lynch, who had represented Mississippi in Congress in 1873, had been nominated by Theodore Roosevelt to be temporary chairman of the Republican Party in 1884, and had held several other appointed positions under the Republicans.[91] Lynch argued, not surprisingly, that black Americans should continue to vote solidly Republican.[92] And finally, John Mitchell Jr., editor of *The Richmond Planet*, wrote that when black Virginians divided their vote, they had suffered because of it: "The unity of action in the black race [...] has been dissipated now. Advantages gained have been lost apparently never to return."[93]

These discussions in *The Southland* thus brought Livingstone students into a lively debate already taking place on the national scene. Perhaps some of them also noticed that although the editors had put Cooper's complaint about being relegated to "women's issues" at the beginning of this edition of *The Southland*, the debate on the vote at the end of the volume was a debate between men.

That summer, six months after his arrival at Livingstone, Trent had to leave the campus and find work so he could earn enough money to support himself at school and send money back to his family. He took whatever work he could find—working on farms, taking odd jobs. At one point he walked the railroad right-of-way from Pineville to Rock Hill looking for a job. In an interview years later he recalled, with some humor, that long walk under a hot North Carolina sun: "It was 15 miles," said Dr. Trent. After a pause he added: "Still is!"[94]

Years earlier, in July 1874, the writer Charles Chesnutt had paid one dollar to rent a horse for a day so he could ride around the Pineville area looking for a teaching position.[95] But Trent didn't even have a dollar to spare as he went looking for a job: he had to walk. He did get a job in Rock Hill, but gave it up when he learned that for the monthly salary of $6.50 he would have to work in the field all day, plowing, then work in the dining room of an inn in the evening.[96]

It is very likely that presidents at the black colleges gave their students suggestions about places where they might find work. It is also very likely that students gave each other tips about where to get a good summer job. They often went north in the summer, to work in expensive restaurants in the large cities, or in resorts on the East Coast. President John Hope of Morehouse College helped students find summer jobs on tobacco farms in Connecticut, in restaurants and the meat-packing industry in Chicago, and in insurance companies in Durham and Atlanta.[97] Some Livingstone students taught during the summer in the rural areas.[98] Other men students supported themselves and their families by working as Pullman porters.[99]

Trent heard that he might be able to get a summer job waiting tables in Asheville, a fast-growing resort city in the mountains of western North Carolina, where waiters were earning twenty-five dollars a month plus meals, tips, and sleeping quarters. During the job interview, when the head waiter asked him if he had any experience waiting on tables, Trent said "yes," that he had a lot of experience "waiting." Actually what he meant, he later said, was that he had been "waiting" a long time for a job that paid twenty-five dollars a month, plus tips, meals, and a place to sleep! Even though the headwaiter immediately recognized that Trent didn't know anything about the job, he still hired him, and taught him how to wait tables in fine hotels.[100] Trent spent the summers of 1891 and 1892 and the spring of 1894 in Asheville, working as a dishwasher at the Swannanoa Hotel, as a waiter at the Grand Central, Battery Park, and Oaks hotels, and as a bellman at the Kenilworth Inn.[101] He later worked at hotels in New York City.[102]

We can only imagine his reaction at his first view of New York City. As late as 1900 Pineville had only 585 residents and 10 stores.[103] Both Charlotte and Salisbury were larger, with about a thousand inhabitants. But New York City! In 1890 there were over a million people within its borders.[104] The city was mammoth, crowded with people moving quickly and aggressively, and tall buildings, some with 9 stories, some with even more. There were cable cars, elevated trains, streetcars, and trains running up and down Manhattan. The elevated trains alone carried 30 million people every year, carrying New Yorkers to work, then back home, carrying also noise, cinders, and soot. The city was exciting, and electric in more ways than one. Electricity was rapidly replacing gas lights all around the city—in factories, homes, theaters, and restaurants.[105]

Perhaps young Trent took a day off every now and then to explore the city with friends, fellow students from black colleges. They might have taken a ride on the trains. Using the new free-transfer system, they could have traveled from borough to borough for only a nickel. As they rode, they might have passed street markets run by New Yorkers who had just immigrated from southern Italy, Russia, Poland, Germany, and China. They might have seen Coney Island or the Statue of Liberty. Or perhaps as they walked through Manhattan they saw St. Patrick's Cathedral, or the new Metropolitan Opera House, a massive building that could seat 3,600 people. And if they walked over to Fifth Avenue and 52nd Street, they would have been dazzled at the sight of the home that William Kissam Vanderbilt had just had built for his wife Alva—a house that copied King Francis I's sixteenth-century Château de Blois.[106]

The black population in New York City was small in the late nineteenth century. In 1900, black people still made up less than 2 percent of the population.[107] But Trent would have still been able to find a welcome at one of the member churches of the AME Zion Church, which had more parishioners than any other black church in the city.[108] He might have also found friendship, as well as a place to sleep, in one of the black Young Men's Christian Associations (YMCAs, or Ys) in the city.[109] Perhaps the New York City Y had housing for young men by the time Trent arrived in the 1890s. But even if it didn't, church members and Y members there would have been able to offer housing suggestions. And as for work, black waiters in New York were earning between $25 and

$30 a month, plus food and housing. A head waiter could earn up to $70 more.[110] There was much to like about the city.

But it was a time of great migration—migration of blacks from the South to the North, migration of foreigners from Europe. Already unsettled by the massive European migration, white New Yorkers acted in ever more racist ways as the century drew to an end. They showed it through employment discrimination, exclusion from unions, and discrimination in housing, all of which led to low incomes and unemployment, as well as bad housing, overcrowding, and high rents, for blacks in the city.[111] Police harassment made a bad situation worse.[112] In 1895, New York State passed a law providing equal access to all public facilities—inns, restaurants, bathhouses, theatres, and music halls, as well as all "public conveyances on land and water."[113] This was an important step forward, but it also tells us how badly whites were treating blacks throughout the state.

Trent worked only one summer in New York City. Perhaps he left the city because white employers were moving blacks out of jobs in order to hire white immigrants. Black waiters specifically were being forced out of the better hotels, the ones with good wages.[114] Perhaps other black students explained that he might be able to make more money as a Pullman porter, if he could figure out how to get the good tips. Or perhaps he had just seen enough of the city and was ready to move on.

He made the most money during his student years working for the railroad. He entered the sleeping car service with the New York Central Railroad as a Pullman porter and was soon in charge of drawing cars going north to Niagara Falls and Chicago, and even further north into Canada, as far as Ottawa and Montreal.[115] In the black community in those days, working as a Pullman porter was considered prestigious work. The job got young men out of the fields and into a good-looking uniform, and it got them a steady wage, albeit a low one.[116] But the working conditions were generally bad. Even on long runs, there was no place for the porters to sleep. They had to sleep sitting up in the smoking room behind a screen. They also had to endure the racist comments and behavior of white patrons and supervisors. And the work was exhausting. Thirteen-hour days were common, but, of course, the porters were on call whenever there were patrons on the train.[117]

Porters greeted the riders, carried the luggage, made the beds, polished spittoons, cleaned shoes, lit and extinguished the lights, and brought food and drink from dining cars. Sometimes they helped the crew load wood for the engine, and sometimes they even had to help the crew gather the wood before loading it onto the train. They also had to do "indelicate work"; that is, work involving alcohol or sex. They had to control "disorder" in the car, tend to the sick, take care of babies and young children, clean up diarrhea and vomit, and scrub toilets and washbowls in the smoking room, which doubled as the men's bathroom. Sometimes they even helped deliver babies. It was not uncommon for the porters to have to deal with sexual advances from both women and men.[118] And when there were long layovers, they had to find lodging in the nearby town, a task that was always problematic, but which also became dangerous once they stepped off the train in the Deep South.[119]

In 1879 porters earned only ten dollars a month.[120] This was not a very big salary. So if a porter was going to make a decent wage, he would have to do it through tips. Tips were generally a nickel or a dime, but sometimes a porter could get more. And if the porter was lucky enough to be chosen for a "choice route," tips were higher.[121] Porters devised their own systems for getting good tips, and for tracking down those travelers who wanted to leave the train without leaving any tip at all.[122] Another way to earn more money was to move up and become the porter in charge of a car, who earned ten to fifteen dollars a month more than a regular porter.[123] But these jobs were not plentiful.

The railroad companies preferred hiring porters with dark skin, whom they considered more manageable. They also feared that porters with light skin might be confused with patrons, and used dark skin as a marker to distinguish between the two groups.[124] One former porter said that the company first refused to hire him because his skin was too light, saying: "You might get too friendly with our wives."[125] In the dining cars, however, the railroad companies preferred to hire light-skinned black people as waiters. Since the work in the dining cars was easier and tips were higher,[126] this undoubtedly created tension between porters and dining-car workers, thus creating tension between black employees with light skin and those with dark skin.[127] It is not often that we can see the hand of white America creating anger, resentment, separation, and class differences in the black community based on skin color. But we can see it here.

Trent's mother had dark brown skin, his father was white, and he himself had light brown skin. Thus, because of his skin color, he was able to get a job in the dining car and make better wages than his coworkers and friends with dark skin. So when he was working for the railroad, he had to manage the racism and insults of his white clients, in order to keep his job and get good tips. But in order to minimize trouble on his runs and maximize profit, he also would have had to manage his relationship with the porters, who knew that he was making more money than they solely because of the color of his skin. But he was in his twenties by then, and had undoubtedly been addressing issues of race and color for many years.

Spending a summer in New York City, working in dining rooms in resort towns and on the railroad—all this very likely gave Trent a broader view of both the world and his own life possibilities. He would have had the opportunity to observe white people who were wealthy, powerful, or famous, and would have learned how to work with them in a way that kept them happy and kept him safe. We can tell that he learned this lesson well because by the time he finished his studies at Livingstone in 1898, he was earning $150 a month from his work in railroad dining cars, and was thus able to make an important contribution toward the support of his mother and grandmother.[128] By the time he left Livingstone, he had lived and worked in New York City, and had traveled to other cities in the North and in Canada, where he would have undoubtedly noticed that black people there lived better and were treated better than they were in the American South. Like black American soldiers who returned from Europe after the Great War with a new understanding of who they could be in the world, Trent too might have come away from this experience with a new vision of possibilities for his life.

At the beginning of his second year at Livingstone, in January 1891, Price and Atkins published another edition of *The Southland*, and copies would have been circulating on the campus. This edition contained the papers presented during the second annual meeting of the American Association of Educators of Colored Youth, held in Atlanta a month earlier. A look at the names of the officers and members of the board of directors of the organization gives us an idea of the network of black and white educators and activists within which President Price worked. Ida B. Wells, then co-owner and editor of a newspaper in Memphis, was one of the officers. The board also included President Price and Simon Atkins, as well as other scholars, educators, and activists—William Sanders Scarborough, classical scholar and professor at Wilberforce College;[129] George Whipple Hubbard, founder and first president of Meharry Medical School;[130] Horace Bumstead, president of Atlanta University;[131] Lucy Ellen Moten, principal of Miner Normal School in Washington, DC;[132] and Francis James Grimké, a Presbyterian minister active in organizations working for equal rights for black Americans.[133]

In its opening "Address to the Public," the organization presented a brief statement of the concern that defined its existence: "We stand face to face with the question, What shall we do to prepare an enfranchised people for the proper performance of the duties of citizenship?" In view of the appalling situation of black education, they made an appeal for increased philanthropic contributions, more scholarships and endowments for black schools, and increased industrial training. The association was also very concerned about the discriminatory state funding of black schools in the South.[134] As Price stated at the meeting: "Instead of saying 'the Negro cannot learn,' it is now sometimes said 'how can he be *kept* from learning?'"[135] The organization believed that black schools would get more equal funding if the federal government gave the southern states more money for education. To that end, the group chose five members to present this concern to Congress.[136]

At the conference, six churches and the American Missionary Association had presented reports on their education work for black students. This edition of *The Southland* included those reports. They described an impressive effort since emancipation. The Presbyterian Church, for example, which came south right after the war, by now had eighty schools for black youth, including parochial schools, general schools that focused on industrial education, three "seminaries" for women, and, as well, two universities, Lincoln and Biddle, for men. In 1890 they were teaching more than 10,000 black students.[137]

In its work for "the colored people in the sixteen Southern States," the Methodist Episcopal Church had a variety of schools, including 8 "collegiate schools," 2 medical schools, a dental school, a school of pharmacy, and a theological seminary. Including the primary schools located in their churches, they estimated that they had approximately 150 schools and 20,000 students.[138] The American Missionary Association (AMA) reported 53 "common schools" and 30 normal schools, as well as Hampton Institute, and many colleges, including Fisk, Talladega, Tougaloo, and Tillotson. In 1889, this organization had over 13,000 pupils in all its schools.[139]

Conference minutes published in this edition of *The Southland* show that the educators were not only teachers, but activists. Before they adjourned they created two committees to follow up on ideas presented before the assembled body. The first recommended the creation of a "Colored Chautauqua," to be held during the summer "somewhere in the South," to improve teacher preparation, "a Chautauqua devoted to moral and mental culture [...] especially from a pedagogical point of view—as it relates to the education of colored youth." Atkins made this proposal, and became a member of the committee of five to explore the matter and report back at the next Association meeting.[140]

Before adjourning, the Association created a committee to contact the Commissioners of the Columbian Exposition of 1892, to be held in Chicago, to petition "for a full and complete exhibit of the general material and industrial advancement of the colored people of the whole country and of the progress of education among the freemen—such exhibit to cover the work of the Industrial, Mechanical, Agricultural, Normal and Academical [*sic*] Schools, Colleges and Universities, and the Literary productions of colored authors." Price was one of five appointed to present these views.[141]

Students reading this volume would have been able to see a large picture of the education of black youth in the South, and think about what role they might play in the future to improve both the number and quality of schools. They would have also seen their professors and college president as organizers and activists for education, for to the extent that the Columbian Exposition would tell a story about the life and work of black Americans in the late nineteenth century, this would be an important teaching moment for white Americans as well as black.

In June 1891, at the end of the semester, Livingstone students had the opportunity to hear Alexander Crummell deliver the commencement address.[142] Crummell was a black Episcopal minister, scholar, intellectual leader, and spokesman of racial solidarity. In 1853 he graduated from Queen's College, Cambridge, with an A.B. degree. In his early thirties he became a proponent of black emigration to Africa, and with the hopes of living a life free of racism, moved from England to Liberia to work as a missionary-educator. He did not return to the United States until 1873. Soon thereafter the Episcopal Church named him "Missionary-at-Large to the colored people of Washington, D.C."[143] It is not surprising that President Price invited him to present this address: he admired Crummell greatly. In a speech he gave in 1879, Price said: "When the iron heel of despotism is grinding the nation, Crummell, with sword, pen and scroll, takes the field."[144]

So when Crummell spoke to the students, he spoke as a much- esteemed elder statesman with worlds of experience behind him.[145] He would likely have begun his speech with an exhortation to the students to aim for excellence. To Crummell, this meant more than getting good grades or a good job. It included at least four qualities: self-possession, that is, the ability to manage one's faculties with the "knowledge of their capacity" and "command of their powers"; exactness, by which he meant "accuracy and precision in one's intellectual ventures"; "facility [...] quickness and promptness"; and taste, defined by Crummell as a "sensitive disdain of the rude and gross."[146] He often emphasized the importance of having a "grasp upon one's intellectual powers."[147] "Accustom yourselves," he once told a group of students, "to fall back upon the mind itself as a main instrument and agency to the end desired."[148]

He would also have likely talked to the students about the obligation of young black people who exhibit this excellence to help bring forth a "revolution" in American society. Who will emancipate the masses of black people, he asked, "from the injustice and grinding tyranny of their labor servitude?" Crummell continued:

> To bring about these results we need intelligent men and women, so filled with philanthropy that they will go down to the humblest conditions of their race, and carry to their lowly huts and cabins all the resources of science, all the suggestions of domestic, social and political economies, all the appliances of school, and industries, in order to raise and elevate the most abject and needy race on American soil. If the scholarly and enlightened colored men and women care not to devote themselves to these [...] duties [...], what is the use of their schooling and enlightenment? Why, in the course of Providence, have they had their large advantages and their superior opportunities?[149]

Although Crummell often emphasized the role of men in this "revolution," he supported the development of black women's intellect, and once told a group of women graduates to strive to make something of themselves, and then strive to make *the most* of themselves. "You have great powers," he continued. "You are responsible both for your powers of mind, and responsible for the training of them. Therefore I say cultivate your powers. Bring them under discipline. Give them strength [....] Use books, literature, science, as the instruments and agents of the intellect."[150]

Alexander Crummell was seventy-one when he presented the commencement address at Livingstone, but he was still actively thinking, writing, and organizing for the betterment of black Americans. The students must have been honored to be able to hear him.

To meet his goal of creating an exciting intellectual community for the students, Price also invited other prominent black intellectuals, activists, and educators to speak to the students, including W. E. B. Du Bois and Booker T. Washington.[151] It is not surprising that both men accepted the invitation to speak at Livingstone. Washington had great admiration for Price, and had invited Price to give the first commencement address at Tuskegee in 1885.[152] And Du Bois held Price and his work in great regard. As he once noted: "The star of achievement which Joseph C. Price [...] hitched his wagon to was the founding of a school for colored youth, a sort of black Harvard."[153] The list of guest speakers at Livingstone also included black lawyer, activist, educator, and legislator John Mercer Langston.[154]

The list of commencement speakers at Livingstone during this period also included both black and white activist women. Frances E. Willard, one of the founders of the Woman's Christian Temperance Union, was one of the white speakers. Mary Church Terrell also presented a commencement address.[155] A teacher and suffrage activist, Terrell was one of the founders, in 1894, of the Colored Women's League, an organization whose goal was "to inform the public about the moral and social progress of the black race."[156] Livingstone also invited Eliza Ann Gardner to present a commencement speech.[157] A prominent Northern abolitionist and founder of the AME Zion Ladies' Home and Foreign Missionary Society, Gardner was considered by church leaders as "the pioneer in our great Southern work and the mother of the conferences in the South."[158]

The selection of the speakers shows the kind of people Livingstone's presidents wanted the students to hear and the lessons they wanted their students to learn. For these speakers were well-educated, well-spoken activists who fought for the rights of black Americans, the rights of all women, and temperance. For students like Trent, who had come from poor homes in the countryside, the Livingstone College administration was demonstrating that the Livingstone faculty was not the only group of well-educated black people in the United States. There was a wider world where many were working hard to improve society, and that activist world included women as well as men, and white people as well as black. And the administration was suggesting that Livingstone students should join this group. [159]

In late 1892, newspapers from as far away as New York, Boston, Detroit, and Philadelphia were praising a new book, *A Voice from the South by a Black Woman of the South,* written by the relatively unknown schoolteacher Anna Julia Cooper.[160] But she would not have been unknown to the students and faculty at Livingstone. They would have remembered the essay she had written for *The Southland* the previous year, in her capacity as editor of the "Woman's Department," the essay in which she had protested being asked to limit her views to the "women's sphere." In this new book, Cooper developed that theme.

"Why are there so few black women with BA degrees?" she asked. From her brief survey, she wrote, she learned that Fisk had twelve women graduates; Oberlin, five; Wilberforce, four; Wellesley, three; Livingstone, only two; and Howard, none.[161] She acknowledged that an education often renders a woman less "marriageable," but the solution, she maintained, was not for women to become less educated, but for the black man to figure out "how he can so develop his God-given powers as to reach the ideal of a generation of women who demand the noblest, grandest and best achievements of which he is capable."[162] Cooper also wrote about the difficulty black women faced when they traveled.

When she arrives at the train station, Cooper continued, she faces a room for women and a room for "colored" and wonders "under which head I come."[163]

And finally, Cooper pointed out that "the colored woman of today occupies [...] a unique position in this country [....] She is confronted by both a woman question and a race problem and is as yet an unknown or an unacknowledged factor in both."[164] And it is here that Cooper continued with language taken directly from *The Southland* essay that Livingstone had published in 1890. Who could forget these words?

> Fifty years ago woman's activity [...] was a pretty clearly cut "sphere," including primarily the kitchen and the nursery and rescued from the barrenness of prison bars by the womanly mania for adorning every discoverable bit of china or canvass with forlorn looking cranes balanced idiotically on one foot. The woman of today finds herself in the presence of responsibilities which ramify through the profoundest and most varied interests of her country and race. Not one of the issues of this plodding, toiling, sinning, repenting, falling, aspiring humanity can afford to shut her out or can deny the reality of her influence.[165]

The students and faculty at Livingstone who had read Cooper's *Southland* essay the previous year would have recognized these words and noticed that, in this book, Cooper was developing ideas initially set out in that essay. But even they would not have realized that Cooper's *Southland* essay was her first published work.[166] Nor could they possibly have imagined that, with the publication of that essay, Livingstone had become a crucible for black feminist thought.

These speakers and publications and ideas interested Trent. He was becoming known as an industrious student, and, also, a student interested in using his Christian training to build a stronger religious community. But he was also known for having fun. In the summer of 1892 he and his good friend John Walker organized Livingstone's football team, the Livingstone Bears.[167] Walker was captain, and Trent was manager, and also played halfback.[168] Each player chipped in a little money to buy the football. They padded their old clothes to make practice uniforms. And since they didn't have special football shoes, they put cleats on their regular shoes for practice and the games, then removed them afterwards.[169]

On December 27, 1892, Trent played in the first intercollegiate football game between two black schools, Livingstone versus Biddle University of Charlotte.[170] There was much excitement at the school in the days leading up to the event. The young women in the sewing classes were making uniforms out of white duck, working hard to finish the uniforms before the big day. Trent later said that he was sure that he had the best uniform since he was "courting" the director of the Sewing Department at this time.[171] While the women were cutting and pinning and sewing, team members practiced their plays.

As time for the kickoff drew near, Livingstone students started gathering at the front lawn for the game, despite the bitter cold, and despite the snow, so they could watch the arrival of others who came to see the game. They came from miles around—some walking, some in wagons, others on mules or horses.[172] The game consisted of two 45-minute periods; each touchdown was five points. In the first half, a Biddle player grabbed the ball and ran to the end zone for a touchdown. During the second period, Walker tackled a Biddle player who had the ball.[173] Trent scored Livingstone's only touchdown on a fumble recovery. But since snow had by then covered the field's markings, Biddle argued that the recovery was out of bounds. The official ruled in Biddle's favor, the touchdown didn't count, and the Livingstone Bears lost.[174] Nonetheless, Trent was recognized as such a good halfback that, later on, Shaw University asked him to join their team in two postseason games.[175]

Many years later Trent said that he had been a "star player" at school because running to catch rabbits when he was in college had kept him physically fit.[176] This is the kind of statement that would make you think someone is pulling your leg, but it turns out that some of the greatest athletes in the National Football League today attribute their skill in part to chasing rabbits when they were young.[177] According to Brian Holloway, a former professional football player and one of Trent's great-grandchildren, this background gives a player "super quick feet, amazing, almost superhuman agility," and the ability to make sudden changes in direction. He continues: "You can't catch him, you can't hit him, and just when you think you've got him, he squirts through [...] and the next thing you know he is running into the end zone." Holloway describes halfbacks as very fast runners, often much smaller than the other players. He also describes them as men with strong personalities and extreme self-confidence—vital traits, he continues, if you are about to step onto the field with "eleven really angry guys who want to attack you."[178]

Trent's role as cofounder, manager, and player on Livingstone's first football team thus provides more depth to our understanding of him as a young man. Creating the team shows us that he was a man with vision and confidence. Playing halfback shows us that he was a man who liked rough-and-tumble sports, and had so much confidence in his physical skill that he wasn't afraid of carrying the ball while eleven men on the other team were trying to tackle him. And finally, since his classmates agreed to join a team he was creating, it is also clear that he had strong leadership skills, and knew, even when young, how to inspire friendship and respect.

Trent was also active in Livingstone's Young Men's Christian Association. Howard University created the first Y branch in a black college in 1869.[179] The national YMCA began sending representatives to black colleges in 1883, to promote Y work and set up branches at the schools.[180] By 1888, there were YMCA branches in twenty-eight black schools.[181] Livingstone had a Y group as early as 1883, perhaps earlier.[182] It also played an important role in the development of the national Y college program. In 1892, it was one of only seven schools present at the third meeting of the black college YMCAs, in Lynchburg, Virginia. It also sent representatives to the fourth conference, in 1893, and to the fifth, in 1894.[183] In 1896, it was one of the eight black colleges that sent delegates to the seventh annual conference (Eastern Section) of Colored Young Men's Associations.[184]

Leaders of the Colored Men's Department of the YMCA thought it was "of strategic importance" to concentrate on building Y associations in the black colleges and universities. William A. Hunton, former head of the Norfolk YMCA, and now head of the "Colored Men's Department," stated in 1899:

> These men, who are soon to become centers of influence among the millions, by forming voluntary classes for the devotional study of the Word, engaging in personal and organized work among their fellows at school, and by studying the condition and need of their people, are strengthened in Christian character and become competent leaders of Young Men's Christian Associations[....] These thousands of intelligent and consecrated young men, dispersing, year by year, into all sections of the country, will lead in the development of a deeper and purer religious life, and in raising the standard of character among their people.[185]

In December 1899, fifty-two of the seventy-one associations of the "colored" YMCAs in the country were affiliated with either a black college or university.[186]

The purpose of YMCA college associations at that time was "to promote spirituality and Christian fellowship among its members, and aggressive Christian work by and for students."[187] College groups were to hold Bible-study classes and gospel meetings, and individual members were supposed to engage in "personal work," defined as "the effort of one man to bring one other man to Christ."[188] One way to do this was to welcome new students to the campus and introduce them to the YMCA. Members of the Y were also supposed to engage in work in the college neighborhood, by leading Sunday school groups and prayer meetings, and, as well, by visiting jails, hospitals, and "alms houses."[189]

In 1894 the Livingstone Y had forty-six members, thirty-six of whom were active.[190] It was considered a strong group because of the "devotion" of a group of seven young men, a group which included Trent.[191] As a schoolmate later wrote: "Trent took an active part in the YMCA work of the school. Mr. Trent is not a minister, but he is very useful in Christian work."[192] The young men in the Livingstone YMCA held weekly services at the county poorhouse: on Thanksgiving Day they took food and other supplies with them. They also held weekly prayer services with the chain gang at the local jail.[193] And they very likely also had Bible classes and tried to convert their classmates.[194] As President Price noted in 1884, the goal of the Association was "to help make secure, as well as to reclaim, young men."[195]

The national offices of the YMCA soon realized that sending representatives to the black colleges was an ideal way to recruit directors for the black Ys around the country. They could reach large numbers of young men without having to travel very much, and at the same time they could reach the educated elite, the type of men they wanted to hire as leaders.[196] Before 1890, the Y international secretary for "Colored Work" had always been white. But in 1890, when Trent arrived at Livingstone, YMCA headquarters finally hired a black man, William A. Hunton, for that position.[197] So if the YMCA leadership visited Livingstone while Trent was there, it was Hunton who would have made the trip. Perhaps he met Trent on one of those trips. If so, it may well have been important to Trent that the person who came on campus to discuss the importance of YMCA work was a black man—yet another important example of black manliness and black leadership.

Trent sang in several music groups at the school, and many thought that even though Trent was known as a good student, he would be most remembered for his singing. As one classmate later wrote: "He had a sweet pathetic voice that drew you in spite of yourself." He and his friend John Walker sang in the Atkins and Battle Quartette, organized by one of his classmates.[198]

The school not only had musical groups and a football team: it also had literary societies and a baseball team, as well as other social clubs created by the students. Members of the Athletic

Club performed tricks on a trapeze, walked a tightrope, and did "jumping acts." The Gallant Six were a group of six young men who took as their inspiration the age of chivalry. One student wrote that "it was a sight worth going hundreds of miles to see a lady drop a pin and six young men [...] make a dive and all six come up with that pin and present it to the lady." One of the women's clubs was The Royals, whose members wore little blue bows to show that they were in the group.[199]

Trent and his friend Walker, although serious students, were not above participating in pranks. They were members of the "Reception Committee," a free-floating group of students in the higher grades who posed as professors to "inspect" new students when they arrived at school. The duty of the "Food Inspector" was to take away and "inspect" whatever food the new student brought to school; the "Examiner" asked the student very hard questions very quickly, to determine what class he should be assigned to; and the "Music Examiner" made the unfortunate student sing, in order to "try out" for the chorus. The "professors" then retired to another room, purportedly to discuss their "verdict," but, in reality, to eat the food they had taken from their hapless victim.[200]

Trent and Walker were also "prominent members" of the Dixie Coon Club, which "swore eternal vengeance on that grinning varmint." One of the members was "Axe-man," and another, "Torchman."[201] It sounds like it was a hunting club, where the most important part of their activities was going out at night for the hunt and the kill. Livingstone had a farm that grew much of the food for the students and faculty, and raccoons were known to cause crop damage and spread disease. But many hunting clubs in the South at this time had stopped hunting, and had become social clubs instead.[202] So we don't know if the men in this club were hunting raccoons for food, for fun, to protect the school's crop, or whether they were even hunting at all. But we do know that for Trent this must have been at least a tip of the hat to his farm-boy days. He had grown up hunting for food, and would continue hunting into his later years.

By the end of 1892, Trent had completed both the B and A grammar classes and was ready to move on to the normal school.[203] But as he moved up in the school, in 1893, the Livingstone community had a moment of great joy, and suffered great sadness. It was a joyous time because in May the school held its decennial commencement. The baccalaureate sermon was presented by Bishop Hood, pioneer missionary of the AME Zion Church to North Carolina. The celebration continued a few days later with a speech by President Price and a series of shorter addresses. Livingstone's Professor Atkins spoke on "The Work of the Negro Teacher." And it must have had some meaning for Trent to hear the talk "The Negro and Business Enterprises"—not because he had any particular interest in business enterprises, but because the speaker was Rev. Josiah Caldwell, who had so many years before suggested to Trent's mother that she send him to Livingstone.

After the addresses, the day concluded with twenty toasts, including toasts to the Alumni Association, to "our college journals," to "the Negro in the legal profession," to "our women," to "our guests and their work," and to "our women in the temperance movement."[204] It was very important, of course, for the school to honor women with two toasts. But it would have been a greater honor if more than two of the twenty-seven speakers that day had been women.

Even as they celebrated the decennial of the school, the students all knew that their beloved president was ill. Price had been invited to give a speech in August at the World's Fair in Chicago, but he had not been strong enough to travel there. Frederick Douglass presented the address in his place, where he told the assembled audience: "This is Price's day. I am here as a substitute. Since I have grown old I was one time disturbed about the cause of my people on the American platform, in leadership and organization. Since the rise of Joseph C. Price, I have dismissed all fears. I am willing to die and leave the race in his hands."[205] But it was Price who would die first.

In August, Price's doctor had sent him to New York City, then Saratoga Springs, for medical treatment, but he soon returned home, very sick. He arrived on Friday, October 6, just a few days after the beginning of classes. Even during his last days, he showed his commitment to Livingstone and to his students. For, despite his weakness, he nonetheless met with the students a few days later for Sunday school, and again the following morning, for devotional exercises. He did not have the energy to lead the exercises, as was his normal practice, but his strong desire to be with his students led him there.[206]

When Price was dying, he called Goler to his bedside, put his arms around him, and said, "Goler, you have been a true friend. I could not have done this without the work you have done here. I want you to take my place; God's blessings be with you." Later recalling Price's promise his first year at Livingstone that the school could not afford to give him a salary, Goler said: "And [...] there I received my pay."[207]

Price died a few weeks later, on October 25, at the age of thirty-nine.[208] His death was an enormous loss to the school, and must have been keenly felt by many students. For those Livingstone students who truly considered their school a family, they had just lost their father. The presidency of the college would now pass to Professor Goler.

Price died during the semester, so it is very likely that Trent attended the funeral services along with his schoolmates, the faculty, church leaders, and presidents of other black colleges.[209] The white community also came to pay its respects. The mayor and the entire city council of Salisbury were present, and four of the leading white lawyers in town asked permission to act as pallbearers.[210] Price was buried on the college grounds in front of Huntington Hall. In a telegram of condolences to Mrs. Price, Frederick Douglass wrote: "The race has lost its ablest advocate."[211]

Years later, in a speech at Livingstone, Trent explained what Price had meant to him:

> I love Dr. J. C. Price for what he was in himself, for his greatness of heart, for the ideals in his life. Thousands have heard the eloquence of his voice and sat with

breathless attention to catch every word that fell from his lips. Two continents have been charmed by his sweeping oratory [....] I have sat beneath its spell and seen men wild with enthusiasm, and yet those who have only heard him speak, caught but a glimpse of the real man. To know him in his true greatness and goodness, ask those who lived under his care, who received his fatherly counsel, who knew something of his philanthropic spirit, who sacrificed with him in this education work.[212]

Reading these words leads us to think that there must have been times when Trent saw in Price the father he would have liked to have—the father who taught him to aspire to "true greatness and goodness," the father who would never abandon his son.

Three years after Price's death the school created a singing group, the Price Memorial Concert Co., to raise money for a memorial to their president. It must have meant a lot to Trent to be a member of this group. When Livingstone held its first Founder's Day celebration, on February 10, 1895, their singing made up the entire program.[213] They performed at various events around the country, including at the Atlanta Cotton States and International Exposition, where, in October 1895, Booker T. Washington made his famous "Atlanta Exposition Address."[214]

At school Trent became good friends with classmates George C. Clement and John W. Walker. Clement, two years older than Trent, had become a minister in 1888, when he was sixteen, and was ordained a deacon several years later.[215] Walker had been his roommate, perhaps the person who inadvertently "shared" his toothbrush with young Trent.

Interestingly, two of Trent's good friends during this period were Africans. Kwegyir Aggrey, from the Gold Coast (now Ghana), arrived at Livingstone in the summer of 1898, right after Trent's graduation. He had been invited to the school by one of the AME Zion bishops, who had traveled to Ghana to establish a mission.[216] Aggrey had already taught school before leaving Ghana: by the age of fifteen he was in charge of a school of about thirty-five boys. By sixteen, he was preaching; taking lessons in preparation for the Cambridge examination; translating sermons and the Bible from English to Fanti; and also composing type, writing articles, and editing copy for the *Gold Coast Methodist Times*.[217] Educated in the classical tradition, Aggrey called Trent "Zeus," and considered him one of his best friends.[218] The second African who became Trent's friend was Simon Fuller, raised and educated on his family's coffee plantation in Liberia, near Monrovia. Fuller came to the United States to continue his studies at Livingstone when he was seventeen.[219]

And it was perhaps at some point during this period that Trent became friends with William Jacob Walls. Walls began his grammar school studies at Livingstone in 1899, at the age of thirteen, and was ordained at Hopkins Chapel in Asheville the following year.[220] While still a student, he pastored at a nearby church.[221] Walls and Trent met early on, for many years later, in a letter to Trent, Walls recalled "how faithfully you helped and guided me from a child in my striving on the upward way."[222]

"Tell me who your friends are, and I'll tell you who you are" is a saying in so many cultures that it is worth paying attention to. Here we note that three of Trent's closest friends were already Christian leaders by time they arrived at college. Of course, Livingstone was a church school, so perhaps this is not as surprising as it would be in a secular school. Nonetheless, these were not students in the school of theology: they were men he met at college and chose as his friends. These choices give us something to think about as we watch the development of Trent's character and see the decisions he will make in his life.

After finishing grammar school, normal school, and college, it was time for Trent to leave this community he had grown to love, and move on. During the last few months at school he might well have reflected on what he had learned over the years.

He would have been thinking about the five school leaders who had so influenced him during his stay: President Price; Professor, then President Goler; Professors Moore and Noble; and school matron Tucker. We can't tell precisely how each of these five would have inspired him. But we can see that they all had a formidable belief in education. It is almost as if, through their lives, they were saying: "Don't stop with a college degree: keep studying! Keep learning!" Both Price and Goler had B.A. degrees, then went on to get degrees in theology. After receiving his B.A. degree, Moore went to medical school, became a doctor, then went back to school and earned a doctorate in classical languages. Noble, who taught mathematics and science, also taught himself the law, and became a member of the North Carolina state bar. And Annie Tucker went on to get an M.A. degree.

Not only did they never stop studying and learning; they also worked very hard to not let life's problems get in their way. Did Goler want to pastor in Winston and teach in Salisbury at the same time? Then he would just ride thirty-six miles on horseback every Sunday night in order to make that possible. Did Price want to continue his devotional exercises with students even though he was suffering with a grave illness? Then he would simply continue to go to chapel services. These five were all pioneers. They were all indefatigable. And they all had in common seriousness of purpose and devotion to learning, to Livingstone, and to the young people in their charge. Price in particular was known for his sense of optimism, for his sense of the possible. Despite all the difficulties in creating and maintaining the school, his favorite saying was this: "I care not how dark the night: I believe in the coming of the dawn."[223] All five must have shared this belief. By spending eight years with them, Trent would have learned something important about dedication, commitment, and friendship. Since Price was president of Livingstone during Trent's first three years as a student, and Goler, the last five, Trent would also have been able to see how they interacted with students and teachers, and to study their different styles of leadership.

Trent would also have been thinking about what he had learned in the classroom during those years. When he began school at Livingstone, he was reading an elementary textbook about the continents, rivers, and oceans of the world, a basic history of the United States, and a fourth-grade reader. Since then, he would have very likely studied astronomy, geology, physiology, botany, and chemistry; algebra, geometry, and trigonometry; social science and political economy; and navigation and surveying, moral philosophy, logic, and rhetoric. He had also probably studied six years of Latin and four years of Greek.[224]

Mastery of these subjects put him in an elite group of classically educated men in the country. This would provide him with not only a certain stature, but also irrefutable proof that white people were no smarter than he. His mastery of Greek and Latin would be especially difficult for many whites to accept. As late as 1904, James Y. Joyner, head of public education in North Carolina, justified the lower per capita spending for black school children, in part, with these words: "As long as we are appropriating only this much money for this number of children, nobody need have any real concern about turning the negro's head by the study of Latin and Greek and other higher branches of learning. The statistical tables of this report show that not a single [N]egro is reported as studying Latin in a single public school of the State."[225] Well-educated men like Trent would cause them "real concern," indeed.

And now, during his last semester in college, he would probably be reading Butler's *The Analogy of Religion, Natural and Revealed, to the Constitution and Course of Nature*, a very long and very dense book on morality. He would also read Homer's *Iliad* in his Greek class; and in Latin, the history of the Roman Empire, by Tacitus.[226] And he must have wondered many times during these final months where he would be going after he left Livingstone, and what kind of work he would be doing.

As noted earlier, YMCA representative Hunton visited black schools every year to look for potential Y leaders. In 1890 he wrote that, during those visits, "the most likely men might be picked out, set apart, and directed in a course of study and line of work." He also thought it important for YMCA workers to spend several weeks at the school "inspiring, instructing and encouraging the candidates."[227] Just as the AME Zion Church was trying to build leaders, so too was the YMCA. Indeed, in a sense, the Y was competing with the black churches for leaders.

Hunton already knew that finding new Y leaders would be difficult. As one black Y leader stated: "My heart is depressed with the burden of the need of a few good men for our work. We must find them."[228] Historian Nina Mjagkij described what they were looking for: the men "had to represent a unique blend of Christian social worker and business manager [....] They had to be willing to work as janitors, librarians, teachers, preachers, counselors, accountants, fund raisers, athletic instructors, and song leaders. They also had to assist men in finding housing and employment. In addition, African-American YMCA secretaries had to be prepared to work for little money."[229]

During their campus visits, Y representatives interviewed potential candidates. If a student looked promising, they would ask him to provide information about his personal and educational background; his employment history, religious affiliation, and previous Y work; his ability to teach athletics and Bible classes, to lead in singing, and to play instruments; and his ability to handle business accounts. A student who was interested in working for the YMCA also had to provide four character references.[230] For this work, a passion for religion was less important than an ability to work with people. They wanted men who were "prominent in the church and popular among their people"; men with business skills; men who had integrity and were honest. They also needed men who would be able to manage issues of class. For example, on one occasion, when Hunton proposed a local physician as director of the YMCA in Columbia, South Carolina, the former director said that the physician was not a good choice, since he was "'too big for us poor people [....] We want men that stand between all classes of men.'"[231]

In April 1898, just a few months before Trent's graduation, the United States embarked upon a war with Spain over the Cuban fight for independence from Spain, its colonial ruler.[232] Soon, almost a quarter of a million American men were under arms. The International Committee of the YMCA immediately received permission from the army and navy to send YMCA secretaries to the field to provide services to the white troops. The Y tents provided newspapers and magazines, material for correspondence, and equipment for games and sports. They also provided Bibles and hymnals for Bible study, and for religious services led by the Y secretaries.[233] Hunton decided it was important to provide these same services to black soldiers. On June 6, 1898, he wrote that he had "nearly secured" a tent to go up at Fort Macon, Georgia.[234] By the end of June, he described his visit to a Y tent near Washington, DC, where he saw 6,000 troops on parade, and a visit to Fort Macon, North Carolina, where he noted that the "North Carolina Colored troops" appeared to be "proud of having colored officers."[235] In July, Hunton and his Y committee set up a tent for 800 soldiers near Richmond, and equipped it with an organ. They also sent a Y secretary, and provided books, writing material, Bibles, and hymnals for the men.[236] It was an exceptionally busy time for Hunton, who was trying to create YMCAs in the camps, raise money for them, and find the men to direct this work, while at the same time carrying on with his regular YMCA work.[237]

It would have been surprising if Hunton had not already considered Trent as a likely prospect for the position of Y secretary even before the outbreak of the war, for Trent was well known on campus for his YMCA leadership. The two men might also have met earlier at one of the annual conferences of the Colored Men's Department of the YMCA, since Livingstone sent student representatives to these conferences as early as 1892, and we know that Hunton attended at least the 1896 conference, when Trent would have been engaged in Y activities at Livingstone.[238]

And, as we have already seen, Trent possessed the traits that the YMCA was looking for in its leaders. His work with the YMCA showed not only his strong interest in religion, but also his work while at school to develop a Christian community. His membership and leadership position on the football team and in the singing groups showed his ability to lead and to get along with others, as well as his ability to organize and teach music and sports. A fellow student later wrote that Trent "grew popular with all classes of students."[239] So there was no doubt but that he was well liked on campus, and that he had learned how to successfully mediate differences of class, gender, and color.

There can also be no question of whether he would have been able to provide four character references. The teachers and administrators at Livingstone would have taken good notice of Trent well before his senior year because of his consistently high grades, because there were so few students in the college, and because of the leadership qualities he showed in campus activities. If Hunton hadn't noticed Trent on one of his trips to Livingstone early on, it is likely that either the president or a faculty member would have pointed him out as a potential Y director.

At some point during the spring of 1898, the national office of the YMCA asked Trent to be YMCA secretary, after graduation, for the Third North Carolina Volunteer Regiment, men who had volunteered to fight in the Spanish-American War.[240] The first black regiment in United States history commanded entirely by black officers, the Third North Carolina Regiment had 1,100 soldiers.[241] Trent's job would require him to set up a tent for the men wherever they were located, and to provide the social and spiritual services which were the hallmarks of the Y community. He accepted the offer. His salary was probably very low. Indeed, it is likely that he could have earned more money after graduation by returning to work in railroad dining cars. But he had been raised by his family to be a leader of his people, and he had been inspired by the AME Zion Church and the Livingstone community to enter a life of Christian service.

Commencement exercises took place Wednesday, May 25, 1898, at two in the afternoon, in Huntington Hall. Rev. Cicero Harris delivered the baccalaureate sermon.[242] Trent graduated as valedictorian of his class with an A.B. degree, at the age of twenty-five.[243] It must have made his heart very full to have his mother, Malinda Dunn, present for the ceremony, for even though she had not been able to get an education, she had always wanted him to have one. When he received his diploma, everyone there heard her shout, in a loud, joyous voice: "Thank you, Jesus!"[244] It must have also been very meaningful to share the event with so many of his good friends, including classmates John Walker and George Clement.[245] Indeed, the celebration continued on into the evening when Trent stood as best man at Clement's wedding to Emma Clarissa Williams, who had graduated from Livingstone's Normal Department the same day.[246] Livingstone might have had strict rules forbidding men and women students from speaking with each other, but the heart has rules too.

When Trent graduated, he was one of only thirty-seven Livingstone graduates with an A.B. degree.[247] But he would be taking more than a college degree with him when he left. He would also be taking friendships that would develop and endure, although he could not know at the time that these friends who had supported and encouraged him at Livingstone would continue to support and encourage him in his later life. Nor could he know how these friendships would travel down through generations in his family.

Along with deep friendships, he would take with him a reputation as a hard worker, a skilled leader, and a man of Christian character. He also took Livingstone's name and reputation. For even though it was a very small school, Livingstone was widely known and respected. So when Trent left Livingstone, he moved out into a network of Livingstone graduates, people who knew and respected the school, and people whose lives had been somehow transformed by the school.

Trent's Livingstone patrimony also included the fact that he had been at the school when Price was president. The fact that he had known Price, this man so widely admired, the fact that he had been in his presence, spoken with him, heard him speak—all this gave Trent a certain standing that would only grow over time as the number of those who had known Price grew smaller.

He would be leaving Livingstone not as a new person, but as a person who had been acculturated into a new language and a new culture. If he arrived at school speaking accented English, he would have left without it. Even though he arrived not knowing what a toothbrush was, by the time he left, he had learned new ways of presenting himself. Before he came to the school, he would have surely seen men and women working together: to be successful on a farm, everyone has to pull together. But at Livingstone, he saw black men and women teachers working together in a professional organization, and had the chance to observe their interaction.

He would have met President Price's wife, Jennie, a graduate of Scotia Seminary, in Concord, North Carolina.[248] This women's school was modeled on Mount Holyoke College in Massachusetts, and thus had modern ideas of what an educated woman should learn. Her studies would not be limited to music, needlework, and cooking: she would also study Latin.[249] Trent would have noticed how President Price treated his wife; he would have seen him outside in the evening playing ball or croquet with their children.[250] And all this must have given him much to consider, as he contemplated the kind of life he wanted to lead, and the kind of woman he might choose for a wife.

Finally, as he left the school, he was anchored, recognized, and valued in the three institutions that would provide him work, status, and a sense of purpose for the rest of his life: the AME Zion Church, Livingstone College, and the YMCA. But of course, this is hindsight. He could not have known then that the foundation was set and the path would be straight. All he knew was that he was leaving school. He was leaving his second home.

Chapter 3

Uplift in a Segregated World:
Trent, the Young Men's Institute, and the YMCA

JUST AS TRENT'S LIFE WAS opening up to the world during these years at Livingstone, just as he was beginning to think about the possibilities for his future, the world for black Americans in North Carolina was starting to close down. As Joseph C. Price once explained: "The Confederacy surrendered its sword at Appomattox, but did not there surrender its conviction."[1]

The signs were everywhere.

Southern states began to enact laws separating blacks and whites in public conveyances in 1881. The first was Tennessee, and other states rolled along behind: Florida, Mississippi, Texas, Louisiana, Alabama, Kentucky, Arkansas, and Georgia. Whites in North Carolina soon started pushing for the same kind of legislation. In 1893 Price led a delegation to the state capitol to lobby against the passage of any such Jim Crow law.[2] Three years later the United States Supreme Court ruled that states did not violate the U.S. Constitution when they required carriers to segregate railway cars, as long as the cars were "equal," thus offering even more encouragement to those who wanted segregated trains in North Carolina.[3] By 1898, when Trent graduated, whites in the state were increasing the pressure on the legislature to segregate not only the trains, but also hotels and restaurants.

In the early 1890s, when Trent was beginning his studies at Livingstone, black people in North Carolina had played an influential role in state politics. They still had the ballot. There were blacks representing North Carolina in Congress, as well as many black officeholders around the state: magistrates and councilmen, members of municipal committees, commissioners. But when Democrats lost the elections in both 1894 and 1896, they became determined to remove blacks from North Carolina politics in the November 1898 election, and used race-baiting as their tool of choice.[4] As election day grew closer, white leaders created a "black-on-white" rape scare in order to destroy the black/white political alliance that had been growing.[5] Every day, the frenzy grew. So even as Trent was celebrating graduation with his friends and family, even as he was moving on to a new job with the Young Men's Christian Association (YMCA), racial hatred throughout the state was growing.

At the same time that North Carolina was gearing up for the election, the United States was in a deepening conflict with Spain over the Cuban struggle for independence from its colonial ruler. Cuba was winning, and the United States, which had long wanted to own Cuba, decided to take steps to ensure that neither Spain nor Cuba itself retained control of the island.[6] On April 11, President McKinley sent a message to Congress requesting congressional authorization to begin a "forcible intervention" in the Cuban conflict, stating only that the sole purpose of this "intervention" was to stop the fighting between Spain and the Cuban insurgents.[7] Seven days later Congress authorized the president to "use the entire land and naval forces of the United States, and to call into the actual service of the United States the militia of the several States" to get Spain to withdraw its forces from Cuba.[8]

In late April 1898, right before Livingstone's commencement, President McKinley authorized the states to recruit volunteers to add to the regular army, as the country prepared for war.[9] More than 200,000 men volunteered for service.[10] Of that number, 10,000 were black.[11] As a representative of the YMCA, Trent would be working with some of these men.

North Carolina's Republican governor Daniel L. Russell authorized the creation of an all-black battalion, the Third North Carolina Voluntary Infantry, that same month. He appointed a prominent black Republican, James H. Young, as commander, with the rank of major. Young, a graduate of Shaw University and editor of the *Raleigh Gazette*, was a former member of the state legislature, and had been acting as liaison for the governor with his black constituents.[12] In May, the battalion was expanded to regimental strength, and had 10 companies with 100 men in each company.[13] In June, Major Young was commissioned colonel, and the governor appointed a full roster of officers to the Third North Carolina, all of them black.[14]

There were three all-black volunteer regiments with black officers during the Spanish-American War, but the Third North Carolina was the only one in the South.[15] For Governor Russell, this was a reward for the black voters who had helped him win the gubernatorial election in 1896.[16] The appointment of black officers was a source of great pride to the soldiers in the Third North Carolina, and to the larger black community. Indeed, some black soldiers in regiments with white officers complained mightily about that situation. In the Sixth Virginia, for example, a black regiment, the soldiers were upset when all the black officers were replaced by white officers, saying that they had only signed up because they were assured that they would have black officers.[17] Not surprisingly, the existence of a black regiment with all-black officers created hostility in the white community.

There were mixed opinions in the black community about participating in this war. Some thought it was a way to show whites that black people were good citizens. Some also thought that victory in the war would lead to increased economic opportunities for black people once Cuba came under American influence. Others considered it hypocritical to try to free Cuba from Spanish rule while black people were not free at home.[18]

Even though the American government was intervening in Cuban affairs for commercial and political reasons, there were those in the black community who saw this war as a way to support the liberation struggle of black Cubans.[19] Indeed, on April 21, 1898, the Board of Bishops of the AME Zion Church adopted a resolution supporting President McKinley's efforts "to give liberty and peace to the long oppressed people in the Island of Cuba."[20] Many remembered Afro-Cuban freedom fighter Antonio Maceo, who had led the long struggle of the Cuban people for independence from Spanish rule and for the end of slavery, earlier in the century. For them, Maceo, often called "the bronze Titan" for his African ancestry, represented the continuing liberation struggle of African people all over the world.[21] Inspired by Maceo's leadership, Captain Thomas Leatherwood, the black officer in the Third North Carolina Volunteer Infantry who had organized the Asheville company of volunteers, named that group "the Maceo Volunteers."[22]

By mid-July, the volunteers had mustered into the army as the Third North Carolina Volunteer Infantry at Fort Macon, North Carolina.[23] But on August 12, just as the soldiers were starting to settle in, Spain and the United States reached an armistice. Although some soldiers were mustered out, soldiers in the Third North Carolina were not.

In September the men traveled by rail to their new home at Camp Poland in Knoxville, Tennessee, for more training, and for garrison duty.[24] The camp was stretched out with a broad road in the middle and with side streets off of the road. The soldiers' tents and the canteen were on one side of the road, and on the other were officers' housing, the hospital, and the YMCA tent.[25] The soldiers' days all had the same basic structure: reveille at 5:45 a.m., followed by breakfast; camp cleanup and fatigue duty; drills, practice marches, and target practice; lunch at 12:15; more fatigue duty and drills, plus classes for some of the soldiers; dinner; then tattoo at 9:00 p.m.; and finally, taps.[26] As the soldiers settled into the new camp, they also had to cut ditches, make sinkholes, build shanties for the kitchens, help lay waterpipes to run into the company kitchen, and lay floors for the tents.[27] The routines would be broken up by sports, inspections, and parades.[28]

The black community in Knoxville provided some support for the soldiers and officers. They welcomed them at the black churches in town and invited them to dinner at their homes.[29] But for many of the soldiers, this did not make up for the unpleasant work they were now being asked to do.

Trent joined the men in Knoxville and immediately set to work in the YMCA tent on the grounds. A major part of the secretary's work was to provide a home away from home for the soldiers, a place for them to sit and read, to write a letter, to visit with friends. For many, it was "a place of rest [and] relaxation, [with a] serene atmosphere and freedom [....] Warmed and lighted during the winter evenings, it was a great gathering place [...] both to keep warm, and indulge in interesting conversation."[30] Some soldiers and officers felt so comfortable there that they stayed in the Y tent until taps called for lights out. The Y secretary was to be a friend, teacher, and guide. As one Y secretary wrote: "Men crave sympathy, advice, encouragement and instructions along moral lines."[31]

The tents were fairly large, forty by sixty feet, with tables, chairs, and, often, an organ. In the Y tent soldiers could find games like checkers, chess, and dominoes, as well as barrels of ice water and sometimes even barrels of iced oatmeal water, considered a healthy and refreshing drink. The Y also provided paper, envelopes, and pen and ink, for those men who wanted to write letters home.[32] And there were books, as well as subscriptions to magazines like *Sporting Life, Army and Navy Journal,* and the black newspaper *New York Age.*[33] But it is very likely that some of the soldiers in the Third North Carolina were unable to read or to write letters home.[34] In July, as the federal government was starting to recruit for the war, a white officer contacted the Office of the Adjutant General to ask if "colored men [...] unable to read and write" could enlist. The reply came back quickly: in time of war, there was no requirement for literacy in black volunteer units.[35] So we might imagine that Trent also organized literacy classes, asking those men who could read and write to teach others, and to write letters home for them as well. He probably taught at least one of these groups himself.

The Y directors also provided entertainment for the men. There was equipment for outdoor sports; baseball was especially popular. And there were concerts where groups of the men would sing, get-togethers when all the men would join in to sing hymns and patriotic songs or tell stories, and talks by one of the men who had a particular area of expertise. Sometimes the tent was so crowded that the event had to be held outside, under the trees. Remembering Trent's Livingstone days and how much he liked to sing, one can easily imagine that he immediately organized musical programs and began to sing in a quartet.

But the YMCA was at its base a religious group, and religion was an important part of Trent's work. There would have been Bible classes and religious services. Perhaps he had Bibles to distribute to the men. He would have worked very hard to encourage conversion.[36] Y secretaries on military bases were expected to work closely with the base chaplain. In this regard, Trent was in luck, because the chaplain for the Third North Carolina, Henry Durham, had spent four years at Livingstone, graduating from its Normal Department before attending theological school at Central Tennessee College.[37] Since Durham had completed his studies at Livingstone in 1892, he and Trent had been on campus at the same time and knew each other.[38] Their common experience might well have made it easier for them to work together.

Military chaplains performed many tasks on the bases. On October 6, Chaplain Durham provided this report of his September activities: "Held religious services twenty-four times; visits to sick officers, six; visits to enlisted men, 100; visits to prisoners in the guardhouse, ten; held service [in guardhouse] twice. Number seeking advice, 150. Personal visits to men in tents, 1,000.

Married, one. Buried, one. The amount of money deposited with me by the men, $200. There have been eight soldiers tried before a general court-martial for whom I appeared as counsel. The number converted during the month of September was eighty-five."[39] Trent would have helped Durham with all these tasks.

Y activities were extremely popular on the army bases. Many camps had so many soldiers that there was more than one Y tent. At Chickamauga, in Georgia, there were eighteen Y tents; Camp Alger in Virginia had twelve.[40] And those tents were busy. In a report from the Seventh Ohio Regiment, a Y secretary provided the following brief, but telling, report: "There have been fully 550 visitors in the tent today; 330 letters were written. We need a much larger tent and more chairs. Fourteen men personally dealt with; ice water barrel filled three times; one man called down for swearing, just came in to ask my forgiveness; one visit to a sick officer."[41] The Y secretary at Camp Alger reported that on one day alone, over 9,000 men visited the tents, and wrote 4,944 letters; 2,684 soldiers went to gospel meetings; 64 asked for prayers; there were 5 Bible classes, which 130 soldiers attended; and 57 of the men "professed conversions." In Tampa, there had been as many as 1,500 men at one YMCA meeting.[42]

Unfortunately, in a summary of Y activity in eight camps, including Fort Macon, we learn nothing about Y activity there. We learn only that "the headquarters of the Colored Troops is provided with the same equipment as are the other camps."[43] There is no reason to suspect that Y activity at Fort Macon was different, or any less popular than it was at white military camps. But clearly the YMCA headquarters was less interested in Y activities in black regiments than it was in protecting itself from claims of discrimination against the black troops. Perhaps Y headquarters had good reason to be anxious about such claims.

Trent would have worked well in this environment. He would have felt comfortable with the enlisted men, and they would have felt comfortable with him. Many were illiterate unskilled workers; perhaps many were farm workers. But it was not that long ago that Trent, too, was a fifteen-year-old barely literate farm boy.

He would also have been comfortable with the officers, a very talented group. Of the 40 officers in this battalion, we find a group of artisans, including a shoemaker, a cooper, a tinsmith, a carpenter, and a blacksmith. Also, of the 40 officers, 16 had graduated from normal school. Half of that group went on to finish college studies, and of those 8, 6 completed advanced degrees: 2 received an M.A. degree, 4 completed medical school, and 2 of them had doctorates. We should not be surprised to find that 10 of the 40 officers had attended Shaw University since Colonel Young, the gubernatorial appointee who headed the regiment, was a Shaw graduate.[44]

The officers of the Third North Carolina had held various positions before mustering in. There were several teachers and principals, a lawyer, two college professors, two editors and publishers, and a trustee of one of the black colleges. Several had held elected positions—on a board of aldermen, on a city council, as justice of the peace, and as a member of the state legislature. And one had been appointed by President Cleveland to serve as minister to Liberia between 1888 and 1890.[45]

Thus the black officer group included the most successful black men in the community—college graduates, lawyers, doctors, by virtue of their education and professional status; and artisans, by virtue of their income, for during this period the wages of black artisans in North Carolina far exceeded those of, for example, teachers. Carpenters at this time earned one dollar and sixty cents a day. So a carpenter who worked six days a week for a month would earn about thirty-eight dollars, whereas black school teachers earned about twenty dollars a month.[46]

Trent had connections with some of the officers that would likely have proved helpful to him in his work, connections built at Livingstone College and in Asheville, where he had worked several summers.

Rev. Durham was not the only officer who had attended Livingstone: First Lieutenant E. L. Watkins had also graduated from the school's Normal Department. Another graduate of the Normal Department was Captain Joseph J. Hood, who had continued his studies at Shaw University's medical school and practiced medicine in Concord, North Carolina. The most interesting thing to note about Captain Hood, however, is that he was the son of Bishop Hood, who had come from Nova Scotia to eastern North Carolina at the end of the Civil War to do missionary work for the AME Zion Church. And finally, Adjutant E. E. Smith was another Livingstone connection—not because he had attended Livingstone, but because it was Livingstone founder and president Joseph Price who had earlier recommended to President Cleveland that he appoint Smith as minister to Liberia.[47]

Captain Thomas L. Leatherwood from Asheville had taught school for several years, and had also established a drugstore. Active in the Republican Party, Leatherwood had been appointed to federal positions in Washington, DC.[48] He was also active locally in Asheville affairs, and, in 1898, was president of the Young Men's Institute,[49] forerunner of that city's YMCA. Along with his friend First Lieutenant Harrison B. Brown, Leatherwood had a successful publishing business and published several newspapers, including *Free Man's Advocate*, *Business Enterprise*, and *The Colored Enterprise*. Brown had served as principal of a public school in Asheville, then worked in the Office of the Collector of Internal Revenue from 1889 to 1893. He then turned to the study of law and was admitted to the bar in the mid-1890s.[50] Trent became friends with these two officers. They would grow to like and admire him, and would, later on, prove helpful in furthering his career.

The soldiers had mustered in at Fort Macon, North Carolina, in July 1898, then moved by rail to Camp Poland in Knoxville, Tennessee, in mid-September, where Trent joined up with them. We can imagine that by November Trent was learning his way around camp, getting to know the men, thinking of new programs to carry out his mandate, and enjoying his work. It doesn't seem too far-fetched to think that the work he was doing as a black Y secretary with black soldiers would be much the same as the work of white Y secretaries with white soldiers. But it was not. Unfortunately, like other black Y secretaries, Trent had another, more difficult task: he would have had to figure out how to counsel the black soldiers when they were attacked by white soldiers, for while they were at Camp Poland, white soldiers in the First Georgia attacked the men of the Third North Carolina Volunteers over and over—with words, with rocks, and finally, with guns. The racial attacks were so serious that the Second Ohio, a white unit, was assigned to protect them. The white attackers, however, escaped punishment.[51]

Matters became even more desperate in November, when white men in Wilmington, North Carolina, attacked the black community in that city. The threat of massive white violence had been building up throughout North Carolina for a long time. Democrats were determined not to lose the statewide election in November 1898, and used race-baiting to get voters to support them. The closer it came to election day, the greater the frenzy of white hatred. Even Salisbury, home to Livingstone College, was not immune: in late September, men in white sheets rode through town terrorizing the black community.[52] But it was in Wilmington, two days after the election, two days after the Democrats and their white extremist friends took power back from the Republicans, that the most shocking violence took place.

How can we imagine the terror of black people in Wilmington who looked out of their windows on a Thursday morning and saw 500 armed white men marching four abreast through the city past their homes, past markets, past the schools—a group of 500 that soon swelled to 2,000? They marched toward the publishing house of Wilmington's black newspaper editor, burned it, and then ran wild, shooting black people wherever they saw them, shooting as they ran, shooting them in the back, shooting them in the head. Other white men joined in the fight: armed white men from Ku Klux Klan–type groups, some on horseback; armed soldiers from Company K of the Wilmington Light Infantry, recently returned from the Spanish-American War, who brought two cannons with them. And they were serious about their task. A commander of one of the infantry units told the soldiers: "When I give the command to shoot, I want you to shoot to kill."[53]

Many black Wilmingtonians tried to fight back, but they were both unprepared for the attack and massively out-armed. And so they fled. Those who were poor hid in the woods, taking their children and old people with them, living in the cold for days with no shelter, no food, no bedding. Those who had resources fled by horse, by wagon, or by railroad. By the end of December, 1,400 black people had left the town. Two weeks later, railroad companies were still adding extra cars on trains for black people fleeing the madness of white Wilmington.[54]

How can we imagine the terror of the black citizens of Wilmington—and how can we imagine the rage and fear of the men in the Third North Carolina, stranded in Tennessee, when they learned of the race hatred building up across North Carolina, and then, when they learned of the massacre in Wilmington? Many in the Third North Carolina had family and friends there. Indeed, Wilmington had provided a company of black volunteers, and was home to at least one of the officers, Major Andrew J. Walker. Two officers, Captain J. T. York and Captain Samuel O. Mason, were from New Bern, eighty-seven miles northeast of Wilmington.[55] But when black people from Wilmington fled to that city to find safety, they were not safe: white men had climbed the railroad water towers so they could see better how to shoot them when they got off the trains.[56]

So there they were, the men of the Third North Carolina, stranded in Tennessee, having given up their homes and family and work to fight for their fellow countrymen, black and white, yet now unable to even help their own people. How could they begin to comprehend that the white soldiers they were supposed to fight with in Cuba, the soldiers in Company K, had been mustered out, and were now slaughtering their friends, neighbors, and family? Company K never got to fight for the United States in Cuba, but they got to kill black people—fellow citizens—back home.[57]

This must have been an important test of Trent's Christian beliefs, and a test of his relationship with the men. He too would have likely had friends in Wilmington and feared for their survival. How would he counsel the soldiers who were frightened for their families, who wanted to desert the army and go back home to protect them, who wanted to kill white people in revenge?[58] Would he be able to persuade them that violence was not the answer to violence? And would he even be able to persuade himself? The camp must have been a somber place indeed.

About two weeks after the Wilmington massacre, on November 23, Trent traveled with the Third North Carolina as they moved once more, this time from Camp Poland, Tennessee, to Camp Haskell, near Macon, Georgia.[59] And a little over two weeks after that, on December 10, the United States and Spain signed the Treaty of Paris. The war was over.

The men in the Third North Carolina were distressed when they learned of the move to Georgia, the Deep South. They knew that the harassment and violence against them would only increase. And in general, they were tired of it all. Some had already written to the secretary of war complaining about bad food, poor housing, insufficient clothing, and the kind of work they were being asked to do. "We the undersigned," they wrote, "did not join the service for garrison duty."[60] The war was over, and they wanted to go home. Unfortunately they would have to remain in Camp Haskell a little longer.

The monotony of camp life was broken toward the end of December when Charles Francis Meserve, the white president of Shaw University, made an unannounced visit to Camp Haskell. He wanted to investigate the charges made in the Georgia press that the soldiers in the Third North Carolina were "turbulent, [...] obstreperous," prone to "drunken brawls," and "worse than useless." Since so many of the officers, and Colonel Young himself, were graduates of Shaw, these charges were in a sense an attack on the quality of men produced by that school. Instead of finding drunken, brawling, "useless" soldiers, Meserve found quite the contrary, noting that "the spirit and discipline of officers and men was admirable." He praised the leadership of Colonel Young. And, without mentioning Trent by name, he also praised Trent's work when he wrote in his report that "the YMCA tent is a great blessing to the regiment and is very popular, and aids in every possible way the work of Chaplain Durham."[61]

But even as the soldiers of the Third North Carolina were waiting to be mustered out, violence against them did not stop. White people in Georgia killed at least four of the soldiers because those soldiers would not accept the insults hurled at them nor follow the Jim Crow customs of that state. Street car conductors killed another three soldiers who refused to ride in the black car. All of the murderers were tried by white juries, and all of the murderers were acquitted.[62] And once more, it was Trent and Chaplain Durham who would have listened to the fear and the rage of the black soldiers, trying to figure out how to counsel them, how to comfort them. There may have been some training for Y directors before they took over their duties during the Spanish-American War, but it is unlikely that there was training for this.

Finally, during the first week of February 1899, the entire regiment mustered out of service.[63] Finally, the soldiers of the Third North Carolina could go home. They never saw combat. They returned home from Georgia by troop train, but since they had been discharged, they were, like all people not in the military, subject to control by local police. The police in Macon harassed the discharged men as they were leaving, then contacted the police in Atlanta, told them that black soldiers were on the way, and warned them that there would be trouble unless the police prevented it.[64] When the train reached Atlanta, the police boarded and clubbed the unarmed men: as one observer tells us, there were "many bloody heads."[65]

The soldiers were returning to a different North Carolina than the one they had left the previous August. The Republicans had lost at the polls, and Reconstruction in that state was over. Ten days after they mustered out, on February 18, 1899, the North Carolina legislature approved an amendment to the state constitution that would disenfranchise the majority of black voters through poll taxes, literacy tests, and a grandfather clause. The vote on the amendment would take place the following year. Less than two weeks later, on March 1, the legislature enacted a Jim

Crow law for railroad cars.[66] Any dreams the black soldiers of the Third North Carolina Volunteer Infantry might have had, that their voluntary military service would enhance their position in this country, were long gone.

Despite the constant grind of racism in his life and in the life of his soldiers, Trent would have loved this work, for it gave him the opportunity to put together many things he loved—manly fellowship, the Christian religion, music, education, and sports. Although he was with the regiment less than a year, it would have been an important time for him. In a sense, it was a test: could he go into a new environment outside of North Carolina, live with strangers, and lead them? This was not like college, the protected environment so near his home in Charlotte, with friends and teachers guiding him. Now it was up to him to guide the men in the regiment. The soldiers were in a strange new place in their lives, and so was he. Hunton was counting on him, hoping, and expecting, that he would do a good job for the YMCA: Trent would not want to let him down. Nor would he want to let down Livingstone president Goler, who would also have been counting on him to do this right, for Trent represented Livingstone at its best.

This was the first time he was in charge of a big project: he was not waiting tables or working in a cotton field or managing a football team. It was a time when he could show others what he was capable of. The reputation he had built at Livingstone for character, intelligence, and an ability to work well with others now moved from a small school to a larger stage. His work with the soldiers confirmed Hunton's belief that Trent was capable of doing good work for the YMCA, and was therefore a good prospect for further Y work. And the soldiers from Asheville, as well as two of the black officers, would remember him and his work, and later recommend him for a position in that city. They had liked working with Trent and wanted to continue their friendship after the war.

The question before him now, however, was what would he do next? Most of the soldiers he worked with would return home and try to fit back into their old lives. But Trent had just graduated from school: he didn't have an "old life." He would have to create a new one.

Five officers of the Third North Carolina accompanied two black regiments when they were moved to the Philippine Islands. The YMCA offered Trent the position of Y secretary with these troops, but he turned it down.[67] He very likely contacted President Goler at Livingstone to see if he knew of a position for him. At Tuskegee University, graduates who had been teaching and creating new schools would get in touch with President Booker T. Washington when something went wrong with that job and they needed another position. In a sense Washington functioned like "an informal board of education."[68] Perhaps Goler operated in the same way.

In any event, it is clear that the leaders at Livingstone and in the AME Zion Church immediately saw where Trent could meet an important need for the church and its institutional development, for they offered him the position of president of an AME Zion school in Greeneville, Tennessee.[69]

But as he traveled by rail from Savannah to Charlotte, he would have noticed, quite painfully, that he too was returning to a different North Carolina than the one he had left. When he left to join the troops, he was a full citizen of the state, with the right to vote and the right to ride in whichever railroad car he could afford. But when he took the train back home to North Carolina, his right to vote was being threatened, and he was riding in a Jim Crow car.

The AME Zion bishops created the Greeneville Normal and Industrial High School in 1887, and built it to accommodate 300 students.[70] Five years later, with classes in Latin, Greek, literature, and higher mathematics, it was called Greeneville College.[71] As head of the school, Trent would be hiring teachers; supervising teachers, students, and support staff; choosing curriculum; and overseeing school finances.

At some point in early 1900, two of his friends from the regiment, Harrison Brown and Thomas Leatherwood, contacted him about the opportunity to move to Asheville and head the Young Men's Institute (YMI) there.[72] Leatherwood, who had been president of the organization in 1898, feared that it might not be able to stay open. There appeared to be a failure of leadership: the institute had had four directors in seven years.[73] Trent was intrigued by the idea. He had probably already heard of the institute and its connection to millionaire George Washington Vanderbilt when he worked in Asheville during his summer school breaks.[74] He might even have participated in some of its activities.

In 1889 Vanderbilt began the construction of his new summer home, Biltmore House, in Asheville, which would be situated on his 125,000-acre estate.[75] It was an enormous construction job, as the house, which would cover 4 acres, was to have 255 rooms, 43 bathrooms, 288 lighting fixtures, 67 fireplaces, and over 6 miles of wire for the phone system.[76] For 6 years, workers baked 32,000 bricks daily, milled oak and walnut for the floors, cut stone, created 30 miles of roadways, and built a railroad spur 3 miles long to bring building supplies to the construction site.[77] They moved between 106,000 and 181,000 cubic yards of earth just to level the ground where they would build the house.[78] A thousand workers were needed to complete the construction, and many of those workers were black.[79]

Because the black workers had no place in Asheville to gather, relax, and socialize, in 1890 Edward Stephens, principal of the "colored graded schools" in Asheville, got together with other black leaders in the city to organize a YMCA for the black people of Asheville.[80] As the local newspaper stated, the purpose of the organization was "to establish a Christian institute and attract to it the young men of the colored race in the city who are now beset by almost every form of temptation, [...] [to] [...] make the colored men studious, healthy, clean and godly—keep them out of the way of temptation and away from the evil resorts."[81]

In order to fund the construction of a building for Y activities, Stephens got Vanderbilt interested in this project. Northern donors provided money for the lot, Vanderbilt provided brick for the construction of a two-story building in downtown Asheville, and his mother furnished the money to complete the building.[82] But although this appeared to be a gift, it was not:

Vanderbilt was clear that he was loaning the money to erect the building "to the colored people of Asheville who are at the head of this project."[83] The plan was that income from membership dues and income from rent from the stores and offices on the first floor of the building would eventually yield enough money to pay the money borrowed for the construction, plus interest.[84] In the meantime, the estate would pay the utilities, and pay, as well, for big repairs to the building.[85] Trustees appointed by Vanderbilt would retain title to the property and collect the money. They would eventually convey title to the institute, if a corporation was formed to hold the title.[86]

By 1893 the building was called the Young Men's Institute.[87] It was under the supervision of two men in Vanderbilt's employ. The first was New York City attorney Charles McNamee, who had moved to Asheville to help Vanderbilt with the construction of the estate. McNamee, Vanderbilt's cousin by marriage and right-hand man, was widely considered Vanderbilt's "on-site alter ego." He was also one of the trustees of the YMI property.[88] More directly, the YMI was under the supervision of Rev. Rodney Rush Swope, rector at All Souls' Episcopal Church in Biltmore Village.[89]

Brown and Leatherwood told Trent that the current director of the YMI was about to leave the organization. Was Trent interested in applying for the job? Indeed, he was. On February 17, 1900, Trent wrote to McNamee inquiring about the position. He noted his previous work with the YMCA and the time he had spent in Asheville, and listed as references men we have met before: President Goler of Livingstone, William Alphaeus Hunton of the YMCA, and Simon Atkins, former Livingstone professor, now head of Slater Academy in Winston-Salem.[90] The following month he provided as references the names of two of his Livingstone professors, B. A. Johnson and D. C. Suggs, who was by then vice president of the A&M College in Savannah, as well as E. E. Smith, former minister to Liberia, adjutant in the Third North Carolina Volunteer Infantry, and, in 1900, principal of Fayetteville Normal School.[91]

Trent was thus interested in leaving Greeneville after only a short stay. He would have been pulled toward the YMI because that work was be similar to the YMCA work he so loved. And life in Asheville must have been attractive to him because he knew the town, knew the people, and had good friends there who would welcome him.

In March, Rev. W. B. Fenderson, president of Asheville's Colored Ministers' Union, sent a letter to Rev. Swope, stating that the ministers in that group "unanimously endorsed" Trent.[92] This was important information as black ministers were often jealous of the YMCA in their community, concerned that that organization would take members away from their church. McNamee also received a letter of recommendation from Carrons Robinson, a soldier who had worked with Trent. Robinson wrote that Trent "seems to have a natural tendency to gain influence generally among the people."[93]

By May, Trent's candidacy was moving along quickly. On May 14, McNamee invited him to come to Asheville for an interview.[94] A week later, McNamee offered him the position for fifty dollars a month, with a probationary period of three months. McNamee emphasized that he and Swope would cooperate fully in the YMI project. "I should expect you to advise me pretty frequently," McNamee wrote, "as I have the interests of the Institute greatly at heart, and I wish no stone left unturned during the next three months to make a success of it."[95] By May 26 Trent was sitting in his office at the Young Men's Institute, writing his correspondence on YMI stationery.[96]

In 1880, when the railroad line finally arrived in Asheville, the city's year-round population was only 2,600. Ten years later, that number had grown to 10,000. And by 1900, when Trent arrived to head the Young Men's Institute, there were 15,000 year-round residents,[97] and 50,000 visitors a year. The city had street lighting, telegraph lines, phone lines, a public school system, and a public hospital. The main street was covered with crushed gravel. There were tobacco warehouses, a tobacco factory, an ice factory, a cotton factory, a tannery, and carriage and wagon makers. There were also several newspapers and literary clubs. Business was booming, and the life of the city was focused on Pack Square.[98]

You only have to walk for a few minutes from Pack Square to get to the Young Men's Institute, which is located on the corner of Eagle and Market streets, not far from what used to be called Negro Road. Designed in an English Tudor Cottage style, like many of the buildings on the Biltmore Estate, it is a two-and-a-half-story building made of coarse stucco, with accents in stone, brick, and wood. When you enter the main door, on Market Street, you enter a large hall that has rooms off the sides and, toward the back, a stairwell with turned balusters. There is something about the space that feels solid and sturdy.[99]

When Trent arrived, there were rooms on the first floor, on the Eagle Street and Market Street sides, for shops, for a doctor's office, and for the janitor. Halfway up to the second floor, on the left, is a large assembly room, 48 by 65 feet, with a ceiling 25 feet high. On this floor we also would have found, in 1900, the library and reading room, the boys' room, and the parlor. Continuing up the stairs, arriving at the top floor, we would have seen the residence rooms, which were sometimes rented out as housing and sometimes used as Asheville's black hotel. Back downstairs again, the basement contained the coal bin and boiler room and had tubs so the men could take baths.[100]

It must have been fairly easy for Trent to settle in. He already had friends in Asheville from his days with the Third North Carolina Infantry, as well as friends from his earlier college days when he worked in the city. And he had very likely spent time at the Young Men's Institute during those periods. He joined Hopkins AME Church, the church of friends William Walls and Thomas Leatherwood.[101] And he decided to live at the YMI, in one of the rooms on the top floor.[102] Thus he would be able to closely supervise the work at the institute and save money at the same time.

He had his work cut out for him. There had been four directors within eight years, the building was run down, and the institute was facing a financial crisis. When the institute was initially created, money for its support was to come from two sources: membership dues and rent for the stores and offices on the first floor. The institute was successful financially in its early years primarily because Vanderbilt required all black men working for the estate to become members, and took the dues out of their paycheck. But by 1895, when construction of the Biltmore Estate was over and the black workers had left town, there were no more automatic deposits into the YMI account.[103] Trent would have to build up the membership in order to get dues, and would also have to find other sources of income for the organization.

When he arrived, Trent had two official roles. First, as landlord for Vanderbilt, he would have to decide who would be a good tenant, make recommendations about those tenants to the estate, make sure the tenants paid the rent on time and evict those tenants who did not, keep up maintenance on the building, get estimates for repairs, and discuss the estimates and maintenance issues with people at the estate.

He also had to report periodically to the estate on the financial affairs of the institute. Every month he prepared a written report, then presented the report in person to a representative of the estate. At that time, he would give the estate most of the money remaining in the institute account to pay down the loan for the construction of the building, keeping out some money for small repairs.[104] At the end of each year, he prepared a written annual report for the estate. As we can see, this role as landlord required him to stay in close touch with the representatives of the estate who had oversight over the institute: McNamee, Rev. Swope, and Edward J. Harding, the estate treasurer.[105]

His second official role was to develop programs for the black men and boys in town. This would not be new to him: he had already set up similar programs for the soldiers of the Third North Carolina Volunteer Infantry—sports, lectures, concerts, classes, Bible studies, a place to read. He would already have some sense of what would work and what would not. Now he would have an opportunity to try something new in his work with men, and would, as well, have the chance to work with boys.

His most immediate task, however, was to ensure the survival of the YMI. It was on the brink of disaster: could he bring it back? Would he be able to gain enough support from the black community to make it financially viable? Would the boys and men get involved in YMI programs? Would the women in the community support it? Was there that much interest? He would have to create the kind of interest that would bring money to the institute, then maintain that interest. Ensuring that there were a lot of dues-paying members, making sure that the offices and stores were rented out and that rent was being paid on time, organizing fundraisers: this would be an arduous ongoing task. In order to do this, he would have to develop and keep good relations with several constituencies: with Asheville's black community in general, and, specifically, with Asheville's black ministers; with black women, always active in community work; and with his white supervisors at the Biltmore.

And so, he got to work.

There was a musical tradition at the YMI. Every Sunday, at four or five in the afternoon, after church was over, and after Sunday dinner with the family, hundreds of black people in Asheville gathered in the institute auditorium to sing their favorite songs. Trent began work at the institute the week of May 22, and decided to introduce himself to the community the following Sunday during the song service.

As he prepared his first talk to the community, Trent also met with several men to see who would like to sing in a quartet with him. That Sunday, one of the largest meetings in the history of the institute was held. And on that very first day in Asheville, when the black community as a group finally met him, Trent sang with the quartet.[106] Those in the audience could immediately see how much he loved singing, and how much he enjoyed manly fellowship. But they could see more, for when one sings in a group, the only way to make beautiful music is to listen carefully to the others. To make beautiful music in a quartet, one singer cannot try to overshadow the others: each must participate as an equal. So in a sense, then, by singing in a quartet for the community, Trent showed the community that although he would be leading the institute, he would not be setting himself apart from the men. He would work with them. And he would listen.

Trent found success right away. When he arrived in late May 1900, the YMI had only fifty-one members. Three months later, at the end of his probationary period, membership had increased to ninety.[107] His work during these first three months gives us a sense of what his work at the institute would be like for the next eleven years. Before his arrival, some programs were already in place at the YMI. There were already lectures, games, athletics, and the Sunday song service. There was also a Bible class for boys, a kindergarten for twenty children that met every morning from nine to noon, and a "bathing department"—tubs, soap, and water, so that men with no access to baths could get clean.[108] It was up to Trent to strengthen these programs and to create more.

In August 1900, after three months on the job, Trent reported that he was meeting with 40 boys for one hour every Thursday evening. He was "very anxious about the boys' department [...] [and would] spare no pains in developing it into a healthy state of activity." He had recently started a Bible class, and had already held nine meetings, with a total attendance of 65. The Sunday song service continued, with about 350 men, women, and children attending each Sunday. He also had organized a baseball team and planned to begin a night school in September for those who could not attend school during the day. Finally, he reported that he was holding a weekly meeting "of a religious nature" with the men only. "We feel, after all," he wrote, "the chief aim of a work like this is to bring men into a closer touch with the Higher Power."[109]

During those first three months, we also see the beginning of what would be regular and frequent written correspondence between Trent, McNamee, and Harding. Much of it centered on leasing out the office space: an offer to rent space for an ice cream store; an undertaker who wanted to take over a business; a music teacher who wanted to rent space for piano lessons; a man who wanted to open a restaurant. The correspondence was about the suitability of the tenant and the amount of rent. There was also some discussion about YMI membership dues. How should they be assessed for men who worked in Asheville only part of the year?

The financial reports Trent provided the estate also help us see what was going on at the institute during that period. And they show us the level of detail the estate required for its records. We see, for example:

Receipts:

Five dollars, each, received for renting the hall to the Woman's Christian Temperance Union (WCTU), the Baptist Church, the AME Zion Church, St. Luke's Church, and the ME Church; seven-dollar rental fee from the Odd Fellows; two-dollar fee for renting the parlor for a social; four dollars paid for renting chairs, and four dollars for renting a stove. Dr. Bryan paid four dollars' rent for his office, and the undertaker paid an eleven-dollar rental fee. Membership fees received: $52.71.

Debits:

Fifty cents for a broom and twenty cents for a mop; ten cents for car fare; thirty cents for stamps; one dollar and fifty cents for Mrs. Martin who played piano for the institute; seventy-five cents for refreshments at a YMI members' meeting, and two dollars and fifty cents for the purchase of soap and eleven towels.[110]

McNamee was a stickler for organization, progress reports, and records. Even before construction of the house began, he created a system of numbering outgoing memoranda and filing incoming mail alphabetically, then by subject. He maintained control over the extensive work of the estate by requiring this level of detail for all estate work, not just for the institute. He also sent weekly reports and invoices to Vanderbilt's private secretary in New York, who then made deposits in McNamee's name so he could pay salaries and local accounts in Asheville.[111] Working with McNamee, watching McNamee's system in operation, might well have been Trent's first training in administration.

By June 1901, at the end of his first year at the institute, Trent reported that membership had grown to 150 boys. He had started a night school, which had 14 members. Four hundred thirty-five young men had attended Bible classes, and there was also a Bible class for boys. The institute was buzzing with activity, day and night, during the week and on weekends. On Monday afternoon, the Minister's Union met; the Woman's Christian Temperance Union met on Tuesday; Wednesday evening was time for the boys' meeting. The Working Men's Club met two nights a week, and the song service continued every Sunday afternoon at five, attracting about 300 each time.

There were now two baseball teams, one for the boys and one for the men, teams that had given a "social" to raise money for uniforms. Every store room had been rented out: there was a cooking school for girls, an ice cream parlor and restaurant, and an undertaking company. The newspaper, magazines, and books in the reading room were in great demand. And the facilities for baths were so popular that on Saturday evenings men had to wait for their turn. Trent also reported that in May he had taken twenty-two small boys "up the Swannanoa River" for an outing.[112] We might imagine them boating, fishing, and swimming; we might envision little boys jumping in the water and laughing, out of sheer joy.

Around this time McNamee sent a note of praise to Trent: "I appreciate the successful work that you are doing in the Institute, and so far as the finances are concerned you have done better than any other secretary."[113] Six months later, he raised Trent's annual salary from $600 to $720. In a letter about the raise, Harding added his own words of praise: "Both Mr. McNamee and Dr. Swope recognize and appreciate the excellent work which you have done since taking charge of the affairs of the Young Men's Institute. In offering my congratulations I desire to add my own testimony to your efficiency."[114]

Thanking McNamee for the raise, Trent took a moment to reflect on his role at the institute: "The position of General Secretary of the YMI is not an easy one by any means. He must present many sides in order to hold the interest of the people. So far I have had their support, and yet there is room for improvement."[115] He continued in this thoughtful vein a few months later: "One hundred and sixty-five men and boys is a small number compared with the whole number in Asheville, yet we feel that if these can be trained to higher ideals; to have a proper self-respect; to grow up into law-abiding citizens with a true conception of life and its responsibilities, every cent spent in such a manner will have ample returns."[116]

The kind of activities Trent engaged in during his first year would continue during his eleven years at the institute. In his role as landlord, he would have to address the continuing maintenance issues every homeowner faces—a broken furnace, plumbing problems, a roof that needs repair. And there would be continuing efforts to get and maintain responsible tenants. The institute would eventually also house an oyster parlor and a drugstore; school principals and doctors would rent offices; the Bonn Soda Water and Ice Cream Parlor would find a home.

In his role as YMI director, Trent would continue to create new programs, welcome new guests, and develop the institute library. Over the years he added a Choral Club and a Boys' Brass Band, both of which gave concerts to raise money for the institute. Other groups that rented the great hall for their events included the Shaw University Singers, the colored Elks lodge, the organization of county teachers, and every June, a cluster of black schools, for their end-of-year programs: Catholic Hill Street School, Calvary School, St. Mathias School, Mt. Zion School, Miss Dole's School. And when Hopkins Chapel burned down in 1907, the congregation held Sunday school and church services at the YMI for three years until the new church was built.[117] In the YMI auditorium the black community heard speakers; they celebrated Emancipation Day and the anniversary of the institute; and they gave benefits, both to raise money for the institute and for the black orphanage. Trent also created an Education Department at the institute. At one point, when he was the only instructor, he was teaching twenty-eight men, most of whom were over the age of twenty-five. One of his former students had just "made an excellent record" in college, and he was preparing three more to enter college in the fall.[118]

Although the focus of the institute was on men and boys, women and girls were connected to its work. Women took their babies to the doctor at the YMI; girls took cooking lessons there; and men took their girlfriends to the YMI ice cream parlor. A woman rented at least one of the stores; the WCTU and the Y Girls rented space for their meetings.[119] Women were present for the Sunday song service, as well as all the celebrations, commencements, and church activities held in the auditorium. Surely they were pleased that the institute was there to support and encourage the men and boys in their families—their husbands and sons, their nephews and cousins. And they showed their support through contributions, both with items for the institute and with money. The Girls' Industrial Club and the Ladies' Auxiliary worked hard to raise money for the institute. In 1910 they turned over $203 for that purpose.[120] In a sense, then, the institute was for all of the black community, the institute was the center of the black community, and Trent directed it all.

While working to develop the YMI, Trent continued his own professional growth. He attended conferences for the YMCA and the AME Zion Church in Salisbury, Atlanta, and St. Louis.[121] In May 1902, Livingstone College asked him to return and present the address at the school's annual Founder's Day program.[122] This invitation was a great honor, and showed his standing in both the AME Zion community and the Livingstone family. A few months later he was invited to present a paper at the Negro Young People's Christian and Educational Congress in Atlanta, a conference designed to include as presenters "the progressive side of the Negro race," "able Christian leaders," and "the wisest thinkers of the Negro race."[123] His speech was published a few months later.

In his brief essay, "What Improvements Should Be Made in Our Churches?," Trent focused on two areas of change. The first was the "display" he saw in some churches when "the financial claims of the church" were presented. In Trent's view, the "marching to the tables" to donate money, the "commotion and restlessness"—all this detracted from the "soul stirring service which has taken our minds entirely away from the trials and disappointments of this life, has lifted from our shoulders and made lighter the burdens that must be borne [....] Would that we could go back to our respective homes in this state of mind, and, in the midst of the deepest reflections, put into practice these sublime truths." It is the church's duty, he continued, to "take our thoughts away from the material side of things."[124] Trent was not writing here about Jesus chasing the money changers from the temple, but his theme was much the same.[125]

His second point, we should not be surprised to note, involved music. He argued that much was being lost by using new songs, and by having the congregation listen passively instead of singing together. "Those old hymns we heard sung with so much feeling in our younger days possess a great history that we can least afford to do without in our religious growth," he wrote. "Bring back congregational singing [....] We long for those times when these sacred hymns, the outpouring of the soul to its Maker, went up from many voices, making the welkin ring with their sweetness." He also emphasized the value of what he called "emotionalism" in the religious life, "a fiery enthusiasm for the salvation of the world." "This is a peculiar characteristic of the race," he wrote. "Cultivate it; it is a precious inheritance."[126] In these suggestions about the church, then, we are not surprised to see a certain simplicity, and a harking back to plain country ways. There should be no showing off when donating money. The congregation should sing the old hymns together. And people should not hold back their emotions, but express their spiritual beliefs with power.

Trent was particularly interested in developing the institute's reading room. He loved reading and he loved books. He knew how education had changed his life, and he wanted to provide the same opportunity for Asheville's black community. Although white Asheville had had a public library since 1870, there was no public library for its black citizens.[127] So the YMI library was crucial. It was, in effect, black Asheville's public library.[128]

In September 1902, Trent bought *History of the Nations*, a thirty-two-volume work, for the library.[129] A few months later, after a fair at the institute raised $42.11 for the purchase of books, Trent added eleven more. Some of the titles are not very surprising: *Plutarch's Lives* (three volumes); the works of Theodore Roosevelt (fifteen volumes); *The Strenuous Life*, a collection of speeches and essays by Theodore Roosevelt. But what is particularly notable here is that for the first time we are seeing a cluster of books by black Americans:

Paul Lawrence Dunbar, *Lyrics of Lowly Life* (1896)

W. E. B. Du Bois, *The Suppression of the Slave Trade* (1896)

Booker T. Washington, *Up from Slavery* (1901)

Charles Chesnutt, *Frederick Douglass: A Biography* (1899) and *The Marrow of Tradition* (1901)

Daniel Wallace Culp, *Twentieth Century Negro Literature; or, A Cyclopedia of Thought on the Vital Topics Relating to the American Negro* (1902)[130]

This list of works by black authors calls to mind the material assigned when Trent was a student at Livingstone: Greek, Latin, the literature and history of white America. Through this list of new books, then, we can see that either Trent is educating himself about the literature and scholarly work of black Americans, or he has already educated himself and wants others in the black community to learn this too. Fiction and poetry, history, essays, biography—he knew they should read it all.[131] The task of undoing the harmful lesson of white America—the lesson that African Americans were people of no worth, who had written nothing, and had done nothing worth writing about—unlearning this lesson would be the task of a lifetime, but Trent was on his way.

In the fall of 1902 the institute welcomed two new tenants: a pharmacy, and Dr. John Walker, Trent's college roommate, friend, and fellow football player, who had just received his medical degree from Leonard Medical School at Shaw University in Raleigh, the first four-year medical school in the nation.[132] His new office in the YMI would be just down the hall from Trent's. These friends would work together to make the YMI a success. Walker would be a trustee of the institute for many years. They also worked together as trustees of Hopkins Chapel.[133] In addition, Trent and Walker supported their alma mater by creating the Trent-Walker Award, "a gold medal for excellence in oratory in the Freshman Class."[134]

And they worked together to support individual young men in the community. For example, Walker and Trent provided support to Ernest McKissick, a young man who found himself "adrift." Both men took him into their homes to stay for a while, where he earned his keep by helping around their houses. Later on, Trent, Walker, and two other men active in the institute told McKissick that if he worked hard during the summer and saved all he could, each of them would give him ten dollars, and they would try to raise more money, in order to send him to Livingstone.[135]

It might have been about this same time that Trent started to think about getting married. He must have been considered quite a catch—a young, handsome black man with a college degree and a good job. Not only that: he was also a property owner. He had been able to save money by living at the institute, and, soon after his arrival in Asheville, used some of his savings to buy property on Blanton Street.[136] One can just imagine all the mothers in town, all the fathers who worked with him at the institute, all the grandmothers who attended the Sunday song service, who invited him to Sunday dinner after church to meet their unmarried daughters!

But the woman who caught his eye was Anna Belle Mitchell, a teacher at the Catholic Hill Elementary School in Asheville. She was born in 1882 in Raleigh, the daughter of William Mitchell, a brick mason, and his wife, Altona Anderson Mitchell, both also born in Raleigh.[137] The Mitchell family was considered an important one within the black community.[138] Perhaps the father's income played into their importance, for of all the black artisans, the best paid were brick masons. In 1900 they earned $2.15 a day, which yielded a little over $50 a month.

Compared to domestic workers, who were earning about $8 a month, and teachers, who earned around $20 a month, this was serious money.[139] There were six children in the family. Anna Belle was likely very close to her sister Eleanora, only three years older. Both girls graduated from Shaw University, and both learned to play the piano, more signs of the family's prosperity.[140]

Anna Belle was likely in the YMI auditorium January 1, 1904, when 500 people gathered to celebrate Emancipation Day. They would have heard a speech by Rev. D. Samuel Orner, "Thirty-Nine Years a Freedman: The Status of Affairs in This Country as It Affects the Negro," as well as a recitation of the poetry of Paul Laurence Dunbar, and music by several choruses, including a chorus of 100 school children. Two women read papers. Miss Ada Young read a paper entitled "The Educational Status of the Negro." Then Miss Ida Briggs, a teacher at the Biltmore School, read "Domestic Science and Its Relations to the Home," in which she made a plea for well-trained mothers in every home, linking such work to "the shaping and moulding of character." At the end of the program, those present contributed money as a "New Year's offering" for the Colored Orphans' Home. In the next day's newspaper report, the writer noted the high quality of this celebration, adding that the Asheville community should thank the committee and Trent for their united efforts.[141]

Almost immediately afterwards, on January 4, the YMI hosted a week of prayer, organized by the local churches. Speeches, prayers, conversions—Trent wrote about all this during the week in three newspaper articles designed not only to report on these activities, but also to encourage participation: "Don't miss these services. We call upon you young men who are out of the ark of Christ to come and be saved, for there is nothing so powerful as that of a pure heart."[142] The following month the YMI was filled once more when seventy-five guests were invited to celebrate the eleventh anniversary of the institute.[143]

Trent's courtship must have been going along very well, for, in early March 1904, he sent McNamee a note, in which he wrote: "I am requesting a leave of absence for a week beginning April 4th as I am to be in Raleigh at that time, where I am hoping to be married."[144] Livingstone friend Kwegyir Aggrey was best man at the wedding, and Anna Belle's maid of honor was her longtime friend and Shaw University classmate, Rose ("Rosebud") Rudolf Douglass, a niece of Frederick Douglass.[145] Charles F. Meserve, the white president of Shaw University, was one of the witnesses to the marriage.[146] Meserve's presence at the wedding is both an indication of the standing of the Mitchell family in Raleigh and a sign of respect for Trent, whom Meserve had met when he observed the Third North Carolina Volunteer Infantry during the Spanish-American War.

That same summer William and Anna Belle Trent purchased and moved into their new home on Hill Street, right next to the school where Anna Belle taught. [147]

In one of those coincidences that delight the heart, while Trent was courting Anna Belle, his friend John Walker had been courting Anna Belle's sister Eleanora, who was teaching mathematics in Raleigh.[148] And on Sunday, June 2, 1904, only three months after Trent's wedding, Walker and Eleanora were married. Two men friends married two sisters, and became family. We might imagine the pleasure these two couples took in visiting each other over the years, attending church together, celebrating birthdays and holidays together, going on picnics together. And surely there were musical soirées, for both Anna Belle and Eleanora were excellent pianists, and their husbands had sung together since their days at Livingstone—Trent, tenor, and Walker, bass. The Walkers would remain in Asheville, where John was becoming a specialist in the treatment of tuberculosis, and Eleanora would teach mathematics at the local high school.[149]

During the Trent wedding festivities, when best man Aggrey first saw Rose Douglass, the maid of honor, he said to himself: "That's the girl for me." The following year, they wed. Two good men friends, Trent and Aggrey, had married two longtime women friends, and Trent's friendship network became even richer. Aggrey was at Livingstone College at this time, teaching and playing a role in administration, so after the wedding the young couple returned to Salisbury.[150]

Several months after his wedding, Trent noticed that the *Asheville Gazette-News* was holding a contest. The organization that won the contest would receive a large collection of books. As the "public library" for black Asheville, the reading room at the YMI was very important, but its collection was woefully inadequate. Trent wanted the YMI to win the contest, and was working with Rev. Swope and his wife to that end. He contacted Harding and asked that the Biltmore Estate vote for the YMI. "[Dr. Swope] thinks that we have a good chance to win. And oh! How sorely we do need such a collection of books."[151] Harding replied that he had been casting his votes in favor of a local hospital, but would, at Trent's request, vote for the YMI in the future.[152]

Almost two months later Harding wrote Trent again, stating that although he had been casting his votes—"a good many thousand votes"—for the YMI, it seemed a waste of votes since the institute was so far behind in the contest, "a hopeless cause." He asked Trent to release him from his promise, so he could cast the Biltmore Estate votes in a more productive direction, adding: "I shall not change my vote, however, without your permission."[153] Trent asked Harding to wait three weeks more.[154] He agreed to wait two weeks only, pointing out that the YMI was 90,000 votes behind the two institutions leading in the contest.[155] By October, Trent had given up on what he called "a brave fight," and decided to cast the institute's votes for Asheville's white YMCA "because it is a similar work as ours and needs these books."[156]

This is a story that can break one's heart: Trent's longing for the books was so powerful and the black community's need, so great. In a generous spirit of brotherhood, Trent gave the votes of the black community, the YMI, to the white YMCA, an organization already so wealthy it had been able to purchase its building in 1901, in a town that had had a library for the men and boys of the white YMCA for decades.[157] The YMI did not win the contest. But the YMI was never going to win the contest. For although the contest was written in terms that were facially neutral, in a city that was more than 80 percent white, in a state where black people were forced to travel in Jim Crow cars and had lost the right to vote, in a country where separate never meant equal, facially neutral did not mean *really* neutral.

Despite this disappointment, Trent was seeing increasing satisfaction in both his personal and professional life. Life was becoming financially problematic for Vanderbilt, however, as he had recently made some disastrous investments and lost a large part of his fortune. In fact, Vanderbilt had been in financial trouble since 1900, when he started spending more money than he was earning. Some of the rooms in the Biltmore House were never finished. He cut the annual expenses for the estate from $250,000 to $70,000. There were no more elaborate parties; the private car was sold; and the Vanderbilt family moved to Europe in 1903 to save money, for when the Biltmore was open, its expenses were about $6,000 a month. Vanderbilt's financial situation only grew worse.[158] This would have a disastrous effect on the black community in Asheville, as many black people either worked for the Vanderbilts or worked for people or companies that provided goods and services to the Vanderbilts. Indeed, in October 1903, in his monthly report to the estate, Trent noted that it had been hard for him to collect money that month, as so many of the young men were not working.[159]

Trent was facing financial difficulties too. He and Anna Belle had bought a house in July. It had been sold by the court to pay the debts of a decedent, and the court allowed only twelve months to complete the payment. Trent asked Harding for a loan of $225 to be repaid monthly with interest, because, as he explained, this rapid house payment "will cause me to make some unusual sacrifices."[160] Harding replied that although he would like to help, he could not make such a large loan without Vanderbilt's permission. He suggested that Trent put his request to Vanderbilt directly.[161]

On November 3, Harding wrote to say that Vanderbilt had approved a one-year loan to be repaid at the rate of $20 a month, with 6 percent interest, to be deducted from his monthly salary.[162]

Since Trent was only earning $60 a month, he would thus see his monthly salary cut by over a third. Nonetheless, he must have breathed quite a sigh of relief. Given the important position he held in the Asheville, Livingstone College, and AME Zion communities, given the fact that he was newly married and now had a child on the way, what a profound embarrassment it would have been for him to be put out of his house.

In November 1904, the estate started to take a serious look at the expenses of the YMI. Was Vanderbilt beginning to think that, with all his financial losses, he could no longer support the institute? At Rev. Swope's request, Harding prepared a report of the "regular running expenses" of the Young Men's Institute for the previous fiscal year. His report showed the following:

salary of secretary	$720.00
salary of janitor	396.00
plate glass insurance	33.10
coal	253.65
electricity	196.08
water	65.05

TOTAL $1,663.86

In addition, the estate had paid for fire insurance on the building and had budgeted $156 for special repairs.[163]

All Vanderbilt's financial issues seemed to come to a head in 1904. That same year, McNamee resigned and moved to Washington state, where he tried to salvage both his investments and Vanderbilt's. Before he left he donated seventy-five books to the YMI library. Rev. Swope then took over supervision of the YMI.[164]

Trent was surely worried. What would happen to the institute if Vanderbilt was no longer willing to support it? Anna Belle was teaching and made a little money giving piano lessons and playing piano for the institute, but surviving on her income alone was not a realistic option. Despite these worries, December must have been a joyous month for the couple because a few days before Christmas Anna Belle gave birth to their daughter, Altona Malinda Trent, named surely out of love for her mother, Altona, and his, Malinda. The following year Trent sold the Blanton Street property and paid off his debt to Vanderbilt, thus easing a little the family's tight financial situation. He took the occasion to thank Harding for his kindness, writing, "I shall never forget it."[165]

But Trent's joy would be short-lived. Without knowing it, in September 1905, he had delivered his last report to the Biltmore Estate. For in November, Vanderbilt decided he wanted to be relieved of his financial obligation to the Young Men's Institute and announced that he would not maintain it after May 1, 1906.[166] He gave the black community six months to buy the building for $10,000 cash. If they failed to buy it, he would put it on the market for $15,000.[167]

After six months, the black community had raised only $2,500, $1,000 of which had come from white people. The black community asked Vanderbilt to accept this amount, and let them pay $1,000 a year until the total was paid off, but he refused. The YMI board of directors then created a subcommittee of three—Trent, Rev. C. B. Dusenbury, and John Walker, then president of the institute, to decide on the next step. One of them, perhaps Walker, decided that telling the truth would not be a good negotiating strategy. As a result, when they met with Rev. Swope at the Biltmore, Walker, speaking for the group, stated that they had raised all $10,000, but asked for thirty days, until May 31, 1906, "to get up the proper papers" and have time to mortgage the property. Swope called Vanderbilt with the proposal, and he agreed. The YMI then borrowed $7,500 from white businessman Mike Kelley and bought the building, saddling itself with a debt and an agreement to repay $1,000 a year at 6 percent interest.[168]

It is distressing that Vanderbilt would not give the YMI to the black community outright, either when it was first built or later. It is distressing that he would not even allow them to pay it off over seven-and-a-half years. In 1883 his father, William Vanderbilt, then the richest man in the world, was worth $194 million. When he died five years later, his son George inherited $5 million, which he added to the million dollars he had inherited from his grandfather—the million his father gave him when he turned twenty-one—and the income from his $5 million trust fund. He had homes in Asheville, Washington, DC, and New York City, as well as a "summer cottage" at Bar Harbor, Maine.[169] George Vanderbilt was quite comfortable.

He would have been hard pressed back in 1896, when the institute was built, to say he could not afford a gift of $32,000. He even had the example of his father, William H. Vanderbilt, who, in 1884, gave $300,000, plus land worth another $200,000, to the College of Physicians and Surgeons in New York City.[170] He also had the example of George W. Pack, who, in 1890, had given a building worth $20,000 to $30,000 to the Asheville Library Association "with the understanding," Pack wrote, "that the corporation shall be free from debt when it receives the conveyance of the property."[171] Perhaps George Vanderbilt thought that he was teaching a lesson in values by making the black community work to pay for the building: they would appreciate it more. But George Vanderbilt never worked for the millions of dollars he was given. He never worked at all.

In any event, the YMI assumed the debt. And on May 8, 1906, along with forty-eight of his colleagues, neighbors, and friends, Trent signed the Articles of Incorporation of the Young Men's Institute. Signatories include the black men of some standing in Asheville at the time. We would expect to find doctors, ministers, teachers, and school principals on this list, and we do. But we also find men with other professions including, for example, contractors, a musician, and a barber; a tailor, a porter, and a peddler in the best vegetable market in town. Finally, in this list we find Harrison Brown, Esq., former lieutenant in the Third North Carolina Volunteer Infantry, and Trent's friend since those days.[172]

On June 12, 1906, the *Asheville Citizen* spread the news in an article entitled "YMI Pays Mr. Vanderbilt $10,000 and Secures Title":

> The property is held by the YMI Incorporated in association with fifteen directors. J. W. Walker is President, John W. Nipson Jr., recording secretary, and W. J. Trent,

Secretary. It is intended to increase the receipts and decrease the expenditures where possible but as interest charges must be met some hard work is ahead for the association. [....] [It] is expected that Secretary Trent will do much. He had expected to go the first of June to St. Louis to take charge of the YMCA there, but since the urgent insistence of the YMI management, he is now corresponding to obtain a release from this engagement.[173]

Trent had obviously been looking for ways to support his family should plans to purchase the YMI fall through.

The YMI was now financially independent. This meant that the Biltmore Estate would no longer be looking over the shoulder of the institute director. But it also meant that the institute would have to raise more money than before. Not only would the black community have to pay off the purchase debt, with interest, but it would also now have to pay for the maintenance and upkeep of the building, as well as salaries—expenses formerly borne by the estate. In addition, the YMI would have to continue paying for the small repairs it had always covered. As noted earlier, in 1904 the amount for upkeep and salaries alone was $1,563. This would therefore present an enormous problem, for in 1904 the YMI only cleared $1,207.60.[174] The black community would struggle with this financial burden for years.

By 1906 Trent had arranged for the YMI to become part of the Colored Men's Department of the national YMCA. In 1905, there were forty-one black Y city associations across the country. Only twenty of them had full-time secretaries, and only thirteen had their own building.[175] Thus it is clear that the black Y world in America's cities was fairly small, and that Trent held a rare position within that world. Around that same time Moorland and Hunton announced that the seventeenth annual conference of the Colored Men's Department would be held at the Young Men's Institute in early December: "The Young Men's Institute of Asheville, which recently joined our brotherhood of Young Men's Christian Associations and purchased the handsome building erected several years ago by Mr. George Vanderbilt, was awarded the privilege of entertaining the conference in response to their urgent petition to 'come over and help them.'"[176] Clearly Trent wanted and needed their support.

Every month the secretaries of the black YMCAs around the country sent a report of their activities to the Colored Men's Department. Then, either Hunton or Moorland put the reports together, added an introductory message, and sent the combined reports out to all the secretaries as a newsletter.[177] In this way, the black secretaries could keep in touch with their colleagues around the country, and learn which activities in other Ys had been successful and which ones had not. The newsletter thus both reduced the secretaries' isolation from their colleagues and provided helpful advice.

But there must have been things the men wanted to talk about together that were too important, or too hard, to put in a brief note. During the December 1906 conference, when they got together in Asheville, the black Y secretaries were surely talking about the loss of civil rights in their state. North Carolina had finally amended its constitution to limit the black vote with literacy tests and a poll tax. Other states had done the same and had also, like North Carolina, segregated railroad cars. And it didn't stop there. In 1900 Mississippi had required that black corpses be removed from white cemeteries to black ones. The following year, in Little Rock, Arkansas, black people had to use a separate room in the library.[178] Trent in particular would have been talking about the lynching of three black men in Salisbury that August, men imprisoned because their white neighbors, with whom they had had disputes, had been murdered. It has been estimated that some 5,000 white people came out to watch them being lynched. Then, after killing these men, some in the white mob cried out: "Now let us go and burn up the nigger college!" Livingstone came very close to being attacked that night, but after some in the mob recalled the kindness of one of the Livingstone professors, the assault was called off.[179]

They would have also talked about the terrible white riot in Atlanta in late September. It started the same way as the

Wilmington riot, with a race-baiting campaign in the white press at election time, then a mob of white men running in all directions attacking black businesses and trying to find black people to beat and kill—a white mob that grew to more than 10,000, a riot that has been called one of the worst riots in U.S. history.[180] In the October secretarial letter, Moorland wrote: "Pray for Mr. Hunton and his family. They were all in Atlanta during the riot—were in the midst of it but God preserved them."[181] After the riot, the Hunton family left Atlanta and moved north.[182] According to his wife, Addie Waite Hunton, her husband never recovered from the shock of that lawlessness and violence, from the understanding that all they had worked for could be lost in a moment.[183] Were some of the other Y secretaries in the South also thinking of moving?

How could these men live their professional lives in dignity and safety? How could they protect their families? This may well have led to a discussion of the great migration of black people out of the South. Between 1900 and 1910, 27,827 black people migrated from North Carolina alone.[184]

Trent wrote his last report for the Biltmore Estate in September 1905. In March 1907, three months after the Asheville conference, he wrote his first report for the monthly secretarial letter of the Colored Men's Department of the YMCA, a report both upbeat and touching: "Since putting in basketball the membership has been increased by twenty-five. We challenge the entire YMCA of America for a contest [....] Twenty-five boys of the Junior Department gave a concert for the benefit of the Building Fund February 20th, and cleared $105. The entire door receipts were $143. How is that! The people see the importance of the work here now, since the Conference, as never before. The Conference helped us far more than we (Asheville) were of service to it." But in that same secretarial letter, Moorland wrote a more somber note: "Pray for Mrs. Trent who is quite ill."[185]

The following month, Trent had only sad news: "I have no notes to write this month. My wife does not now seem to be holding her own in the great struggle with her illness. So you must know that I am in no mood for work. Pray that God may restore her if it is His will."[186] A few weeks later, on May 1, 1907, Anna Belle lost her great battle, and died.[187] Their baby girl, Altona, was just two-and-a-half years old.

It must have felt impossible to continue living in their home without his wife—their home, the site of such hopes and joys. And there was also the problem of his daughter: who would care for her while he worked? For he worked all hours of the day and, often, evenings and weekends too. Anna Belle's sister Eleanora and her husband, Trent's friend John Walker, must have thought about this too. During that time of great loss and confusion, while Anna Belle was dying, before Trent could even think about how he would be able to continue on without his wife, John and Eleanora would have likely said to him: "Come and stay with us." And that is what they did. Trent and his daughter left their home on Hill Street and moved in with the Walkers, who shared their sorrow and provided solace and comfort.[188] Thus, with the support of this family and friends in Asheville, Trent went on with his life and continued his work.

At the same time that he was continuing his work at the institute—finding tenants, maintaining the building, developing programs, and trying to raise money for both daily expenses and the debt—he was becoming more involved in the work of the Colored Men's Department of the national YMCA. Because his organization of the Y conference in 1906 had been so successful, the secretaries returned to the YMI for their annual conference in July 1908.[189] This session was the first summer training session for the secretaries and new recruits to be held in Asheville.[190] It was still a small group, as there were only twenty-five black secretaries in 1908.[191] Over the years these men would get to know each other very well.

When Trent decided it was time to wed again, he began to court Margaret ("Maggie") Hazel Tate of Charlotte. He would have known the Tate family through his visits to his family in Charlotte, and through the AME Zion network in western North Carolina. He would have also known Maggie's father, Thad Tate, since his school days in Charlotte, in the late 1880s. By the time

Trent started to court Maggie, Tate had become even more successful and an even more important player in Charlotte's black community. He, his wife, Mary Butler Tate, and their ten children lived in an elegant brick home on Seventh Street.[192] With a group of Charlotte's other black businessmen Tate had formed the Queen City Real Estate Agency, a development company, as well as the Afro-American Mutual Insurance Company and the Mecklenburg Investment Company.[193] He also helped found, and was on the board of, the newly created Brevard Street Library, the first public library for black people in the South.[194]

Maggie Tate, born in 1887 in Charlotte, was the first of the Tate daughters.[195] A graduate of Scotia Seminary, she taught for a while at the Myers Street Elementary School in Charlotte, the first black graded school in the county.[196] If any young single woman knew how to be a parent for little Altona Trent, it was Maggie. She was also used to being in a family that was important in the black community; her father was involved in many different community uplift projects. She had, in effect, been raised for this marriage.

On June 30, 1909, in the evening, Trent and Maggie Tate were married at Grace AME Zion Church Chapel, in Charlotte. So many attended the wedding that the crowd overflowed into the Sunday school classrooms. There were black guests and white guests, poor guests and rich ones, guests in the professions and guests in the trades. Many schools of higher learning were represented, including Biddle, Shaw, Howard, Fisk, and Atlanta universities, Livingstone College, and Scotia Seminary. People were dressed in their finest attire, the women wearing dresses made of "lawn, dimity, organdie, mull, silk chiffon, [and] satin."[197]

Miss Hattie P. Neal sang two or three songs as Miss Essie Grigg accompanied her on the piano. Then Miss Grigg played the wedding march while four bridesmaids with pink ribbons walked down the aisle, followed by four bridesmaids with blue ribbons, all carrying rings of daisies. Finally Maggie appeared and, on her father's arm, walked down to the altar, which stood under an arch of make-believe angels. She had sprigs of orange blossoms pinned to her veil, and to her dress, which was made of white satin and trimmed with Irish lace. She too carried a bouquet of daisies, along with a white prayer book.

The pastor at Grace, Rev. W. O. Carrington, presented the first and last parts of the ceremony. But it was Rev. George Clement, Trent's classmate and good friend, who pronounced them husband and wife. After the ceremony there was a reception at the Tate home, where the family displayed the many wedding gifts the new couple received. At ten in the evening, undoubtedly tired and happy, Trent and his new wife left on their honeymoon tour.[198]

The following day, Trent's friend Kwegyir Aggrey noted in the Charlotte newspaper that both Trent and Maggie Tate Trent "belonged to the very best social circle among colored people in the State."[199] Thus, this is a story about a marriage, but it is also a statement about class and status within the black community. It reminds us how far Trent had come from that boy picking cotton in the hot North Carolina fields, the young man cleaning spittoons and slop jars on Pullman trains. And it also tells us how far he had wanted to come.

Two weeks after the wedding the Colored Men's Department of the YMCA held its summer institute for secretaries in Asheville once more.[200] Perhaps the summer institute was held in Asheville because of its pleasant summer climate. But it was certainly also due to Trent's effectiveness as a Y leader and organizer. And these skills were being recognized more and more. For, a few months after the conference, in November, the YMCA announced that "Mr. W. J. Trent, the successful General Secretary of the Asheville Young Men's Institute Association, has been engaged by the International Committee to give a part of his time during the next six months to work in North and South Carolina. Trent is General Secretary at Asheville and Special Agent of the International Committee."[201] So Trent now had a new title, new duties, and greater responsibility within the YMCA added on to his YMI work.

We see even more clearly his growing role in the national YMCA effort the following month, when he attended the annual conference of the Colored YMCA in Louisville, Kentucky. At that event, the local newspaper reported that "all phases of YMCA work will be discussed and will be in charge of International Secretaries Hunton, Moorland, Watson and Trent."[202] This is a remarkable statement. At this time the YMCA had only three black international secretaries. Hunton, the first, was hired in 1888, and Moorland, the second, in 1898.[203] At the time of this conference, John B. Watson was the third international secretary.[204] So if Trent was being named in the same breath as these three leaders, he clearly had very high standing within the Colored Men's Department of the YMCA. The conference also gives us an opportunity to see his skill in working with a group, and the affection his fellow Y leaders had for him, for on Sunday, December 5, the local newspaper reported that "W. J. Trent [...] led in singing and the whole association joined in what proved to be one of the happiest moments of the two-day session."[205]

After the wedding, Trent had moved back to the house on Hill Street with his wife and daughter.[206] And soon, Maggie was pregnant. Their joy could not have been greater when, on March 8, 1910, Maggie gave birth to a son, whom they named William Johnson Trent Jr. Trent's mother, Malinda, was in Asheville with them when the baby was born, perhaps to help the new mother.

Because the Trents' home church, Hopkins Chapel, had burned down in 1907, the baby was baptized in August in the Young Men's Institute. Bishop Cicero Harris performed the service—Harris, who had left Cleveland as a young man so many decades before to teach freed men and women in North Carolina; who had become the principal of Wesley Institute, the precursor of Livingstone College; who had been one of the first teachers at Livingstone in the 1880s; who had given the commencement address when Trent graduated in 1898.[207] By choosing Bishop Harris to baptize his son, Trent linked the past of Livingstone and the past of the AME Zion Church, through his present, to his son— the future. This must have been a powerful moment indeed. That same year, in a sign of great respect, Livingstone College invited Trent to return to receive an honorary M.A. degree.[208]

At the same time that Trent was maintaining his duties at the Young Men's Institute and developing his career with the YMCA, he continued to add professional responsibilities. By 1911 he was also editor of the *Western North Carolina Advocate.*[209] His friends were advancing in their careers too. In 1911 Kwegyir Aggrey was teaching at Livingstone College and working on his doctorate at Columbia University. He had also been ordained an elder in the AME Zion Church.[210] Rev. George Clement was editor of AME Zion weekly *Star of Zion* and had received both an honorary M.A. degree and an honorary doctorate in divinity from Livingstone.[211] In 1908 he was appointed a member of a committee to develop a new AME Zion publishing house in Charlotte. [212]

Young "Willie" Walls, Asheville's "boy preacher," received his license to preach in 1899, when he was fourteen, and was ordained deacon in 1903. Trent probably visited with him many times during his Asheville years, as they both attended Hopkins Chapel. As Walls later wrote, Trent had offered him guidance since he was a child.[213] Walls was not only preaching at Hopkins from time to time; also, in the fall of 1903, he gave a sermon at the Young Men's Institute.[214] In 1905, he too was ordained an elder in the AME Zion Church. He received his A.B. degree from Livingstone in 1908, then began his studies at Hood Theological Seminary.[215]

John Walker, still practicing medicine in Asheville, was, as noted earlier, specializing in the treatment of tuberculosis.[216] Simon Fuller, who had come from Liberia to study at Livingstone, completed his medical studies at Boston University School of Medicine, where he became interested in neuropathology. In 1899 he became chief of pathology at Westborough (MA) Hospital, where he had interned and taught. He left the United States a few years later for postgraduate work at the University of Munich's Psychiatric Clinic, where he studied under Alois Alzheimer.[217] In 1909 he married Livingstone graduate Meta Vaux Warrick, a prize-winning sculptor who had studied in Paris, where she was sponsored by French sculptor Auguste Rodin.[218]

While Trent was working hard in Asheville, focusing on the YMI debt, Hunton, Moorland, and Watson were in despair over the YMCA in Atlanta. Such a large and vibrant city held so much promise! But between 1907 and 1910 there had been three Y secretaries in Atlanta. When the second secretary arrived in June, 1909, he described a building filled with "an accumulation of dust, dirt and disorder," torn wallpaper, and broken bathtubs.[219] And the third director lasted only a year.[220] Hunton, Moorland, and Watson had their hands full trying to organize the Atlanta Y and keep up with the work of the other Y organizations at the same time. Toward the end of 1910 Watson wrote: "At present my time is taken with an effort to revive the work in the Atlanta city Association." The plan was to pay off the debt of the Atlanta Y and get that organization ready for a new director.[221] But who could manage this difficult situation and turn it around? Who would last longer than a year?

They offered the job to Trent, and he accepted. It was a big step up—a move into a larger city, a larger black community; indeed, a very important, well-educated, prosperous black community, and the center of black higher education in the United States—"the black Athens," people called it, the home, even in 1911, of many black schools of higher education: a university, three colleges, and three seminaries.[222] But it would mean uprooting his family, leaving friends in Asheville, leaving the Walkers, Trent's good friends, and little Altona's aunt and uncle. And Maggie would be leaving behind her family in Charlotte.

As he was getting ready to leave North Carolina, Trent's thoughts went to those friends who would now be farther away. On June 3 he sent a message of gratitude to friends Kwegyir and Rose Aggrey, in Salisbury: "I want to thank you both so much for the kind hospitality which is always shown me under your vine and fig tree."[223] In his letter he touched on themes dear to his heart: their mutual love of classical literature, their desire to improve the lives of black Americans, the hope that there would be a new generation to take up this task. Here is an excerpt from the letter:

There is no home outside of my own where I feel so free and at ease as I do when with the Aggreys. Some of these days Fortune will smile upon us all, then we will spend more time together in an atmosphere equally as conducive of "sweetness and light" as the present. Then we will talk of the great and mighty men of old, who drunk delight of battle with their peers, far on the ringing plains of windy Troy. And then as a climax of it all we will, under the guidance of those we love, help shape the destiny of a race. And I am sure, from all indications, there will be still some young Trent and young Aggrey to swell the chorus either in song or with a cry.[224]

On July 3, 1911, William and Maggie Trent sold their home on Hill Street.[225] Trent resigned from the Young Men's Institute three days later. When he left, the YMI still owed $2,000 for the purchase of the building.[226]

In 1900 Trent had arrived in Asheville a single man, well educated, but with a limited professional background. After only eleven years, he was leaving Asheville a widower, a new husband, the father of two, and a leader with a national reputation for professional excellence. It must have been hard for William and Maggie to leave good friends, but clearly Trent wanted more. And the YMCA leadership was encouraging him to go after it, and take a larger leadership role.

But even as Trent moved on in his career, we can see the limitations of his effort. For even as young black men fought in the armed forces and participated in organizations that prepared them to become citizens and Christians who were strong in their faith, violence against black people continued, civil rights were lost, and segregation grew. Nonetheless, Trent continued his work with the YMI and the YMCA—both segregated institutions—in his effort to form black men of the highest character. In a state where black men had lost the right to vote, this might well have represented the best strategy available. At the same time, Trent had to be attentive to the fact that white people provided an important financial base for these institutions. He thus had to walk a fine line in order to continue his uplift work and maintain the support of the black community, while at the same time not alienating white donors.

Class of 1898
Livingstone College, Salisbury, N.C.
left to right: John W. Walker, William J. Trent, George C. Clement

Students, Huntington Hall
Livingstone College, Salisbury, N.C.
(1903)
(courtesy of General Research & Reference Division, Schomburg Center
for Research in Black Culture, The New York Public Library, Astor,
Lenox and Tilden Foundations)

Teachers and Administrators
Livingstone College, Salisbury, N.C.
(1903)
front row, middle: W. H. Goler
front row, right: Edward Moore
2nd row, 2nd, 3rd, and 4th from left:
Mary A. Lynch, Annie C. V. Tucker, Victoria Richardson
top row, far right: Kwegyir Aggrey
(courtesy of General Research & Reference Division, Schomburg Center
for Research in Black Culture, The New York Public Library, Astor,
Lenox and Tilden Foundations)

Brass Band of the Young Men's Institute
Asheville, N.C.
(ca. 1905)
seated on floor, left: William J. Trent
(courtesy of Heritage of Black Highlanders Collection, D. H. Ramsey
Library Special Collections, University of North Carolina at Asheville)

Altona M. Trent, Maggie Tate Trent, William J. Trent Jr.
Atlanta, Ga.
(ca. 1913)

Mary Estelle Trent
(ca. 1945)

William J. Trent and Langston Hughes
Andrew Carnegie Library
Livingstone College
Salisbury, N.C.
(1950)
(courtesy of Livingstone College, Salisbury, N.C.)

William J. Trent
New York, N.Y.
(July 15, 1952)

William J. Trent and Cleota C. Trent
in front of President's home, Monroe Street
Salisbury, N.C.
(ca. 1955)

United Negro College Fund
left to right: William J. Trent Jr., Rufus E. Clement
New York, N.Y.
(1963)
(Bill Anderson, photographer; photograph courtesy of
Linda Anderson Cook and Darian W. Swig)

Chapter 4

The Roots of a Black Middle Class:
Trent at the Atlanta YMCA

ATLANTA IN 1911 was the commercial center of the South, a boom town bursting with energy.[1] There were almost 155,000 people in the city, one-third of whom were black.[2] It must have been quite a change for the Trents since Asheville's population was only about 15,000 in 1910. Moving to a town with so many black colleges and universities would have surely delighted Trent.[3] There had been no college or university for black people in Asheville. He only knew Livingstone College, and he had loved that life. He had learned there, he once wrote, "an undiminishing delight in a great love for classical literature and art and music."[4] Thus, he would also love what these Atlanta schools offered—a world of debates, concerts, speeches; and a world of black men, college teachers and administrators, who read and loved books, and loved learning, as he did.

But by the turn of the century, Atlanta was also the most segregated city in Georgia.[5] Movie houses, public accommodations, housing, downtown stores, streetcars—all were segregated.[6] Black Atlantans had various ways to respond to these humiliating circumstances. Martin Luther King Sr. refused to ride the streetcar at all. Benjamin Mays, then a professor at Morehouse, rode the streetcar as little as possible. But when he had no choice and had to sit in the back, he once said, "my body was there but not my mind."[7] And black people did not forget that Atlanta was also the city of the 1906 riot, when white people attacked black men and women for days, using hatchets, iron bars, knives, and guns. Two dozen black people were murdered, and hundreds more were injured.[8]

Georgia had abolished convict leasing in 1909, but it made convicts, mostly black, available to work in chain gangs on state roads, thus replacing private brutality with state brutality.[9] As for the vote, black Georgians had essentially stopped voting. Georgia had enacted so many voting restrictions that although the state black registration in 1904 was 28.3 percent, by 1910 black registration had dropped to 4.3 percent.[10]

But this would not have surprised the Trents, for black people in the South had been losing their recently gained power and status, and any sense of safety, for decades. So the attractions of a city with many black schools of higher education, and the daily humiliation of being treated as an inferior being, went hand in hand.

Most black people were poor. The women did domestic work, and the men, when they could find any work at all, worked mainly for the duration of a particular contract. They lived in slum areas with falling-down houses and schools, areas that lacked basic city services like lighting and sewage removal. Some of these districts were filled with bars and houses of prostitution, violence, and crime.[11] Trent's work at the Atlanta YMCA was an effort to address some of these problems by providing healthy surroundings and important support for black men who were trying to make their way in a rapidly urbanizing city.

His work thus put him at the center of the creation of a black middle class in the South's fastest-growing city. He would be working in tandem with other black actors in the city whose organizations provided much-needed services for the black community—actors like Rev. Henry Hugh Proctor at First Congregational Church, and Lugenia Burns Hope, who created the Neighborhood Union—important representatives of both the Progressive and Social Gospel movements. Atlanta's many black schools of higher education—Atlanta University, three colleges, and three seminaries—also played an important role in creating a burgeoning black middle class.

When they arrived in Atlanta, the Trent family moved into a house on Johnson Avenue in the Fourth Ward, long considered the best residential area for black people, the home of those older black Atlantans who had made up the city's black aristocracy.[12] By 1900 this professional group was made up largely of a new group of blacks, who were by and large new to Atlanta.[13] It was also the heart of the black business district.[14]

According to W. E. B. Du Bois, "the best Negro homes in Atlanta" at this time were fairly large, and had both running water and bathrooms in the home. The houses generally had seven or eight rooms, all with windows, curtains, and shades. And somewhere in the house was a piano or organ.[15] The Trent house was probably much like this. It was likely made of wood, as were most homes in the Fourth Ward.[16] It sat up on brick pillars, creating an area underneath where children played during the hottest days of summer. The family used gas lights and had coal stoves for heat.[17]

We can be sure that one of the first things the Trents did when they arrived in Atlanta was choose a church. Surprisingly, they did not choose an African Methodist Episcopal (AME) Zion church for the family, but chose, rather, the First Congregational Church—the church of the "wealthy and well-connected" black people in Atlanta, the church of the black aristocracy in that city around the turn of the century.[18] Atlanta University had been created by Congregationalists. As a result, the black professors and administrators at that school tended to go to First Congregational.[19]

But Trent was not affiliated with Atlanta University, and the Trent family was profoundly linked to the AME Zion Church.

Trent's mother, Malinda Dunn, had been one of the early founders of the China Grove AME Zion Church in Pineville, North Carolina, and Maggie's father, Thad Tate, had been one of the founders of Grace AME Zion Church in Charlotte. So changing denomination was a deep break in family history.[20] It was also a change in liturgical style. The AME Zion churches were black-created and imbued with an emotional liturgical style. But in the Congregational Church, black people prayed in a rigid and rational white New England tradition. [21]

It is very likely that the Trents chose this church out of admiration for Rev. Henry Hugh Proctor, the first black pastor of this church, who played an important role in the black political leadership in the state through sermons, speeches, publications, and petitions that he and W. E. B. Du Bois sent to the state legislature.[22] Proctor also saw the church as an important center of community activities.[23] By 1912 First Congregational had a library with 3,000 volumes, a kindergarten, a gymnasium, an auditorium that seated 1,000, a ladies' parlor, and a kitchen and sewing room for teaching domestic skills to young girls.[24] Because of its services for black girls and women, it served, in essence, as the Young Women's Christian Association (YWCA) for the city's black girls and women.[25] Before there was a Young Men's Christian Association (YMCA, or Y) in Atlanta, First Congregational had also offered a gymnasium for black men.[26] The church also had an employment bureau and an outreach program for prisoners.[27] In addition, Proctor developed music festivals for the black community.[28] His example of "applied Christianity" would win the approval of many leaders in the Social Gospel movement.[29] Clearly, Trent would have immediately felt a kinship with this man and his work.

Part of getting the family settled was finding a school for Altona, who was almost seven when they moved. They decided to send her to the Ogelthorpe School, a private school created in 1905 to provide practical experience for students in Atlanta University's Normal Department.[30] Altona would remain in the Atlanta

University system throughout primary school, secondary school, and college.[31]

Trent's introduction to Atlanta and to the YMCA community would have been facilitated by his Y friends and colleagues William Alphaeus Hunton and John B. Watson. Although Hunton had moved his family north to safety after the 1906 riot, Trent would still be able to rely on Hunton's many friends and colleagues in the city. He could also count on Watson, who started his Y work as international secretary in 1908 and had been working in the black Atlanta community since 1909.[32]

John Hope, who had become the first black president of the Atlanta Baptist College in 1906,[33] would have also welcomed and aided Trent as he and his family settled into their new life. Hope was well acquainted with Moorland and Hunton and very active in Y work. He was faculty adviser to the YMCA on the college campus and regularly participated in the city's black Y by teaching night classes. Over the years Hope was often a member of the Y's management committee.[34] Indeed, it is very likely that Hope participated in the selection of Trent for the position of secretary of the Atlanta city Y. Hope and his wife, Lugenia Burns Hope, had two young sons. In July 1911, when the Trents arrived, young Edward would have been nine years old. John Jr., the Hope baby, was just one and a half, and William Trent Jr. was three months younger.[35] The Hopes must have made an important effort to welcome the Trents into their community and their family life, for these two babies would grow to be fast friends.

Finally, after getting everyone in the family settled in, Trent got down to work. His office was in the YMCA on Wheat Street—later renamed Auburn Avenue—in a house between Courtland Street and Piedmont Avenue.[36] Much like Asheville's Young Men's Institute, the Atlanta Y, founded in 1894, provided educational programs for men and boys, as well as athletics, Bible study, and bathing facilities. It also had space available for a few young men to stay when they first moved to the city.[37] This would have been very familiar to Trent. But it must have been a relief that in this new position he would no longer have to act as a landlord to businesses within the YMCA building, as he had in Asheville.

Indeed, there was no need for stores and businesses within the YMCA building at all, for within just a few blocks of the Atlanta Y, on Auburn Avenue, one could find almost everything: Annie Epp's lunchroom, Bethel AME Church, Henry Alexander's shoemaker shop, the Gate City drugstore, and the Atlanta Mutual Insurance Company, as well as medical offices and grocery stores, a barber shop and a tailoring shop, a notary public, an undertaker, a furniture company, a cigar store, and a meat market. And there was more. In 1909 there were sixty-four black businesses, seven black professionals, and fourteen white businesses on Auburn Avenue, the commercial, social, and entertainment center of black Atlanta.[38] This was the "talked about" street in Atlanta. People used to say that if you were black and went to Atlanta but didn't go down Auburn Avenue, you hadn't really been to Atlanta.[39]

Trent's tasks at the Atlanta Y were in many ways like his tasks when he arrived in Asheville at the Young Men's Institute—to get the building cleaned and repaired, to continue the ongoing programs, and to create new programs. Much like the work in Asheville, too, was the important task of raising money. Only, this time, it was not to pay for a building that had already been built: it was to pay for the construction of a new, modern, fully furnished, and up-to-date Y building. In 1910, of the forty-four black city YMCAs in the country, only twenty-one of them owned any property.[40] Surely Atlanta's black community was large enough, and important enough, to have its own building.

In December 1910, white businessman and philanthropist Julius Rosenwald had offered to contribute $25,000 to every black community in the country that raised $75,000 toward building a YMCA. But he would give the money only after the community raised $50,000 and actually spent that sum toward land and the construction of the building. The Rosenwald offer would last five years. This offer led black Ys across the country to start money-raising campaigns to meet the Rosenwald criteria. In 1911, it also led the International Committee of the YMCA to hire three more

African Americans as international secretaries for Y work: Channing Tobias, David Jones, and Robert P. Hamlin.[41]

Thus, more precisely, then, when Trent arrived in 1911 his major task was to raise $50,000 for a new building within five years and, at the same time, raise money for programs, building upkeep, and his own salary.[42] Trent and Watson would be working on this project with Woods White, the white chairman of the Georgia State Committee for the YMCA and a member of the Y International Committee. White was also a businessman, and very influential with public leaders and newspapers in Atlanta.[43]

Trent's primary effort in the fundraising campaign would be through Atlanta's black churches. The plan was to obtain promises to contribute to the building fund, and then to collect based on those promises. In order to do this, Trent, Watson, and White first created pledge cards, obtained pledges, then determined the church of each person who had pledged a contribution. Next, Trent sent the pledge cards and list of names to each pastor with instructions for collecting the money. The pastor was to give the card of each person who made a pledge to a "captain"—a church member who would pass them on to the church members ("canvassers"), who would then collect the money. Some churches had many canvassers. For example, Friendship Church had 240 members who made pledges, and 24 canvassers. The Y committee of management also played an important role in this project. Each committee member was assigned a group of churches to keep in touch with about collecting on the pledges.

After working out this system, Trent, Watson, and White held an instructional meeting for the ministers and other prominent men in Atlanta. They then visited the Ministers' Unions in the city and visited, as well, each church, during both Sunday morning and Sunday evening services. And they periodically called all the workers together for reports or for more instructions.[44]

This was their primary effort—to reach as many black people in Atlanta as possible through their churches. A secondary effort was an agreement signed by 100 Atlanta men to continue working on the fundraising project and to attend all Y meetings about fundraising, until the building was finished.[45] And, of course, they would also reach out to wealthy individuals, both black and white, in and out of Atlanta, to try to reach their goal.

With respect to leadership roles in this project, the "leader and general advisor" of the fundraising effort was White. Trent was considered "his man to know everything." Watson's role was to help Trent with the "multitude of details," to keep the preachers "corralled," and to inform White of any disaffection among preachers, so that he could give personal attention to a particular church. Watson was also head of the Y's Bureau of Publicity and Education for this effort. The three men met at least two or three times a week, and sometimes several nights in a row. White, Watson noted, attended all meetings, and was always the last man to leave.[46]

The appearance of a white man as head of the black fundraising project is at first surprising, then understandable. Of course Trent would need a point of entry into the wealthy white Atlanta community in order to raise money for the building, and White could make those contacts for him. He would also be able to use his connections with the white newspapers to gain favorable publicity for this fundraising effort. In both black and white communities, an important white person leading the effort would give the building project more credibility and importance. But it was not always easy for black Y leaders to work with White. Although they were convinced that White was sincere in his interest in this project, Watson noted that at times he lacked "many courtesies that he should show Colored men." Despite this rudeness, they decided to ignore it and work with him "for the greater good."[47]

YMCA reports that follow the creation of this fundraising project document the monthly progress. In January 1912, six months after Trent's arrival in Atlanta, Watson reported that he had been spending a lot of time in Atlanta helping collect pledges, organizing workers, and "securing the cooperation of men of special influence."[48] By February, Watson had announced that Trent was "pulling things together in Atlanta."[49] In September,

Watson and his wife moved to Atlanta.[50] Thus, he would be able to spend more time on the Atlanta Y building fund. In November, Channing Tobias asked Trent's fellow Y leaders to pray for Trent in the building campaign.[51] In December, Trent started a sixty-day "50 cents" rally, an attempt to get every black churchgoer to contribute that amount to the YMCA building fund. At this time, there were "at least twenty thousand communicants" in "the forty Negro churches" in Atlanta.[52] That same month Watson wrote that "Trent is one of the hardest worked men in the entire brotherhood at this time."[53]

In January 1913, Watson had more to say about him: "Trent is a man greatly to be loved, and I believe today he would be voted by the Colored men of Atlanta the best loved man in the city. He has his weaknesses, many of which have cropped out in this campaign and for which some of the white men have jumped on him with both feet; but most of us have no doubt that today he is the best man that can be found for the piece of work he is trying to do."[54]

But collecting the money people had pledged was not easy. By March 1913, about two years into the drive, the team had collected only $8,000.[55] Trent, however, was indefatigable. Toward the end of the year Watson reported: "Mr. Trent is planning a great mass meeting for the evening of the Second Sunday in December. Every church in the city will close its doors that night. Mr. Trent is as fresh on the job as if he had started yesterday. His resourcefulness and Christian manhood are still impressing themselves on the people of this great city."[56]

In mid-January 1914, the *Atlanta Independent* decided to print the name of every person who had made a pledge to support the new Y, listing both the amount pledged and the amount paid on that pledge.[57] This was the beginning of a five-week campaign to get pledges fulfilled.[58] And the money started to come in, from 25 cents on a $25 pledge, to $390 on a $1,000 pledge.[59] The final report of the rally listed 35 churches. Of those churches, 20 donated less than a $100, and 7 donated less than $10. Trent's church, First Congregational, however, came in second to

Friendship Baptist, with $2,241.39.[60] This shows both the wealth of those who attended the Congregational Church and the support Rev. Proctor and his congregation provided to Trent and his work.

And, finally, we learn from this rally the great forbearance of those black Atlantans working for the new Y building in dealing with some of the white people who supported the project, because, at the last meeting of this five-week campaign, Woods White said, in a speech, "that the Negro, by his own admission, was the weaker race." The following speaker, Bishop C. K. Nelson of the Episcopal Church, made bad matters worse by beginning his speech with comments about his "old Negro mammy, whom he loved as a mother," and ending with a statement that he supported public playgrounds and parks for black children since "even the lower animals thrived and prospered in having plenty of space in which to take recreation."[61]

It might seem incongruous that these white men who had been supporting Trent's campaign made such racist statements. We should remember, however, that White and Nelson were supporting the construction of a black YMCA within a segregated Y system in a segregated city. Given this context, then, their racist words and their support of Trent's fundraising campaign were in accord.

Moorland knew that the Y secretaries often worked themselves to exhaustion, and encouraged them to take the time to rest. "Take a vacation," he told them. "If you are not tired of your work, the work may be tired of you, and it might be restful to both to have a separation for a few weeks at least. You will do better work if you rest a while."[62] He also reminded them to read: "Do not fail to keep abreast of the times by systematic study. You must take a little time for the improvement of the mind or you will soon be a back number."[63]

Summertime was often a quiet time in the Trent household, as Maggie took the children to spend summers with their relatives. From the age of two until he was ten, Bill went to Charlotte, where he stayed with his grandparents; Altona spent many summers with her aunt Eleanora and uncle John Walker, and the Walker children—her cousins—in Asheville.[64] Without the presence of the children, the house in Atlanta was calm and restful. In September 1914, Trent let his colleagues know that he had taken at least some of Moorland's advice: he read "for his vacation," and sent them the list of books he had read during the summer, "in the evening, at the close of work."[65]

He read the gospel; that is, the first four books of the New Testament, the teachings of Jesus in Matthew, Mark, Luke, and John. It is easy to understand this selection given his upbringing, his conversion, his work with the chaplain during the Spanish-American War, and the religious component of his YMCA work. It would not be surprising if he reread the gospel every summer.

He also read John Daniels's report of his research, *In Freedom's Birthplace: A Study of the Boston Negroes.*[66] In many ways, this is good scholarship. For example, Daniels presents data distinguishing the lives of black immigrants from the South from the lives of those born and raised in Boston, as well as the lives of "Negroes of foreign birth," thus allowing himself to discuss differences within the black community. The book also includes data documenting employment in Boston by classes of work and by race. But even within these discussions, there are thoughtless stereotypes, stereotypes that are not even consistent, stereotypes that undermine his thoughtful research and confuse the reader, who is trying to sort out what is intelligent work and what is not. For example, Daniels writes that black people are jealous, and "conspicuously deficient" with respect to social cooperation, yet writes, at the same time, that black people show a "high degree of [...] human kindness, ever ready to help their fellows in time of need."[67] He also fails to support his damning indictments of the black community. For instance, the only evidence he offers for his statement that blacks are "morally backward" and show "extreme sexual laxity" is "common report [...] confirmed [...] by scrupulous observation," since, he notes, collecting good statistical data to support this assertion would be "next to impossible."[68] So we wonder how Trent read this book and what he took from it. And we wonder if he, like many black people, had learned to read around the racism in order to gain some benefit from the scholarship.

Trent also read "a volume of John Hay's addresses," referring perhaps to the recently published collection of essays by one of Lincoln's secretaries, as well as the science fiction novel *The World Set Free*, by H. G. Wells.[69] There were three more novels on Trent's summer reading list. The first, Frances Hodgson Burnett's *The Dawn of a To-Morrow*, is the story of a wealthy businessman on the verge of suicide, who is saved when he meets a group of very poor people who share their meager meal with him and teach him about faith. The author called this "a Christmas story," and it has that simple flavor.[70]

But the books that may have meant the most to him that summer were two novels by John Fox: *Little Shepherd of Kingdom Come* and *The Trail of the Lonesome Pine*.[71] These are stories of two very poor youth—a boy and a girl living in the isolated Appalachian countryside, young people whose lives are transformed by education. They then begin to look in a different way at the people and the life they loved and left behind, and they wonder where they now fit: in the simple life in the countryside, or in their new sophisticated world. More specifically, in *Little Shepherd*, as the boy grows up, we see him trying to choose between the uneducated country girl who loves him and the rich girl he adores, the one who lives in the world of his aspirations. As a country boy who had left old ways behind, a country boy who had married educated city girls from prosperous families, Trent must have found that this book resonated at some level in his mind and spirit.

So we see that Trent read a variety of literature that summer: fiction, essays, social science research, and the Bible. By telling his colleagues that he had read these books, he was showing them both that he kept up with what was being published and that he had broad intellectual interests. He did not read only the magazines and books published by the YMCA: his world was bigger than that. He would not be, in Moorland's term, a "back number."

Not only did he take time to read: Trent also took the time to keep in touch with his friends from college and from his Asheville years. He returned to Asheville in 1913 to join the celebration when the Young Men's Institute burned its mortgage.[72] He wrote a letter to Dr. Torrence in Asheville in February 1915, showing concern for Torrence's health.[73] He corresponded with his friend Kwegyir Aggrey when the latter was studying at Columbia.[74] And he was undoubtedly still in touch with classmates Walker and Clement. As he wrote many years later, these three remained close friends and discussed their problems with each other throughout their lives.[75]

He was also making new friends in Atlanta. As noted earlier, John Hope was very likely one of them. Even though he was a college president, Hope had initially come to Atlanta to teach Latin and Greek, and while a professor he introduced football to the school.[76] So, beyond their common work for the YMCA, Trent and Hope were both college men with other shared interests.

Trent also became close friends with Truman Kella Gibson Sr., who had become vice president and secretary of the Atlanta Mutual Life Insurance Company the year before the Trents arrived in Atlanta.[77] Gibson too was involved with the YMCA and spent some time on the board.[78] Gibson and his wife had a son, Truman Jr., who was almost two years younger than Trent Jr. Even though the Gibsons would move to Chicago when Truman Jr. was in the fifth grade, the two couples' sons developed a deep friendship which they continued over the years.[79]

Gibson was a close friend of Alonzo Herndon, and thus, through this connection, Trent might well have become Herndon's friend too.[80] Like the Trent family, the Herndons attended First Congregational Church.[81] And like Trent, Herndon was a self-made man. Born a slave, Herndon made his way first as a barber, then as owner of the largest, most luxurious barbershop in Atlanta. He parlayed the money earned through the barbershop into the ownership of a few small black insurance companies in 1905. Six years later his Atlanta Mutual Life Insurance Company had 84 branch offices and 70,000 policy holders. When Trent arrived, Herndon was well on his way to becoming very rich.[82] Herndon also supported the black community with charitable contributions, as well as in the political sphere.[83]

All these men supported Trent in his effort to raise money for the new Y building. But the deadline for the Rosenwald grant was fast approaching. In order to receive the grant, Trent and his team would have to raise $50,000 by 1916. In September 1914, Trent reported that they had raised almost $17,000 "from the Colored people."[84] But they could not meet their goal. At the end of the five-year fundraising period, only seven cities had been able to meet the goal of the Rosenwald grant. Rosenwald then decided to grant five-year extensions to six cities, including Atlanta.[85] So this massive, laborious, grinding effort to raise money for the new Y building in Atlanta would go on.

As he continued this fundraising effort, Trent and Maggie both took great interest in their children's schooling. It is very likely that, in the fall of 1915, five-year-old Bill began elementary school. He attended the Houston Street School, about a twelve-block walk from their home.[86] When the school was built in 1881, it was the first new schoolhouse for black children in Atlanta and the first school staffed entirely by black teachers. Well lit and well ventilated, with eight rooms, it was the pride of the community. But by the time Bill started school some thirty-five years later, the Houston Street school was badly maintained and run down. There was no indoor plumbing, and for heating in the winter, janitors carried big stoves from room to room. Because there were so few schools for black children in Atlanta, it was also overcrowded. As a result, the students studied in double shifts, there was a shortage of supplies, and the staff was overworked.[87]

Ten-year-old Altona would have likely taken the streetcar to the Ogelthorpe School, the feeder school for Atlanta University, which was located on the university campus. One might wonder why Trent didn't send his son there too. Perhaps it was because the family couldn't afford to pay private school tuition for two children, and, if put to the choice, the parents wanted their daughter in the more protected environment. Or, perhaps, the Trents might have already planned that their son would go to Morehouse Academy for secondary school, then attend Morehouse College, where Hope was president.[88] There was a reason, then, to avoid having him develop an attachment to Atlanta University's campus and community.

In 1917, Trent was working hard at the Y, going to church, visiting friends, attending concerts and plays, keeping an eye on his children's studies, but paying more and more attention to events in Europe, for the sounds of war were growing loud. Germany had declared war on Russia, then France, then Belgium—which brought Great Britain into the war to support the Allies. In 1915 Germany had attacked the American ship *Lusitania*, and, since then, Americans had been wondering if America would go to war too. On April 6, 1917, they learned that the answer was "yes," when the United States declared war on Germany. President Wilson explained that the country entered the war not to gain land or wealth, but specifically to make the world "safe for democracy."[89] Only five weeks later, on May 18, Congress enacted the Selective Service Act of 1917, setting up the first draft call in June.[90]

The black community in Atlanta must have been very anxious when newspapers announced the passage of the new law: were its husbands and sons, brothers and fathers going to be sent away to fight and die in a foreign land? But even as those in the community were talking about this, they faced another crisis when, only three days later, on May 21, an all-encompassing fire struck the city.

It began about eleven in the morning, on a windy day, which made everything worse. Because so many homes in the Auburn district were made of wood, and close together, the fire jumped easily from house to house. There was smoke everywhere; there were roofs caving in, fire wagons going in every direction, sirens blaring. The schools let the children out early, and they ran home to help their families save whatever they could. Some who feared the fire was coming close, and others who had already lost their homes, went to the churches for safety. Rev. Proctor was one of the ministers who opened their churches that Monday. Since First Congregational was made of brick and stone, it could withstand the fire. Other city residents, both black and white, stayed together in city parks. Telephone poles burned down; sidewalks buckled; trolley cars could no longer run; power went out in many sections of town. The National Guard was called in, and firefighters from other towns came as well. But it wasn't until about ten that night that firefighters managed to halt the spread of the fire, by dynamiting houses at the edge of the fire. By that time, it had destroyed 73 blocks, and almost 10,000 people, mainly black, no longer had homes.[91]

We know the Trent family lived in the Auburn area, one of the places seriously damaged by the fire. The parents must have been terrified until Bill and Altona arrived safely from school, then terrified again, perhaps, as the firefighters seemed unable to get the fire under control. Perhaps they were among those who walked to First Congregational to wait out the fire. It is unlikely that they lost their home, but it might well have been damaged.[92] Late that night, when the fire was finally under control and they could return home, we might imagine that the Trent family gave thanks together in prayer.

As for the war, the black community had been right: the men in their families would be called to fight in Europe. Although the black population was only 10 percent of the total American population, black men would eventually make up 14 percent of all men drafted into the military.[93] They expected that their service in the military would help them gain equality when they returned.[94] But even though the black soldiers were going to fight "to make the world safe for democracy," they would fight in segregated units. Jim Crow was going to war, too.

There is a strong and important relationship between military service, manhood, and citizenship.[95] As a result, America's military leaders decided to strip black men of the dignity and status afforded soldiers: by keeping them in labor groups and out of fighting units altogether. Therefore, most black men who served in the military during World War I served as noncombatants. One hundred seventy thousand of the 370,000 black draftees stayed in the United States during the war, where they worked as laborers—loading ships, hauling material, constructing buildings. The same was true when the black soldiers served in France. There, they worked as cooks, stevedores, mechanics; they dug trenches, laid railroad tracks, built dams, and buried the dead.[96] To remind black men that they were only laborers, and not true soldiers, the military often denied them uniforms, and had them wear either work clothes—blue overalls made of denim—or their own clothes.[97]

American military leaders did finally create two black combat units—the Ninety-Second and Ninety-Third Divisions. But it then put four regiments of the Ninety-Third under the control of the French military, thus putting them "outside the American army, and, in a symbolic sense, outside of the nation itself."[98] This turned out to benefit the black American soldiers, however, since the French soldiers treated them as comrades.[99]

America's military leaders had been concerned that the French might treat black troops in France as true soldiers and true citizens of America; that is, as men entitled to be treated with dignity and respect. They immediately foresaw the problem this could cause when the soldiers returned home. Therefore, in August 1918, a few months after the arrival of black troops in France, American military officials had the French issue to their officers a memorandum entitled "On the Subject of Black American Troops." This memorandum called for the French officers to "prevent the rise of any pronounced degree of intimacy between French officers and black officers" and, as well, to keep the French people from "spoiling the Negroes."[100] But they were too late, and this directive wouldn't have helped, anyhow, for the French were already noticing that the black American troops were much more agreeable than the white soldiers, who held the French in some contempt. Because of the way the French welcomed these black soldiers, the soldiers suddenly had a new idea of who they were as men, and what democracy could look like.[101] The American political and military leadership was right: this would be problematic when black soldiers returned home.

That same month, August 1918, Morehouse president John Hope left Atlanta to work for the YMCA in France, where he would remain for almost a year. As "Field Secretary for Work among the Colored Troops," he was responsible for all of the Y war work with black troops in France. He visited camps, investigated soldiers' complaints of discrimination, and addressed plans to create a separate leave area for black soldiers.[102] These were matters he would talk over with Trent when he returned.

One month after Hope's departure, the Selective Service System required that all men between the ages of eighteen and forty-five register for the draft, and Trent signed up.[103] Very soon thereafter, on November 11, 1918, the fighting was over.[104] What a relief this must have been for everyone back home And what a relief for Trent, who would not have to go to war, and who had already seen way too many young men from the Butler Street Y go away to war and return damaged—in their body, their mind, or their spirit—or not return at all.

Despite the war, there had been good news for the Trents during those years. They celebrated the birth of their second child, a daughter, Mary Estelle, named certainly for Maggie's mother, Mary, and Maggie's sister Estelle. They also celebrated when their good friend George Clement was consecrated as a bishop in the AME Zion Church.[105] And even though Trent was still struggling to raise money for the Y, he must have found it most enjoyable when, in October 1917, he sang in concert before 4,000 people at the Atlanta Auditorium-Armory to raise money for the Y.[106]

Finally, by 1918, there was good news about the Y, for Trent had raised $50,000. Thus the Y had been able to receive the Rosenwald matching funds, and construction had begun on the new Y building on Butler Street, just a half-block off Auburn Avenue.[107]

People must have expected that the end of the war would begin a time of peace, a time for the country to heal and rebuild. But that was not to be. There was labor unrest all over. During the war, hundreds of thousands of black people had moved north. They had been, in a sense, "pushed" out of the South because of the collapse of the South's cotton economy, caused both by the crop devastation due to the boll weevil and by the loss of an important cotton market in Europe due to the war. The war then "pulled" black Southerners north, because of a labor shortage in the North created by both the draft and the steep decline in European immigration.[108] Almost half a million black Southerners moved north in only one year, between 1916 and 1917.[109] So as the white soldiers were returning from the war, the North looked different and the job market looked different. But these white men now wanted their jobs back.

Black men had returned from the war with a new sense of self. And black people had a new sense of hope. They had believed President Wilson when he said that the country was fighting for democracy, and to black Americans, that meant at home as well as abroad. They also felt that they had paid enough dues in that war to be entitled to unquestioned citizenship rights. "We return," wrote Du Bois. "We return from fighting. We return fighting. Make way for Democracy! We saved it in France, and by the Great Jehovah, we will save it in the United States of America, or know the reason why."[110]

There were welcome-home parades for the black soldiers around the country: Chicago, New York City, throughout the South. Disciplined, strong young men in uniform marched in parade formation. Sixty thousand came out to cheer them on in Chicago; 250,000 welcomed them in New York City.[111] But the pride felt by the black community and the returning soldiers would only anger and frighten the white community. These men had new, dangerous ideas about their value as men and as citizens of this country. And they had been trained in the art of warfare and the use of weapons.

Thus we come to what NAACP officer James Weldon Johnson called "the Red Summer" of 1919—"red" because of all the blood of black people that flowed as a result of crazed attacks by their white fellow citizens, a "red summer" when white people

A Black Man's Journey from Sharecropper to College President

acted out their rage and their fear. The terror was everywhere. In July, hundreds of white veterans, soldiers, and civilian workers from Camp Meade near Washington, DC, gathered to take revenge on the alleged attack on a white woman by black men. For four days white mobs invaded the black community, beating and shooting black people wherever they found them. By the fourth day, Congress had ordered 1,000 troops into the city to stop the rioting. Six people lay dead; several hundred were wounded. That same month, in Chicago, a young black man, Eugene Williams, swimming near Lake Michigan's 29th Street beach, crossed the imaginary line into "white" water, was stoned by outraged white people, and drowned. After his murder, black threats were met with white violence, which continued for two long weeks. Thirty-eight people died, black and white, 17 of them the first day alone. More than 500 were injured.[112]

And the violence continued not only around the country, and not only throughout the summer of 1919, but for two more years. Tyler Station, Kentucky; Pensacola, Florida; El Dorado, Arkansas; Pickens, Mississippi; Pope City, Georgia; Norfolk, Virginia; Longview, Texas; Star City, Arkansas; New Orleans, Louisiana; Charleston, South Carolina—the names of the cities of white terrorism and violence kept on rolling out. The period beginning with the end of the war and ending with the Tulsa riot of 1921 was a period of the worst violence against black people since Reconstruction. There were twenty-five race riots, large and small, and seventy-six black victims of lynching, at least eleven of whom were veterans.[113] Their service to their country did not save them.

The terror was particularly intense in Georgia, where, during the Red Summer—between April and November 1919—there were seven major riots and lynchings, more than in any other state.[114] During the previous year, white Georgians lynched nineteen black people, more than double the number of the previous year.[115] This should have come as no surprise: in 1918 the NAACP reported that there had been more lynchings in Georgia between 1889 and 1918 than in any other state.[116]

On April 22, 1921, at a conference he called in Atlanta, Georgia's governor presented a document entitled "A Statement from Governor Hugh M. Dorsey as to The Negro in Georgia." In this document he listed 135 examples of egregious cruelty of white Georgians toward black Georgians within the previous two years: black people lynched; black people held in peonage; black people chased out of their homes and towns by organized lawlessness; black people subject to individual acts of cruelty. "In some counties," he wrote, "the [N]egro is being driven out as though he were a wild beast. In others he is being held as a slave. In others, no [N]egroes remain [....] We stand indicted as a people before the world."[117] Four weeks later, the newly revived Ku Klux Klan held a large parade in downtown Atlanta.[118]

It is hard to imagine how Trent and Maggie coped during these years. They must have thought the world was spinning out of control: a war, a fire, riots, lynchings. Every day there was more terrifying news. Did they try to keep this information from their children? This would have been difficult, for Altona was fifteen and Bill was ten, so they would have heard of all this from their classmates. They might have tried to keep their children home more. Perhaps they started traveling around town in a different, more secretive manner. Did they think of moving north?

We know one way that Trent responded. Along with John and Lugenia Burns Hope, he became a member of the newly created Commission on Interracial Cooperation (CIC).[119] Inspired by the CIC, more than half of all counties in the South organized similar interracial committees.[120] The goal of the CIC was to develop training schools so people could learn both how to gather information about race conditions in the South and how to cope with racial conflicts within their own communities.[121] Groups formed by the commission monitored Klan activities and allegations of police brutality, headed off race riots and lynchings in their communities, and even managed to get twenty-two indictments in lynching cases in the early 1920s.[122] The CIC supported the end of peonage and the creation of truly equal schools, as well as equal accommodations for travel. It did not, however, fight for the end of segregation, or for giving the right to vote to black Americans.[123] But the NAACP did. And Trent was an active member of that organization, and helped organize the South's first national NAACP meeting.[124]

Years had passed since Trent had arrived in Atlanta with the mandate to raise the money for the construction of a new Y building. Finally, on Sunday, May 16, 1920, at 3:30 in the afternoon, Trent's dream came true with the dedication of the brand-new Butler Street YMCA. John Hope, chairman of the board of managers at the time, presided over the event, which was held in the Y gymnasium and open to all members of the public. Speakers included J. E. Moorland, Woods White, and Robert Russa Moton, principal of Tuskegee Institute.

The celebration continued all week long. Monday night the Y held exercises celebrating its work with schools, colleges, and veterans. Tuesday evening there was a program about business concerns and fraternal orders, as well as postal clerks and carriers. "Industrial concerns" were on the program Wednesday. Thursday night was the time for exercises by churches and Sunday schools. Ladies' night was Friday night. And Saturday, "the biggest night of all," was boys' night.[125] Reporting after the dedication about the effort it took to build the new Y, the *Atlanta Independent* stated that "Professor Trent [bore] the heat of the burden and [acquitted] himself well. His services have been strenuous and in every instance he has done honor to the movement and reflected credit upon himself."[126]

But all were not pleased with the way the Y leadership had managed either the Y or the fundraising. The day before the dedication, the editor of the *Atlanta Independent* wrote that he could not understand "why it took ten years to do what we ought to have done in two years." He thought "that there was an air of selfishness about the management of the institution which handicapped it in its work, that the people did not take to the movement for the reason they did not believe that the management of the institution stood for the interest of the people, and that the institution was being used for the benefit of the few at the expense of the many."[127]

We don't know to what the editor was referring. Certainly, knowing Trent's background as a poor country boy; knowing about his Y work at college, where he visited men in jail and on chain gangs; remembering his work in Asheville—we find this surprising. John Hope would later describe Trent as a "servant of the community, going into factories, business houses, dens, dives [...] to bring out men; [...] giving a Thanksgiving dinner to a group of hungry boys."[128] Nonetheless, the men who would be on the podium during the dedication must have read this editorial, because they took care, in their talks, to advise the management "not to make the institution a gentlemen's club," emphasizing that the work of the YMCA "was not to save those who were already saved; in other words, the bath tubs, reading rooms and all of the other paraphernalia were not provided for those who have this equipment at home, but for those who did not have these things at home and need a better environment in order that they might recognize Jesus Christ the Savior of the world."[129]

There must have been hundreds of guests at the dedication—members of the Y, the Y board of managers, the ministers who had worked so hard to encourage their membership to contribute, all those who had contributed to the building fund, the hundred men who vowed to never give up on this project, and all their families. And there would have been even more people present, for, as the newspaper announced, the public was "cordially invited" to all events surrounding the dedication.[130] How proud they must have been to see this fine building and know that they had played a part in its construction.

That Sunday afternoon, as the guests approached the building, they would have seen a six-story tan brick building, built in the classical Georgian Revival style.[131] The front door had columns on both sides and a cornice decorated with molding. The windows were arranged symmetrically, three on each side. And, as is common in Georgian Revival style, the top floor had dormer windows.

To get to the auditorium for the dedication, guests would have walked up the curved double staircase to the building entrance on the second floor. As soon as they entered the building, they would have noticed the high ceilings and the spacious hallway. It is a building that feels open, light, and accessible. Immediately they would have seen, on the right, a large room that has the feel of a parlor. Opposite the entrance to that room, above the fireplace, visitors would have seen a large framed bas-relief sculpture of a man crouching, nude, his body facing forward, head turned to the side—a man surrounded and embraced by angels. The rays of the sun burn bright around him. This sculpture, *Paul*, tells the story of Paul on his way to Damascus, when "suddenly there shined round about him a light from heaven and he fell to the earth."[132] It tells the story of Paul's sudden conversion from a man who persecuted early Christians to a believer in the teachings of Jesus. Trent commissioned sculptor Meta Vaux Warrick Fuller, wife of his friend Simon Fuller, to create this work for the new YMCA.[133] Given what we know about Trent's own conversion, and what we know about the work of the YMCA at this time, a sculpture about Paul and his miraculous transformation to a life of Christian living was the perfect choice for this new building.

Walking past the parlor, the guests would have seen offices, then arrived at the gymnasium, which served as an auditorium that day. The next floor up contained classrooms and meeting rooms. And the top three floors held forty-eight dormitory rooms as well as bathrooms, with a lounge on each of the three floors. A pool and showers were located on the ground level.[134] The building also had a restaurant.[135] After all the dedication speeches, and after the tour of the new building, the guests must have been tired when they headed home that Sunday, but they also must have felt a profound sense of satisfaction with this new building, and a great sense of accomplishment.

Since the Butler Street Y was only two-and-a-half blocks from the old Y, and just a half-block off Auburn Avenue, Trent was still working in the heart of commercial black Atlanta. If he walked from the new Y down Butler Street and turned right onto

Auburn, he would have been at the Odd Fellows' building and auditorium, both constructed soon after his arrival in Atlanta. In these two buildings alone he would have found dentists, doctors, and lawyers, a bakery, a barber shop, a soft-drink shop, a tailor, and a photo studio, as well as the Gate City drugstore, a branch of the Poro College Beauty School, an insurance company, and the Masonic Relief Association. These two buildings also contained two banks and two insurance companies.

If he turned left onto Auburn after leaving the Y, in that first block he would have seen more shops, including the Herald Book and Publishing Company, Lum Sing's laundry, a stove repairer, and a meat market. But the most amazing and wonderful new shop for Trent in this block now, in 1920, must have been J. A. Hopkins's bookstore.[136] We know how much Trent loved to read. What a wonderful development for him, then, to have a bookstore so close. It was also, apparently, quite a temptation. As his son later recalled, it was not uncommon to hear a version of this conversation when his father returned home after work: "Will," Maggie would say, "did you bring the meat home for dinner?" "Law, Ma," he replied, "I forgot it. I stopped by Hopkins's bookstore and got another book."[137]

There were now more black businesses and more black professionals on Auburn Avenue than there had been in 1909: 72 black businesses, compared to 64; 20 black professionals, instead of 7; and 16 white businesses, instead of 14.[138] And Trent, as director of the Y right off Auburn Avenue, was in the middle of everything.

In the Trent family everyone worked. The 1920 census tells us that Maggie was working at home as a seamstress, which was considered an appropriate job for middle- and upper-class black women at the time. It also tells us that Altona, now sixteen years old and a junior in high school, was giving private piano lessons.[139] She probably also played piano at tea parties to supplement the money she earned giving lessons.[140] At the age of ten, Bill was chopping kindling for neighbors to make money. The children also helped out at home. Bill's chores were bringing in kindling and coal and cleaning the yard and bathroom. Altona very likely helped Maggie with cleaning the house, cooking, and laundry. The children worked together too: Altona washed the dishes, and Bill dried them.[141]

Besides working as a seamstress, Maggie was taking care of the household and the family and sewing her family's clothes. She also took time to visit with her new Atlanta friends. One of these friends was Alberta Dickerson Gibson, from New Jersey, wife of Trent's close friend Truman Kella Gibson. Since the Gibsons also had a little boy, the women visited each other with their children.[142]

Maggie was also very likely friendly with John Hope's wife, Lugenia Burns Hope. The two women had some things in common: prominent husbands who worked together for the YMCA, an important institutional role helping their husbands, and little boys. But Lugenia was always deeply involved in civic projects and in activities on the Morehouse campus, so she might have had little time for social visits with women friends.

Lugenia had heavy responsibilities in her role as the wife of a college president. There were often overnight guests to care for: black visitors to Morehouse stayed with the Hopes as there was no hotel for black people, and white and foreign visitors stayed with them simply because of the Hopes' hospitality. Even though she had hired help as well as student workers, the responsibility was on her shoulders.[143] As wife of the president, she had to be a role model, a mother figure, and an official college promoter and hostess. She cared for the live-in students and women faculty. She was dorm mother at Graves Hall, where she made daily room inspections. It was her task to supervise the cleaning of the buildings and grounds and, in the early years, to keep the college accounts. Lugenia also taught a sculpture class for students at Morehouse and Spelman, and a millinery class at Spelman.[144]

But even with all these chores, it was Lugenia's civic and political activities that took most of her time. In Atlanta she worked to raise money for a free kindergarten for black children; she worked to establish a black YWCA for young girls. But her most important and influential activity was the creation of the Neighborhood Union, a women's social welfare agency that provided medical, educational, recreational, and civic activities for the black community; she headed the organization for twenty-five years. She was also, among her many activities, one of the founders of the Southeastern Federation of Colored Women's Clubs, and assistant to Mary McLeod Bethune at the National Youth Administration.[145]

As the wife of a YMCA director, Maggie too had to play a diplomatic role and serve as hostess to those friends, relatives, AME Zion ministers, and fellow Y workers who were visiting town. She likely played a leadership role in the YMCA women's auxiliary, participated in fundraisers, prepared food for Bible classes, and taught Sunday school. Her role was also a sacrificial one, as her husband's Y work took him away from his wife and family long hours during the day and evening, all week long.[146]

Maggie was perhaps involved in women's activities at First Congregational too. Other than that, we know nothing of her activities outside of the home. Was she involved in Lugenia Hope's Neighborhood Union? In the summer of 1920, the campaign to get the Nineteenth Amendment ratified was in full swing.[147] Had Maggie been active in this effort? Did she even think that women should have the right to vote? As with Anna Belle Mitchell, Trent's first wife, we have only a faint idea of the shape of her life.

If we think about the Trent family when they were not working, it is easy to first think of Altona, for Altona at the piano was the heartbeat of the household. She loved the piano and played for hours every day. Her brother Bill's first memory was sitting under the piano while his big sister played.[148] Sometimes her father sang along with her, and very likely the rest of the family joined in. As for social activities outside of the home, the black campuses offered a plethora of interesting events for the Trent family: theater, concerts by glee clubs and orchestras and bands, speakers, and sports events.[149]

First Congregational Church also offered activities for the family. In 1910, Rev. Proctor organized the Atlanta Colored Music Festival Association, in order to bring to Atlanta "the best musical talent of the race." Over the next five years black people in Atlanta could hear, among other artists, baritone Harry T. Burleigh, tenor Roland Hayes, soprano Rachel Walker, and violinist Clarence Cameron White. They also heard the Fisk Jubilee Singers and, from Tuskegee Institute, its band, orchestra, male glee club, and mandolin, guitar, and banjo clubs. Every concert included music by black composers, most commonly Afro-British composer Samuel Coleridge-Taylor.[150] The Trents must have looked forward to the festival every year.

In 1920 the Butler Street Y was dedicated. But Trent had even more good news that year, for that was when John Hope appointed him to the first board of trustees of the newly created Atlanta School of Social Work. Both John and Lugenia Hope were also on the board.[151] And in a sign of Trent's popularity and status in Atlanta, that same year he was invited to become a founding member of Atlanta's Kappa Boulé.

The Boulé, otherwise known as Sigma Pi Phi, was the "first elite national black men's club."[152] An organization for professional black men, it is older than all the black college fraternities. The organization began in Philadelphia in 1904, when Dr. Henry Minton asked five of his doctor colleagues to help him gather together "'a selected group of men [...], men who were congenial, tolerant, and hospitable,'"[153] men who had graduated from college and had already made significant achievements in their careers and their communities.[154] There was no application process: men were nominated and voted upon with no knowledge that they were being considered.[155] As the first Boulé, the Philadelphia group was Alpha Boulé. The Atlanta Boulé, the tenth, was therefore called Kappa Boulé. By then there were chapters in, among other cities, Chicago; New York; Washington, DC; Baltimore; and Detroit.[156]

Harry Pace, who decided to organize the Boulé in Atlanta, chose what he called "as fine a group of men as any that have ever had the privilege of entering our cherished council."[157] In this group we find two college professors, a college president, the president of a graduate school, five dentists and doctors, both the medical director and the vice president of Atlanta Mutual Life Insurance Company, and a lawyer. We find men with degrees from Harvard, Colgate, Brown, and Michigan Law School. We find Truman Kella Gibson and John Hope. And we find Trent.[158]

According to historian Nina Mjagkij, the position of a black Y secretary during this period was "equal in importance to that of the Public or High School Teacher."[159] But Kappa Boulé was a high-powered group, and half the men in this founding group belonged to the old elite families of Atlanta.[160] Seeing where Trent's peers placed him in Atlanta society both develops and modifies Mjagkij's statement. Her assertion may be correct in some settings, but Trent's Boulé membership suggests it is not correct where there is a Y secretary with Trent's scholarly and professional background, intelligence, and personality traits.

Trent was also a member of two black fraternities, the Prince Hall Masons and the Odd Fellows.[161] In 1924 there were 24,000 black Masons in Georgia.[162] But the state's largest and wealthiest black fraternal order was the Odd Fellows. By 1916, the Odd Fellows had 1,100 lodges and 33,000 members in Georgia, with assets of almost $1 million. In 1912 the fraternity purchased almost an entire block on Auburn Avenue and erected an office building and auditorium, both paid for in advance.[163]

Black men created these two fraternities as soon as the fraternal orders crossed the Atlantic from England in the eighteenth and early nineteenth centuries.[164] They were mutual aid societies that provided benefits when members were sick and couldn't work, and provided funeral and death benefits as well. But their benefits were more than monetary, for they also provided safe spaces where black men could experiment with political leadership free of racism.[165]

Although Trent was a member of both fraternities, he might well have been more involved with the Prince Hall Masons, for in North Carolina, Trent's home state, the Masons had strong historical ties to the AME Zion Church. In 1864, that denomination had sent James Walker Hood to North Carolina as a missionary to the newly freed people in the South. Ten years later he had created 366 AME Zion churches with over 20,000 members.[166] But when Hood left for North Carolina, he had yet another task, for the Prince Hall Masonic Lodge in New York City commissioned him to establish Masonic lodges in the South as well. Thus, he was simultaneously creating AME Zion churches and Masonic lodges. By 1874, he had established 18 Prince Hall lodges in North Carolina with 478 members, and one-third of the leaders of the North Carolina AME Zion Church were Prince Hall Masons.[167]

But even as Trent was making new acquaintances and developing new friendships in these groups, he still kept in touch with old friends. In July 1920 Aggrey took a leave of absence from his duties at Livingstone and left the United States to serve as a member of the Phelps-Stokes Commission. The commission, sponsored by the Phelps-Stokes Foundation, was to survey educational needs in Africa to see how the foundation could help. Over the next year Aggrey would travel to Sierra Leone, Liberia, the Gold Coast (now Ghana), Nigeria, Cameroon, the Belgian Congo (now the Democratic Republic of the Congo), Angola, South Africa, and England.[168]

By 1920 Trent's friend William Walls, the "boy preacher" from Asheville, had completed his studies at Livingstone and received a B.D. degree at Hood Theological Seminary. In 1920 he was elected editor of the *Star of Zion*, the newspaper of the AME Zion Church.[169] Given the editor's power to select articles and write editorials, he had the power to shape the thinking of the entire church community. Also, the position of editor had often been a stepping stone on the path toward becoming a bishop.[170] There was every reason to think that Walls's career in the church would follow the same trajectory. Walls was also a member of the board of trustees of Livingstone College in 1920, as was Trent's great friend and classmate John Walker.[171] As we can see, then, by 1920 Walls was already in a powerful situation, and was positioned to become even more powerful within the church.

In 1920, the Livingstone College board of trustees was discussing the problem of low teacher salaries and the possibility of raising tuition.[172] At the same time, everyone involved in the construction of the Butler Street Y was thinking about money problems too. For although the building had been dedicated and some portions of it were in use, the top two floors—the dormitory spaces—had not been completed.[173] And money was very tight. In October 1920 the Mell Plumbing Company wrote to Hope, complaining that Trent had not yet paid an overdue bill. Hope replied that Trent would pay the bill as quickly as he could, adding that the Y would pay interest on the debt.[174] Two months later Hope wrote Moorland about the problem raising money for the new building. "The South has been hard hit on account of cotton," he wrote, "and now Christmas is upon us. I do not think that you are going to get a single colored man in Atlanta just now to give a hundred dollar pledge [....] I write to let you know that we are willing, but may not be able to accomplish as much as we wish."[175]

The financial situation didn't improve over the next fifteen months. In March 1922 Moorland and Tobias visited Atlanta along with new black international secretary for the Y, John H. McGrew. They met with the YMCA's committee of management, and, on Sunday afternoon, Moorland and Tobias addressed a mass meeting at the Y, trying to encourage support for the local YMCA. They were struck by the enthusiasm they saw there, and thought this should help make possible the completion of the building, and "lift a considerable portion of the heavy burden from the shoulders of the faithful and efficient Secretary, Mr. W. J. Trent[,] and the Committee of Management standing solidly behind him." Despite this sense of positive energy, they decided that it didn't make sense to do financial canvassing then due to "all the needs, bank failures, and abnormal economic conditions."[176]

The following month Trent himself expressed his frustration with the financial situation at the Y, as he suggested the impact it had had on his life and the life of his family. In correspondence with John Hope about a staff person who had just resigned, Trent wrote that this person might well have stayed on staff "if he had been getting his salary regularly and had not gone so far in debt last summer [....] I agree with you that we need a first-class man for the place," he continued, "but of course we must be able to pay a man a good salary. I shall not pass through again in a personal way what I have passed through during the past twelve months. I would not have gone through this if it had not been that I can't get myself to the point to leave a job when it is passing through a crisis. However I am too old now to forever remain in a crisis. I know I can do better."[177]

Long hours and the lack of a steady salary led 25 percent of all new Y secretaries to resign within the first year.[178] There is a sense in which it is amazing that Trent lasted this long with so much personal financial worry. We know that he had other job offers during this time, jobs with better salaries.[179] It must have been difficult to be in need, and to see his family in need. Nonetheless there were times when Trent could find humor in the financial crisis. I recall my father, Bill Trent, telling me that at one point the YMCA committee of management, impressed with Trent Sr.'s commitment and determination, voted to raise his salary. In response, he asked them not to raise his salary as he was having a hard enough time raising the money to cover the salary he already had!

At the same time that Trent, Moorland, Tobias, and Hope were struggling to raise enough money to finish the Y, problems continued to surface at Livingstone. At the board meetings in 1921, the trustees emphasized that the school needed to make a greater effort to get a class-A rating from the state. They also noted that there were problems with the library, repairs were needed, and there were serious sanitation issues, including insufficient sewer pipes, outhouses still on school property, and hog pens on the school's farm too close to school buildings. Dodge and Hood Halls needed toilets, and both Hood and the auditorium needed heat. The board's alumni committee had even more concerns: a lack of discipline at the school; the lack of a librarian; poor teachers; low teacher salaries; and poor recordkeeping. The alumni also noted a lack of cooperation between teachers and Livingstone president

Suggs, adding that it was "imperative that the President live at the school."[180] The first two school presidents, Price and Goler, had lived on Monroe Street, right across the street from the college.[181] Not only did Suggs not live on Monroe Street; he didn't even live in Salisbury: he commuted to Livingstone from his home in Greensboro—today, on a fast-moving highway, an hour-long trip.[182]

In April 1923, the trustees discussed the continuing need to repair old buildings and build new ones.[183] The following month the board listened once more to the concerns of Livingstone alumni, who noted particularly that the institution lacked equipment, the dormitories were unsightly and unsanitary, and the buildings and campus were generally poorly kept. Continuing on, the Alumni Association suggested that it be allowed to play a more important role in the affairs of the school. The representative for this group stated that the alumni were willing to finance the construction of a gymnasium on campus. But they also wanted the board to name alumni as two of its twenty-four members. In an effort to "assist" the board in this effort, the Alumni Association, headed by William J. Walls, unanimously recommended that Trent be one of those representatives.[184] The board accepted this recommendation.[185]

So we see now that Walls had even more power than we thought. Not only was he editor of the *Star of Zion* and a member of Livingstone's board of trustees, he was also chairman of the Livingstone Alumni Association, putting forth the name of his friend Trent to become a member of the board.

There is little doubt but that he and Trent had discussed this move. If Trent joined him on the board, Walls would have one more vote he could count on, as the two friends very likely shared a philosophy about the future of the school. But perhaps the two men were thinking even then about putting forward Trent's name during the election for the presidency of the school the following May.

Success as a Y secretary often opened important positions for these men. Several went on to obtain good positions with the federal government.[186] The step from Y secretary in a large city to college president should not surprise us, for a successful secretary has already shown many of the qualities needed by a college president: administrative skills, as well as the ability to guide youth, to relate to several different constituencies, and to raise money for the institution.

Back in Atlanta, there was finally good news: in December 1923, there was enough money to complete the two top dormitory floors.[187] YMCA international secretary Tobias told the secretaries in the field that Trent "deserves great credit for sticking to a hard job."[188] The building project was more costly than expected. The original cost of the land, building, and equipment was approximately $141,000. Julius Rosenwald contributed $25,000 toward that goal; the local black population contributed another $35,000, and the remaining sum was contributed by others. The building was paid in full when complete: there was no property debt.[189] David T. Howard, born a slave, gave $1,500 to the building fund, the largest contribution given by a black person. In a speech in one of Atlanta's black churches, he explained why he made such a large donation: "All that I am and all I have my people have helped me get and be, and it is my duty to help other men and boys to be all that God wants them to be."[190]

This was a very important moment for Trent. His work of twelve years was coming to fruition; the task of raising money for building construction was over. This would also be an important year because it was in 1923 that his mother, Malinda Dunn, moved to Atlanta to live with him and his family. She would spend the last ten years of her life with them, much of the time as an invalid. But there is no doubt that she helped Maggie with the housework however she could. And when there was spare time and she had the energy for the task, she made quilts for her friends.[191]

By this time Altona was in college at Atlanta University, Bill was a student at Morehouse Academy, the private high school affiliated with Morehouse College, and Estelle was five years old. What a shock it must have been to Malinda Dunn to live with these children who had lives so different from her childhood, and from her son's childhood. These children had never worked in a field. These children had never been so poor they had to catch, trap, or grow their own food if they wanted to eat. These children could read and write, and had known only a protected childhood: school every day, music lessons, visits with friends, Sunday school, books everywhere.

The children adored their grandmother, but her ways and theirs were sometimes different, and at times that difference manifested itself in church. I recall my father saying that when she was moved by the service, sometimes she would stand up and shout; sometimes she would get up from her seat, raise her long skirt up off the floor, and do a little shuffle dance down the aisle. The shout and the shuffling dance tradition were old ones in black churches, older than slavery, African in form and tradition.[192] But the Congregational church had strict, controlled forms of worship, and young Bill was embarrassed. One day, after Malinda had shouted in church, he said to her—very carefully, we might imagine—that people didn't shout out in that church. She replied that she didn't care what other people did: if the spirit moved her, she was going to shout!

In a sense, this is the story of all immigrants to a new land, or a new life. The first generation from, say, Senegal, still speaks Wolof, the language of the old country, as they are learning English and American ways. Similarly, Trent was the first generation in his family to leave life on a farm, to go to school, and to learn new ways, and, in a sense, a new language. But his children, Malinda's grandchildren, had only heard about the old country, or, perhaps, visited every now and then. Thus are old languages and old ways lost.

Trent continued to keep in contact with his friends of long standing. In January 1924, Walls was in Atlanta where he addressed the YMCA.[193] He surely stayed with the Trents, where the two men talked way into the night about the problems at Livingstone, for by the end of the month, the *Star of Zion* announced that the school needed emergency money.[194] Was the current president, Daniel Cato Suggs, doing all that could be done to save the school?

Suggs had earned a B.A. degree from Lincoln University in 1884, at the age of eighteen, graduating a few years after Price, Goler, and Moore. After teaching several years in public schools, he became chairman of the Department of Natural Sciences and Higher Mathematics at Livingstone, serving in that position between 1887 and 1891, and overlapping for a year with young student Trent. He then moved to Savannah State College as vice president of the school and professor, and became president of Livingstone in 1917.[195] By the time he arrived at Livingstone, Suggs was also a rich and successful businessman. Indeed, he was a millionaire.[196] Livingstone's trustees had assumed that he would both donate money to and raise money for the school, but he did neither. He was also criticized for devoting too much time to his personal business interests and for being aloof from the students, faculty, and staff.[197] As Trent and Walls discussed the problems with Suggs's performance, they very likely also talked about ways to promote Trent's candidacy for the presidency of the school before the quadrennial election in May.

In order to even be considered for the presidency, Trent would have to be prominent in the consciousness of the AME Zion community, in general, and in that of the Livingstone board of trustees, in particular. Walls was at that time still editor of the *Star of Zion*. In May he would step down from that position when he was consecrated as a bishop in the AME Zion Church.[198] But he still had time to use his position as editor to put Trent's name in the paper and in people's minds. In April the *Star of Zion* announced that Trent was planning to attend the general conference "of his beloved Zion."[199] That same month Walls published two brief articles by Trent in the newspaper.[200] He thus used his position as editor to help Trent, and just in time for the election, which would take place the following month.

We can't tell the importance of the *Star of Zion* in making Trent a visible and viable candidate. But we do know that on May 27, 1924, the Committee on Nominations of the Livingstone

College board of trustees presented three names for consideration for the presidency of the school: current Livingstone president Daniel Cato Suggs, Kwegyir Aggrey, and Trent.[201]

Aggrey, Trent's longtime friend, was much loved by the Livingstone community. Since his graduation, Aggrey had not only taught and handled administrative matters at Livingstone, but also, as an ordained elder of the AME Zion Church, had taken over the pastorate of two country churches. The education he received from these rural church people led him to create Farmers' Clubs, along with Thomas B. Patterson, an agriculturist at Livingstone. At club meetings the two men gave talks on improving farming skills, as well as on developing the home and social life. The success of these clubs led them to then develop the community-based Negro Community League to address issues of education, health, and agriculture. They also created both a credit union and a realty company to help black people buy land.[202]

At the time of the May 1924 election, Aggrey was in Nyasaland (now Malawi) and Rhodesia (now Zimbabwe), with the second Phelps-Stokes Commission, and would not return to the States until July.[203] The school sent a formal invitation to Aggrey, inviting him to take the presidency. But he declined the offer. As he wrote to a friend: "In the United States Livingstone stands first in my heart. I love her. God's choicest blessings attend her. But in the whole wide world, Africa, my Africa comes first." He then recommended Trent for the position.[204] With Aggrey out of the running, the competition was between President Suggs and Trent. President Emeritus Goler pleaded with the board to allow Suggs to continue. On the seventh ballot, Suggs was elected over Trent, eleven votes to nine.[205]

As bishop, Walls was no longer editor of the *Star of Zion*: that position had gone to William H. Davenport, who had been active in YMCA work with Trent at Livingstone during their college days.[206] On January 1, 1925, eight months after Suggs's reelection, and two weeks before the Livingstone board of trustees was to meet, Davenport put a brief article by Trent in the *Star of Zion*.[207] The following week, he placed a letter critical of what was taking place at Livingstone on the front page: "Livingstone is not a class 'A' college," it said. "Livingstone will never reach the A class under the present administration. The present administration has failed [....] No board of trustees, except the trustees of the AME Zion Church would tolerate such a condition."[208]

Board minutes do not tell us what happened between May 1924, when the board elected President Suggs to another four-year term, and January 1925, when this letter was published. Apparently things at Livingstone got much worse, while President Suggs kept informing the board that things were getting better—because at the January 15 board meeting, board member Bishop Kyles stated that he had received information about conditions at Livingstone that was contrary to the information presented by President Suggs in his semiannual report. In his view, Suggs should resign at once. Suggs then offered his resignation.[209]

The following week the *Star of Zion* announced the news: Suggs retired after deliberation by the bishops, his retirement to become effective June 1, 1925, at the end of the school year. The *Star of Zion* also reported that day that Bishop George Clement, who graduated with Trent—the friend who had asked Trent to stand best man at his wedding—George Clement, now a member of Livingstone's board of trustees and a bishop in the church, had just been elected chairman of the board of bishops for six months.[210] Trent's friends Walls and Clement would thus be powerful voices during the selection of the next president of the school.

Finally, on May 27, the board of trustees met to select Livingstone's new president. Once more, Trent was in the running. Bishop Walls presented the case for Trent, and Bishop Kyles did the same for Dr. Innes.[211] Eighteen ballots were cast, fourteen for Trent. The board then voted once more in order to make the vote for Trent unanimous.[212] When notified of the vote, Trent didn't hesitate in accepting the appointment. That June, at commencement, Livingstone formally announced that Trent was the new president.[213]

It is clear that Trent's election was furthered through the efforts of his longtime friends William Walls and Davenport. Livingstone's board of trustees also included Trent's classmates and longtime friends John Walker and George Clement, of the famous class of 1898, as well as Bishop Josiah Caldwell, who had suggested so many years earlier that young Trent study at Livingstone. [214] All three would likely have supported Trent. But it was the effort made by Walls as head of the Alumni Association, Walls as editor of the *Star of Zion*, and now as bishop, who presented the argument for Trent to the board of trustees, which led to the successful vote. In a handwritten note to Walls years later, Trent stated: "It was you more than anyone else that got me into this college."[215]

On the day that the *Star of Zion* carried the story about Livingstone's commencement, Davenport wrote and published a touching and heartfelt editorial about the new president:

Mr. W. J. Trent, A.M., of the famous class of '98 [...] we salute you. You have been elected President of Livingstone whose founder, Dr. Jos. C. Price, made famous. You are the first of the alumni to achieve this enviable and honorable distinction and we expect you to wear it honorably [....]

We know you; we have known you for more than thirty years. We knew you when a student from the woods, you chased rabbits for a diversion. You were young, clean, healthy, ambitious, studious, alert, idealistic. [....] In your manhood you have translated your youthful ideas into activities. As President of Greeneville College, [in the] YMI work in Asheville N.C., in the YMCA work in Atlanta [...] you have done considerable constructive work, impressed hundreds of young men with your noble purposes, high sentiments, splendid circumspection and disciplinary and organizing abilities.

It is in organization and discipline where you will be put to immediate test [....] And we expect that you shall maintain discipline [...] or send the offenders home on the next train [....] In the enforcement of discipline you must not have regard for person or position. The bishop's child must be dealt with as promptly and as severely as the boot black's. In this you will have the support of all of us.

You will inspire the confidence of the public if the books of the College are audited annually by a public accountant and left open for the inspection of anybody who cares to look at them[....]

These are just a few hints, Mr. President. You have the good-will of the Denomination in which you were born and reared and for which you have made social and financial sacrifices. We believe in you. We trust you. You have our cooperation, our best wishes, our prayers. Much depends on you. You cannot fail us.[216]

The welcome came from Livingstone. The farewell from Atlanta followed. J. B. Anderson, editor of *The Atlanta Independent* newspaper, wrote: "Mr. Trent has fought a good fight among us and indelibly impressed his personality in the community life of Atlanta [....] We believe that William Johnson Trent leaves the community without a real enemy. And Mr. Trent has not achieved this great accomplishment by bowing or vacillating with his 'hat in hand' to white or black. He has been the same manly William Trent to all men [....] He is fair in debate and criticism and in his relation to his fellowmen [....] He concedes to you the honesty of your views and purposes and vigorously prosecutes his own." Alonzo Herndon added: "I don't know a single man I would sooner follow."[217]

Leaders in the Y's Colored Men's Department gave their own farewells. In July, in one of his final messages to the field before retirement, Moorland announced that Trent was leaving Atlanta, and described him as "one of the pioneers of the years when only thorough consecration would hold a man to the difficult task of promoting the Association program."[218] Trent's efforts and the efforts of other Y leaders had paid off, for, by the time he left Atlanta, the Y had anchored itself in black communities around the country. There were 25 city Ys and 128 Ys in black colleges, with a total membership of 28,000.[219]

That same month, J. B. Watson wrote a letter to the *Star of Zion* about Trent, with whom, he noted, he had been "closely connected" for seventeen years. His letter gives us more insight into Trent and into the decisions he had made: "Mr. Trent, personally, is one of the best men I have ever known [....] He is patient, longsuffering, a friend to everybody and a never tiring servant wherever he works [....] All of this you probably know [...] already, but there is one thing it is barely possible you do not know, and that is that Mr. Trent is one of the foremost scholars of the Negro race [....] In History and Social Economics, I am sure he has very few equals in our country. He reads extensively and critically and is an intelligent student to what he reads."[220]

Watson then expressed the hope that the Livingstone community would put politics aside and give Trent a fair chance to do his work, noting that there were many other places where Trent could have worked. "To my personal knowledge," he wrote, "during the past ten years, he could have gone to a half-dozen places with better salary and better living conditions. But he has refused to leave Atlanta when the work in that city was so much in need of him."[221]

The receptions, the accolades, the awards, the praise— finally, all that was over, and it was time to begin work as college president. Trent spent much of that summer at church district meetings, talking about his plans for Livingstone and trying to gain support for the school.[222]

Trent had not hesitated to accept the position as president of Livingstone, but when Maggie learned of it, she wept. The school was desperately poor, and it was not clear that salaries would be paid on time, or that they would be paid at all.[223] Perhaps she was also sad to leave behind her home and her good friends: she had lived her entire married life, and raised three children, in Atlanta. She might also have found it disheartening to leave such a large, vibrant city, Atlanta, with a population of over 200,000, for Salisbury, which had fewer than 14,000 people. She might have been saddened at the thought of the loss of privacy that would come with her new role as wife of a college president in a very small town. And perhaps she wondered if the role of the wife of a college president was a role she wanted.

Nonetheless, Maggie would be packing and moving and trying to set up their new home in Salisbury, with their daughter Estelle, now eight. The two older children would stay in Atlanta. Altona had just graduated from Atlanta University with the highest grade point in the entire school, and the third highest in the history of the school. She would be staying on at the university as a professor of Latin.[224] Bill was entering his senior year at the Academy of Morehouse College and would finish high school there, living in a dormitory under the sound supervision of President and Mrs. Hope, whose home was on the campus. Fortunately, Bill, as top student in his class, had won a scholarship for that year.[225] This would have certainly helped the family financially, as the fee for tuition, room, board, and incidentals at Morehouse Academy for one year was almost $185.[226] After graduation Bill would join his family in Salisbury and begin college at Livingstone.

On September 16, at the opening ceremony of the school year, Livingstone's president emeritus Goler introduced incoming president Trent. Seated next to Trent was Dr. Edward Moore, who, along with Goler, had come to Salisbury with Joseph Price more than forty years before to create this new school. Also on the platform were two of Trent's good friends: Bishop George Clement and Kwegyir Aggrey, who had recently returned from Africa to visit his family in Salisbury.[227] Trent's heart must have been very full that day. He had finally come back home.

Chapter 5

Sustaining and Improving Black Schools: President Trent at Livingstone College

IT IS EASY TO IMAGINE Trent walking around the Livingstone campus early one morning that first summer, walking around so early that the dew was still on the grass, so early that no one else was out and about, so early that all was quiet. As he looked around he was remembering: over there was the field where he had played football, and here were Dodge Hall, the boy's dormitory, and Ballard, which had held the industrial classes. Huntington Hall had burned down in 1918. He must have been sad not to see it, for that was Livingstone's first building, where the earliest students lived and studied with their professors. As he walked, he would have also been taking in the new buildings on the campus. Two were named after men we have already met, men he so admired: Goler Hall, a dormitory for girls, and Hood Building, which had been used for administration and for the Hood Theological Seminary. He would have also walked by the new chapel and auditorium, and the new building that must have made him smile, the Andrew Carnegie Library.[1] Although it had a capacity for 15,000 books, it held fewer than 7,000 now.[2] Even sadder, the library was not even in use.[3] He would have to hire librarians and get the building cleaned, organized, and open.

And across from the library, on Monroe Street, Trent would have passed by the homes of Livingstone people he knew so well. There was the Joseph Price family home, the home of his good friends Rose and Kwegyir Aggrey, the home of Bishop Cicero Harris, who had died a few years before. As he continued walking, he would have passed the homes of President Emeritus Goler and Professor Moore, the men who had started the school with Price in 1882. He walked by the home of Victoria Richardson, who had been teaching at Livingstone since its beginning, and the home of Mary Lynch, who started the Young Women's Christian Temperance Union for Livingstone women in 1891, while teaching there.[4] The history of the school was on this street, and now Trent and his family would join them.

There had been many changes since his graduation in 1898. In 1902, Livingstone had joined with the East Tennessee Industrial School, the two schools operating as separate departments with headquarters in Salisbury. There had been five departments of instruction at Livingstone then: Grammar, Normal, Classical, Theological, and Mechanical and Agricultural. The Mechanical and Agricultural Division had had nineteen departments of industry, including Shoemaking, Tanning, Nurse-Training, Painting, Plastering, and Raising Poultry.[5] But less than ten years later, the Livingstone catalog didn't mention the East Tennessee Industrial School at all.[6]

Over the years Livingstone had created Hood Theological Seminary, turned it into a graduate school, then seen President Suggs suspend its operation.[7] The elementary grades had been eliminated, and there was a new emphasis on social sciences in the college. Rufus Clement, son of Trent's friend and classmate George Clement, and now a professor of history at Livingstone, was teaching an exciting new course entitled "The Negro in American History."[8] Clement, who had graduated from Livingstone in 1919, also had an M.A. degree in history and a B.D. degree, and was working on his doctorate.[9] Trent was glad to find him there. He knew he would need a good right-hand man when he started to address Livingstone's problems. Having known Rufus and his family for so long, he had complete faith in Clement's ability and loyalty, and made Clement dean of the college.[10]

But he was going to miss his good friend Kwegyir Aggrey, who was leaving Livingstone and returning to the Gold Coast (now Ghana), the country of his birth, in October. Aggrey had been named assistant vice-principal of the Achimota school, an institution that would go from kindergarten through college and was specifically designed to be a synthesis of European and African cultures. Aggrey was very excited about this concept and had been helping plan the school for several years. Upon his return to the Gold Coast, he would give sermons and continue developing the school through speeches and letters and by encouraging African leaders to send their children to school there.[11] So Aggrey was busy in Salisbury, packing 2,000 books to take back with him. His wife, Rose, would accompany him.[12]

As he walked, Trent also would have thought about two fairly recent studies of the school. The first was a 1917 evaluation by the Federal Bureau of Education and the Phelps-Stokes Fund, which found good instruction at the school, but noted that the school had management problems. The report recommended that Livingstone create a better accounting system, which would include an annual audit by an accredited accounting company.[13] The second was a 1922 report by the General Education Board (GEB), a foundation created by John D. Rockefeller Sr. to promote education. The GEB found that the school was doing well with respect to buildings and grounds, recordkeeping, teachers, and student body, but that it needed a larger endowment and needed to improve its laboratory facilities. The evaluators also stated that the library needed to be overhauled and enlarged.[14] The most important evaluation was by the North Carolina State Department of Education. When Trent became president, that organization had given Livingstone only a C rating. This meant that a student graduating from Livingstone with a B.A. degree, having paid for four years of study, would receive credit for only two years of college work.[15] Livingstone graduates would thus have to study for two more years at a school with an A rating before entering graduate school.

Not surprisingly, most of the school's problems revolved around money. Considering Trent's work at the Young Men's Institute and the Butler Street Young Men's Christian Association (YMCA, or Y), the major tasks of his life had been not only to develop and guide black youth, but also to develop and maintain those black institutions that served them. Thus his work in Asheville and Atlanta can be seen as training for the work he would do at Livingstone, this school he loved so much. For he would have to work hard to raise the money to maintain and improve it.

This was a serious problem, indeed, for, at Trent's arrival, the school was carrying a debt of $150,000.[16] So he would not only have to find the money for the school's ordinary expenses—maintenance, salaries, utilities, equipment, and food—he would also have to raise money to pay down the debt while at the same time looking for money for new buildings. This task was made even more problematic because, although the AME Zion Church was supposed to give monthly payments to Livingstone from its annual appropriation of $30,000, it did not always make those payments on time.[17]

Although Livingstone was an AME Zion school, the church had recently shown little interest in developing either the college or the seminary. As a result, other than the monthly payments, Livingstone received limited contributions from the church. Small appropriations did come in, generally at Easter and on Children's Day, in June. But when Trent became president that summer, both days had just passed. All of the church's spring conferences had been held; and the school was scheduled to open before fall conferences met. This is why Trent had visited church school conventions and district conferences as soon as he was elected president—to let ministers and church leaders get to know him, to remind them about their college and its needs, and to get a little "running expense money" before school opened in the fall.[18]

Even though Livingstone produced many of the state's black elementary school teachers and about 10 percent of its black high school teachers, little money was coming from the state of North Carolina. Its 1921 appropriation to Livingstone was $1,000. In 1923, that sum was reduced to $250.[19] It must have also been frustrating for Trent to see the strong financial support that other black colleges received from the churches that created them. In 1922, the Baptists gave Shaw University $150,000; Presbyterians gave the same amount to Biddle University; and the Methodist Episcopal Church gave $100,000 to Bennett College.[20] But these were majority-white denominations, which had members with more money than did the black AME Zion Church.

This situation was made worse because of the overall bad economy in the United States that began at the end of World War I. These are, of course, overlapping problems. Low interest by the church and a bad economy mean less money, which means it is hard to pay the teachers, improve the library, buy science equipment, or keep up the buildings—all of which eventually leads to a low rating, which leads to poor morale among the administrators, teachers, and students, which once more leads to low interest from the church. So when Trent arrived, morale at the school was very low. The teachers were distressed because the school owed them so much back pay;[21] the students were anxious, because they knew the low value their degree would have, coming from a class C school. And everyone on campus—students, faculty, staff—everyone was demoralized because President Suggs had seemed so uninterested in their lives and in the life of the college, showing his lack of interest by not living near the campus, as had former presidents. Clearly, Trent had a lot to do for Livingstone to succeed.

When he spoke with the ministers at the church conferences that summer, Trent pledged honesty with respect to the school's funds, and said that he would treat all students fairly—this latter, with respect to disciplining students by sending them home. As one scholar noted, this statement "caused almost a revolution in sentiments overnight throughout the General

Church," as President Trent "had begun to operate on the heart of the sick patient to remove two of the major causes for the many ills of Livingstone College and the Seminary."[22] Thus, the major issues, as perceived by the AME Zion community, were issues of integrity with regard to school finances and of fair play with respect to discipline.

Hopefully, a change of perception within the church would mean more donations for the school. But Trent also launched the Price Memorial Campaign to raise $250,000. The money would go toward building the Price Memorial Building for school administration, a gymnasium, and a central heating plant, as well as additional dormitory space for boys. It would also go toward liquidating the school's debt.[23] There would be many more campaigns before the school's debt was paid down and the Price Building, constructed.

Trent looked for donations from individuals and from foundations like Rockefeller's GEB, the Slater Fund, and the Duke Foundation. Sometimes an individual made a gift, such as the $25,000 sent by B. N. Duke of New York City in 1926.[24] Sometimes the gift came from a foundation, but with a condition attached. In 1927, for example, the GEB offered Livingstone $75,000 for construction of the buildings, but "with the proviso that payments by the Board are to be made [...] only when said College shall have no outstanding indebtedness.'"[25] It would be quite a while before the school would see that money.

Trent made speeches everywhere. He gave a speech before Salisbury's Rotary Club.[26] He traveled with the Livingstone Octet along the East Coast, into New England, to churches, conferences, and the homes of wealthy white people, where students would sing and he would give a speech.[27] At one point, within a two-week period, he gave speeches in Winston-Salem and Greensboro, North Carolina; and in Mobile, Alabama. Bishop Walls traveled several hundred miles to join him for the Mobile effort, and Bishop Clement accompanied him and the Livingstone Octet in Greensboro. After these presentations, although the three communities pledged to later send a total of $2,230, when he was there he only received $661 in cash.[28] At this rate, only a determined optimist would believe that he could ever meet the school's financial goals.

This must have reminded Trent of his college days, when he was a member of the Price Concert Company, the group that traveled around the country, singing, to raise money for a Price memorial right after Price's death. And yet the effort to raise money for the Price Building continued. Early on in his presidency Trent expressed his frustration: "We have talked enough about the wonderful Price. We have talked now for thirty-three years, as he passed to the great beyond in the year 1893. Unless we do something tangible and worthwhile, we will make ourselves ridiculous in the eyes of the sober thinking people of this country."[29] But the Price Memorial campaigns would continue for years, becoming an important benchmark of his administration.

As he sought contributions, Trent was very savvy about marketing the school, for many white philanthropists did not want to support higher education for black people.[30] One brochure for the Price campaign emphasized that over a thousand men and women had graduated from Livingstone's college. The photographs in this brochure showed dormitories, the library, the seminary, and Ballard Hall, which was then being used for classrooms, offices, and laboratories, not industrial trades, as in the past.[31] But another brochure, for a different audience of potential donors, showed photographs of the college farm; pointed out that the school had just purchased two mules, a barn, a molasses mill outfit, and a disk harrow; and stated that the school's immediate needs included a dairy, a poultry farm, and a tractor.

> We are fortunate in having a 269-acre farm which is being developed as rapidly as possible [....] We have the best college farm in the South [....] For quite a while there was a tendency to divorce college life from anything that looked like agriculture [....] Those were the days when the idea of education was a knowledge of a few facts taken from books, but education at Livingstone College is being

expressed in terms of service to those in the greatest need [....]

> In a co-educational institution an ideal home life must be the goal [...] so why not carry in our program sufficient equipment to teach self-help, to teach in a practical way a knowledge of the soil, how to run a truck garden [....] Any people who get too far away from the soil [are] [...] throwing away an opportunity to develop economic independence.

> Several of our students work on the farm during the summer months [...] and this helps them to get through College [....] With such a plant well developed and better equipped, a much larger number could be given employment which would not only help the individual student, but would help to raise enough food stuff to feed the entire school.

The brochure included a testimonial from a former mayor of Salisbury, who recommended Livingstone to any "disposed to bettering the condition of the colored people through industrial and Christian education."[32]

We can see, then, that the college was speaking in two ways to potential donors. In the first, it emphasized that Livingstone offered a classical liberal arts education; in the second, it emphasized agricultural training. But even then, the brochure noted that many Livingstone students worked on the farm to pay their way through college. Thus, although the brochure dwelt on farming, its underlying focus was on helping students gain a liberal arts education.

During that first school year, as he began his search for money for the school, Trent managed to pay the teachers their unpaid back salaries, thereby greatly improving their morale.[33] He also encouraged the faculty to get graduate degrees. Rufus Clement later said that he had settled into the groove of an ordinary teacher until Trent encouraged him to study further. He completed his doctorate within three years of Trent's arrival on campus.[34] Not only did Trent encourage faculty to return to school; he told them that he would do the same. Thus they would all learn and grow together.

Trent lifted the students' morale by improving living conditions in student housing and by promising the students that the class of 1927 would be graduating from a class-A school.[35] He also imposed higher intellectual standards on the students. Between scholastic year 1925–1926, when he arrived, and the following year, there were 30 percent fewer students at Livingstone because of new requirements.[36] He also hired a librarian, an assistant librarian, and four student assistants.[37] Under a Trent presidency, the library would be open and would be in use.

One of the complaints about Suggs was that he was aloof from students, faculty, and staff, but this was not true of Trent. This was not his way. Former Livingstone student, Blanche Sherrill, recalled that Trent walked through campus two or three times a day and greeted the students. According to Rev. Andrew Whitted, another former student, when Trent walked by Dodge Hall, the boys' dormitory, he would stop and talk with the young men. Sometimes he would ask questions about the Bible, just to see if they were studying the Bible as they should. Other times he would talk about how to treat girls and women. Whitted also noted that Trent was down to earth, that he loved the students and they loved him even though he was strict, like any good parent. In his view, Trent took special care of the poor students. Eliza Miller, a former faculty member, pointed out that Trent got along well with the faculty. If there was a problem, she continued, he could talk about it in such a way that the teacher wasn't offended.[38]

Rev. J. A. Armstrong, a former Livingstone student, recalled the following: "We had nicknames for him: we called him 'Country' and 'Prexie.' We also called him 'President William J. "go home" Trent,'" because if you broke school rules, he would definitely send you home. If you saw him coming towards you with an apple and a package of peanut butter crackers, you knew that he was about to drive you to the train station, and you were going home."[39]

Years after graduation, a Livingstone alumna wrote a fictional account of life on Livingstone campus, which included this statement by a student: "Yesterday [President Trent] got after me for not picking up some paper from the campus. He just said, 'Young man, how can you walk over that paper?' I picked it up and carried it to a trash can. An hour after that he said, 'Mr. Barber, thank you for what you did. I'll tell your mother and grandmother about you next week when I go to Spartanburg. Your grades are improving: keep it up!'"[40] The community Trent was creating thus extended beyond the borders of the campus to include students' families.

According to an historian of the AME Zion Church, Trent was "like a sympathetic father" to the students. He tried to find work for them, and always tried to make newcomers feel welcome. Interestingly enough, he extended himself more for the seminary students, because, as he well knew, without the support of the ministers, Livingstone could not survive.[41]

Rev. Vernon Shannon, Livingstone alumnus and AME Zion minister, told me that Trent often ate with the students in the dining room. He also remarked on Trent's sense of humor. According to Shannon, one day, when a speaker was about to address the students, he turned to Trent from the podium and asked how long he could speak. Trent replied that he could speak as long as he wanted: they would listen for twenty minutes!

President Trent liked his students. He knew them, encouraged them, and taught them. And he had dreams for them, dreams about what they should do with their hard-won education. He once explained his vision to a group of students:

> As a minority group in this nation we have a definite contribution to make, and our grandfathers and grandmothers felt, and our fathers and mothers feel that the best contribution their children can make [...] will be through Christian education in heart, head and hand. Many of us do not know what our parents have gone through and are now going through that you might get the best in the field of education, but in the midst of it all their prayer for

you is the same as that of Hector, the Homeric hero, who, just before going to battle with Achilles, took his little son up in his arms, turned his face to Olympus, and prayed to Zeus to make his son better than his father.[42]

Standing on the shoulders of their parents and grandparents, then, Livingstone graduates were expected to use their Christian education to become men and women of character, and to make an even larger contribution to society than did their forebears. Through their effort they would be helping create a black middle class based on education, thus strengthening the larger black community.

Within a year of Trent's arrival, there were reports of great change. In February 1926, the *Star of Zion* published an article about student life on campus: "The students are applying themselves as never before to the intellectual, moral and social betterment of the school [....] The opening of the Library has done much to create a real genuine student atmosphere on the campus. The president is sparing no pains in seeing to it that our library keeps up to the standard."[43]

A few weeks later, Bishop Walls issued his report:

The Theological Department [...] has fifteen promising students, one of whom is a woman [....] The College department [...] is in its halcyon era. Especial emphasis is placed upon science as never before there [....] The High School [...] is on the A class list of the state [....] The library [...] is open from 8:45 a.m. to 9 p.m. A visit there at 7:30 in the evening found every chair occupied [...] and perfect order [....] There is marked harmony and respect between President W. J. Trent and workers from the Deans to the teachers in the culinary department and the manager of the ground [....] President Trent's office is working overtime.[44]

And then, in early April, came the news they had all been hoping for: the State Department of Education had just changed Livingstone's rating from C to B, thereby allowing the school's graduates to receive three years of college credit instead of two.[45] All hoped that an A rating would not be far behind.

On Tuesday, May 25, 1926, during commencement, Trent was inaugurated as president of the college. Bishop Caldwell, president of Livingstone's board of trustees, presided at the event, his presence a reminder of that day so long ago when young pastor Caldwell had said to Trent's mother: "Send your son to Livingstone."[46]

In his inaugural address, "An Appeal for the Church School," Trent talked about the importance of merging the academic and the spiritual within a scholarly environment. "Every department of a Church school," he said, "should be a department of religion [....] The halls of schools, colleges and universities are crowded with the best brains of the youth of our land. It is not ability that we lack [...] but a new type of education [....] This world is built on moral foundations [...] and this, I say, is to be the contribution of the Church school."[47]

Fannie C. Clay spoke for the school's alumni, noting that within only months Livingstone had gone from a class-C to a class-B school, with "wonderful prospects" of a class-A rating:

> One year ago it seemed that we faced the setting sun; but today by a wonder which came directly from the man we honor [...] we turn to the rising sun [....] President Trent's success has been due to [...] meekness of spirit, devotion to duty, love of character and worth, the bundle of sunshine and smiles that he carries day by day, his personal contact with teacher and taught and finally his living example of righteousness, unselfishness and goodness. He has won the student body not so much by sweetened or honeycombed phrases, but by presenting them with sound doctrines, good counsels, and useful services.[48]

The following day, after the first report on the Price Memorial Campaign, there was music. And we should not be surprised to note that the music was provided by the original Price Memorial Quartet and the original Price Memorial Concert Company, which included members Dr. John W. Walker, Mrs. Emma Clement, and President Trent.[49]

Trent appointed two new librarians, Victoria Richardson and Josephine C. Price, the youngest child of Joseph C. Price, founder of Livingstone. During the summer of 1926 they made their first annual report, noting that, since Trent's arrival, the library had added over 1,400 books. "A change in the administration has brought about improved conditions and the outlook for the future is bright," they wrote.[50]

Also, during that summer, all seven faculty members in the college did indeed attend graduate school. Two went to Harvard University; two to Columbia University; two to Northwestern University; and one to the University of Chicago; whereas, during the two previous summers before Trent's presidency, only three faculty members had attended graduate school.[51] Trent attended school that summer too, thus teaching by example the value of continuing to study and learn. While at the University of Chicago, he took two courses: financial administration of higher education, and administration and supervision of academic work in colleges.[52] The college students were thrilled by all this, and when they returned in the fall, they expressed their pride: "All members of the Faculty did Summer School work and have returned with new energy and zeal to take up their task and to pour out their knowledge to us."[53]

Rev. Davenport, editor of the *Star of Zion* and Livingstone alumnus, summed up in passionate terms the general response to the work of Livingstone's new president: "Dr. W. J. Trent has so completely revolutionized Livingstone that it is a pleasure to walk its grounds, an elixir of life to breathe its atmosphere and a revival of the most glorious days of the college when intellect glittered in every sunbeam, wisdom lit upon every swaying tree-top, and every student was a hope and ideal of the highest possibilities of the race."[54]

Fannie Clay's address at Trent's inauguration and the students' report about their teachers both appeared in the October 1926 edition of *The Living Stone*, a monthly student publication. The "Freshman Notes" for that edition were written by Trent's son, William J. Trent Jr., class of 1930, who had just finished high school at Morehouse Academy in Atlanta.[55] He had enjoyed that year—living in a dormitory with his friends, attending chemistry lab, playing clarinet in the Morehouse Orchestra and Glee Club, preparing for debates, going to dances.[56]

One week after Trent's inauguration as president of Livingstone College, his son, William, the top student in his graduating class at the Morehouse Academy, gave the valedictory address at his commencement.[57] What a week that must have been for the Trent family! Surely they all traveled to Atlanta for commencement and to visit old friends. We can only imagine their joy and their pride.

Trent Jr. would not have known it then, but Morehouse Academy and College were incubators of leadership for the black community. W. E. B. Du Bois had taught there earlier.[58] Sociologist E. Franklin Frazier was currently teaching at the college.[59] And Benjamin Mays, who would go on to become president of Morehouse College, taught Trent Jr. algebra at the Morehouse Academy.[60] Trent Jr.'s schoolmates included Albert Walter Dent, future president of Dillard College in New Orleans, and Howard Thurman, who would one day be an important preacher and theologian, and influence a young Martin L. King Jr. by teaching him about Gandhian nonviolence.[61]

After moving to Salisbury, Trent Jr. became close friends with the Aggrey children and with Rufus Clement, whom he had known since childhood. He also met and became close with the Duncan family. Samuel E. Duncan Sr., head of Livingstone's Mathematics Department, lived just a few blocks from the Trents on South Caldwell Street.[62] Several of his children would become well known. Elizabeth Duncan Koontz became president of the National Education Association, then head of the Women's Bureau under President Nixon. John B. Duncan, an attorney, was selected by President Kennedy to join the board governing the affairs of the District of Columbia. Julia Bell Duncan served for fifty years as registrar, then registrar and treasurer, of Livingstone.[63] And Dr. Samuel E. Duncan Jr., teacher and administrator, would one day play an important role in the life of this school.

Like her younger brother, Bill, Altona Trent had left Atlanta. She had just started teaching music at Bennett College, a black school in Greensboro, North Carolina, only a few hours away from Salisbury. In the fall of 1926, at the very time that Altona joined the faculty, Bennett became a women's college.[64] There are several possible reasons for why Altona decided to leave her teaching position at Atlanta University. Perhaps she wanted to be closer to her family; perhaps she liked the idea of a women's school; or perhaps she had only stayed in Atlanta while her younger brother was there, to provide him with family support.

It was also that fall that David Jones became president of Bennett College. Jones had been one of the leaders in the black YMCA back in 1911, when Julius Rosenwald made his offer to support the construction of black Ys. So Trent had known Jones for many years. Indeed, it is very likely that the two men discussed a teaching position for Altona, and that since Jones had known her father for many years, he did not hesitate to hire her.

Trent's younger daughter, Estelle, would have started school that fall at the J. C. Price School, a black public elementary school built just a few years before.[65] As for Maggie, she would have been working hard trying to get her family settled into their home. She would have also started to meet Livingstone's faculty and staff and learn what would be expected of her in her new role as president's wife. She remembered that in Atlanta, Lugenia Burns Hope was expected to be the official college hostess, role model, and mother figure, and take care of the women faculty too. Perhaps Hope had given her some idea of the problems she might face as wife of the president, and suggestions about how to address them. Maggie was also still taking care of Trent's mother, Malinda Dunn, who had been living with them in Atlanta. And with Salisbury just a couple of hours' drive from Charlotte, Maggie must have relished being able to renew her ties with her family there.

Of course Maggie knew some of the Livingstone women already. She knew Rose Aggrey, of course, since Maggie's husband and Kwegyir Aggrey had been close friends for so long.

And her aunt Sallie Butler Rattley had been friends with both Victoria Richardson and Mary Lynch in Charlotte, way back in the 1880s, even before Maggie was born.[66] Although Richardson and Lynch were elderly when the Trents arrived in 1925, these two women had surely known Maggie all her life and would have played an important role in helping her get settled in the Salisbury community.

These three women would have also introduced her to Salisbury's community of clubwomen, as all three were active in the Salisbury Colored Women's Civic League, founded in 1913 by Lula Kelsey, a mortician who worked with her husband in the Noble and Kelsey Funeral Home. Some of the League programs— like participating in a citywide cleanup day and lobbying city officials for legislation requiring "sanitary privies" in the city— involved public health. In other efforts, they lobbied city officials for better services for the black community, including maintenance of the black cemetery and development of a public playground. They organized a "baby day," to provide free access to a doctor for mothers who could not otherwise afford it, and they visited the city jail, chain gangs, and the county home for the indigent. Although they were turned down when they asked for permission to use the public schools for evening classes, they simply moved evening classes to Lula Kelsey's living room. Indeed, without money, publicity, or public aid from their husbands, black women in the South were engaging in many of the same reforms of the Progressive Era as white Southern women, who were working with all those benefits.[67]

There were other ways that Maggie might have been involved in women's club work. Rose Aggrey was active in the Women's Home and Foreign Missionary Service of the AME Zion Church. Victoria Richardson expanded the reach of this club by creating a division specifically for teenaged girls.[68] Temperance was an issue that concerned black club women in Salisbury. Mary Lynch served for a while as president of the North Carolina Woman's Christian Temperance Union, and Richardson served as state president of the Loyal Temperance League.[69] And these women would have all known Charlotte Hawkins Brown, founder and principal of the Palmer Institute in Sedalia, North Carolina, who built the North Carolina State Association of Colored Women's Clubs in 1909. Rose Aggrey was at one time president of this organization.[70] So Maggie would have had activist clubwomen in her Salisbury circle of friends. We don't know specifically what clubs she joined. But we know that she was also active in club work and, like Rose Aggrey, served for a while as an officer of the state's Association of Colored Women's Clubs.[71]

One of Maggie's new responsibilities would be to serve with Trent in the college's Sunday school: Trent was one of the teachers, and Maggie was treasurer.[72] She also would have been active in Soldiers Memorial AME Zion Church, which they had chosen as their church.[73] This was not a surprising choice, for Soldiers had long ties with Livingstone. Joseph Charles Price joined the church in 1882 when he came to Salisbury. He also had his office there, thus demonstrating the close link between Livingstone and the AME Zion Church. Goler was also a member of Soldiers, and served as pastor there for three years. Kwegyir Aggrey served as pastor of several churches in the Salisbury area, but his first pastoral assignment was at Soldiers in 1903. And William J. Walls was pastor there between 1910 and 1913.[74] Rev. Dr. Grant Harrison, pastor of Soldiers, told me that Trent, too, had his office for a while in Soldiers—perhaps in order to maintain a tradition—but he soon returned to the campus.

A look at Livingstone's catalog for 1926–1927, the second year of the Trent presidency, shows us the shape of the school. We see familiar names, going back decades: Rufus Clement was serving as dean of the college, and Rose Aggrey, who had an M.A. degree from Shaw, was teaching English. She had returned from the Gold Coast after several months, pregnant, and resumed her position as chair of the English Department in Livingstone's high school.[75] The school offered both B.A. and B.S. degrees. One big change since Trent's student years was that the college no longer required the study of Latin and Greek language and literature. He would have likely seen this as a sad change, loving ancient literature as he did. Livingstone also offered a High School Department and a theological seminary. Although the school had both a Commercial Department and a Home Economics Department, the catalog no longer mentioned farm or industrial work.[76]

Trent created a Lyceum on campus, a program of cultural events and speeches by black artists and scholars. Students were required to attend the events, and town members, both black and white, often came too. Indeed, both black and white people in Salisbury helped sponsor these programs.[77] In both 1926 and 1928, contralto Marian Anderson gave concerts at the school.[78]

In spring 1927, W. E. B. Du Bois wrote about Livingstone in the national NAACP publication *The Crisis*. He described Trent and his administration in glowing terms, then mentioned the school's higher rating, as well as its quarter-million-dollar campaign. "Already," he wrote, "thousands of dollars have been spent for equipment in new science laboratories, in the purchase of the best of recent books for the library, and in general equipment." He also noted that the Slater Fund planned to make annual donations to the school for teacher salaries.[79] That June, Du Bois delivered Livingstone's commencement address.[80]

But the very best news that year came in a two-sentence telegram Trent sent to Davenport, editor of the *Star of Zion*, on December 14: "Livingstone received A rating today. Let us rejoice." The following day, Davenport replied, in the newspaper: "Certainly, let us rejoice." He then reminded his readers of the great distance the school had come: "The rating of the Institution was low, very low, when Mr. Trent took charge, and all of us were ashamed of it. But in [two] short years, as if by magic, Livingstone has risen from its ashes."[81] Graduates of the school were soon accepted for advanced study by Boston University, the University of Cincinnati, Fordham University, and Northwestern University.[82] The school was truly on the rise. Trent was elected president of the North Carolina Association of Negro Colleges that year, a sign of respect by his new colleagues in the state.[83]

June was a particularly joyous time for Trent, for that's when Kwegyir Aggrey returned to Salisbury, to be with his family and see his new baby, Orison Rudolf Aggrey, for the first time. If we recall the letter Trent wrote to Kwegyir and Rose, explaining how important they were to his life, we can imagine how happy Trent was when his good friend returned home. For his son's baptism, Aggrey had brought a bottle of water from the sacred spring in the Gold Coast in which he himself had been baptized. But he did not stay in Salisbury long: he left two weeks later to go to New York City, where he would give talks, work on his doctoral dissertation at Columbia, and preach at "Mother Zion," in the heart of Harlem.

No one could have expected that Aggrey would suddenly fall ill. And no one could have expected that this illness would be fatal. But suddenly, on July 30, Aggrey died, in New York City, far away from home, of pneumococcal meningitis. The funeral service was held in New York, then his body was taken to Salisbury for a service at the college and interment.[84] Like Rose and her children, Trent suffered a great loss when Aggrey died— Aggrey, the friend he called "a man of great and lasting good."[85] But this was only the first in a string of personal losses that would continue for almost ten years.

There would be another change in the family's life six months later when Altona left Bennett College at the end of one semester and married Vernon Johns. When they met, Johns was pastor of the Court Street Baptist Church in Lynchburg, Virginia, and a teacher of theology at the Virginia Theological Seminary and College, also in Lynchburg.[86] Johns had briefly attended Virginia Seminary, earned a B.D. degree from Oberlin Seminary, and done graduate work in theology at the University of Chicago.[87] Considered "one of the most brilliant scholar-preachers of the modern age," Johns was also considered one of the three great black preachers of this period, along with Mordecai Johnson and Howard Thurman.[88] He was also a forceful and provocative activist for black rights.

The wedding ceremony, performed by Rev. Goler, took place on Altona's birthday, December 21, at the family home in Salisbury. Her aunt and uncle, John and Eleanora Walker, came from Asheville; President and Mrs. David Jones of Bennett College came from Greensboro; and some of Maggie Tate Trent's relatives came from Charlotte. After the wedding the couple drove to Charleston, West Virginia, where Johns was then pastor.[89] Their first child and Trent's first grandchild would be born the following December.[90]

In 1929, the Bureau of Education in the U.S. Department of the Interior issued a report on Livingstone, based on research conducted there in 1926 and 1927. The report made several suggestions for improving the school. As to structure, the Bureau suggested that Livingstone concentrate on the college and emphasize teacher training. It should eliminate the high school, except for a few courses to provide practice teaching for those students majoring in education. It should, as well, drop the theological seminary as a separate institution, and create a department of theology within the college instead. The school should give more care to the upkeep and repair of buildings and campus grounds. With respect to the library, the agency strongly recommended that Livingstone replace its "older, more obsolete" reference books.[91]

The report noted that the teachers earned between $1,200 and $1,600 a year, and the president, only $2,500, "without perquisites."[92] This was an astonishingly low rate for college graduates. For example, at this same time, a black postal clerk in Washington, DC, earned $2,200 a year.[93] These salaries, the report indicated, should be "substantially increased." Finally, the Bureau noted that of the ten college faculty members, only three had graduate degrees. The investigators wrote that the school should encourage more faculty members to go to professional conferences and attend graduate school, all the while noting that with the low salaries they received, it would be very difficult for them to do that.[94]

Much of the recommended action depended, of course, on Livingstone's finding money for increased salaries, better library books, and building maintenance. As a result, there was little the school would be able to do about these particular problems at the time. However, in July 1929, the board of trustees did increase Trent's salary to $3,000 a year, and added the money necessary for maintaining the president's residence.[95]

With respect to school structure, the board of trustees decided to eliminate the first year of high school, then drop a class each succeeding year until all were dropped except for the senior year, which would be retained as a college preparation class.[96] But as for theological studies, Trent was in favor of establishing a "full-fledged" theological department—that is, reopening Hood Seminary. It is very likely that he wanted Livingstone to prepare ministers, not only because he wanted well-trained ministers, but also because he wanted future AME Zion ministers to know the school, love it, and want to support it.[97] Livingstone would indeed reopen Hood Seminary, but not for several more years.[98]

Also, in 1928, the school added, along with studies for the B.A. and B.S. degrees, a two-year premedical course that would qualify students to enter medical school.[99] During this same period, the administration dropped Latin and Greek completely from the curriculum, replacing them with Spanish. It also put more emphasis on mathematics and science: in 1932, five of the seventeen faculty members taught science and math courses.[100]

The intellectual life of the school was greatly enhanced when, on March 17, 1929, Livingstone hosted guest speaker Alain Locke. The school brought Locke to Salisbury, and Locke brought the Harlem Renaissance to the school. Just hearing Locke's background alone would have dazzled the students: the first black Rhodes Scholar, he graduated from Harvard Phi Beta Kappa and magna cum laude in only three years. He also studied at the University of Berlin and the Collège de France, and earned a doctorate in philosophy from Harvard in 1918.[101] Widely considered the "leading spokesman of the Harlem Renaissance," Locke was also a historian of black America, a supporter of writers and artists, and editor of *The New Negro: Voices of the Harlem Renaissance*, a compilation of essays, poetry, fiction, literary analyses, and art by contemporary black artists—a book created to give readers an idea of what the term "Harlem Renaissance" meant.[102]

The Harlem Renaissance was not a phenomenon of black people as a whole, or even of Harlem as a whole, but was an artistic movement encouraged by leaders of the National Urban League and the NAACP through their publications *Opportunity* and *The Crisis*, in an effort to improve race relations during a time of extreme backlash against black people at end of World War I. Thus the movement was created by what W. E. B. Du Bois called "the talented tenth," the educated elite in the black community who developed and spread the ideology of a confident race of black people.[103]

In his talk, "How to Be a Negro," Locke stated that the students should be proud of their race. In order to do that, they should emphasize the positive aspects of black culture. The students must know their history, and all Americans should know it too. One duty of students as future educators, therefore, was to present this information to the larger society.[104] These were provocative ideas at Livingstone at the time. Professor Clement had offered a seminar titled "The Negro in American History," one of the most popular courses with students, between 1924 and 1927. But only Clement, Trent, and a few other faculty members were interested in having students learn black history.[105] The others thought that in order for black youth to fit into the larger American society, they had to reject their own racial heritage.[106]

Only two years later, Livingstone no longer offered "The Negro in American History," but it had a new sociology course entitled "American Race Problems."[107] Locke would have viewed this as a step backward, and Clement and Trent might have agreed. For Locke had written earlier, in his essay "The New Negro," that it was important for black Americans to view themselves not as social problems, but as complete people with their own identity, history, and literature. Indeed, this was the thrust of the Harlem

Renaissance. He wrote: "The Negro today [...] resents [...] being regarded a chronic patient of the sociological clinic, the sick man of American democracy [....] By shedding the old chrysalis of the Negro problem we are achieving something like a spiritual emancipation."[108] While at Livingstone, Locke gave both students and faculty a lot to contemplate.

By 1930, Livingstone had collected half the money it needed for the construction of the Price Memorial Building, and decided it was time to start construction.[109] Founder's Day, February 10, 1930, was a day of great celebration, when Josephine Price-Sherrill, youngest daughter of Joseph C. Price, took the shovel and broke ground for the new building.[110] It finally seemed that the Price Memorial Building would really be built. At the board of trustees meeting that June, Trent gave what the secretary called "the most heartening and illuminating report of his administration," as Trent described Livingstone as now "in the ranks of pre-medical institutions," as he told of an additional gift from the Duke Foundation, and as he spoke of a visit from a former member of Britain's Parliament, Dr. John Murray, principal of the University College at Exeter, who was so impressed by the ability of the student body that he offered a prize in the English Department. The grateful trustees appointed a committee to prepare an "appropriate resolution expressive of the great accomplishments of President Trent to be read at Commencement."[111]

But this excitement would not last long, for the financial situation of the school would now start to spiral down as the economy of the country spiraled down. Trent soon had to use money collected for the building to pay the school's debts, liens, and contracts.[112] And so the Price Building would stand incomplete for many years, a sign of the school's financial weakness.

Although we use the date of the Wall Street crash, October 24, 1929, to mark the beginning of the Depression in this country, it was not the cause of the Depression. There were many causes, including agricultural stagnation during the 1920s, which had a terrible impact on black Americans, as more than 80 percent of black people worked on farms.[113] The crash of October 1929 created more problems: flattened sales in the housing and car markets, abuses on Wall Street, the disappearance of asset values, and weaknesses in the country's banking system. But the Depression became the "Great Depression," an "unprecedented calamity," around 1931, due to the collapsing international economic system. The stage for this collapse had been set by international political decisions made at the end of World War I.[114] And the country wouldn't recover for years.

In the first three years after the crash, approximately 100,000 people in the United States lost their jobs every week.[115] In 1932, in some American cities, black unemployment was over 50 percent. Between 1929 and 1933, agricultural prices declined 61 percent, and one-third of all homesteads were lost due to foreclosures. Over two-thirds of black cotton farmers were working hard and earning no profit at all.[116] By 1932, between 1 and 2 million Americans, including families, were "homeless wanderers."[117] In 1933, a quarter of the American workforce had no work.[118]

During this same period, two-thirds of the black farmers in North Carolina and one-third of the white farmers had no land and worked mainly as sharecroppers.[119] North Carolina's principal crops, cotton and tobacco, provided over one-half of the state's income from agriculture.[120] But prices fell in North Carolina, as they fell elsewhere, when the farmers overproduced both products. In 1919 ginned cotton brought thirty-five cents a pound; by 1931, it brought less than six cents a pound.[121] In 1933, over a quarter of all North Carolinians were on relief.[122]

The impact of the Depression on Livingstone would be hard to overstate. The dream was for the school to be a black-owned school, largely financed by the black community. But black people were barely surviving: they had no extra money to contribute to the church, no extra money to pay college tuition for their children. The white community in Salisbury tried to help: they contributed almost $10,000 to Livingstone during the Depression. As a white businessman noted: "The true worth of the college is the immediate relations—business and cultural—that take place from day to day. This relationship has added in no small way to the business prosperity."[123] But many wealthy white donors, also harmed by the Depression, decreased their charitable gifts.[124] Trent, however, would not give up. When he learned that Livingstone would not be getting the $75,000 GEB grant for the Price Memorial Building because it had not met the conditions of the grant, he said to Walls: "I just do not believe Livingstone College is going to fail. There is too much blood and tears of the fathers stored up in the brick and mortar of those buildings for God to let it fail."[125]

Nonetheless, the school was sinking fast. In January 1932 Trent told the board of trustees that the school was approaching "financial embarrassment." Its accounts with Wachovia Bank and North Carolina Bank and Trust were overdue, and, since former president Suggs had paid no interest on the farm loan when payments came due, this account was also in arrears. The board passed a motion to ask N. C. Newbold, then director of the Negro Division of the State Department of Education, for help. They also formed a special committee to look into satisfying the banks "by notes or short mortgages on the College property."[126]

Six months later the situation was critical: the school needed $6,000 immediately, and called for a special meeting of the board. At that meeting President Emeritus Goler offered the school a loan of $4,000, and Bishop Mason offered to loan another $1,000. Adding the $1,000 received from the church during a special "Livingstone College night," the school reached its goal. In his annual report at that meeting, Trent noted that the church's Women's Home and Foreign Missionary Board had also donated $1,000, and that the school had received some help for teachers' salaries from the Slater Fund. The board agreed that Livingstone needed a minimum of $50,000 from the entire church body.[127]

Also present at this meeting, sadly, was an attorney hired by former president Goler. Over the years, Goler had loaned $20,000 to the school, and was concerned that the debt had not been written down in the proper legal form. At the meeting,

Goler's attorney and the board formalized an agreement to protect his client's interests.[128] How sad that this man, one of the school founders, now eighty-six years old—a man who had ridden his horse through the night so many years ago to get from his church in Winston-Salem to his Monday morning classes at Livingstone; who had taken the helm after Price died, and kept school going for twenty-three years as president; who had loaned money to the school time and time again—how sad that he now had to hire a lawyer to protect his interests from the school he so loved.

The financial situation did not improve. In January 1933 the board held a special meeting to discuss a letter from the teachers, who had written that as much as they loved the school, appreciated the work of President Trent, and would like to continue working at Livingstone, the school owed them thousands of dollars in unpaid salaries. They were being pressed by creditors for board, lodging, and various bills, which made their situation extremely "embarrassing among strangers," they wrote, "making it impossible to maintain personal self-respect and public confidence." The board decided to hold a special rally for the teachers at Easter, in April, and agreed to send them a letter letting them know that financial relief would soon be on the way.[129] While the Easter collection generated $16,000 for the teachers, the board treasurer announced at the board's June meeting that the AME Zion Church was far behind in making its monthly payments to Livingstone from the church appropriation, and, indeed, that the church had paid less than half the amount it had promised to give to the school that year.[130]

In May 1936, the church directed the bishops to organize a $100,000 campaign, which would require church members to raise $25,000 each Founder's Day for four years. If the school received this money, it would allow Livingstone to pay down its debts, then approximately $168,000.[131]

The problems continued. It should come as no surprise that at some point between 1932 and 1934, the Southern Association of American Colleges and Secondary Schools moved Livingstone's rating down to C because of its lack of faculty and staff, and for insufficient course offerings, buildings, and physical equipment—weaknesses caused surely in part by the Depression.[132] A few years later, in December 1936, that accrediting body sent a letter to Trent announcing that it had removed Livingstone from probation and restored a class-B rating, "based on [...] the evidence of substantial improvements during the past year. We trust," the association continued, "your supporting constituency will continue to increase your annual income so that you can make the further progress necessary to retain this rating."[133] How painful this must have all been for Trent, who had struggled so hard at the beginning of his presidency to gain a class-A rating for his students, only to see it disappear. With a B rating, students graduating from Livingstone would once more receive only three years of credit for four years of work and four years of tuition payments.

Immediately after receiving this letter, Trent wrote a statement for the local Salisbury newspaper, which noted that Livingstone was making only its second appeal to the general public for financial help in its history. According to the newspaper, the AME Zion Church had just authorized the issuance of $100,000 in bonds to help the school pay down its debts. "Every citizen who is a friend to the college," the journalist wrote, "is urged to cooperate by purchasing these bonds."[134]

But the bond campaign was not very successful, and the need for money for the school was sometimes an emergency. In late summer 1937, Trent and Walls corresponded about the school's problematic financial situation. Trent wrote that he needed money by the opening of school in the fall.[135] But Walls replied that although he would do his utmost, "I cannot promise that we will have the money at the opening."[136] Walls must have addressed this problem fairly quickly, for two weeks later Trent wrote back that he was glad to hear that the church had launched a campaign for $25,000 for the immediate relief of the school, and that the church would deliver the first installment of the money at the school opening, September 15.[137] "You have been consistent in your interest in Livingstone College," Trent wrote, "and I want you to know how much I appreciate it."[138]

At around this same time, Walls told Trent how he understood Trent's role in the history of both the church and the school: "Everybody knows you must either save Livingstone College or the Zion Church will not be worth talking about in this country. Lose Livingstone and we lose all. You are our servant and we are yours."[139] By 1939, the school's outstanding debt had been reduced to approximately $61,000, a sum that might, some thought, be adjusted with creditors so that only a $41,000 debt remained.[140]

If the Depression was hard on the school, it was also hard on the Trent family. In May 1931, all Trent's personal notes were called in, including the note for his car. In July the North Carolina Public Service wrote Trent to say that he had owed ninety dollars since 1929, and that his latest payment on the debt was only three dollars and sixty cents in August 1930. Trent replied that he couldn't pay any more at the time. By December of that same year he had received no salary in three months.[141] I recall my mother, Viola Trent, saying that, like many other families, the Trents had a vegetable garden, and that Trent always kept hunting dogs—although she did think it strange that the guests were served only vegetables, while the meat went to the dogs! But a country boy who knew how to farm and hunt knew he could always keep food on the table. The family had been living in a rented house since their arrival in Salisbury. So it was very helpful when, several years later, the board of trustees began to discuss providing housing for the president and reimbursing him for past rent paid.[142] I recall my mother telling me that during these hard times, Maggie, an excellent seamstress, sewed items to sell, such as embroidered linens.

Estelle was the only child at home during this period. Altona was teaching music at Virginia Seminary, where her husband was then president. In June 1930, Trent Jr. ("Bill") graduated from Livingstone, and delivered the "oration, with valedictory." It must have been very moving for Trent Sr. to see his son graduate with top honors from the school he so loved, the school he too had graduated from as valedictorian. His son was moved, too. In the commencement program Bill Trent saved, one of his sisters wrote: "Bill and Dad both cried."[143]

Upon graduation, Bill left Salisbury to begin his studies at the Wharton School of Business, University of Pennsylvania. Although he received at least one fellowship, it was still hard to make ends meet.[144] I remember my father telling me that one day when he returned home from Philadelphia, he noticed that the pants to his father's suit were worn and patched. Shocked, he told his father that, as a college president, he had to dress better than that. In response Trent asked Bill to think about how he was able to send his son money for food and housing in Philadelphia. Trent Sr.'s values were always clear.

So Altona and Bill had both left home. It was very likely a loss to the family, to Trent, and to the school, then, when, in 1931, family friend Rufus Clement resigned from Livingstone and left Salisbury to become head of Louisville Municipal College, the black school set up as a part of the University of Louisville. He would continue to teach history, and would become president of Atlanta University only six years later.[145]

Clement's departure was a loss to the school and to the Trent family. But nothing could have prepared them for the loss they would suffer the following year when, on March 28, 1932, John Walker killed himself. "Pistol shot wound in head self-inflicted": these are the words on the death certificate.[146] This was Altona's uncle in Asheville, Trent's classmate and best friend for many years. The shock was almost insurmountable. Trent must have wondered why Walker had not turned to him if he felt he was facing a situation he considered hopeless. Or perhaps Trent knew the reason for Walker's despair and had been unable to help his friend. Some in Asheville thought Walker killed himself because he never recovered from his grief after the death of his four-year-old daughter, Anna Belle, several years earlier.[147] But these are only guesses. We have no answers.

Less than a year later, in January 1933, Malinda Dunn, Trent's mother, died of breast cancer, at the age of seventy-eight.[148] And the following year, on June 1,1934, only eighteen months after his mother's death, his wife, Maggie Trent, died. She had been ill for five days, had undergone emergency surgery for appendicitis, rallied for a day, then relapsed and died. Had she lived until the end of the month, they would have celebrated their twenty-fifth wedding anniversary.[149] The funeral was held June 4 at Livingstone College Chapel. Bishop Caldwell, chairman of the Livingstone board of trustees, presided.[150] And Charlotte Hawkins Brown spoke a few words to express the sentiments of the North Carolina State Association of Colored Women's Clubs. The newspaper account of her death tells us that during her stay in Salisbury she made many friends, was active in church work, and was an "ideal companion to her husband."[151]

How quickly could so many loved ones be lost, and at such young ages. Maggie was only forty-six when she died, and Walker, fifty-seven. The loss of a friend, the loss of his wife, his mother— to whom could he turn to now for solace? Aggrey was gone. Walker was gone. His wife was gone. Trent would have needed support from the church, but also from his friends, so he very likely turned to George Clement, his one remaining friend from the class of '98. But life was cruel to Trent during these years, and he would lose even Clement, who died only months later, in October 1934.[152]

There is no way to replace a mother, or a wife of twenty-five years, or friends one has known over thirty-five years. But we should remember that Trent had also known Bishop Walls, Asheville's "boy preacher," since the turn of the century. He would always be able to count on this friendship. And he had certainly made new friends in Salisbury since his arrival in 1925. One of these friends was William F. Kelsey Sr., a partner in the Noble and Kelsey Funeral Home.[153] Perhaps Samuel Duncan Sr. was another friend. Duncan was at one time a professor of mathematics and science at Livingstone, then head of Livingstone's Mathematics Department. The two men had been students at Livingstone at the same time, Duncan graduating in the class of 1900, two years behind Trent.[154]

Rev. Wiley Hezekiah Lash—founder of several Lutheran congregations in Rowan County, minister of St. John's Lutheran Church in Salisbury, and head of the church's parochial school—was also a friend. He and his wife, Mayzonnetta Grundy Lash, had been in Salisbury since the early 1900s, and had established a chain of grocery stores there. They were thus leaders in both the black community's religious and business communities.[155] The Lash home was also on Monroe Street, where the Trents lived. Just as Bill Trent was friends with the Aggrey and Duncan children, so too he became friends with the Lash children.[156]

It is a sign of Trent's great resiliency that in 1935, only a year after Maggie's death, he married Hattie Covington of Rockingham, North Carolina, who had graduated from high school in Rockingham, then attended Fayetteville Normal and Industrial School. Beginning in 1915, she had taught in the public schools of Richmond County for many years, then worked as a social worker until her marriage. She had always been active, and a leader, in her local AME Zion Church; thus it is very likely that she and Trent met through the church.[157] But Hattie had other interests too. Whereas Maggie had been the wife who raised three children, Hattie was the wife who would be known for her efforts to beautify the college grounds with shrubbery and flowers.[158]

But the many losses, the continuing effort, the anxiety of trying to find the money to support his family as well as the school—all these things finally took a toll on Trent's health. We should not be surprised, for, as president, Trent was doing more than running the school and searching for funding. He taught Sunday school and was a preacher steward at Soldiers Memorial Church. He also was active in the college's YMCA and in the temperance movement. At times, when no faculty member was available for a particular course, he also taught at the seminary.[159] In June 1937 he went to Hendersonville for a rest.[160] A small town just south of Asheville, in the Appalachian Mountains, Hendersonville provided a respite from the daily stresses of work, in the beauty of the mountains. But the stay wasn't sufficiently healing, and the following month his doctor ordered him to bed. "I am suffering from an abcess," he wrote to friend Walls, "which is sapping my strength."[161] Within two weeks he was in the hospital.[162] The following year, in December, the student journal reported that Trent had stopped work due to illness, then was taken to the hospital for a few weeks. He returned home from the hospital, then was hospitalized once more.[163] He seemed unable to regain his energy or his health.

Some years later, the *Star of Zion* spoke about Trent's health in a way that doubtless referred to those years of continuing illness: "President Trent has enjoyed the richly deserving honor of seeing Livingstone College come to the greatest development it has known. Richly deserving, we say, because he came very near to sacrificing his life in the interest of the College. What else could it have been but the Providence of God that saved his life, because He knew that William Johnson Trent loved the College more than he loved his own life."[164]

During these stressful times, Trent continued to show interest and pride in his children's activities, as they forged new paths in their young lives. Estelle, the baby of the family, graduated from high school, then entered Livingstone College in 1933. While there, she was an honor student. She also, like her father, had a beautiful voice, and was a member of the college octet. Also like her father, she sang solos in public, and performed "Forever Thine" when Narvie A. Purifoy married Livingstone dean Frederick Douglass White in 1935.[165] Estelle thus followed the family traditions of music and scholarship.[166] She graduated in 1937 and continued her studies at the University of Pennsylvania, where she received an M.A. degree in 1939. She then returned to North Carolina and taught in public schools in Greensboro for the next several years.[167]

As for Altona, in 1934, she taught for several months at a one-room schoolhouse near Prospect, Virginia, then began teaching in the public schools in Farmville, Virginia, where the Johns family had a farm. But this was only the latest move in a married life filled with moves. Two years after their marriage, in 1929, Johns left his pastorate at Court Street Baptist Church in

Charleston, West Virginia, and returned to Lynchburg as head of the Virginia Seminary. While there, Altona taught music at the seminary. Five years later, Johns left his position at Virginia Seminary and began touring around the country, preaching and giving lectures. This is where we meet up with Altona, teaching at the small schoolhouse in the country, then in Farmville. In 1937, when Johns returned to Charleston's Court Street Baptist Church as pastor, she remained in Farmville.[168]

Trent had had high hopes for the marriage of his daughter to Vernon Johns, a brilliant minister and scholar. But he was beginning to see a pattern in Vernon's career and the effect that was having on his daughter as Johns went from job to job; as he traveled around the country, preaching and giving speeches; as he worked on the farm. Trent would have wanted more stability for his daughter—stability both in the financial sense and in the sense of being able to settle into a home and into a community.

Johns's mother had advised Altona to get a job,[169] and so in 1934 she had begun her teaching career. But what would it have meant to Trent that his brilliant daughter had gone from teaching Latin and music at the college level to teaching reading and writing at a one-room schoolhouse, then teaching at public schools in rural Virginia? Would he have been proud of her dedication and love for these students? Or would he have seen her slipping down in terms of class, when he had struggled so hard to raise his position, and his family's position, within America's class system? Trent had worked very hard to move from his position as a sharecropper and become part of the black "better class," a group marked by education, wealth, property ownership, morality, self-discipline, and social decorum.[170] Would his children maintain themselves and future generations in this class, or not?

We do not get the sense that Altona was unhappy teaching in rural areas. Indeed, while teaching and raising her children, she wrote a book of the songs she had learned from her young students.[171] At the same time, she began what would be for her the lifelong pleasure of summer graduate study and music workshops at various schools around the country, including the universities of

Pennsylvania, Maine, and Vermont, the Juilliard School, the Eastman School of Music, and the Kodály Institute, at Stanford University.[172] But, still, her father worried. Altona had been the main support of her family since 1934, when Johns left the presidency of Virginia Seminary, and in Trent's view, supporting the family was the husband's job.[173] Perhaps Altona's father had begun to question his daughter's choice for a husband.

In August 1932, Trent Jr. received his M.B.A. degree from the Wharton School of Business. When asked years later about disappointments in his life, he told the interviewer that although he graduated second in his class at Wharton, the white recruiters who came to the school would not interview him.[174] As a result, his father gave him a job at Livingstone, where he spent two years teaching economics and coaching basketball.[175] At the same time he was working on a doctorate in economics at the University of Pennsylvania.[176]

While teaching at Livingstone, he started dating Viola ("Vi") Magdalene Scales, the youngest child of Mary Mosby Scales and William Samuel Scales of Winston-Salem. Vi had graduated from Howard University in 1932, but because of the Depression, was unable to find a teaching job.

Vi's mother, Mary Mosby Scales, and her sister, Ella Mosby Haith, were very close, and always lived near each other. As a result, the Scales and Haith children were more like siblings than cousins. At the same time that Trent Jr. was courting Vi, Ella Haith's daughter, also Ella, a speech therapist, was being courted by Robert C. Weaver, who was teaching at North Carolina Agricultural and Technical College (A&T) in Greensboro while finishing his doctorate in economics at Harvard.[177] Trent Jr. and Weaver, both students of economics at universities in the North, both now teaching at black colleges and living near each other in North Carolina—one in Greensboro, one in Salisbury—these two men were at the same time traveling to Winston-Salem to court cousins, and grew to be friends. But Weaver soon left A&T, left teaching, and moved to Washington, DC, to work in the federal government, where he hoped to help to ensure that black people benefitted from the New Deal.[178]

In 1932, when the country elected Franklin Delano Roosevelt president, his mandate was to turn the economy around and find jobs for people. He had said, in a speech: "I pledge you, I pledge myself, to a new deal for the American people."[179] And the American people expected him to deliver. Within a hundred days of his election, he sent fifteen bills to Congress to improve the economic situation and eliminate the Depression. The first two created the Civilian Conservation Corps, which would hire a quarter of a million men to work on flood control and forestry projects, and the Federal Emergency Relief Administration, which transferred federal relief money to the states.[180] The following year Congress enacted the National Industrial Recovery Act, which included the creation of the Public Works Administration (PWA), a construction project that would create jobs throughout the country.[181] The statute provided money for a staggering amount of construction, construction that included public housing, schools, hospitals, highways, roads, bridges, railroad crossings, power plants, airports, sewage disposal plants, and recreation centers.[182] Roosevelt put Harold Ickes at the head of this agency. In September 1933 Ickes issued an order that prohibited discrimination based on color or religion in all PWA projects.[183]

Ickes, who was white, hired Clark Howell Foreman, also white, as his special advisor on the economic status of Negroes. The black community, as we might imagine, was in an uproar over the choice of a white person for that position. But Foreman persuaded Ickes to allow him to hire a black assistant, and selected Robert C. Weaver for the position.[184] Weaver viewed the role of the PWA leadership as ensuring that the various relief operations included black people and treated them in a nondiscriminatory fashion. He also recommended to Foreman that their office work to expand opportunities for black people in the federal government. One of the ways he and Foreman did this was by getting other departments to hire advisors on Negro affairs.[185]

While Weaver was in Washington, DC, in the fall of 1934, Trent Sr.'s YMCA colleague and friend, President Jones of Bennett College, hired Bill Trent as a teacher. Bill would thus be following in the footsteps of his sister Altona, who had taught there seven years earlier. Trent Jr. taught economics, ran the college bookstore, served as official greeter and photographer, and also coached the basketball team, which, he was always proud to say, had two undefeated seasons while he was their coach.[186] In 1937 and 1938, he also served as acting dean of the college.[187]

Bill Trent had left Livingstone because he had not been receiving a salary, and he would receive one at Bennett. That salary, however, was not large: he earned $80 a month, and he had to pay Bennett half of that for rent.[188] But once he had a salary, he could start to think about getting married, and he wed Vi Scales in December 1934, in her parents' home in Winston-Salem. Good friend Samuel Duncan was his best man.

I recall my mother telling me that Trent was not pleased when his son chose her as his wife. Although her parents were wildly successful entrepreneurs in Winston-Salem—wealthy enough to keep three of their children in college during the Depression—neither parent had gone to school past the second grade. The Scales family had property and wealth, but this would very likely not, in Trent's eyes, have been able to overcome their lack of education and professional status, markers of membership in the black "better class." For although some of their wealth came from the Howard, Blackburn and Scales Funeral Home, from investments in the Forsyth Savings Bank, and from real estate, part of their wealth derived from a bail bond business, a pool hall, a restaurant, and movie houses, businesses frequented by black people not in the "better class," and perhaps used by the latter to mark a lack of morality in the former.[189]

Trent Sr.'s friends were college presidents, college professors, ministers, doctors—men with college degrees and advanced degrees, members of the black "better class." And they had daughters. Why couldn't his son choose one of those young women? What made Vi's position worse, in Trent's view, was that she had no plan to transcend her background with graduate school and a profession. Her dream was to make a home and raise a family with her husband. And this must have been Trent Jr.'s dream, too, for despite his father's disapproval, they wed, and raised three daughters together. A year after Bill Trent married Vi Scales, Weaver married her cousin Ella Haith.[190]

In 1936 Weaver asked Bill Trent to work with him on a research project that would survey the training and employment of white-collar and skilled black workers. Trent served as assistant administrator and regional director of the project.[191] Two years later Weaver transferred to the newly created United States Housing Authority, as special assistant to the administrator on race relations. The agency's mandate was to increase the amount of public housing.[192] As Weaver was leaving his position at the PWA, Ickes asked whom he would recommend to take over his position, and Weaver recommended Trent. On July 19, 1938, Ickes appointed Bill Trent as his adviser on Negro affairs.[193]

Trent Sr. could hardly have been more proud of his son. A few weeks after the appointment, he wrote his son a letter about this new position: "Let me add my congratulations to [...] the many I know you must have received up to this time [....] I am sure you will make good on the job, and that you will carry your honors meekly. It has been my experience in contacts with the really big people, that they never get puffed up over anything that may come their way. It may be that you will be needed in some other department of the government in the years to come, because of the high type of work you will do in this position. However that may be, let each day take care of itself."[194]

Describing his work, Trent Jr. noted that the focus was on "securing maximum Negro participation" in all programs within the Department of the Interior and the Public Works Administration. This meant integrating black people into all activities of these agencies, including employment by the agencies and employment on all projects financed by the agencies.[195]

He later gave an example of this work: "We had a situation where money was given to Fayetteville, North Carolina, for a black school and a white school, and it turned out that the white school was going to cost more than they'd anticipated, so they started taking money away from the money for the black school. This was called to my attention by a black principal and Ickes investigated. I went down and we told them to put the money back, and not only that, but to stop work on the white school until they got started on the black school."[196]

The nature of his work meant that Trent Jr. traveled extensively to monitor projects around the country, including the construction of the Grand Coulee Dam in Washington State. Here, for example, is his travel schedule for the three weeks between October 30 and November 23, 1938: Chicago, Illinois; Oklahoma City, Oklahoma; Ardmore, Oklahoma; Santa Fe, New Mexico; San Francisco, California; Seattle, Washington; Spokane, Washington; Grand Coulee, Washington; and St. Louis, Missouri.[197] Trent Jr. was also trying to get the government to integrate the national parks and campgrounds.[198] This got to be such an important part of his portfolio that even after he left the Department of the Interior and his work with Ickes, Ickes would ask his staff to meet with Trent for advice on the issue.[199]

By 1937, only five of the New Deal agencies did not have a "Negro advisor." Along with black officeholders with prominent positions, like William H. Hastie Jr., this group sometimes called themselves, and were called by others, "the Black Cabinet," even though this was an informal, amorphous group of black federal government workers with no group-based authority in the Roosevelt administration and no formal contact with the president.[200]

Early on some in this group decided that it would be helpful to get together every now and then to brainstorm about problems in one or more of the agencies. How should the problems be addressed? There were several avenues these black advisors might pursue. They might develop and present information to government officials; they could contact the black press, black churches, and black leaders to create outside pressure; or they could do both. Sometimes they would all take the same proposal to the head of their agency at the same time. At other times they would prepare information for Mary McLeod Bethune, whom they considered the head of this group.[201] Bethune was especially important for her nationwide contacts in the black community and for her friendship with Eleanor Roosevelt, who was known to have some influence over her husband, President Roosevelt, with respect to race issues. As Bethune often said to "her boys": "Use me."[202]

Since, by and large, those in the Black Cabinet held only advisory positions and could make no policy decisions on their own, some in the black community wondered if they had any impact at all. Did they get a lot done, or were they just window-dressing? Historian Nancy Weiss maintains that these two judgments are not inconsistent, for, as she suggests, "the symbolism of the Black Cabinet may have been its most important substantive achievement." It was the first time that so many black people had access to such a variety of government positions; the first time black people had penetrated this far into government; and the first time that the federal government had indicated that it was paying attention to the lives of black America in a broad-based way.[203]

As Trent was celebrating the work of his children, he, along with other Americans, was also watching Europe head once more toward war. And he was angry at the stupidity of a world that was gearing up for another global war so soon after the end of World War I. He spoke about this in a speech at North Carolina A&T University: "We went into the world war in 1917 to make the world safe for democracy and to end war. But what do we find seventeen years after? The nations are spending more for armament than ever before in the history of the world, and the methods of warfare have so radically changed that in the next war, the civilian at his peaceful labor, the mother with her babe in her arms, the aged and afflicted will suffer as much as the soldier on the firing line, for much of this warfare will be fought in the air."[204]

Germans, remembering their defeat in World War I, started to talk about "victory next time," as Hitler marched into the

Rhineland in violation of the Treaty of Versailles, which had marked the end of that war. Trent would have been reading the newspapers anxiously as Hitler took over Austria in 1938 and the United States slid back into isolationism. Would there be another Great War? Would the United States join in it once more? And, if so, would his son be drafted? Mussolini invaded Ethiopia, then Albania; Germany invaded Poland, Finland, Denmark, and Norway. Then came the Blitzkrieg in 1940, and the German conquest of Holland, Belgium, and Luxembourg—all of which led to the easy conquest of France in June 1940.

As Roosevelt was trying to decide how to help the Allies overseas without joining them in the war, in another part of his administration, Trent Jr. was still working on behalf of black Americans. In a 1939 reorganization of the executive branch, the PWA was moved into the newly created Federal Works Agency (FWA). The following year Trent Jr. became race relations officer for that agency.[205] His work remained essentially the same.

One of his new responsibilities was the chairmanship of an interdepartmental committee that was arranging an exhibit for the American Negro Exposition to be held in Chicago during the summer of 1940.[206] It was during this exposition that he renewed his friendship with Truman Gibson Jr., a friendship that dated back to their childhood in Atlanta, and back to their fathers' friendship.[207] In the fall of 1940, Trent Jr. called Gibson to see if he would be interested in moving to Washington to work as an assistant for William Hastie, who was then civilian aide to the secretary of war. He was, and joined them in D.C.[208]

Around this same time, Hitler attacked the Soviet Union, swept through Yugoslavia, chased the British from Greece, and started sinking American ships, while Japanese troops were moving into China and South Indonesia. On December 7, 1941, the Japanese bombed American ships in Pearl Harbor. The United States declared war on Japan the following day. Three days later, both Germany and Italy declared war on the United States. That same day, the United States declared war on those two nations.

Trent Sr. was immediately worried about two of his grandsons, Increase and William Trent Johns ("Billy"), Altona's oldest children, who were in the military: Billy had been drafted into the army, and Increase was in the navy, stationed in the Philippines.[209] He must have also been fearful for his son, who was eligible for the draft.[210] He would never have imagined that he would have to worry about the safety of his daughters during the war. They would surely remain home in the States. But no, Estelle would not be safe—for she left teaching, left North Carolina, left the country, and joined the Red Cross. Between 1943 and 1945, as the war dragged on, she worked in London and Paris as a Red Cross Service Club director.[211]

The Red Cross hired only college graduates over twenty-five years old.[212] Their job was to raise the morale of American troops, soldiers generally younger than the Red Cross women, and generally homesick. To accomplish this, the Red Cross created hotels and recreation centers wherever there were soldiers. For example, there were eight Red Cross sites in London. At one of them, the "Rainbow Corner," soldiers could find American food and music, movies, dances, French lessons, and young American women to talk to. For soldiers in the field, the Red Cross used "club-mobiles," outfitted buses that took coffee and doughnuts out to the soldiers wherever they were stationed. They carried, as well, cigarettes, magazines and newspapers, a phonograph, and records.[213] As one Red Cross worker explained, their job was to talk with the soldiers: "Doughnuts and coffee were our props."[214] Like the American military, Red Cross facilities and workers were segregated. Thus, black Red Cross workers like Estelle would be working with other black Red Cross workers, and serving only black soldiers.[215]

There was a great shortage of Red Cross workers and facilities for the black soldiers.[216] According to the Red Cross, very few, "if any," of the black clubs were completely staffed.[217] In March 1945, the Red Cross had only thirteen clubs with black staff in Great Britain and Western Europe, and sixty-eight black club staff members.[218] Thus, black women like Estelle worked within a relatively small group. In February 1944 the Red Cross directed that black soldiers be served at all Red Cross clubs, black or white. But the black soldiers reported that they were made to feel unwelcome, or were turned away, when they approached white Red Cross facilities.[219]

We can get an idea of what Estelle's life might have been like overseas by looking at the experiences of a battalion of black women in the Women's Army Corps (WAC) who served in France and Britain when she was there. In interviews long after the war, these women said that they were struck by how well the British and French treated them, and described situations where the British and French intervened when the black women were being badly treated by white soldiers or white Red Cross workers.[220] This must have given these women a new sense of self, much as it did for black soldiers who served in Europe during World War I. The women also enjoyed being able to travel around Europe and see the sights.[221]

By and large, the black WACs got along well with the black soldiers, who were glad to see them. However, the women did note some tension with these men at times, perhaps because they were successful women who outranked most of the men.[222] This is not surprising, as more than half the black soldiers during World War II had not gone beyond grade school.[223] This kind of tension might well have also existed between black soldiers and the black Red Cross workers, since the Red Cross recruited only women with college degrees. But the only specific information we have about Estelle during this period comes from Leslie Stokes, one of the black soldiers stationed in England during the war, who said that everybody loved her, and that even the white officers admired and respected her.[224]

A Red Cross club provided services much like the YMCA. It was a place for the soldiers to eat, sleep, and wash; it was a home away from home. The clubs generally had a lounge, a library, music rooms, and rooms for games. Program activities might include talent shows, band concerts, dancing, tours, movies, group singing, and religious programs.[225] Estelle's work overseas, therefore, was much like her father's work during the Spanish-American War, when he was Y director for the Third North Carolina Volunteer Infantry. He should have been pleased to see his daughter follow in his footsteps. I recall my mother saying, however, that he was not. He very likely thought that if his youngest daughter was going to work with the army, she should be working with the women in the army, not the men, even though being a Red Cross worker was considered a very respectable position for a woman: Eleanor Roosevelt used to wear a Red Cross uniform when she visited the troops.[226] But at a more elemental level, Trent probably thought that she should be home teaching, doing social work, or working for the church, happily married, and not off in another country working with soldiers.

Trent would also have been unhappy because his youngest child was working in Paris and London, both dangerous places between 1943 and 1945. Even though the German blitz of air attacks in 1940 and the Luftwaffe attacks of 1941 were over, in 1944 Germany started firing V-1 rockets with bombs over London.[227] On just one day, July 31, 1945, over a hundred of these bombs hit London alone.[228] The rockets caused over 5,000 deaths before the end of that campaign and flattened several dozen Red Cross buildings in London.[229] Estelle would have also been in danger when she was working in France, as hidden ground mines could explode at any time.[230] And as if all this were not dangerous enough, many Red Cross workers died in plane crashes during the war.[231]

But even though Trent Sr. might have been worried about his daughter and grandsons during this period, he was president of a college and had to maintain his focus on the school. One newspaper item that caught his attention was the story of Lloyd Gaines, a graduate of Lincoln University, the state-supported black school in Missouri. Gaines had applied to the white University of Missouri Law School and been rejected solely because of his race. Missouri at the time had no state-supported black law school for Gaines to attend, but, according to state law, Missouri would still pay for his legal education if he would attend graduate school at "the university of any adjacent state."[232] Gaines refused this option, insisting that the refusal to allow him to attend the state's only law school solely because of his race was a violation of his constitutional right to the equal protection of the laws, under the Fourteenth Amendment to the U.S. Constitution.[233]

The Supreme Court agreed, noting that a state can provide the equal protection of laws only within its own jurisdiction: it cannot shift that burden to another state. The court also pointed out that it didn't matter if Gaines was the only black student in Missouri who wanted to go to law school in Missouri: the state was still constitutionally required to provide it for him.[234]

This case attracted Trent's attention because he could immediately see the ramifications of this ruling for Livingstone. Since Southern states were now constitutionally required to build public colleges and universities for black students, this was wonderful news for the black community. But since the states had greater financial resources than the smaller, private black colleges and universities, this meant a new source of competition for these schools, which, in most cases, would not be able to provide the same level of scholarship money, curricular development, or faculty salaries as the state. No longer "protected" by segregation laws, Livingstone was being forced into a more competitive educational arena.[235] And it was up to Trent to figure out how to enable the school to compete more effectively.

He must have been pleased when, in 1941, his old friend William Walls became chairman of the board of trustees of Livingstone College, as Walls was now in a position to provide even more support for the school. When Walls took this position, he wrote Trent a letter addressing their new relationship:

> I trust you do not suspect any officiousness beyond the duties of my conscience in the new position on my part [....] This correspondence is strictly private and confidential and you must never suspect me. I will always be advised by you, as I trust you will let me give any experience from the field which seems to me to be a resource of helpfulness. I want us to have personal freedom of intercourse and

exchange and I do not want that there shall be anything come between us and cause any retardation to the success of the school, which for the first time has an alumnus as president and one a chairman of the trustees [....] I am conscious of this opportunity to make history [....] I have always been and will always be glad to cooperate with you, my friend Trent.[236]

The following year brought great excitement to the campus when Trent and Livingstone hosted the Quadrennial Christian Education Convention of the AME Zion Church. On the evening of August 12, North Carolina governor J. Melville Broughton made a welcoming speech to the 1,500 young delegates.[237] Mary McLeod Bethune also spoke to the convention that evening.[238] But they were only the warm-up acts, for everyone was waiting for the following day, when Eleanor Roosevelt would arrive.

Early the next morning President and Mrs. Trent got up early to get ready for this exciting day. They put on their Sunday-best clothes, had breakfast, then drove to the Salisbury train station, where they joined dignitaries of the AME Zion Church, Salisbury's mayor Ramsey, and, as a journalist noted, "a member of the white reception committee of the local YWCA." The train was late. When it finally arrived, the group walked quite a distance, past many cars filled with soldiers and sailors, to get to the last coach. And then there she was, Eleanor Roosevelt, standing alone, in a navy dress with white polka dots, and, of course, a hat and white gloves. She shook hands with everyone, and then they all took the long walk back to the station.[239]

It must have been an early arrival, because Roosevelt had a very busy schedule that day. In the morning, the women of the YMCA gave her a tour of the city, then hosted a luncheon for her at the Yadkin Hotel restaurant. Guests invited to the luncheon represented local religious and civic groups, including, among others, the YWCA, the Girl Scouts, the United Daughters of the Confederacy, and the Daughters of the American Revolution.[240] All these organizations, as well as North Carolina restaurants, were still segregated in 1942, so we can assume that all the guests were white.

Roosevelt arrived around two in the afternoon at Livingstone, where, in a panel discussion, she spoke out for equal opportunity in education, nondiscrimination in employment, equality under the law for each citizen, and equal participation in government, including the right to vote. She also spoke about the war, saying that it was a war for the freedom of all people, no matter what their race, color, or creed. "Boys are now scattering all over the world," she continued. "They are meeting new people, seeing new things, new conditions and [experiencing] new feelings [....] I think you young people will come out of this war with new rights acquired."[241]

After the panel, she attended a seminar at the local black high school, reviewed the AME Zion parade, returned to the hotel for dinner, then went back to Livingstone to make a speech. After an introduction by Bishop Walls, she spoke mainly about the war effort and about the four freedoms President Roosevelt had named months earlier: "freedom of speech, freedom of worship, freedom from want, and freedom from fear." During this evening session, Trent read a telegram from President Roosevelt, who offered his congratulations on the success of the conference and asked for the AME Zion Church's help in the war effort. Then, before Mrs. Roosevelt left, Lula Kelsey made a presentation to her, very likely as a representative of the black women's clubs in Salisbury.[242]

Eleanor Roosevelt must have been very tired by the time she returned to the train that would take her home. Trent must have been tired too. But how proud he must have been to host the wife of the president of the United States, and to read a telegram from the president. And how proud he must have been that the day's events went well, showing his school and his people in such a bright and positive light.

The previous day, Governor Broughton had told a local journalist that "nothing exists in our state but a harmonious and friendly relationship between the races."[243] But no black person was fooled by that. For they all knew that, despite Mrs.

Roosevelt's heartfelt speech about equality, the state of North Carolina had forced the president's wife to spend a segregated day in a segregated town.

Many of the black colleges felt the impact of the war. One effect was declining enrollment. In school year 1940–1941, black colleges had enrolled 39,793 students; by 1943–1944, that number was reduced to only 27,371, a loss of about one-third of the student population.[244] Livingstone too had been changed by the war. There were fewer students in general, and fewer men students in particular. In the 1942–1943 scholastic year, the school's total enrollment included fewer than 200 students: 48 men and 148 women. There were only 4 men in the senior class out of 28.[245] During those same years, 21 of the 141 courses listed in the school catalog were identified as war related. They included courses as varied as quantitative analysis, general physics, the historical backgrounds of World Wars I and II, community health, histology, war mathematics, and childcare in wartime. And all men students, however few there were, had to take 2 courses in physical education.[246]

In a speech he gave during the war, Trent pointed out that he and the other leaders of the black colleges had "come forth [...] to offer their physical equipment, their teaching staffs, their student bodies and their own great abilities for the service of the nation." They had adjusted their schools' programs, were active in the community to support the Red Cross and the sale of war bonds, and, even more significant, he said, "these colleges have provided a reservoir of trained men and women of color" for the armed services.[247] Perhaps he thought that this would—and should—redound to the benefit of the larger black community at the end of the war.

As the rising tide of U.S. military spending began to "float" the economy out of the Depression, so too did Livingstone slowly recover from the Depression and become solvent. War orders were flooding the large industrial cities. There were also 1 million draftees, pushing unemployment below 10 percent for the first time in a decade.[248] So, finally, black people were getting jobs; parents and students would be able to pay Livingstone's tuition; and foundations and individual donors would have money to give. As the editor of the *Star of Zion* noted: "The enormous increase in circulation of funds, incident to the war, has not been lost to the benevolent causes of the church."[249]

As the school's survival began to seem possible, many saw Trent in a new light. AME Zion historian George Alexander Brooks Sr., for one, described him as "the right man in the right place at the right time. Like the captain of the ship, he was determined to remain on board even if the ship went down. He was a Moses."[250] J. L. Fisher, a white official at Salisbury's Wachovia Bank and Trust Company, concurred: "I can testify to my own personal knowledge that that educational financial wizard actually worked a miracle in delivering the college from an almost certain financial collapse."[251]

And so Livingstone moved into better years. By 1939 the school's indebtedness had been reduced to $61,129.[252] They were almost at their goal, and continued to reduce the debt slowly, slowly from that amount. And then, in 1942, Bishop Walls led a campaign that raised $30,000, which finally wiped out all of Livingstone's debt.[253] As a result, the school had finally met the condition of the GEB, which had promised so many years earlier to give Livingstone $75,000 for completing the construction of the Price Building as soon as the school had cleared all its debts.[254] That proposal had expired decades before. But Trent returned to the GEB. He told foundation officers that he recognized that Livingstone had no claim on this money, but asked them nonetheless to take up the case of Livingstone once more, and make a new appropriation of $75,000 to complete the Price Memorial Building.[255] On March 15, 1942, the GEB informed Trent that it had granted his request.[256] And so Livingstone began the final work on the construction of the building.

The board of trustees was so grateful to Trent for shepherding the school safely through the Depression, and for raising the money to finish the Price Building, that they decided to hold a testimonial service for him. February 10, 1943, was Trent

Day on campus. The event included gifts, as well as statements by the students of both college and seminary, to show their appreciation for President and Mrs. Trent. We do not have a copy of Trent's speech that day, but a reporter at that event quoted a few sentences from his speech, words that help us see how he thought about the relationship between the individual and the community. "We are members of one great body," he said. "Nature planted in us a mutual love and fitted us for a social life. We must consider that we were born for the good of the whole."[257]

Finally, that same year, during commencement, the Price Building was dedicated.[258] The commencement speaker, Dr. Jackson Davis, associate director of the GEB, spoke of Livingstone's efforts to eliminate the debt as "the successful culmination of one of the most heroic efforts ever witnessed among Negro colleges."[259]

But even though Livingstone was moving out of a potential financial disaster, the extraordinary financial difficulties that the black colleges had faced during the Depression led Dr. Frederick Douglass Patterson, president of Tuskegee Institute, to think about creating a group solution. To begin a discussion of the issue, he wrote an article in January 1943 in the *Pittsburgh Courier*, urging private black colleges to put their resources together and "make a unified appeal to the national conscience."[260] A few months later, he discussed the idea with representatives of the GEB to see if the foundation considered the concept worthwhile and viable, and important enough to support. The foundation was indeed interested, and decided to endorse and financially support the organization.[261] Patterson then invited nineteen presidents of the black colleges to meet and discuss the proposed new organization.[262] It would be the "first cooperative fund-raising venture of educational institutions in America."[263] They would call it the United Negro College Fund (UNCF, or Fund).

The initial meeting of the presidents took place at Tuskegee on April 19, 1943. An exploratory committee formed at that meeting met two months later. Included in both committees were Rufus Clement, president of Atlanta University, and Albert W.

Dent, president of Dillard University.[264] One of the issues they addressed was the choice of an executive director. Who would go to New York City to head this new organization? That person would have to have strong interpersonal skills, since he would be trying to get all the presidents of the black colleges to work together. He would have to have good business skills, to keep the organization functioning. He definitely should have attended one of the black colleges, so he would have an insider's knowledge about the weaknesses and strengths of the schools.

That fall, Rufus Clement suggested to the committee that Trent Jr. head this new fundraising organization. Al Dent said, "Yes, yes, I know Bill Trent. He was at Morehouse with me." And Patterson agreed.[265] Although Patterson didn't know Trent as well as did the other two, he did know him a little—both through Trent Jr.'s federal government work, when Trent Jr. had visited Tuskegee, and through his father, Trent Sr., fellow president of a black school.[266] Trent Jr. accepted the offer.[267]

Bill Trent was well qualified for the position. He had attended a black college, had taught at two black colleges, and had an M.A. in business administration. These qualifications, and the fact that, as the son of one of the presidents of the black colleges, he had been raised within Trent Sr.'s network, made him a logical choice for the position. In 1943 William J. Trent Jr. became the first director of the United Negro College Fund. He would be continuing the legacy of his father—his love for, and commitment to, one black school, Livingstone College. Trent Jr.'s task would be both to expand this commitment to all the black colleges in the Fund and to move the issue of their survival to the national stage.

Black men networking with each other has been an important theme in this story. Trent Sr. nurtured and developed his college friendships over the years—friendships with Clement, Walker, Walls, Aggrey, and Davenport. This group of friends then worked together to gain the presidency of Livingstone for him. And he walked into a ready-made network of black men leaders when the Young Men's Institute joined the national black YMCA. Years later he and others in this network used this connection to help the generation that followed. David Jones helped the Trent children by giving them jobs at Bennett College. He then made Trent Jr. dean of the college, just as Trent Sr. had made Rufus Clement, son of his friend George Clement, dean of Livingstone College.

Like his father, Trent Jr. also developed a rich network of black men friends of his generation. He got his job in the federal government through Robert C. Weaver, a friend, and cousin by marriage. And his high-school schoolmate Albert Dent supported his candidacy to be head of the UNCF some twenty years after their graduation. But a particularly interesting variation on the theme of networking occurred with second-generation networking—that is, when Trent Sr.'s son and the sons of Trent Sr.'s friends networked with and helped each other. We have seen it twice so far: when Trent Jr. helped Gibson Jr. get a job in the War Department, and when Rufus Clement recommended that Trent Jr. head the UNCF.

When Bill Trent began to work with the presidents of the black colleges in the Fund, he moved into the rich network of black men that his father had nurtured for decades. In the initial group this included not only the black college presidents he had become acquainted with, but also at least two men Trent Sr. knew from his YMCA network: David Jones at Bennett and Mordecai Johnson at Howard. The Fund was thus building on middle-class connections Trent Sr. and others like him had been creating for years.

The creation of the United Negro College Fund was itself a brilliant example of networking within the black community, only this time we see it at the institutional level. For even though these black schools represented various Protestant denominations, various philosophies of education, and various organizational styles, their presidents and trustees were willing to transcend their differences to make sure that all their schools survived, and to educate those young black women and men who would become leaders in the next generation.

The job of executive director of the Fund may have been a complicated position for Trent Jr., as some of the presidents were much older than he. But, along with the position, he was inheriting whatever goodwill his father had built up in his networks over the years. President Lyndon B. Johnson used to say that "the richest inheritance of any son is his father's friends."[268] This was not true for Trent Sr., but it was definitely true for his son.

It is somehow fitting that Bill Trent was the first director of the UNCF, for the Fund both advanced his father's dream and used his father's strategies to achieve them. The dream William Johnson Trent had been following all his life was to guide and educate black youth, and to make the lives of succeeding generations better than his. He remembered "the privations and hardships" he had suffered to get an education.[269] He remembered his schoolmates who had been forced to give up their dreams of an education for want of money. But money from the UNCF would allow black colleges to provide lower tuition and more scholarships. The Fund was thus crucial for the realization of his dream.

The Fund also used the same strategies that Trent Sr. had found successful throughout his life, for his effort had always been to bring people together—whether by organizing a football game, leading Sunday's song service, or networking with other members of the black middle class. As he once stated: "We are members of one great body [....] We must consider that we were born for the good of the whole." And so it was by all the schools working together as "one great body" that the success of all the schools in the Fund—"the good of the whole"—would be achieved, and Trent's dream might become a reality.

In early 1944 Bill Trent moved to New York City to begin to set up the Fund. He was both excited and anxious about this new project, for he knew that this organization might not take hold, and that he was leaving his present job for a position that might only last one year.[270]

On March 25, 1944, an editorial in the *Norfolk Journal and Guide* addressed Trent Jr.'s departure from the Federal Works Agency: "The addition of Trent Jr. to the staff of the UNCF is the gain of that agency and the loss of the FWA [....] Few have worked more energetically and with more substantial achievement through the years of their services than did Mr. Trent [....] Mr. Trent worked without fanfare and without an appetite for glory. He was a man of action."[271] At about the same time, in a personal letter to Trent Jr., the editor wrote: "Your leaving the Federal Works Agency is a real loss to our people. They do not know, [and] probably never will know, how well you have served them."[272]

In February 1944, at the same time that the *Norfolk Journal and Guide* was addressing Trent Jr.'s work, the *Star of Zion* wrote a front page "salute" to Trent Sr.:

It is probable that President Trent, next to Bishop William Jacob Walls, has been more thoroughly indoctrinated with the Price Spirit than any man in Zion Methodism. Like the illustrious first president he refused to believe that Livingstone College did not have a great destiny [....]

Dr. Trent is an educator [...and] a man of many admirable qualities. He knows the history of education in America, particularly, as few men know it. His mind is brilliant and clear, and his memory one of the most remarkable we have ever observed. To hear him speak [...] is one of the rarest of inspirational moments. Although not an orator of the Pricean school, President Trent grips his audiences with a pleasing fascination [....] And what he says is buttressed with a deep sincerity, a character of sterling quality, and a sense of humor which makes him a friend beloved [....]

And so, in testimony of a grateful constituency, the *Star of Zion* [...] salutes Livingstone College and President William Johnson Trent, whose labors for Our Livingstone have been so abundant, so unselfish and rich in results.[273]

The following month President Trent reported to Livingstone's board of trustees that the school had paid all its debts, the central heating plant was completed, Dodge Hall had been remodeled, and new sidewalks had been installed. The school had increased the salaries for the faculties of both the college and the seminary, Hood Seminary was growing, the college teachers were publishing, and one of them had received a fellowship.[274] One can only imagine their joy at hearing all this good news, after years of not knowing if the school would even be able to stay open. That same month, the board of trustees voted to join the United Negro College Fund.[275]

The work of father and son came together that May, when Bill Trent invited his father to give a speech in New York City at the event that launched the Fund's first annual drive.[276] This was a new beginning for them. They would work together as college president and UNCF director for the next thirteen years.

Chapter 6

The Legacy of Decades of Struggle:
The Trents and the United Negro College Fund

IN EARLY 1944 William Johnson Trent Jr. left the federal government to head the United Negro College Fund (UNCF, or Fund), an organization that would make a united appeal for the member colleges. This appeal would lessen competition between the schools for funds and would, at the same time, make black colleges more visible to the wider public, hopefully encouraging more financial support.

But achieving this goal would not be easy. The creators of the Fund wanted Trent to take "a pious hope" and turn it into "an institution of indispensable worth and national recognition."[1] He had watched his father struggle for years to raise funds to keep Livingstone College operating. Now he was trading a safe government position for the burden of raising funds for all the black colleges in the UNCF. He understood that this was a daring venture.

The first task of the Fund organizers was to find space to house the organization. They knew they wanted to be in midtown

New York City, but property owners in the city did not want to rent to a black organization. It was only through the intervention of white architect Julian Whittlesey that they were able, finally, to rent the Fund's first office, on East 57th Street.[2]

Staff was small at first. Paul Franklin, from John Price Jones, a fundraising organization, went to the Fund, bringing his secretary, Betty Stebman.[3] And Trent Jr. brought two of his secretaries, Josephine Davis and Edna Jones, from the Federal Works Agency in Washington, DC, to work with him.[4] Other than that, there were only two temporary workers in the field.[5] As a result, the presidents of the black member colleges were initially required to play an important role in raising money for the Fund. They were expected to raise a certain amount each year in their school city. They were also assigned a campaign city, where they were to make calls on individual and corporate prospects, discuss the work of the Fund, and request financial support.[6]

By May, Trent Jr. had put together the Fund's first annual drive and was drafting a report of activities to deliver at a UNCF meeting in Atlanta in June. In the report, he discussed staffing issues and presentations to foundations, corporations, and labor organizations, as well as the selection of thirteen large cities where the Fund was already conducting intensive campaigns.[7]

But all thoughts about the Fund must have disappeared on June 6, when Americans woke up to stunning news about the war: the United States and its allies had invaded Normandy, in France, opening a western front in the war against Germany. This was welcome news for Russia, which for years had been fighting Germany on the eastern front and asking the Allies to come in on the west.[8]

It was a massive invasion. On that one day, 6,483 vessels landed on the Normandy coast, dropping off more than 100,000 men, and Allied pilots flew 15,000 sorties to protect them as they landed. But the casualties were massive too: more than 2,000 young men died that day trying to land on Omaha Beach alone.[9] This would be a critical moment in the history of the war. The Allies had already won ascendancy in the European air war.[10] Now they would use their colossal force to win on land. Allied troops moved on to Paris, which they liberated in August. By January 1945, at the Battle of the Bulge, in Belgium's Ardennes Forest, they wiped out what remained of Hitler's reserves of men, aircraft, and armor.[11] Finally, on May 8, 1945, less than a year after the Allied invasion, Germany surrendered.[12]

But the war in the Pacific was not yet over. At the same time that the United States had been fighting Germany in Europe, it was also fighting Japan in the Pacific. Between 1942 and 1945, important sea battles were taking place, including the campaigns at Guadalcanal, Iwo Jima, Okinawa, and Leyte Gulf, the largest sea battle in history.[13] Although the United States was winning these campaigns, they were very costly in terms of American lives lost. As a result, the United States decided to take the war to Japan and bomb Japanese cities, not just military targets. In March 1945, the United States began a systematic air campaign and firebombed 66 of Japan's largest cities. In just one attack on Tokyo, 90,000 died, and, because houses were mainly made of wood, 1 million Japanese were suddenly homeless. Between March and July, as a result of these attacks on cities, 900,000 Japanese were killed, over 1 million were injured, and 8 million lost their homes.[14] On August 6, the United States dropped an atomic bomb on Hiroshima, killing almost 40,000 Japanese immediately: another 100,000 died within a few days. Three days later it dropped an atomic bomb on Nagasaki, killing another 70,000. The following day, Japan surrendered.[15]

Trent Sr. might well have been thinking about a speech he gave before the war, in which he had prophesied that this war would be fought in the air, with disastrous consequences: "The civilian at his peaceful labor, the mother with her babe in her arms, the aged and afflicted will suffer as much as the soldier on the firing line."[16] And so it was, and his own country, in the final months of the war with Japan, killed almost one and a half million Japanese—children, women, the elderly, the infirm—in cities throughout the country. It would not have gladdened Trent to know that his prophecy came true. But like all Americans, he would have been greatly relieved that the war was over. It brought not only an end to the fighting, but also an end to his fears for his family, for two of Altona's sons were in the military, and Estelle had been in England and France since 1943.

Having now lived through both World War I and World War II, Trent was thinking about war and Livingstone's role in creating a new future. In a radio speech about "the devastation of modern warfare," he said: "There is much thoughtless talk of world war number three [....] Here at Livingstone College we are attempting through religious and scientific training to give the youth under our charge a new point of view [...] [which is] that intellectual training alone will not save us; material wealth alone will not save us. There must be a new creature with a changed heart who will practice democracy as well as preach it, if civilization is to be saved for us and for our children."[17]

At the same time that the war was winding down, the new United Negro College Fund was working out systems of organization. The structure of the Fund was fairly straightforward. It was headed by a board of trustees that included the presidents of all twenty-seven member colleges and twelve lay members.[18] The board decided issues like the formula for distributing money among the member schools and the criteria for deciding which schools could become members of the UNCF. It also decided where the college presidents would campaign.[19] Thus the college presidents would be working in cooperation for the good of all the schools in the Fund.

One of the first questions the board had to address was which black colleges and universities could become members of the Fund. It decided that in order for a school to join the Fund, it had to have an A rating from the Southern Association of Colleges and Secondary Schools. It also decided that only private schools could become members. When the Fund began, then, it included twenty-seven private accredited colleges, twenty-three of which were church related.[20]

The next key issue before the board was how to distribute the money raised by the Fund. Should the larger schools receive more than the smaller ones? They decided to divide 45 percent of the income equally between the schools, which would favor the smaller schools. The remaining 55 percent would be distributed based on both a school's enrollment and its income from gifts, grants, and endowments: the greater a school's enrollment and income, the greater its contribution from the Fund. While this favored the larger schools, it also encouraged smaller schools to recruit more students and seek more money from their supporting church in order to obtain a larger distribution from the Fund.[21]

The goal of the organization was to raise 10 percent of the current operating expenses of the member schools. Thus, the Fund would solicit money for current purposes only, to pay, for example, for teachers' salaries, library books, administrative expenses, scholarships, and the operation of the physical plant.

Since the member schools created the Fund to solicit money for current operating expenses, they would no longer be able to solicit money for this purpose, with the exception of the church-related schools, which were free to solicit more current funds from their founding church at any time. But the colleges could still solicit for special projects, like school reunions, endowments, and buildings. Soliciting funds from alumni was also limited to certain specific events, like Founder's Day and school reunions. Otherwise, alumni who wanted to raise money for their school were required to work through the Fund's national Intercollegiate Alumni Council.[22]

As executive director, Bill Trent managed the day-to-day operation of the Fund, with the advice and counsel of the board of trustees. Some years later, when he described his duties in that role, he wrote that he had to "hire the staff [...] assign responsibilities [...] 'ride-herd' on the fund-raisers [...] determine what the public relations aspect would be in order to be sure that it was in keeping with the operating philosophies of the colleges [...] watch costs [...] determine the question of organizing for fund-raising [...] and work out working relationships with the Presidents."[23] He also had to pressure the presidents to take charge of the Fund's campaign in the cities assigned to them.[24]

Working with the college presidents would have to be managed very carefully. Many were used to running their institutions all by themselves, and with a powerful hand. As sociologist Charles S. Johnson of Fisk University wrote in the early days of the Fund: "There are still too many presidents [...] who mistake omnipotence for omniscience; who assume that because final authority rests with them, ultimate wisdom does also; who confuse educational dictatorship with educational leadership."[25]

As director of the Fund, Trent Jr. would also have to develop a good working relationship with its staff. His philosophy of administrative leadership was to hire people who could do the job, give them the authority to do it, and then let them do it. If they did the job well, he would compliment them. If they didn't, instead of criticizing them publicly, he would go into their office, call them into his office, or invite them to lunch, so they could discuss the problem. He later explained: "I was in and out of offices on all the floors all the time to talk to people about what they [were] doing [....] It's sort of a direct personal relationship with every member of the staff. That went to the clerks down in the file department [....] I don't know where I picked it up [...] but it just seemed to me in a small tight organization like that, that personal relationships were very important."[26] Bill Trent might not have known where he learned an administrative style based on personal relationships, but having seen Trent Sr.'s administrative style, we do.

Bill Trent would also have to develop good relations with white donors and volunteers, especially with John D. Rockefeller Jr. and Lindsley F. Kimball, Rockefeller's right-hand man and his liaison with the Fund, for Rockefeller's participation in the work of the Fund was crucial.[27] He not only donated money; he also spoke publicly about the work of the Fund, thus linking his name and prestige to its work. He was key in recruiting chairs for the national campaign and in recruiting chairs in campaign cities— well-known, wealthy corporate leaders who were powerful in their communities, and who, in vouching for the Fund, encouraged other wealthy people to donate.[28] He wrote letters for the Fund, not only soliciting money but also suggesting how much money to donate.[29] His power to persuade was very strong. For example, after Rockefeller asked Walter Hoving, president of the Lord and Taylor department store, to be the Fund's first national campaign chair, Hoving accepted, summing up Rockefeller's influence by asking: "Who can say 'no' to Mr. Rockefeller?"[30]

Because of Rockefeller's participation in, and close supervision of, the work of the Fund through Lindsley Kimball, Trent Jr.'s position at the Fund would be much like his father's position at the Young Men's Institute, where his range of action was closely supervised by Vanderbilt and his right-hand man, Charles McNamee. This close supervision by a wealthy white donor might have been difficult for Bill Trent. But he knew that the money he raised for this organization was important: it would initially benefit young black men and women in the member schools and would ultimately increase and strengthen the educated black middle class.

Trent Jr. became the face of the Fund and spent much of his time traveling around the country giving speeches about its work. In the Fund's first year it raised $765,000, more than three times as much as all twenty-seven schools had raised through their own individual efforts the previous year.[31] While the bulk of the money came from corporations, businesses, labor unions, and foundations, the conservative estimate is that black Americans contributed about $95,000, and, of that, $25,000 came from black servicemen, with one army unit, the Ninety-Third Division, giving well over half that amount.[32] In its second year, the Fund raised almost $1.1 million. Five years later it raised over $1.2 million.[33]

As a member school of the Fund, Livingstone was entitled to distributions from that organization. In 1945, after receiving the Fund's initial contributions, Trent Sr. was able to buy equipment and furniture for the school and hire five new faculty members.[34] So he understood immediately how valuable Fund membership would be for Livingstone, and was diligent about doing his part to support the organization. In 1944, as president of a member school, he was expected to raise $1,000 in the Salisbury area. But, as he wrote to his friend William J. Walls in October, since the white people in the community had already donated $1,000 to the Fund, "we should raise a thousand from among ourselves."[35] The following year he spent a month in his assigned region in Connecticut, raising money for the Fund.[36] He attended the meetings of the Fund's Executive Committee.[37] And he reminded the Livingstone College board of trustees that if Livingstone could not maintain a sufficiently large endowment, it would not receive an A rating from the Southern Association and would no longer be eligible for membership in the Fund.[38] He thus put pressure on the board to maintain or increase its contribution to the school.

In 1950, in a fundraising speech on a local radio station, President Trent described the importance of the Fund's work, especially for small schools. He noted that between 1949 and 1950, although all the five black colleges in North Carolina combined gave a little less than $12,000 to the Fund, they received more than $125,000 from the Fund during the same period. More precisely, Trent was supposed to raise $2,500 in the Salisbury area between 1949 and 1950. He managed to raise only $2,172, but Livingstone received $22,697 in return.[39] As Trent later explained to the board of trustees, this money "saved us from being in the red."[40] In 1951 the UNCF began a five-year capital campaign to raise $25 million for the schools.[41] Between 1952 and 1956, Livingstone received $357,628 from this campaign. The school used the money to build Harris Hall, which was a men's dormitory; to pave the campus roadway; to build gates at the entrance to the campus; and to improve the athletic field.[42]

We can only imagine how proud Bill Trent felt when he signed the first check distributing UNCF money to Livingstone—his alma mater and the school where his father was president. And we can only imagine the pride Trent Sr. felt, watching his son direct the Fund and receiving money from the Fund. It is a reminder of the many years that Trent Sr. supported his son, wearing a patched suit in order to be able to send him money when he was in graduate school at the University of Pennsylvania. But now the roles were reversed, and the son was sending money to the father. Because the Fund was also sending money to other colleges, the presidents of those schools were getting to know Bill Trent, and were perhaps seeing Trent Sr. in a new light, for it was his son who was making possible all these improvements in their schools. The Trent men did good work.

However, there was more going on at Livingstone during this period than its work for the Fund. Trent Sr. was still dealing with the aftermath of the war. He was appointed to Salisbury's Post-War Planning Commission to represent the black community and black veterans as the city dealt with postwar conditions.[43] After the reduction in the number of male students during the war, black veterans returned to black colleges in massive numbers. In 1946, 31 percent of all students in black colleges were veterans; the following year, the number rose to 35 percent.[44] Trent worked for and with black veterans on Livingstone's campus too. Because there was insufficient housing, the school built fifteen housing units for them.[45] Perhaps placing them in separate housing also met Trent's goal of keeping the veterans separate from other college students, for even though, or because, these men were older and more mature than the other men students, they were closely supervised by the administration.[46]

The school also created special admission provisions for veterans, who could be admitted without a high school diploma if they could show that they were at least eighteen years old and had completed twelve units of high school, including three of English, with above-average grades. They had to show sufficient evidence of scholarship ability, as indicated by the quality of work on Livingstone's entrance and placement exams. And finally, they had to provide a recommendation of sufficient maturity to be able to profit from college instruction, from their high school principal or another responsible person.[47] Some of these veterans would prove to be outstanding students. In the fall of 1950, three students who received straight A's tied for first place on the dean's list: two of them were veterans.[48]

These were the lucky black veterans, who were able to go to college and have their education paid for by the G.I. Bill.[49] Many others who wanted to attend college could not. Because white schools would often not accept them, 95 percent of black veterans who went to college under the G.I. Bill used their higher education benefits in black colleges and universities, which had very limited space. Another problem was finding housing in the segregated South, where most of the black colleges were located.[50] It is estimated that black colleges and universities had to turn away 20,000 black veterans because of insufficient facilities and resources.[51] Thus, because white veterans of World War II had so many more opportunities to get an education paid for by the G.I. Bill than did black veterans, that legislation increased the education gap between black and white Americans, thereby increasing the difference between the black and white middle classes.[52]

As the veterans were settling in at Livingstone, and as the college began to learn about and address their needs, some 200 students at the college went out on strike. This strike was not like some earlier student strikes in black colleges, when students were protesting Victorian standards and limitations.[53] And it was not led by the men students or the veterans, but by seven women students who were complaining about housing conditions and food in the women's dormitory. Although the unrest began in the fall of 1945, it was on Sunday, January 25, of the following year that Trent sent a letter to the parents of all the students: "We have had considerable trouble this term with the blowing of fuses, clogging of sewer lines, inadequate heat at night, and many complaints about food. I do not feel that all their complaints were wrong." He added that in a meeting with the women boarding students, he asked them to send a committee to his office to discuss the grievances. He had promised that he would address some of the problems immediately, and he did. For example, an electrician came to correct the wiring, and, in order to solve the problem promptly, Trent hired a second man to work the evening shift with the electrician. He also told the women that he would set up a meeting with a representative from the Student Council, the dietitian, and the treasurer to address the issue of food service. Since that meeting, he wrote, the meals had improved.

"You can imagine how surprised I was on Thursday morning," he continued, "to find that the young women would not come to classes and offered no explanation for their actions." The following day, Livingstone's Executive Committee met with the student committee from the women's dormitory to find out why they refused to go to their classes, since the school was addressing their problems. There was no progress, according to Trent, as the young women refused to make a statement or answer questions in a helpful way. Trent wrote that he had just learned that the students were planning demonstrations to begin at the end of the exam period and to continue until Founder's Day in February. He ended his letter to the parents by asking them to urge their children not to participate in demonstrations, noting that all those involved in demonstrations would be dismissed.[54] The following day Trent expelled the seven women leaders of the strike for failing to honor the agreement to return to class if conditions at the women's dormitory improved.[55]

By Thursday, January 30, Trent had announced that he was closing the school between February 2 and February 11.[56] This was not a regularly scheduled holiday. And by then, Bishop Walls, chairman of Livingstone's board of trustees, was on campus conferring with Trent, student leaders, and faculty, in an effort to end the strike.[57] But to no avail.

On February 1, the seven women students who had been dismissed went to the Superior Court of Rowan County seeking a temporary restraining order to prevent Trent from closing the school and expelling them. The court set a hearing for February 14.[58] On February 2, Trent announced that all Livingstone students would have to apply for readmission to the school for the spring semester.[59] The following week he fired two faculty members who had facilitated the strike.[60]

These were bold moves by a president who felt the reins of control slipping from his hands and grabbed them back. It was also a very risky move: suppose only a few students applied for readmission? Suppose none did? Suppose firing those two faculty members hampered Livingstone's ability to hire new faculty in the future?

On February 13, the day before the court was to hear the students' complaint, Livingstone's board of trustees met at the college. The trustees immediately raised the issue of Trent's response to the strike. Had he overreacted to the actions of the students and the two faculty members he fired? Shouldn't there have been differing levels of punishment for different kinds of actions? Was the punishment Trent handed out draconian? The board also met with the seven women students who had been dismissed, who agreed to cancel court proceedings if they were absolved of criminal intent and allowed to take their semester exams. They also asked to be allowed to continue their studies at Livingstone. Finally, all seven signed a statement that they would withdraw their complaint from the court "with no conditions whatsoever attached." The board then remanded their case to the school administration and faculty for review and "final disposition," and affirmed its support for both the administration and the school's faculty committees.[61]

All Livingstone students had to apply for admission to the school for the spring semester. The school refused to accept twenty-nine of the students for readmission.[62] Included in that group were the seven women students who filed the lawsuit.[63] In the previous fall, before the strike, Livingstone had 367 students. But because of a surge in applications, there were 364 students by February 13.[64] In August, Trent summarized the school's situation for the board: "Some thought the institution would go down as a result of the strike, but this is not the case. Because of a lack of dormitory accommodations we have had to refuse admission to approximately 200 applicants for the fall term."[65]

It is interesting to note that Geraldine Gordon, one of the seven women students who were on the strike committee and were refused readmission to the school, was the daughter of AME Zion bishop Buford Gordon, who was also a member of Livingstone's board of trustees. And it was he who filed the lawsuit against the Livingstone administration.[66] This reminds us, then, of Trent's early promise to the church community after his appointment to the presidency, that he would be fair with respect to disciplining students. It also reminds us of the editorial in the *Star of Zion* that asked him to treat the child of a bootblack and the child of a bishop the same way. Some church members must have been shocked when Trent dismissed a bishop's daughter, but he had promised to not favor some students over others, and he did not. He was serious about the school rules, and students who violated them could expect to be sent home.

While Trent was willing to work with the students on valid complaints, he was not willing to have his authority undermined. He was so clear about this that he was willing to anger a bishop of the AME Zion Church who was a member of the school's board of trustees by dismissing his daughter, even though a large part of the school's money came from the church, as solicited by the trustees. He must have felt very secure in his relationship with both the board of trustees and the board of bishops to have taken this step. But, as always, he could count on the support of his friend Walls, head of the board of trustees, to make an effort to understand and support his actions as president.

Despite the stress of the war, the arrival of the veterans on campus, and the student strike, this was a time when good things were happening in Trent's life. In 1944 the school finally provided a home for the president, right across from the school, on Monroe Street, and the Trents moved in. The house was a large brick building, two stories high, with ten main rooms and an attic. Newly remodeled under the supervision of his wife Hattie, most of the rooms were painted in pastel shades with white trim, while the modern kitchen was decorated in red and white. The house had a porte cochère and garage, and in front, a broad, shaded porch, with planters filled with flowers.

On Friday evening, September 29, 1944, President and Mrs. Trent held an open house to welcome the community to their new college home. Trent, in a black tuxedo and bowtie, and Hattie, in a long teal blue gown with shimmering beads, welcomed each guest and showed them the features of the home, assisted by fifteen members of the faculty, staff, and Salisbury community, who were stationed throughout the house. There were flowers in each room, especially roses and gladiolas. On the lace-covered dining room table was an elaborate floral display composed of blue ageratum with strands of ivy spreading all around. Musical selections provided by Mrs. Lucille Satterwhite, wife of the dean of the School of Theology, and Mrs. Van Catledge, wife of a member of the Psychology Department, made the evening even more festive.[67]

When the house was finished, Trent wrote to his friend Walls telling him that the house was ready for his visit, and that he was always welcome as "one of the family."[68] After visiting the Trents, Walls thanked them for their hospitality, noting that he enjoyed his stay in their "palatial" home.[69] During this period Walls also wrote Trent about how much he valued their long friendship: "Somehow I am leaning more and more heavily on you for advice and friendship these days than even in my youth. I feel that I need you more than ever and I do trust you as I can trust only a few men in all my acquaintances, particularly because I believe you love your God, your Church and your Race with all your life."[70] Trent replied: "I wish to thank you for the kind words as to your depending upon me in matters that concern the church. I have been your friend all along, even when we have differed, and will be until the end regardless [of] what may come or go."[71]

A few months later Trent returned to Asheville, where he was the principal speaker at the Young Men's Institute (YMI) as the black community celebrated the renovation of the center. This must have brought back many memories of his years in Asheville—memories of developing programs with the black community; working with the men of the Biltmore Estate, McNamee, Harding, and Swope; celebrating the birth of his first two children; mourning the death of his wife. In his talk he presented a history of the institution from 1890 until his resignation as director in 1911. His presence thus returned YMI history to the community. But his presence did more, for a musical tradition returned with him. As the Asheville newspaper announced: "This afternoon at 5 o'clock [...] the Sunday afternoon song services, which were a feature of the center for many years, will be resumed."[72]

Around that same time, Hattie Trent published *My Memory Gems*, a book of her poetry.[73] By then she had already published two pageants about the AME Zion Church, as well as *A Catechism: Highlights of the AME Zion Church at a Glance*, material that the church was using extensively.[74] Her husband must have been proud of her new publication, and especially proud of her role within the church.

As he entered his seventies, this was also a time of great honors for Trent. In 1945 Livingstone surprised him with an honorary doctor of laws degree. When the board made the announcement at the school's commencement ceremony in June, Trent was "overcome with emotion." The audience, also delighted, used this occasion to express their joy and approval of this honor.[75]

The AME Zion Church also showed its regard for Trent by asking him to play an important role in the sesquicentennial celebration of the church, a fifteen-day event in New York City, in mid-September 1946. As Bishop William J. Walls wrote in his history of the AME Zion Church: "The most puissant leaders of church and state came and participated with the AME Zion Church in her jubilee. Bishop Walls and President W. J. Trent Sr. of Livingstone College introduced the historic celebration over 'the seventy-one key stations of the Columbia Broadcasting System Radio.'"[76] It promised to be a celebration of great proportions: on opening day, Sunday morning, more than 5,000 AME Zion members took Holy Communion.[77] At least seven local churches opened their doors for sesquicentennial programs—not only AME Zion churches, but also Baptist, African Methodist Episcopal, Methodist Episcopal, and Episcopal churches.[78] There was so much planning involved in this event, there were so many participants, that the New York City post office opened a small branch in "Mother Zion," the home of the AME Zion Church, during this period.[79]

On Monday, New York City mayor William O' Dwyer welcomed the delegates.[80] Then, during the week, there were speeches and discussions, roundtables and reports, on varied themes, including Methodism and Christian education, the Negro church, and the African work of the AME Zion Church. Dr. Frederick D. Patterson, president of Tuskegee Institute, spoke during a session on the church's founding fathers.[81]

Halfway through the two-week celebration, on Saturday, September 14, there was a massive church parade and motorcade which zigzagged from 110th Street, up and down 7th Avenue, 135th Street, St. Nicholas Avenue, and 145th Street, until it reached the 136th Street entrance to "Mother Zion."[82] There were cars in the motorcade representing fraternal, civic, business, and social organizations; there were limousines for the bishops and church dignitaries; there were floats showing the history of the church. There were banners, brass bands, marchers in uniform, all escorted by foot police and mounted police. New York City expected so many spectators that it donated a reviewing stand with a thousand seats.[83]

Trent's longtime friend Bishop Walls was the general chairman of the planning committee, so we can be sure that Walls was in the motorcade, in one of the limousines reserved for church dignitaries.[84] It would not be surprising if Trent rode along with him. How thrilling that must have been, to see hundreds and hundreds of people waving and cheering as the cars and limousines and floats passed by.

During the second and final week of the event, delegates addressed various topics, including the urban church, the Christian education of children, the expansion of the AME Zion Church, and ministers' leadership institutes.[85] Roy Wilkins of the NAACP spoke on a panel on social education and action. And New York governor Thomas E. Dewey gave a "rousing address" at Carnegie Hall.[86] During this week there was also a testimonial dinner for Emma Clarissa Clement, widow of Trent's great college friend AME Zion bishop George Clement, because the Golden Rule Foundation had just named her "American Mother" for 1946. It was the first time that the organization had awarded this honor to a black woman.[87]

One evening of the celebration was reserved to celebrate Livingstone College. Virgin Island governor William H. Hastie, Trent Jr.'s friend, made the principal address.[88] When it was Trent's turn to speak, he said that, in his view, "the church was committed to the fundamental belief that its obligations [were] not alone to the Negro people, but to the entire nation."[89] Jackson Davis, vice president and director of Rockefeller's General Education Board, which had earlier funded the construction of Livingstone's Price Memorial Building, also spoke at this event. By concentrating its resources, Davis said, the AME Zion Church had made Livingstone College "one of the fine Negro achievements in education and religion."[90] Finally, to close this event, participants sang the school song, "My Livingstone."[91]

The final event of the two-week celebration was held in Madison Square Garden and began with a song festival by the thousand-voice Sesquicentennial Choir. The theme of the evening was the growth of freedom. Harlem's representative in the U.S. House of Representatives, Adam Clayton Powell Jr., gave a speech, as did Mary McLeod Bethune, educator and activist in the Black Women's Club movement. A church representative presented flowers to Emma Clement, Paul Robeson sang, and the evening concluded in high energy, with the massive choir singing the Hallelujah Chorus from *Messiah*, George Frideric Handel's oratorio.[92]

It is easy to imagine Trent taking Holy Communion with his fellow participants that first Sunday; easy to imagine him singing the Hallelujah Chorus along with the choir. And, during those two weeks, what a great pleasure it must have been for him, as he walked through the halls to panels and roundtables and addresses, to greet old friends, some of them very likely former Livingstone students. They would have been talking about the sesquicentennial program and reminiscing about old times—about the days when Trent was a student at Livingstone, a participant in church meetings in various cities over the years, and, for the past twenty-one years, president of the church college. But he would have been remembering even farther back, to the days when he went to church as a little boy with his family. He was seventy-two years old now, and had been involved in the life of this church for almost half of its one hundred and fifty years.

Trent might also have been reflecting on what the church had meant to him in his life, for its influence was powerful. Had his mother, Malinda Dunn, not been an important person in the founding of the China Grove AME Zion Church in the small town of Pineville, North Carolina; had student-minister Josiah Caldwell not stopped to spend the night at their home when he came from Livingstone to preach on Sundays—then who would have seen the possibilities in this young boy? Who would have said to his mother: "When your son gets through school down here, send him to Livingstone." For it was those words, and that school, that transformed his life.

Trent must have been very pleased to know that the church he so loved had not only lasted so long, but had developed and grown. He must have been pleased to have the church set aside one evening of the two-week event to celebrate Livingstone, its college. But we might also imagine that since he was now in his seventies, he might have found those two weeks not only exhilarating, but also exhausting.

After he returned home to Salisbury, the honors kept coming. In June 1947, at a meeting of Livingstone's board of trustees, one of the trustees read a letter from the president of the student council, a letter signed by 250 Livingstone students, requesting that the school's new gymnasium be named after President Trent. The trustees approved the request and voted to name the new gymnasium the William Johnson Trent Gymnasium.[93]

And finally, in 1950, Livingstone College celebrated Trent's Silver Anniversary, his twenty-fifth year as president. The celebration would last for months. In February, on Founder's Day, friend and sculptor Meta Vaux Fuller, a Livingstone alumna, presented the school with a bronze bust of Trent, to be placed in the William Johnson Trent Gymnasium.[94] It was later announced that there would be a school holiday on Thursday, April 27, so students and faculty could pay tribute to their president.

The Livingstone campus was in bloom that day: dogwood trees, redbud trees, azalea bushes, peonies—all created a festive mood. The activities began at 10:30 in the morning, when the student council conducted a program in the auditorium. William Highsmith read the scripture, and Nathaniel Morgan sang the Lord's Prayer. Julia Battle and Lovelace C. Dillingham gave orations. Parker Bailey presented an orchid to Hattie Trent and a watch to Dr. Trent as tokens of the students' appreciation of their service to the school. Howard Lynch, representing the senior class, made the principal address. In his speech, he quoted Plato's *Apology of Socrates* about the life not examined, then went on to address Trent's important and difficult work at Livingstone during the previous twenty-five years: "He accepted the captaincy of the ship when it was amidst the raging storms; when the sea of events was becoming more vicious and more unmerciful and the waves of formidable circumstances were beating relentlessly upon the ship's deck. But the spirit of the captain was undaunted. He took fearless stand at the pilot's wheel [...] determined to emerge safely with his ship and cargo—the hope of the Negro people." As the program ended, all joined in to sing Livingstone's school song.

The festivities continued at two-thirty in the afternoon in Goler Hall, where the women students gave a tea. There was also an open house of all the dormitories that afternoon. At six o'clock the entire Livingstone community gathered for a buffet supper in the dining hall. The College Choral Union closed out the day of celebration with a concert of spirituals, the music Trent so loved.[95]

The faculty and staff took part in the celebration by creating the "Trent Collection," a group of books to be donated to the Carnegie Library in his name. To memorialize this event, they had a bronze plaque made to hang on the wall in the library above a bookcase filled with books from the collection. Words on the plaque explain that it was given as "a tribute to Wm. Johnson Trent, torchbearer of great books."[96] Along with the plaque, faculty and staff presented a book collection valued at $250.[97] It included biographies of Mahatma Gandhi, Albert Schweitzer, and Ralph Waldo Emerson; a photographic history of the Civil War and a history of the relationship between church and state in the United States; a book about Paul of Tarsus and the story of Jesus in the literature of the world; the collected poetry of Shelley and Keats, *The Brothers Karamazov*, and *War and Peace*; and an anthology of American Negro literature.[98] As part of the festivities, Meta Vaux Fuller returned to the Livingstone campus for the week of May 6, when she discussed art and conducted art demonstrations for the students.[99]

This must have been a time when Trent reflected on his many years at Livingstone—from his student days in the 1890s, studying for Latin tests, playing football with his friends, working as a Pullman porter to pay for room and board; to 1910, when the school expressed its pride in his work by awarding him an honorary master's degree; then to that amazing day in 1925 when the school's trustees told him that they had chosen him to be the school's fourth president.

Walls once called Trent's administration "the redeeming administration," and perhaps it was, for he managed to turn around a failing school, which quickly garnered an A rating from the state; to raise enough money to keep the school going during the Depression; to pay down its huge debt; and, at the same time, to raise enough money to construct the Price Memorial Building.[100] But even as Trent reflected on the school's past and his successes, he knew that the search for money for the school was ongoing and difficult, and that the school's rating could drop quickly without adequate funding.[101] He hoped that the newly created United Negro College Fund would continue to provide money for the school, thus making the school's survival and success more likely.

In 1951 the city of Salisbury showed their regard for Trent by appointing him to the Salisbury city school board: he was the first black person to hold this position. According to one newspaper account, the appointment "signifie[d] this community's love and respect for a great Negro educator."[102] Seen in a negative light, twenty-six years seems quite a long time for the city to wait before appointing a "great Negro educator" to the school board of this very small southern town. In a more positive light, however, the appointment shows white Salisbury trying to make some progress with its relationship to the black community. Times were changing in the white community.

But times were also changing in the black community. It was the black Parent Teacher Association (PTA) that had asked the Salisbury City Council to appoint a black person to the school board. The PTA also asked that the appointment be made from a list of three names it submitted to the council, and Trent's name was not on that list.[103] So the school board was not being entirely responsive to the black community when it chose Trent. By the time the city council was ready to appoint a black person to the school board, Trent was almost seventy-five years old. Perhaps the black community wanted a younger black person on the board, one with more energy to fight for the rights of the black students. And perhaps the white community did not.

Changes in both white and black communities were not limited to Salisbury. After President Harry S. Truman came into office in 1945, he did not hesitate to act in support of black Americans. Within three years he asked Congress to enact an antilynching bill and issued an executive order ending segregation in the armed forces.[104] The Supreme Court, too, was actively protecting the rights of black citizens when it held that white primaries, the enforcement of racial covenants, and segregation in both interstate transport and railway dining cars were unconstitutional.[105] Closer to home, in 1951, the University of North Carolina finally admitted the first black students to its medical and law schools. Trent must have been especially pleased when he learned that this group included Floyd B. McKissick, the son of Ernest McKissick, whom Trent had helped in Asheville so many years before.[106] Perhaps not every black American had heard of these actions taken by the president, the Supreme Court, and the University of North Carolina, but there is little doubt that they all heard the news when, in 1947, Jackie Robinson broke the color barrier and became the first black baseball player in the major leagues.

Like many other black Americans, Trent must have wondered at these changes: did they truly suggest changed thinking in the broader white community? Perhaps so. But sometimes a positive change conceals a sad truth. For example, although proposing an antilynching bill tells us something important about President Truman, it also reminds us that the lynching of black Americans was a national problem of some magnitude.[107]

In February 1952, on Livingstone's Founder's Day, the bishops, officers, presiding elders, ministers, members of the AME Zion Church, and many alumni and friends honored Trent with a testimonial and dinner in the college dining hall to celebrate his twenty-seven years of service to the church and the college.[108]

Trent would have wanted all his children to attend the dinner. And surely they would all have wanted to be in Salisbury with him that day. But it is not clear that all could be present. His youngest child, Estelle, had been moving around quite a lot since she returned from Europe after the war. In 1945 she worked for a while as program director at a veterans' hospital in Alabama, then joined up again with the Red Cross to work on recreational programs in Guam, then Japan. In 1947 she began working for the Army Special Services Division as director of a military service club in Japan, where she received a promotion for her work.[109] She returned to the States in 1948, moving to Petersburg, Virginia, home of her sister, Altona, where she taught for a while at the Virginia State College laboratory school.

The following year, Estelle returned to Japan to be program director at a military service club where, in 1951, the soldiers of the Ninety-Seventh AAA Gun Battalion at Camp Gifu named her "Woman of the Year [...] a lady with a lot of personality and a heart of gold." By this time, she was married to Master Sergeant John J. Stewart, who was then serving with the U.S. Army in Korea.[110] In June 1952 we find her in Fort Sill, Oklahoma, where she likely joined her husband.[111] But Estelle may well not have been in the country in February 1952 when the dinner to honor her father took place.

Altona, who was still teaching, would have been able to attend the testimonial dinner. But, like her younger sister, she too had recently moved. In 1948, she left teaching in public schools near Farmville, Virginia, and moved with her three youngest children to Montgomery, Alabama, where she joined the faculty of Alabama State College. These were productive years for her. While there, she wrote a music book for elementary school children with Vivian Flagg McBrier and received a master's degree at Teachers' College, Columbia University, in music education.[112]

When Altona arrived in Montgomery, the deacons at the Dexter Avenue Baptist Church were looking for a new pastor. She suggested her husband, Vernon, and they hired him to fill that role. As the daughter of a college president, Altona had a background that fit with the status-conscious congregation at Dexter; but church members would soon learn that the words and acts of their brilliant new preacher would not. Vernon Johns pressured the congregation to sing spirituals, which they did not like; he criticized them for clinging to their professional titles instead of building an economic base; he not only preached economic independence, but also brought ham, sausage, and vegetables from his farm to church to sell after Sunday service from the back of his pickup truck; he gave sermons on the rights of black people that caused him to be summoned by the police chief and local judge, and that led the Ku Klux Klan to burn a cross on the church lawn. His years at Dexter were stormy ones, and so Vernon Johns resigned from Dexter Avenue Baptist Church in the summer of 1952.[113] After his resignation, Altona left Montgomery to take a position at Virginia State College in Petersburg, Virginia, where she would teach for the next twenty years.[114]

Altona would likely have attended the testimonial dinner for her father, as would her brother, Bill, for he and his father were very close. They shared professional interests—as president of a black college, and as director of an organization raising money for black colleges. Indeed, their interests overlapped, for there were times when President Trent of Livingstone was on the Executive Committee of the UNCF, and periods when his son, Bill Trent, director of the UNCF, was a member of the board of trustees of Livingstone College.[115] The two men also shared a love for music, and they shared books, sending them back and forth, up and down the East Coast. They took trips together; they even went hunting together.[116] Bill Trent would have made every effort to be present even though he was already traveling a lot for the Fund—meeting with alumni groups, giving speeches during campaigns, discussing problems with the presidents of the member colleges, and helping presidents with their local campaigns.

It would have been important for Trent's children to be at the testimonial dinner, for they, along with the trustees of Livingstone College and the AME Zion Church, had joined in to give their father a six-week tour of Europe and the British Isles. He had always wanted to visit the important European and British educational institutions—the Universities of Oxford, Cambridge, Edinburgh, and Glasgow, and the Sorbonne.[117] He wanted to visit other historic sites too, including Westminster Abbey, St. Paul's Cathedral, the Houses of Parliament in London; the old League of Nations Building in Geneva; and the Scotland home of David Livingstone, after whom Livingstone College was, perhaps, named.

Trent was probably enjoying these weeks as he made plans for the trip, talking with friends who had traveled abroad and working with staff members who were buying the ticket for his trip across the Atlantic on the *Zuiderkruis* and arranging for hotels and tours. Sadly, in the midst of this excitement, in the midst of this continuing celebration of his Silver Jubilee, and only two months after the testimonial dinner, in April, his wife, Hattie, died, after seventeen years of marriage. On April 15, the funeral service was held in the Livingstone College Chapel, where a special Livingstone student music group brought solace to those assembled by singing "I Will Not Leave You Comfortless." Hattie Trent was remembered not only for her church work, but also for her efforts to beautify the Livingstone campus. She was buried in Richmond County, North Carolina, her childhood home.[118]

Despite his grief at the death of his wife, Trent left the States on July 15 for Europe. In later reports to the Livingstone community, he wrote that he had taken a boat ride down the Rhine River in Germany, to Basel and Lucerne, in Switzerland, then gone on to Milan, where he saw da Vinci's painting *The Last Supper*. He went to Rome, spent four days in Geneva, then traveled on to Paris, which he described as "the most beautiful city, I believe, in the world."[119] He also noted that during the six-week trip he stayed at the finest hotels, where he always had excellent accommodations. "During the entire trip," he wrote, "I never saw any signs of discrimination."[120] And in just this one quiet sentence, without saying more, Trent lays out before us a lifetime of insult and humiliation, anger, and fear.

Trent returned from his European tour at the end of August 1952. Within a year, at the age of seventy-nine, he married sixty-year-old Cleota Collins, a friend and colleague of Altona's from the Music Department of Virginia State College.[121]

This would be Trent's fourth marriage: he had been widowed three times. The word "resilient" seems hardly strong enough to describe his ability to withstand and recover from great shocks and severe emotional losses. Perhaps adding "hardy" and "tenacious" to the word "resilient" helps us come closer to describing his remarkable nature. Even at his advanced age, despite having lost three wives, he was still willing to take the chance to wed once more. Perhaps he felt that the president of a college should have a wife; perhaps, even more, the president of a church college should. Or, it might have simply been that he was lonely and wanted a woman's presence in his home.

Cleota Josephine Collins was born in 1893 in Cleveland, Ohio, the daughter of a minister. Her musical training would eventually include study at the Cleveland Conservatory of Music, Western Reserve University, Ohio State University, Columbia University Teachers' College, and the Juilliard School of Music. She was one of the founding members of the National Association of Negro Musicians.[122] At their initial national conference, in Chicago, July 1919, there was a concert at which both Cleota and Marian Anderson performed.[123]

In his 1921 book describing nineteen "famous modern Negro musicians," Penman Lovinggood, tenor and composer, described Collins as "the foremost Dramatic Soprano of her race."[124] Her music teachers included contralto Lila Robeson of the Metropolitan Opera and soprano E. Azalia Hackley, who took Collins on as a protégée and helped her find money to study abroad.[125] In the 1920s Collins created a voice studio in Cleveland, and toured extensively from that city. She began a teaching career in the 1930s. She taught at Sam Huston College (now Huston-Tillotson University) in Texas; Bluefield State College, in West Virginia; Tuskegee Institute; and then Virginia State College, where she was appointed head of the Voice Department in 1940. She retired from teaching when she married Trent.[126] But she did not give up her music. In Salisbury she became director of the Cathedral Choir at Soldiers Memorial Church, and also led a community choir.[127]

We can only imagine Trent's joy at having a musician in the house again, at having a home filled with the sound of the piano and singing. Cleota loved to hear him sing and would often say: "Give us a song!" There must have been many times when she played the piano to accompany her husband, many times when she played the piano and they sang together. Altona visited every summer for a week to give Cleota a rest from caring for her husband. And during those visits, it was Altona who played the piano while her father sang.[128] For he never gave up singing. When his friend William F. Kelsey died in 1944, the Kelsey family asked him to sing at the funeral, and he did.[129] Thus, we know that people in the community had heard him sing and were touched by his voice.

A year after Trent's marriage to Cleota, while the UNCF was raising money in a capital campaign, and while Livingstone was preparing the October dedication ceremony for Harris Hall, the new boys' dormitory built with UNCF money, everything about black schools and the Fund was thrown into question as the U.S. Supreme Court Justices took up the case of *Brown v. Board of Education*. The question before the court was whether public schools violated the United States Constitution when they segregated children into black schools and white schools.

On May 17, 1954, the court issued its ruling. In direct and simple language it stated: "We conclude that in the field of public education 'separate but equal' has no place. Separate educational facilities are inherently unequal."[130] The black community was thrilled with this ruling, which promised to open the door to the end of segregation throughout the country. But, along with their joy, the presidents of the member colleges of the UNCF were concerned. For they could immediately imagine the response of Fund donors, both black and white, to the Court's ruling: "Now that public schools will be integrated, why should there still be black colleges and universities? They are no longer needed. Black students will be able to attend the public white schools now. So why should the United Negro College Fund continue to exist?"

Two weeks after the *Brown* decision, Dr. Frederick D. Patterson, president of the Fund, responded to these concerns. He pointed out that the black colleges now had a new responsibility: to serve *all* the youth of America. Since college and university enrollment throughout the country was increasing rapidly, it was clear that the country would in the future need every accredited school, and that, even then, all those schools would need to expand. For that reason alone, then, the black schools deserved financial support. But there were other reasons to support the Fund, Patterson continued. He pointed out that eliminating racial restrictions would not remove "the dollar barrier" facing black youth who wanted higher education. Nor would it correct the educational deficits that black youth had suffered due to the "long neglect" of black schools. These deficits meant that colleges would have to provide remedial education for many black students before they enrolled. Patterson also noted that it was going to be very problematic to get *Brown* implemented. As a result, he concluded, the major responsibility to provide first-class higher education for black youth in the South would continue to fall on the historically black schools. And these schools would still need financial assistance from the UNCF.[131]

When Patterson wrote about how difficult it would be to get the court's ruling in *Brown* implemented, he was prescient, for the desegregation process would continue for decades. The Supreme Court seemed to recognize, and even support, this possibility when, in 1955, it held that courts with school desegregation cases should not require school boards to proceed with the desegregation process immediately, but only "with all deliberate speed."[132] Many states and local school boards interpreted this ruling as giving them time to stall desegregation. Others would simply create systems to maintain the status quo.

North Carolina, for example, along with Mississippi, Alabama, Florida, and Louisiana, created pupil placement laws designed to maintain segregated schools.[133] In North Carolina this came in the form of a widely supported 1955 amendment to the state constitution that gave the state legislature the authority to permit local communities to close public schools if forced integration proved intolerable; to pay for the private schooling of any child assigned to an integrated school against the wishes of her parent or guardian; and to change the state pupil-assignment law to allow parents to apply for the reassignment of their child if the parents were dissatisfied with the original school placement. Nonetheless, even in North Carolina, there were school systems that did not hesitate to comply with *Brown*. In Greensboro, for example, the day after the Supreme Court's ruling in *Brown*, the Greensboro school board passed a resolution stating that it would abide by that ruling, and directing the head of the board to begin to study how to effectuate these changes.[134]

Because Americans understood that *Brown* set in motion the long-term process of the integration of the country's schools, there was concern that donations to support the black colleges in the Fund would drop after *Brown*. But they did not. Instead we see ever-increasing numbers:

1953	$1,441,220
1954	$1,477,204
1955	$1,631,292
1956	$1,668,317
1957	$1,774,619[135]

The UNCF was producing excellent results. Between 1944, when it was created, and 1958, it raised $17,923,057 for current operations and $17,750,000 for capital purposes. It also received $498,000 in bequests. Thus, during the first fourteen years of its life, the Fund raised $36 million for its member schools.[136]

As we saw earlier, in *Gaines v. Canada* the U.S. Supreme Court ruled that states would have to provide the same educational opportunities for black students that they provided for white students. This meant that states would be building colleges and graduate schools for black youth, public institutions that would have greater financial resources for faculty salaries and scholarships than would the private black colleges and universities. Thus, after *Gaines*, private black colleges and universities had to compete for black students and faculty with the better-financed black schools supported by the state. Indeed, this became a problem at Livingstone, as some of the strongest teachers began to leave for the black state schools.[137]

Now, sixteen years later, the Court's ruling in *Brown* made the competition even more intense, for that ruling meant that public white colleges and universities would no longer be able to refuse to admit black students because of their race. As a result, Livingstone, as well as all other black colleges and universities, would now be competing for black students not only with state-financed black schools, but with all the better-financed white public colleges and universities.[138]

Despite this competition, in many ways the school was in a good place at this time. In a 1955 radio speech to raise money for the UNCF, Trent reported that Livingstone had over 400 students from 22 states and Washington, DC; South America; and Africa. It held an A rating. As president of a member college of the Fund, Trent stated, he had to raise $4,000 in the Salisbury community that year for the Fund. He thanked the citizens of Salisbury for their past help in raising this contribution, and pointed out that the Fund had given more than $300,000 to Livingstone since 1944.[139] It is easy to see, then, the value of the UNCF to Livingstone. At the beginning of Fund activities, in 1944–1945, Livingstone was required to raise $3,000 in Salisbury. That sum had been raised now, in 1955, to only $4,000. Even if we assume that Trent had raised $4,000 each year since 1945, that means that Livingstone would have sent only $44,000 to the Fund during that period, while receiving more than $300,000 from the Fund for its effort.

The school had grown from a ten-room wooden building to eleven brick buildings, which included the new Harris Hall dormitory and the new Edward E. Moore Apartments for faculty. Dodge Hall had been remodeled. There was a new, fireproof wing at the library, which now held over 33,000 books. The librarians were developing an Audiovisual Department, extending the program of library orientation for freshmen, and using a more modern system of recording book circulation. Livingstone also had, in its own view, "one of the better equipped natural science departments in the South." With this equipment, it provided premedical and predental training, laboratory technical training, and training for the teaching of science. Other courses prepared students for careers in social work, secondary and elementary school teaching, and secretarial work. And the seminary prepared students for the ministry and for missionary work.

Students at Livingstone had many extracurricular outlets, including tennis, volleyball, softball, basketball, badminton, varsity football and basketball for men, and varsity basketball for women. Students could also participate in a French Club and Spanish Club, Thespians, the College Choral Union, the school newspaper, Future Teachers of America, the YMCA and YWCA, and fraternities and sororities.[140]

The school also offered the students a rich cultural life. In the period between 1944 and 1957, many artists came to Livingstone to perform. Among the singers we find Paul Robeson, Camilla Williams, Todd Duncan, Carole Brice, Mattawilda Dobbs, and Robert McFerrin. Pianist Hazel Scott gave a concert, as did Natalie Hinderas. As for theater, plays were put on by Livingstone's student theater group (the Julia B. Duncan Players) and by others. For example, Livingstone students presented *South Pacific*, and the Bennett College Players presented *Hedda Gabler*.[141] The students also heard commencement speeches by nationally recognized black figures, including educator Benjamin Mays, president of Morehouse College, and George L. P. Weaver, an important civil rights activist within the labor movement.[142]

By 1956 Livingstone was in a financial position strong enough to enable it to strengthen the position of the faculty. For example, the school now offered retirement benefits for certain faculty and administrative officers, and faculty working toward a doctorate received a one-year leave plus financial assistance. Also, the Ford Foundation had recently given the school a gift of almost $100,000 to be invested, with earnings used to increase faculty salaries over ten years.[143] Other financial data suggests that the school was in a relatively strong financial position. The college's physical plant was valued at $1.5 million, and the school had an endowment of $314,000.[144]

Yet even with these strengths, in 1956, once again Livingstone was finding it hard to meet the standards of the Southern Association of Colleges and Secondary Schools. The Association mentioned several weaknesses. It noted, for example, that the standard for faculty training was not being met, and that other standards were being met only marginally, including those related to the teaching load and the library.[145] So once again we see the school struggling, needing more money, and placing more demands on the school's leadership.

And the struggle for black civil rights continued too. Trent would have been talking with his friends about the bus boycott in Montgomery, Alabama, which began only six months after the *Brown* ruling, when black people—tired of having to stand in the bus when there were empty seats in the white section, tired of being moved to the back of the bus to the black section—simply refused to ride the city's buses. For 381 days, they walked, drove their cars, and set up carpools to give rides to those black people who had no cars, as they went to work, to shops, to doctors' offices, and to church. This was mass nonviolent resistance, a new kind of protest. Over 90 percent of all black people in Montgomery honored the boycott, which was led by the new young preacher at Dexter Avenue Baptist Church, Martin Luther King Jr. Only when the U.S. Supreme Court held the segregation of buses unconstitutional did they begin to ride the city's buses again.[146]

As the civil rights movement found a new vibrant spirit, Trent was growing weaker. His age was beginning to show, and health problems appeared. In March, 1956, when he was 83, his right leg was amputated below the knee due to problems with diabetes.[147] This was clearly a time when he should have at least been cutting back on his work. And he made some effort to do that. In late March, when elected to the Publication Board of the AME Zion Church, he refused the position, saying that his doctor had told him to eliminate some of his obligations and that he had already resigned from his position on the Salisbury Board of Education.[148] But friend Bishop Walls asked him to attend just one meeting of the Publication Board in April, and he did.[149] That summer he also gave a talk in Asheville and attended a meeting of the Committee on Christian Higher Education in Dobbs Ferry, New York.[150] Clearly he was finding it hard to slow down. It would be even harder to give up his professional life completely. But the question was in the air: was it time for him to retire?

The matter came to a head three months later, on June 5, 1956, at a meeting of the Livingstone board of trustees. Trent's good friend Bishop Walls was presiding. Also present were board members Rufus Clement and Trent's son, Bill, who had been a member of the board since at least 1954.[151] As the first order of business, Bishop Spottswood moved that the board reelect Trent unanimously for his ninth term as president of Livingstone. Rufus Clement seconded the motion. The board passed the motion, then applauded Trent for his efforts over the years. At this point Clement raised the issue of retirement. "Now that the election has been completed," he said, "I feel free to raise the question as to the thinking of President Trent as to when he might wish to retire."[152]

There is little doubt that some of the board members, including Trent Jr., had decided as a group to raise this question at that meeting, and to raise it right after Trent's reelection—when it would be clear that Trent had the board's affection and support. It is even likely that it was Trent Jr. who had asked the board to raise this question, in an effort to protect his father's health, as he could see his father tiring and weakening as he aged. They would have chosen Clement to raise the issue, for Clement had just seconded the motion that Trent be reelected, thus showing his support for the president. And Clement, the son of one of Trent's best friends, was a man Trent had known since he was a child. Thus it would not be possible for Trent to think that Clement had raised the question of Trent's retirement with anything but kindness and respect.

Trent replied that he had been thinking about retiring since the surgery, since he hadn't been able to spend full time at his office. He would consult with his family, he continued, then decide and inform the board. Walls, supporting his friend, then reminded the board that Trent had just been reelected president with "no strings attached," and that it would be Trent who would make the decision about retirement, not the board.[153]

There was "wild enthusiastic applause" at commencement later that month when Walls, as chairman of the Livingstone College board of trustees, announced Trent's reelection.[154] Calling Trent "Livingstone's man of destiny," the school's alumni commented on the reelection too:

> This humble "Country Man" has stayed on the job, stuck by his convictions and achieved miraculously for Church and College. Indebtedness has been liquidated, the institution has been awarded the highest rating, buildings have risen on the campus, the Endowment secured, an endless line of ministers and educational leaders have gone out from the school, the physical plant has been beautified, and Livingstone is fast becoming what men dreamed she

would become. As each of these milestones has been reached, William Johnson Trent remained plain Trent [....]

The spirit of this recognition is not to portray President Trent as a perfect man. He has his faults, so do we all. He has his enemies, and what man can boast no foes? This is to give recognition to a life well lived, a job performed with sheer determination and persistence.[155]

We have seen statements praising Trent before. But it is here that we see him described as a "humble 'Country Man,'" "plain Trent." Thus we are reminded that the qualities so many admired in him are those same qualities he learned from his family as a young man working on the farm and struggling to work his way through school: humility, simplicity, discipline, and steadfastness.

Trent retired on July 1 the following year.[156]

He received many letters of congratulations upon his retirement. One of them linked his work at Livingstone with his son's work at the United Negro College Fund. At the request of John D. Rockefeller Jr., Lindsley F. Kimball, Rockefeller's right-hand man, wrote to Trent to express Rockefeller's best wishes and congratulations. Kimball, who knew Trent Sr. from the latter's efforts to raise money for Livingstone, and who had been working with Bill Trent for over ten years as Rockefeller's liaison with the Fund, then continued, writing for himself:

> It is a double privilege and pleasure to write because I have known you now for a decade and would like to add my own warmest sentiments. You have hoed your row with quiet efficiency and unusual courage. Beyond that you have done something else which I cannot refrain from commenting upon [....] Mr. Rockefeller once said to me that he had done more for the world by giving it his five boys than through all of the dollars that he had given throughout his lifetime. You can be equally proud in this respect because Bill has won a degree of admiration and esteem which is as rare as it is well deserved.[157]

And so, after thirty-two years, William Johnson Trent left Livingstone, and Livingstone chose its fifth president, Dr. Samuel Edward Duncan. Duncan had graduated from Livingstone College, earned a doctorate from Cornell University in education, and held positions as both science teacher and principal. In his most recent position before his Livingstone presidency, he had spent twelve years as state supervisor for Negro high schools for the North Carolina State Department of Public Instruction. During this same period, Duncan was a consultant to the Phelps-Stokes Fund for educational projects and a member of the National Committee on the Education of Negroes, which was sponsored by the United States Office of Education.[158]

Duncan's father had been Trent Sr.'s schoolmate at Livingstone and had been head of the Math Department at Livingstone, so Trent Sr. had watched this young man grow up. Duncan and Bill Trent had also been good friends since they were young, such good friends that Duncan had been best man at Bill Trent's wedding. So he was known and respected by both father and son. They surely promoted Duncan's candidacy before the Livingstone board of trustees. Thus Duncan knew he could count on their encouragement and support as he took on this new role.

Three months after Duncan became president, the country experienced yet another spasm of racial violence, as a mob of violent white women and men surrounded nine black high school students who had been chosen to integrate Little Rock's Central High School, when the students tried to enter the school building. Orval Faubus, the white governor of Arkansas, not only refused to protect them from the mob; he also ordered the National Guard to bar them from the school building, thereby refusing to obey the Supreme Court ruling in *Brown*—and, indeed, barring the enforcement of *Brown*. A state governor refusing to enforce a federal court order created a constitutional crisis of national dimensions and led President Eisenhower to send 1,000 riot-trained soldiers from the One Hundred and First Airborne Division to Little Rock to protect the students.[159] America looked on in amazement as the federal government used armed forces to guard nine young black students, to enforce *Brown*, and to protect the civil rights of black Americans. This was a new day indeed.

Upon Trent's retirement, the community in western North Carolina, where he had labored so long, showed him their appreciation. The Salisbury-Rowan County Chamber of Commerce awarded him a citation for distinguished community service; the Laymen's Council of the Western North Carolina Conference awarded him a citation; and Johnson C. Smith University in Charlotte awarded him an honorary doctorate.[160] In 1959 the Board of Bishops of the AME Zion Church, the Livingstone College trustees, and Livingstone alumni held yet another testimonial dinner.[161] Trent was eighty-five now, and those who respected him knew there would not be much more time to honor him.

Although Trent left the presidency of Livingstone, he did not leave his beloved school. As president emeritus, he became a member of the school's board of trustees and attended its meetings, along with his son, Bill.[162] He also donated his personal library, 935 volumes, to the college library, for he was beginning to realize that he would not be reading these books again.[163]

As always, Trent enjoyed hearing from his children and learning about their activities. Altona was still teaching at Virginia State, still giving piano recitals.[164] Sometimes she and her husband, Vernon, performed together: she would play the piano, and he would recite poetry. During one of these presentations, Johns recited poems from the Bible, as well as "Thanatopsis," by William Cullen Bryant, "l'Envoi," by Rudyard Kipling, and "Requiem," by Robert Louis Stevenson. Among her piano selections, Altona played spirituals, as well as Bach's "Jesus, Joy of Man's Desiring."[165]

Trent Jr.'s work with the UNCF was leading him to some interesting places and opening some interesting doors. In the fall of 1960, he made a six-week trip to London, Kenya, Tanganyika, Nyasaland, Uganda, and Southern and Northern Rhodesia (now Zimbabwe), to begin shaping the Fund's African Scholarship

Program. While there, he met with African and British educators and students, as well as African political leaders.[166]

His position also led him to the White House. On February 21, 1962, Trent Jr., along with several presidents of the Fund's member schools, met with President Kennedy at the White House to get his support for their capital campaign. Kennedy agreed to endorse the campaign and invited a group of major corporate leaders to a White House luncheon to help launch it.[167] The following year, on June 19, 1963, at the invitation of President Kennedy, Trent Jr., along with other leaders in the education field, met with the president to discuss "those aspects of the nation's civil rights problem that relate to our schools at all levels."[168]

Like his father, Bill Trent kept his friends close. In December 1960 President Kennedy named Robert C. Weaver to be administrator of the U.S. Housing and Home Finance Agency.[169] To celebrate this event, Trent Jr. organized a dinner at the Waldorf Astoria in New York City. On the invitation list were many friends from their Black Cabinet years: Truman Gibson, Frank Horne, Ted Poston, George L. P. Weaver, Roy Wilkins, Frederick D. Patterson, Ralph Bunche, and Thurgood Marshall. According to Trent's invitation, the event would be "stag, informal, and no publicity; just the gang getting together to honor one of its own."[170]

But it is about this time that we begin to lose track of Estelle, Trent's youngest child. We know that in 1952 she was living in Fort Sill, Oklahoma. The following year she moved to Bamberg, Germany, to be with her husband. And by 1957 she was teaching school in Washington, DC, where she also did volunteer work with the Red Cross.[171] We also know that she struggled with breast cancer for over five years and died sometime in the late 1950s, a deeply sorrowful event for her father, brother, and sister.[172] Other than that, there is no information about her work, her friends, her husband, her joys, or her sorrows.

Trent Sr. lived long enough to see important changes come to Livingstone, for President Duncan came in with a revitalizing energy. His optimism and vitality were contagious. More students began to come to the school, and the faculty became more interested in graduate study.

Duncan had new ideas about governance at the school. He wanted more involvement by the faculty and trustees. Duncan asked the faculty to study the school's instructional program to see where improvements should be made, including changes in the curriculum, teaching methods, and administrative organization. He also had a vision of the faculty and trustees working together, and promoted that goal. He held an educational workshop at the AME Zion Church's Black Mountain retreat for the school's board of trustees and faculty to discuss the roles of the trustees and faculty in promoting the institution's programs. Also during this period, the board of trustees chose a committee to work with faculty committees in a ten-year projection study for the school. At their first meeting, in February 1960, the chairs of these committees discussed the philosophy of the school, as well as the curriculum, staff, endowment, and buildings. They also talked about how the school could contribute to the church and to the nation.

President Duncan also came into office with a $7 million development program. He planned to create ten new buildings on campus within the first ten years of his presidency. His goal was to add a health unit and more dormitory space and housing, and to expand the physical education facilities.[173] Trent lived long enough to see some of these changes at Livingstone.

Trent would have also seen great changes because of the civil rights movement. But he would not have expected that the changes would come from black college students looking for confrontation and violating state laws, as a form of nonviolent civil disobedience. It all seemed to start Monday, February 1, 1960, when 4 black students from North Carolina Agricultural and Technical State University, in nearby Greensboro, sat at the white lunch counter at Woolworth's in defiance of state segregation laws and asked to be served. They would wait a long time, sitting in silent protest, and they would not be served. But they came back the next day, along with more college students, and within three days, they were joined by 80 more students, some white. By Saturday, 400 students were at Woolworth's with them.[174]

Although there had been sit-ins in the South before, for some reason this particular demonstration in Greensboro had a "catalytic effect," and this form of passive nonviolent resistance soon spread to other cities in North Carolina.[175] Within ten days, sit-ins jumped the state line, and black college students were sitting in in South Carolina, then Tennessee.[176] By the end of February, there were sit-in campaigns in 31 cities in 8 states.[177] By the end of March, the movement had spread to Georgia, Texas, Arkansas, and West Virginia, and there were sit-ins in 40 more cities.[178] And, by April, only two months after the sit-in at Woolworth's in Greensboro, there had been sit-ins in 78 cities in the South, involving tens of thousands of protesters.[179] By the following year, representatives of the Student Nonviolent Coordinating Committee (SNCC) were sitting in, in Washington, DC, at the Justice Department, then in the office of the attorney general of the United States.[180]

At the beginning it was hard for the students to get support from the adults in the black community, many of whom thought this might be merely some problematic teenage fad. The black newspapers were initially hesitant in reporting their actions. Who were these young people? Their protests had not been approved by the major black civil rights groups. Indeed, the NAACP Legal Defense Fund did not defend the first students arrested in sit-ins.[181]

Trent must have had many concerns when he read about the sit-ins—concerns about the students' breaking the law, concerns about their being attacked and sent to jail, concerns that the Livingstone students would follow suit. He was no longer a college president, but he immediately understood the various kinds of pressure the presidents of the black schools would be under: pressure from the students' parents, concerned about their children's safety, education, and future; pressure from the larger black community, which feared turmoil, violence, and economic loss; pressure from the white community where the college was located, which also feared violence and economic loss, and had no plans to integrate its community; pressure from white donors, who were willing to support education in black schools but not willing to support lawbreakers or integration; and pressure from the schools' boards of trustees, which took all these concerns into account.[182] Perhaps Trent was relieved that he was no longer a college president.

It is unlikely that Trent would have condoned the student sit-ins and demonstrations when they first began. He had not learned to survive in a hostile, violent white world by taunting it with his black presence in what it considered the wrong place. But perhaps he learned to appreciate what the students were doing. Perhaps he learned to admire their courage. And it is likely that he was impressed by the effect the students were having on segregation, for they were indeed making change: by 1961, almost 200 Southern cities had begun the process of opening formerly segregated public accommodations—including downtown stores in Durham, North Carolina, lunch counters in Virginia drugstores, and restaurants in Trailways bus terminals.[183]

Trent lived long enough to see civil rights gains in Salisbury too. By 1961, picketing had led to the desegregation of lunch counters in the city. That same year, Salisbury's Chamber of Commerce and Merchants' Association passed a "resolution endorsing fair employment of Negroes and the opening of public accommodations to Negroes."[184] In 1962 Livingstone students held a protest demonstration in front of the segregated Capitol Theater, which finally ended segregated seating in Salisbury movie houses.[185] That August—eight years after the Supreme Court ruling in *Brown*—three black children—Anita, Richard, and Ida Taylor—started the school integration process in Salisbury when they enrolled in the all-white Frank B. John Elementary School. According to the local newspaper that day, "there were no incidents."[186] Change was coming to Salisbury slowly, but it was coming.

On December 30, 1961, when Trent turned eighty-eight, friends and neighbors stopped by his home to give him birthday greetings. The local newspaper covered the event and photographed him sitting in an easy chair, smiling, with a book in his hands.[187] He died eighteen months later, on Friday, June 14, 1963.

Funeral services were held the following Monday at 2 p.m. in the James Varick Memorial Auditorium on Livingstone's campus.[188] President Duncan read the Old Testament lesson from Micah, which says, in part:

> [6:] "With what shall I come before the LORD,
> and bow myself before God on high?
> Shall I come before him with burnt offerings,
> with calves a year old?
> [7:] Will the LORD be pleased with thousands of rams,
> with ten thousands of rivers of oil?
> Shall I give my firstborn for my transgression,
> the fruit of my body for the sin of my soul?"
> [8:] He has told you, O mortal, what is good;
> and what does the LORD require of you
> but to do justice, and to love kindness,
> and to walk humbly with your God?[189]

Rev. Herman L. Anderson, the minister at Trent's church, Soldiers Memorial, read the New Testament lesson from 1 Corinthians, which teaches about love.[190]

President Rufus Clement of Atlanta University, son of Trent's classmate and friend George Clement, led the congregation in prayer. Trent's good friend Bishop Walls delivered the eulogy. A special chorus made up of choir members from Livingstone and several local churches provided the music.[191] Trent was buried in the Oakwood Cemetery.[192] On his gravestone are these words from the New Testament: "I have fought a good fight; I have finished my course; I have kept the faith."[193]

Two days after his death, the *Salisbury Sunday Post* published an editorial about Trent that said, in part: "When measured by the obstacles he overcame, Dr. Trent stands tall among the tallest of men. Wherever he went and whatever he undertook, he gained with dignity, wisdom and kindness the respect of all men."[194] Livingstone alumni immediately established the William Johnson Trent Memorial Scholarship "to assist bright graduates of the college in attending institutions of higher learning."[195]

William J. Walls had told Trent years earlier that he trusted him in a way he trusted few men, "because," he wrote, "I believe that you love your God, your Church and your Race with all your life." This was truly so. And this love informed the work he would choose. He would work within Christian organizations—the YMCA and Livingstone College, even the Young Men's Institute, which he treated as a Christian organization—to maintain and strengthen them, in order to prepare the next generation to do more than his generation; he wanted them, as he once said, citing Homer, "to make the son better than the father." And the young men and women in his care would learn to use the same tools they saw him use day after day: hard work and self-discipline; Christian faith; the belief that a task could be accomplished, that a goal could be reached; and the ability to keep on against all odds. It must have been profoundly satisfying to Trent to see over the years the development and growth of the hundreds of women and men who had been in his care, young people who would go on to become leaders in the black community. He never earned a lot of money doing this work. Indeed, he was poor all his life. But he knew that in his long life he had had everything that mattered—his work and his church, deep friendships, the love of his family, the respect of his peers, and the joy and comfort of music and books.

ACKNOWLEDGMENTS

I have loved writing this book, in large part because I have had the great good fortune to work with so many wonderful people along the way.

When I began this biography, I knew that, since I am not a historian, I would need to talk with a historian from time to time about research issues. I asked Glenda Gilmore if she would be willing to answer my questions as I went along. She not only agreed to answer questions, but also offered to read draft chapters, then offered even more guidance as the years went by. Glenda's help, encouragement, and excitement about this project have been constant, and her ideas have helped shape this book. I thank her for both her friendship and her support.

I also want to thank Isabel Marcus who supported this project week by week, since its inception. Every time we got together for coffee or for a talk on the phone, she would ask: "What have you learned this week? What new ideas do you have? Talk to me about the book!" And as we talked, our conversations helped me see new patterns, and understand what I had learned in new ways. Isabel's passionate commitment to this work, as well as her many insights and ideas, have been invaluable.

Thanks go to Grey Osterud for her encouragement and good advice. I am grateful to Bob Banning, Leslie Cohen, and Jean Jesensky for their excellent work copyediting and proofreading the manuscript, and creating the index. I also thank Nancy Cleary of Wyatt-MacKenzie Publishing who helped me turn a manuscript into a book. All errors in the book, of course, are mine.

No one could have asked for better, smarter, or more meticulous research assistants than those I have had during this project. These three—Nicky Fox-Mandelbaum, Mary Kohler, and Hope Russell, then graduate students at the State University of New York at Buffalo—were my constant companions throughout the many long years of research and writing. They loved this project, and their youthful excitement continually renewed my energy. I offer my heartfelt thanks—and best wishes for a great scholarly future—to them all. Double thanks go to Hope Russell, who also helped format the manuscript.

There has been no greater supporter of this project than my mother, Viola Scales Trent. Even as she approached her hundredth year, she never failed to ask about my progress with the book. She also provided much important family history. My cousin Jeanne Johns Adkins patiently answered countless e-mail questions during all the years that I have been working on this book, and with her help, I understood our family history—especially the Asheville and Atlanta years—better. Cousin Adelaide Altona Johns Anderson provided helpful information, too. Through this research, I also learned about, then contacted, cousins in Savannah, Georgia— descendants of George Johnson, one of William Johnson Trent's uncles. Lester B. Johnson Jr., grandson of George Johnson, sent me photographs, notes, and copies of obituaries, all of which filled in many gaps in my understanding of that branch of my family. I take this opportunity to thank them all for sharing information with me, and helping me write this book.

The fine work of genealogist Sasha Mitchell provided valuable information about William Johnson Trent's parents, grandmother, aunt, uncles, and cousins. It was also Sasha who "found" Lester B. Johnson Jr., told me he was a cousin, and put us in touch. I am grateful to her for this important work.

I have always loved books and libraries, but it was not until I began this project that I really understood the important work of librarians and archivists. I want to first thank all the librarians at the School of Law, State University of New York at Buffalo, and especially John Mondo, who managed to find everything I needed to read, found documents I needed to read that I hadn't thought to request, and "saved" me when I didn't meet return deadlines, all with great patience and good cheer. I would also like to thank, in Asheville, North Carolina, Betsy Johnson, at the Pack Memorial Library; Jill Hawkins, at the Biltmore Estate Archives; and Helen Wykle, at the Ramsey Library, at the University of North Carolina at Asheville. I also thank, in Atlanta, Kayin Shabazz, at the Woodruff Library, Atlanta University Center; and Herman Mason Jr., at the Morehouse College Archives. I am grateful for the help provided by Ryan Bean, at the Kautz Family YMCA archives at the E.L. Andersen Library, University of Minnesota at Minneapolis; Joellen ElBashir and Ida E. Jones, at the Moorland-Spingarn Research Center at Howard University, in Washington DC; and Vanessa Sterling, at the Edith M. Clark History Room, Rowan County Public Library, in Salisbury, North Carolina.

I spent many weeks in Salisbury, on the campus of Livingstone College, conducting research at both Heritage Hall and the Andrew Carnegie Library. This would not have been possible without the support of Livingstone president Dr. Jimmy R. Jenkins Sr., who always made sure that I had access to these archival repositories, and always made me feel welcome on the campus. I take this opportunity to thank him. I also express my gratitude to Deborah Johnson, a member of the Livingstone College staff, who accompanied me during my many hours conducting research at Heritage Hall and located much helpful material there.

Raemi Lancaster Evans organized a get-together on Livingstone's campus of several men and women who had been students and teachers at Livingstone when Trent was president. My heartfelt thanks to Raemi and to all those who participated with such good spirit: Jewel Witherspoon Holland, Eliza Miller, Rev. Andrew Whitted, and Blanche and Charles Sherrill. Joseph C. Price, the founder of Livingstone, was Charles Sherrill's grandfather. I thank also Reginald W. Brown—son of Frank R. Brown Sr., the dean of Livingstone's seminary under Trent—who participated in this meeting too.

Rev. Grant Harrison Jr. and Mrs. Joanne Harrison took me through Soldiers Memorial AME Zion Church in Salisbury, while telling me the history of the building and explaining its relationship to Livingstone College. I received a warm welcome from Rev. Carnell Thompson and the congregation at the China Grove AME Zion Church in Charlotte, who listened with great attention and a good many "amens" as I told them of the role my great-grandmother Malinda Dunn had played in the earliest years of their church history. In Atlanta, Rhonda L. Copenny, then executive secretary of the Butler Street YMCA, took the time to walk me through the building and provide an update on the life of the building since my grandfather left Atlanta in 1925. I am grateful to all of them for their encouragement and assistance.

My research was greatly facilitated by grants from the Baldy Center for Law and Social Policy, School of Law, State University of New York at Buffalo, and the North Caroliniana Society, at the University of North Carolina at Chapel Hill, which awarded me an Archie K. Davis Fellowship. I thank all those who made these grants possible.

There were many more who helped and encouraged me along the way. In 2008, while in Paris, I met with a group of French scholars who study, teach, and write about African American history and culture (*Cercle d' Etudes Afro-Américaines et de la Diaspora*). When I told them that I was thinking about writing an article about my grandfather, and explained why, they insisted that I write a book, not an article. I thank them all for their encouragement.

I shared many joyous moments with Jason Ellis, Quynh Dinh, and Anya Quynh Ellis while working on this book. I am grateful for their presence in my life. Thank you, Jason and Quynh, for your loving support. And thank you, Anya, for being the world's best granddaughter.

Finally, let me say that I started writing this book in an effort to understand how my grandfather could have gone from being a sharecropper to being a college president, and many new questions grew out of that inquiry. But I also wrote it as a gift for the younger generations in my family, and the generations to come, and as a way to honor our ancestors, who struggled on so we could see this day.

NOTES

Introduction

[1] "College Pays Tribute to President Trent on 25th Year at Livingstone," *Livingstone College Bulletin* 6, no. 3 (May 1950): 1; "Livingstone College Observes Trent Day: Silver Anniversary," *Star of Zion*, May 4, 1950.

[2] William J. Walls, *The African Methodist Episcopal Zion Church: Reality of the Black Church* (Charlotte, NC: AME Zion Publishing House, 1974) (hereafter *AME Zion*), 43–45.

[3] Heather Andrea Williams, *Self-Taught: African American Education in Slavery and Freedom* (Chapel Hill: University of North Carolina Press, 2005), 206.

[4] Frenise A. Logan, *The Negro in North Carolina, 1876–1894* (Chapel Hill: University of North Carolina Press, 1964), 143.

[5] Ibid., 147–150.

[6] Walls, *AME Zion*, 309–311.

[7] D. Gordon Bennett and Jeffrey C. Patton, eds., *A Geography of the Carolinas* (Boone, NC: Parkway Publishers, 2008), 89.

[8] John Jamison Moore, *History of the AME Zion Church in America* (York, PA: Teachers' Journal Office, 1884), 340–341.

Chapter 1

[1] Leon F. Litwack, *Been in the Storm So Long: The Aftermath of Slavery* (New York: Alfred A. Knopf, 1979), 143.

[2] Heath Thomas, "Appointment to School Board Tribute to Trent," *The Salisbury Evening Post*, July 22, 1951.

[3] The 1870 Census gives her birthplace as North Carolina; the 1880 Census gives her birthplace as South Carolina. U.S. Federal Census, Year: *1870*; Census Place: *Charlotte City Ward 4, Mecklenburg, North Carolina*; Roll: *M593_1148*; Page: *97B*; Image: *198*; Family History Library Film (FHL): *552647*; U.S. Federal Census, Year: *1880*; Census Place: *Sharon, Mecklenburg, North Carolina*; Roll: *972*; Page: *536D*; Image: *0490*; FHL: *1254972*; Enumeration District: 117.

In a 1951 interview, William Johnson Trent said that his grandmother was named Harriet Massey, that his mother was Malinda Johnson, and that he had two uncles, George Johnson and Ben Miller. He further stated that in 1873, when he was born, the family lived in Charlotte, North Carolina, and that Malinda later married Mack Dunn. In the 1870 Census we find a Miller family in Charlotte. The family includes Harriet, 32; Ben, 17; Malinda, 14; and George, 11. The fact that Trent said he had an uncle named Ben Miller suggests that this is, indeed, his family, as does the family structure—despite the fact that every member of this family is named Miller in the census records. Trent's recollection is confirmed as we find Malinda ("Linda") in 1880, married to Mack Dunn, with a six-year old named William Johnson ("John"). Malinda Dunn reappears in both the 1910 and 1930 census, living with her son William Johnson Trent, head of household. The ages for Malinda in the 1880 and 1910 census do not match the age listed for her in 1870. But, in 1930, she gave her age as 74, which matches the age of fourteen-year old Malinda Miller in 1870, sixty years earlier. There are several ways to understand the different surnames in this family—Massey, Miller, Johnson. First, census records often contained errors. Sometimes the information was provided by a neighbor; sometimes the enumerator didn't listen carefully or misspelled names. Also, freed people often changed their names upon emancipation, and women often changed their name upon marriage. But looking at this pattern over time leads us to the strong conclusion that the Miller family we find in the 1870 census is, indeed, the family of William Johnson Trent.

[4] U.S. Federal Census, Year: *1910*; William Johnson Trent; Census Place: *Asheville Ward 3, Buncombe, North Carolina*; Roll: *T624_1099*; Page: *5A*; Image: *358*; FHL: *1375112*; Enumeration District: *0009*.

[5] U.S. Federal Census, Year: *1870*; Census Place: *Charlotte City Ward 4*. See note 3, supra; Thomas, "Appointment to School Board." Harriet Massey might well have had more children than the four listed in the 1870 Census. Many enslaved people were separated from their children when their children were sold away. Although freed men and women searched for lost family members after emancipation, most never found them. Heather Andrea Williams, *'Help Me to Find My People': The African American Search for Family Lost in Slavery* (Chapel Hill: University of North Carolina Press, 2012), 22–25, 172.

[6] John J. Winberry and Roy S. Stine, "Settlement Geography of the Carolinas before 1900," in D. Gordon Bennett and Jeffrey C. Patton, eds., *A Geography of the Carolinas* (Boone, NC: Parkway Publishers, 2008), 73, 77. North Carolina also had an important tobacco crop, which had moved south from Virginia to the northern part of the state, as well as a corn crop, which grew throughout the state. Bennett and Patton, *Geography of the Carolinas*, 73, 77–78.

[7] Larry E. Tise, "Confronting the Issue of Slavery," in Lindley S. Butler and Alan D. Watson, eds., *The North Carolina Experience: An Interpretive and Documentary History* (Chapel Hill: University of North Carolina Press, 1984), 197.

[8] Thomas, "Appointment to School Board."

[9] Jacqueline Jones, *Labor of Love, Labor of Sorrow: Black Women, Work and the Family, from Slavery to the Present* (New York: Random House, 1985), 34–35.

[10] Thomas, "Appointment to School Board."

[11] Alexander Crummell, "The Black Woman of the South: Her Neglects and Her Needs," in James Daley, ed., *Great Speeches by African Americans* (Mineola, NY: Dover Publications, 2006), 75 (speech presented August 15, 1883).

[12] Eric Foner, *Reconstruction: America's Unfinished Revolution, 1863–1877*, Perennial Classics edition (New York: HarperCollins, 2002), 81.

[13] Janette Thomas Greenwood, *Bittersweet Legacy: The Black and White "Better Classes" in Charlotte, 1850–1910* (Chapel Hill: University of North Carolina Press, 1994), 41, 44.

[14] Ibid., 37–40. Because Charlotte was not near the fighting and was located on three railway lines, the Confederate government established several military hospitals there. Janette T. Greenwood, *On the Home Front: Charlotte during the Civil War* (Charlotte, NC: Mint Museum History Department, 1982), 8.

[15] Thomas W. Hanchett, *Sorting Out the New South City: Race, Class and Urban Development in Charlotte, 1875–1975* (Chapel Hill: University of North Carolina Press, 1998), 41. By 1880 there would be 3,338 black people in Charlotte, 47 percent of the total population of the city. Ibid., 41.

[16] Ibid., 32–41; D. A. Tompkins, *History of Mecklenburg County and the City of Charlotte from 1740 to 1903* (Charlotte, NC: Observer Printing House, 1903), 118–119.

[17] Greenwood, *Bittersweet Legacy*, 46.

[18] Ibid., 69.

[19] Ibid., 44–46.

[20] Ibid., 70.

[21] Thomas, "Appointment to School Board."

[22] U.S. Federal Census, Year: *1870*; Census Place: *Charlotte City Ward 4*. See note 3, supra.

[23] Susan Strasser, *Never Done: A History of American Housework* (New York: Pantheon Books, 1982), 105–106, 108–109.

[24] Ibid., 104. Laundresses were paid very poorly for this hard work. As a result, during Reconstruction black washerwomen were among the many black workers who organized collective actions and went out on strike to gain better pay. Tera W. Hunter, *To 'Joy My Freedom: Southern Black Women's Lives and Labor after the Civil War* (Cambridge, MA: Harvard University Press, 1997), 74-77.

[25] Strasser, *Never Done*, 110–111.

[26] Ibid., 33

[27] Ibid., 36

[28] Ibid., 54–55.

[29] Ibid., 61.

[30] Ibid., 86, 95.

[31] Greenwood, *Bittersweet Legacy*, 71.

[32] David M. Fahey, "Grand United Order of Odd Fellows," and Robert E. Weir, "Prince Hall Masons," in Nina Mjagkij, ed., *Organizing Black America: An Encyclopedia of African American Associations* (New York: Routledge, 2001), 252, 593.

[33] Martha S. Jones, *All Bound Up Together: The Woman Question in African American Public Culture, 1839–1900* (Chapel Hill: University of North Carolina Press, 2007), 168–169.

[34] Allison Dorsey, *To Build Our Lives Together: Community Formation in Black Atlanta, 1875–1906* (Athens: University of Georgia Press, 2004), 101–106.

[35] Greenwood, *Bittersweet Legacy*, 71.

[36] Ibid., 71.

[37] Frenise A. Logan, *The Negro in North Carolina, 1876–1894* (Chapel Hill: University of North Carolina Press, 1964), 202–203.

[38] Thomas, "Appointment to School Board." I have no explanation for why William Trent's family used the surname "Trent" instead of "Trant," his father's surname.

[39] As late as 1943, a bishop in the AME Zion Church called George Washington "an ideal American." William J. Walls, *Joseph Charles Price: Educator and Race Leader* (Boston: Christopher Publishing House, 1943), 406.

[40] Thomas, "Appointment to School Board."

41 Edward Lawrence Trant, age and race: U.S. Federal Census, Year: *1870*; Census Place: *Charlotte City, Ward 1, Mecklenburg, North Carolina*; Roll: *M593_1148*; Page: *56A*; Image: *115*; FHL: *552647*. His exact birth date, September 12, 1847, is listed on the headstone on his grave. "Edward Lawrence Trant (1847–1889)—Find a Grave Memorial," http://www.findagrave.com, Memorial #6492458 created 02 Jun 2002. Accessed July 31, 2011. The 1870 Census also indicates that he could read and write. Mildred Trant, real estate, personal estate: U.S. Federal Census: Year, *1860*; Census Place: *King William, Virginia*; Roll: *M653_1357*; Page: *567*; Image *147*; FHL: *805357*. In today's dollars, Mildred's real estate would be valued at $322,185, and her personal estate, $671,220. See "Historical Currency Conversion" at www.futureboys.us. The term "personal estate" would have included the value of slaves.

42 Litwack, *Been in the Storm*, 55. In the 1870 Census, Mildred Trant reported that she had real estate valued at $4,500 and no personal estate. U.S. Federal Census, Year: *1870*; Census Place: *Mangohick, King William, Virginia*; Roll: *M593_1658*; Page: *117B*; Image: *239*; FHL: *553157*.

43 National Park Service. *U.S. Civil War Soldiers, 1861–1865* [online database]. Provo, UT: Ancestry.com Operations, Inc., 2007. Original data: National Park Service, Civil War Soldiers and Sailors System, http://www.itd.nps.gov/cwss/.

44 U.S. Federal Census, Year: *1870*; Census Place: *Charlotte City, Ward 1*. See note 41, supra.

45 William T. Dortch et al., The Code of North Carolina, March 2, 1883, chapter 42, section 1810. Section 1810 was enacted in 1871–1872. It was not until 1967 that the Supreme Court held antimiscegenation laws unconstitutional. *Loving v. Virginia*, 388 U.S. 1 (1967).

46 In 1904 William Johnson Trent noted in a marriage certificate that his parents had been married. "North Carolina, Marriages, 1759–1979," index, *FamilySearch*, https://familysearch.org/ark:/61903/1:1:F8H8-23X, Wm Johnson Trent and Annie B Mitchell, 06 Apr 1904, citing Wake, North Carolina, reference p25a; FHL: 236,325. There is no evidence that this is true, although it might be. It might also indicate that the couple held themselves out as married. Or perhaps Trent simply wanted to present himself as the child of married parents.

47 Thomas, "Appointment to School Board."

48 In the marriage certificate mentioned in note 46, *supra*, thirty-year-old Trent noted that his father, Edward Trant, was dead. Indeed, his father had died six years earlier. In order to have this information, Trent would have had to have maintained some connection with his father, even if only through information passed within the black community.

49 Litwack, *Been in the Storm*, 269–270.

50 By 1880 Edward had returned to Virginia, had married and had another son, and was working as a wholesale grocer. He and his wife went on to have four more children. He died in September 1889, at the age of forty-two. Edward's marriage in Virginia: "Virginia Marriages, 1785–1940," index, *FamilySearch*, http://familysearch.org/. Accessed August 3, 2011. Entry for Edward L. Trant and Rosa N. Harrison, married 02 April 1879, citing Marriage Records, FHL: 0,030,597; index entries derived from digital copies of original and compiled records;

Working as wholesale grocer; one child by 1880: U.S. Federal Census: Year: *1880*; Census Place: *Varina, Henrico, Virginia*; Roll: *1370*; Page: *248B*; FHL: *1255370*; Enumeration District: *71*.

Four more children, firstborn a son: U.S. Federal Census: Year: *1900*; Census Place: *Richmond, Monroe Ward, Richmond City, Virginia*; Roll: *T623_1738*; Page: *3B*; FHL: *1241738*; Enumeration District: *77*.

Died in 1889: See note 41, *supra*.

[51] Litwack, *Been in the Storm*, 301.

[52] Foner, *Reconstruction*, 425–431.

[53] Paul D. Escott, *Many Excellent People: Power and Privilege in North Carolina, 1850–1900* (Chapel Hill: University of North Carolina Press, 1985), 156–157.

[54] Hannah Rosen, *Terror in the Heart of Freedom: Citizenship, Sexual Violence, and the Meaning of Race in the Postemancipation South* (Chapel Hill: University of North Carolina Press, 2009), 182–186, 189–190.

[55] Foner, *Reconstruction*, 454–459.

[56] Charles Lane, *The Day Freedom Died: The Colfax Massacre, the Supreme Court, and the Betrayal of Reconstruction* (New York: Henry Holt and Co., 2008), 65–109.

[57] There is some dispute about how many black people were killed during the massacre. Cf. Foner, *Reconstruction*, 437 (280), and Lane, *The Day Freedom Died*, 265–266 (between 62 and 81).

[58] Foner, *Reconstruction*, 530.

[59] William J. Walls, *The African Methodist Episcopal Zion Church: Reality of the Black Church* (Charlotte, NC: AME Zion Publishing House, 1974) (hereafter *AME Zion*), 43–45.

[60] Ibid., 127, 186.

[61] Some historians have maintained that the Social Gospel Movement began in the mid-nineteenth century, as "American Protestantism's response to the challenges of modern industrial society." Donald K. Gorrell, *The Age of Social Responsibility: The Social Gospel in the Progressive Era, 1900–1920* (Macon: University of Georgia Press, 1988), 3. As Ralph E. Luker points out, however, this analysis ignores the earlier church responses to slavery and to the issues raised by emancipation. Ralph E. Luker, *The Social Gospel in Black and White: American Racial Reform, 1885–1912* (Chapel Hill: University of North Carolina Press, 1991), 2.

[62] Walls, *AME Zion*, 186. Gardner organized the first AME Zion missionary society in New England, which later became known as the Ladies' Home and Foreign Missionary Society. Susan J. Sierra and Adrienne Lash Jones, "Eliza Ann Gardner," in Jessie Carney Smith, ed., *Notable Black American Women, Book II* (Detroit: Gale Research, 1996), 239.

[63] Walls, *AME Zion*, 187–188, 501. Almost immediately upon his arrival in North Carolina, Hood became a leading figure. At the statewide freedmen's convention in Raleigh in 1865, he was elected president. Roberta Sue Alexander, *North Carolina Faces the Freedmen: Race Relations during Presidential Reconstruction, 1865–1867* (Durham, NC: Duke University Press, 1985), 24.

[64] Walls, *AME Zion*, 190.

[65] Heather Andrea Williams, *Self-Taught: African American Education in Slavery and Freedom* (Chapel Hill: University of North Carolina Press, 2005), 206.

[66] Ibid., 20–21.

[67] M. C. S. Noble, *A History of the Public Schools in North Carolina* (Chapel Hill: University of North Carolina Press, 1930), 319–320. His annual salary was $1,250. Ibid.

[68] "Report of Rev. J. W. Hood, agent, to the Hon. S. S. Ashley, Superintendent of Public Instruction and Secretary of the Board of Education (April 22, 1869)," in North Carolina Department of Public Instruction, *Report of the Superintendent of Public Instruction of North Carolina for the Year 1869*, 25. Available at www.docsouth.edu/nc/report1869/report1869.html.

[69] Ronald E. Butchart, *Schooling the Freed People: Teaching, Learning, and the Struggle for Black Freedom, 1861–1876* (Chapel Hill: University of North Carolina Press, 2010), 6.

[70] Williams, *Self-Taught*, 106.

[71] Ibid., 169–170.

[72] Butchart, *Schooling the Freed People*, 19–20.

[73] Williams, *Self-Taught*, 39.

[74] Constance E. H. Daniel, "Two North Carolina Families: The Harrises and the Richardsons," *Negro History Bulletin* 13, no. 1 (October 1949): 5.

[75] Earle H. West, "The Harris Brothers: Black Northern Teachers in the Reconstruction South," *The Journal of Negro Education* 48, no. 2 (1979): 128; Daniel, "Two North Carolina Families," 5.

[76] Walls, *AME Zion*, 305.

[77] Daniel, "Two North Carolina Families," 5–6.

[78] Walls, *AME Zion*, 306.

[79] Ibid., 308.

[80] John Jamison Moore, *History of the AME Zion Church in America* (York, PA: Teachers' Journal Office, 1884), 338, www.docsouth.unc.edu/church/...moore.html.

[81] Walls, *AME Zion*, 308.

[82] Moore, *History of the AME Zion Church*, 338.

[83] Walls, *AME Zion*, 309.

[84] Lenwood G. Davis, "A History of Livingstone College, 1879–1957" (Ph.D. diss., Carnegie-Mellon University, May 1979), 20.

[85] Walls, *AME Zion*, 309; Davis, "History of Livingstone College," 23.

[86] Walls, *Joseph Charles Price*, 235; W. F. Fonvielle, *Reminiscences of College Days* (Raleigh, NC: Edwards and Broughton, 1904), 104.

[87] Davis, "History of Livingstone College," 51; Livingstone College, "William Harvey Goler," in *Administrative Profiles for the Centennial Celebration* (February 6, 1980), n.p.

[88] Walls, *Joseph Charles Price*, 235.

[89] Davis, "History of Livingstone College," 84; Walls, *Joseph Charles Price*, 287.

[90] Davis, "History of Livingstone College," 34.

[91] Fonvielle, *Reminiscences*, 112.

[92] Ibid., 104.

[93] Walls, *Joseph Charles Price*, 42; Davis, "History of Livingstone College," 22.

[94] Davis, "History of Livingstone College," 19, 24, 26.

[95] Ibid., 26–27.

[96] Walls, *AME Zion*, 310.

[97] Rufus E. Clement, "A History of Negro Education in North Carolina, 1865–1928" (Ph.D. diss., Northwestern University, 1930), 125. Despite the church's attempt to avoid

competition with the state normal school in Fayetteville by creating a school in the western part of the state, in 1881 North Carolina opened a normal school in Salisbury. It was closed in 1903. Ibid., 112, 154. Rufus E. Clement was the son of George Clement, a classmate and friend of William Johnson Trent.

[98] Davis, "History of Livingstone College," 66.

[99] Kent Redding, *Making Race, Making Power: North Carolina's Road to Disfranchisement* (Urbana: University of Illinois Press, 2003), 20.

[100] John Jacob Beck, "Development in the Piedmont South: Rowan County, North Carolina, 1850–1900" (Ph.D. diss., University of North Carolina at Chapel Hill, 1984), 142–143.

[101] See, for example, text at notes 152–154, 156, *infra*.

[102] Davis, "History of Livingstone College," 26 ("10,000 dollars above expenses"); Moore, *History of the AME Zion Church*, 339 ("9,000 dollars").

[103] Davis, "History of Livingstone College," 26, 29–30. Some think the school was named after David Livingstone, a British explorer of Africa, both to attract funds and to honor his work "to uplift and educate" Africans. Others say that the name "Livingstone" was chosen to honor Robert Livingstone Vivent and his contribution to the emancipation of African Americans. Robert Livingstone Vivent, David Livingstone's son, died in 1864 in a Confederate prison camp near Salisbury, where he is buried. Ibid.

[104] Moore, *History of the AME Zion Church*, 317, 340.

[105] Walls, *AME Zion*, 310.

[106] Logan, *Negro in North Carolina*, 147–150. These five were Shaw University (Baptist), Bennett Seminary (Methodist Episcopal), Scotia Seminary and Biddle University (Presbyterian), and St. Augustine Normal School (Episcopal). Kittrell Industrial School was founded in 1887 by the African Methodist Episcopal Church (ibid., 150).

[107] Moore, *History of the AME Zion Church*, 340.

[108] Ibid., 341.

[109] Davis, "History of Livingstone College," 84.

[110] Fonvielle, *Reminiscences*, 104–106.

[111] Ibid., 112.

[112] Walls, *Joseph Charles Price*, 257.

[113] Foner, *Reconstruction*, 81–82.

[114] Jim Downs, *Sick from Freedom: African-American Illness and Suffering during the Civil War and Reconstruction* (Oxford: Oxford University Press, 2012), 28.

[115] Litwack, *Been in the Storm*, 345–346; Foner, *Reconstruction*, 82.

[116] Litwack, *Been in the Storm*, 352–353.

[117] U.S. Federal Census, Year: *1880*; Census Place: *Sharon, Mecklenburg, North Carolina*; Roll: *972*; Page: *536D*; Image: *0490*; FHL: *1254972*; Enumeration District: *117*.

[118] W. J. Trent, autobiographical statement, 1950, 1.

[119] Ages of Mack and Malinda Dunn: U.S. Federal Census, Year: *1880*; Census Place: *Pineville, Mecklenburg, North Carolina*; Roll: *972*; Page: *550D*; Image: *0517*; FHL: *1254972*; Enumeration District: *118*. This census states that in 1880 Malinda ("Linda") was twenty years old. However, since the 1870 Census lists her as fourteen, and the 1930 Census lists her as seventy-four, I am assuming that there is an error in the 1880 census

record of Malinda's age. U.S. Federal Census, Year: *1870*; Census Place: *Charlotte City Ward 4*. See note 3, supra; U.S. Federal Census, Year: *1930*; Census Place: *Salisbury, Rowan, North Carolina*; Roll: *1719*; Page: *9A*; Enumeration District: *0037*; Image: *71.0*; FHL microfilm: *2341453*.

Date of marriage between Malinda Johnson (Miller?) and Mack Dunn:
"North Carolina Marriages, 1759–1979," index, *FamilySearch*, https://familysearch.org. Accessed May 10, 2011. Entry for Mack Dunn and Linda Miller, married 08 Apr 1880; citing Marriage Records,
FHL: microfilm 0,502,339.

[120] Litwack, *Been in the Storm*, 1.

[121] Scott E. Giltner, *Hunting and Fishing in the New South: Black Labor and White Leisure after the Civil War* (Baltimore, MD: Johns Hopkins University Press, 2008), 12.

[122] Thomas, "Appointment to School Board."

[123] Joseph D. Reid Jr., "Sharecropping as an Understandable Market Response: The Post-Bellum South," *Journal of Economic History* 33 (1973): 107–108.

[124] Thomas, "Appointment to School Board."

[125] Reid, "Sharecropping," 110; Logan, *Negro in North Carolina*, 78.

[126] Joe A. Mobley, ed., *The Way We Lived in North Carolina* (Chapel Hill: University of North Carolina Press, 2003), 358–359.

[127] Ibid., 361–362.

[128] Karin L. Zipf, *Labor of Innocents: Forced Apprenticeship in North Carolina, 1715–1919* (Baton Rouge: Louisiana State University Press, 2005), 47–48. The author is writing about four-year-old slave children, but young children very likely performed the same kind of work on farms well into the twentieth century.

[129] Benjamin E. Mays, *Born to Rebel* (New York: Charles Scribner's Sons, 1971), 8.

[130] Thomas, "Appointment to School Board."

[131] Giltner, *Hunting and Fishing*, 18, 63, 66, 70, 74, 189 n.86.

[132] Helen Moseley-Edington, *Angels Unaware: Asheville Women of Color* (Asheville, NC: Home Press, 1996), 14. Moseley-Edington's book is an oral history based on interviews she conducted with black women in the Asheville area. This particular recollection is from Katherine Sutson Brown, who was born in 1914.

[133] Lucy S. Herring, *Strangers No More* (New York: Carlton Press, 1983), 16.

[134] Giltner, *Hunting and Fishing*, 21–26.

[135] Ibid., 29–32.

[136] Thomas, "Appointment to School Board."

[137] Ibid.

[138] Herring, *Strangers No More*, 16.

[139] Mays, *Born to Rebel*, 13.

[140] Jones, *All Bound Up Together*, 154.

[141] Mays, *Born to Rebel*; Walter Raleigh Lovell, "Memories of Childhood," *Star of Zion*, January 15, 1925.

[142] Lovell, "Memories of Childhood."

[143] China Grove AME Zion Church, "Our Beginning." Available at http://chinagroveamezion.org/default.aspx.

[144] Ibid. The internet list is of the church's "early founders." But the website gives 1867

as the founding date of the church, when Malinda was only eleven and, obviously, not married to Mack Dunn. So the internet list of "some of the early founders" probably means something like "early leaders," rather than "original founders" of the church.

145 Davis, "History of Livingstone College," 139.

146 Walls, *AME Zion*, 589.

147 Moore, *History of the AME Zion Church*, 341.

148 William Johnson Campbell, "The Origin and Development of Livingstone College and Hood Theological Seminary of the African Methodist Episcopal Zion Church and the Progressive Administration of President William Johnson Trent" (B.D. thesis, Hood Theological Seminary, May 1950), 35.

149 Logan, *Negro in North Carolina*, 139.

150 George Alexander Brooks Sr., *Peerless Laymen in the African Methodist Episcopal Zion Church* (State College, PA: Himes Printing Company, 1974), 1:140.

151 Thomas, "Appointment to School Board." He kept the book all his life. Ibid.

152 Philip A. Benjamin, *The Philadelphia Quakers in the Industrial Age, 1865–1920* (Philadelphia: Temple University Press, 1976), 129–130.

153 Butchart, *Schooling the Freed People*, 64.

154 North Carolina Department of Public Instruction, *Report of the Superintendent*, 22.

155 Herring, *Strangers No More*, 65.

156 North Carolina Department of Public Instruction, *Report of the Superintendent*, 21.

157 In 1880, only one black school in the state was made of brick. Logan, *Negro in North Carolina*, 141–142.

158 Lovell, "Memories of Childhood."

159 Richard H. Brodhead, ed., *The Journals of Charles E. Chesnutt* (Durham, NC: Duke University Press, 1993), 70–74.

160 Mays, *Born to Rebel*, 12.

161 Campbell, "Origin and Development," 35.

162 Ibid., 37.

163 Walls, *AME Zion*, 98.

164 Ibid.

165 Ingvar Haddal, *John Wesley: A Biography* (New York: Abingdon Press, 1961), 72–73.

166 Rev. Andrew Whitted, phone interview with author, July 24, 2010. Whitted also stated that when he learned of Trent's conversion experience, he understood why Trent had been so successful in his work for both the YMCA and the church.

167 William J. Trent, excerpt from unpublished autobiography, in Davis, "History of Livingstone College," 140. As far as I have been able to determine, there is no existing copy of this document.

168 Davis, "History of Livingstone College," 140.

169 Walls, *Joseph Charles Price*, 198.

170 William J. Walls, *The Romance of a College* (New York: Vantage Press, 1963), 22.

171 Glenda Elizabeth Gilmore, *Gender and Jim Crow: Women and the Politics of White Supremacy in North Carolina, 1896–1920* (Chapel Hill: University of North Carolina Press, 1996), 37.

172 Ibid., 40–42.

173 Clement, "History of Negro Education," 123–125.

[174] Robert J. Norrell, *Up from History: The Life of Booker T. Washington* (Cambridge, MA, and London: Harvard University Press, 2009), 39.

[175] Leroy Davis, *Clashing of the Soul: John Hope and the Dilemma of African American Leadership and Black Higher Education in the Early Twentieth Century* (Athens: University of Georgia Press, 1998), 129. Atlanta Baptist College was renamed Morehouse College in 1913. Ibid., 197.

[176] Livingstone College, *Catalogue of the Officers and Students of Livingstone College, Salisbury N.C., 1887–1888* (Greensboro: Thomas Brothers Power Book and Job Printers, 1888) (hereafter *1887–1888 Catalogue*), 7.

[177] Ibid., 35–36.

[178] Ibid., 42–48.

[179] Davis, "History of Livingstone College," 31–32.

[180] Clement, "History of Negro Education," 173.

[181] James D. Anderson, *The Education of Blacks in the South, 1860–1935* (Chapel Hill: University of North Carolina Press, 1988), 189. At the same time 4.4 percent of white youth of the same age attended secondary school. Ibid., 89. Many of the black colleges were "colleges" in name only. In 1899–1900, only 58 of the 99 black colleges had any students at all in the college classes. Ibid., 249.

[182] Ibid., 67.

[183] Joseph C. Price, "Intellectual Culture—A Necessity," 1–2 (some punctuation marks changed). Speech delivered in James City, NC, in 1879. The papers of Joseph C. Price are located in the Andrew Carnegie Library, Livingstone College, Salisbury, North Carolina.

[184] Norrell, *Up from History,* 31.

[185] Butchart, *Schooling the Freed People,* 90–91.

[186] Marcy S. Sacks, *Before Harlem: The Black Experience in New York City before World War I* (Philadelphia: University of Pennsylvania Press, 2006), 58–59.

[187] Paula J. Giddings, *Ida: A Sword among Lions; Ida B. Wells and the Campaign against Lynching* (New York: HarperCollins, 2008), 448.

[188] Norrell, *Up From History,* 72, 97, 200.

[189] Ibid., 97.

[190] Livingstone College, *1887–1888 Catalogue,* 18–21.

[191] Ibid., 21–25.

[192] Fonvielle, *Reminiscences,* 13. Rev. Cicero Harris, one of the founders of Zion Wesley, went on to become a professor of mathematics and homiletics at Livingstone, as well as a member of the school's board of trustees. Ibid., 17; Livingstone College, *1887–1888 Catalogue.*

[193] Foner, *Reconstruction,* 425–429.

[194] Robert L. Zangrando, *The NAACP Crusade against Lynching, 1909–1960* (Philadelphia: Temple University Press, 1980), tables 1 and 2 (n.p.).

[195] Theodore Brantner Wilson, *The Black Codes of the South* (Tuscaloosa: University of Alabama Press, 1967), 107–108. Vagrancy was not the only offense that could send a black man to a forced labor camp. One could find men there who had been convicted for using obscene language, selling cotton after sunset, or violating a contract with a white employer. Douglas Blackmon, *Slavery by Another Name: The Re-Enslavement of Black Americans from the Civil War to World War II* (New York: Random House, 2008), 99.

[196] Blackmon, *Slavery by Another Name*, 55.

[197] Matthew J. Mancini, *One Dies, Get Another: Convict Leasing in the American South, 1866–1928* (Columbia: University of South Carolina Press, 1996), 60, 207.

[198] Blackmon, *Slavery by Another Name*, 90.

[199] "Life-Sketch of President W. J. Trent of Livingstone College," 1935, 1; Thomas, "Appointment to School Board."

[200] Randal Maurice Jelks, *Benjamin Elijah Mays, Schoolmaster of the Movement: A Biography* (Chapel Hill: University of North Carolina Press, 2012), 30–31. Mays did go away to school, and went on to become the president of Morehouse College. He served in that position for twenty-seven years. Ibid., 138, 229.

[201] Thomas, "Appointment to School Board."

[202] Greenwood, *Bittersweet Legacy*, 79, 81, 96; U.S. Federal Census (Washington, D.C.: Government Printing House, 1950).

[203] Charlotte-Mecklenburg Historic Landmarks Commission, "St. Peter's Episcopal Church" (1987), 5, http://www.landmarkscommission.org.

[204] Lemoine D. Pierce, "Charles Alston: An Appreciation," *The International Review of African American Art* 19, no. 4 (2004): 33, 36.

[205] Greenwood, *Bittersweet Legacy*, 98, 103–107. The words *"Deo Religio et Temperantiae"* ("God, Religion, and Temperance") are inscribed on the cornerstone of Grace's second church.

[206] Eugene Stitt, "Mr. Thad Lincoln Tate," in "An Appreciation of Twenty-One Men Who Have Rendered Long and Faithful Service in One Job" (1946), 8.

[207] http://charmeck.org/mecklenburg/county/ParkandRec/TrailOfHistory/ Pages/ThadTate. Tate ran his barber shop for the next sixty-one years. When he retired he simply gave the shop to two of the barbers who had worked with him for over twenty-seven years. Stitt, "Mr. Thad Lincoln Tate," 9. The Levine Museum of the New South in Charlotte houses, as a permanent exhibit, a barber shop with the original sign from Tate's barber shop on the front. The shop has vintage chairs just like those in his shop. The museum display also contains photographs of Tate, his family, and his home, as well as a statement about his contribution to Charlotte's black community. Thomas W. Hanchett, e-mail messages to author, September 19 and 20, 2013. In 2015 Mecklenburg County installed a sculpture of Tate on its Trail of History. See http:// charmeck.org, *supra*.

[208] "Tate Funeral Slated Monday," *The Charlotte Observer*, March 31, 1951; Nina Mjagkij, *Light in the Darkness: African Americans and the YMCA, 1852–1946* (Lexington: University Press of Kentucky, 1994), 34.

[209] Copy of wedding invitation in possession of author; "Mrs. W. J. Trent Passes," *Star of Zion*, June 14, 1934.

[210] YMCA of the USA, *YMCA in America, 1851–2001: A History of Accomplishment over 150 Years* (2000), inside front cover, 2.

[211] Michael McGeer, *A Fierce Discontent: The Rise and Fall of the Progressive Movement in America* (Oxford: Oxford University Press, 2003), 80.

[212] Jelks, *Benjamin Elijah Mays*, 44. The goals and strategies of the Social Gospel Movement and the Progressive Movement often overlapped. McGeer, *Fierce Discontent*, 80–81 (quoting two leaders in the Social Gospel Movement, Washington Gladden and Walter Rauschenbusch); Gorrell, *The Age of Social Responsibility*, 37. Both movements

wanted to transform individuals and American society, and both called for civic engagement to accomplish those goals.

[213] YMCA of the USA, *YMCA in America*, 6.

[214] Ibid., 1–2.

[215] Mjagkij, *Light in the Darkness*, 18.

[216] YMCA of the USA, *YMCA in America*, 4.

[217] Mjagkij, *Light in the Darkness*, 34. The Y movement was an idea that spoke to the spirit of the time: by 1894 there were over 500,000 Y members in 5,000 Ys around the world. YMCA of the USA, *YMCA in America*, 11.

[218] Addie D. Waite Hunton, *William Alphaeus Hunton: A Pioneer Prophet of Young Men* (New York: Association Press, 1938), 13–17.

[219] Ibid., 21.

[220] Ibid., 15.

[221] Thomas, "Appointment to School Board."

Chapter 2

[1] William Jacob Walls, *Joseph Charles Price: Educator and Race Leader* (Boston: Christopher Publishing House, 1943), 487; Lenwood G. Davis, "A History of Livingstone College, 1879–1957" (Ph.D. diss., Carnegie-Mellon University, 1979), 27.

[2] W. F. Fonvielle, *Reminiscences of College Days* (Raleigh: Edwards and Broughton, 1904), 13–14.

[3] Livingstone College, *Catalogue of the Officers and Students of Livingstone College, Salisbury, N.C., 1887–88* (hereafter *1887–88 Catalogue*) (Greensboro, NC: Thomas Brothers, Power Book and Job Printers, 1888), 30.

[4] C. R. Harris, "The Educational Work of the AME Zion Church," in Livingstone College, *The Southland* (January 1891) (hereafter *Southland*, 1891), 76.

[5] Harris, *Southland*, 1891, 79.

[6] According to Livingstone's *1887–1888 Catalogue,* during that academic year, the Collegiate Department had 24 students, 3 of whom were women. The Normal Department had 51 students, split fairly evenly between men and women. The largest department was the Preparatory Department, with 87 students, again split almost equally between men and women. The only department with no women was the English Theological Department, which had only two students. *1887–88 Catalogue*, 11–15.

    The numbers for the Preparatory Department are only suggestive. Grammar school grades started with E and went up to A. Pages 16 and 17 of the catalog are missing. There is, therefore, no record for the D and E classes, the beginning classes, which would have probably been the largest classes in the Preparatory Department.

[7] "Testimonial Dinner for Doctor William Johnson Trent," February 12, 1952, http://toto.lib.unca.edu/findingaids/mss/blackhigh/blackhigh/Biographies/trent_will. Accessed May 17, 2011.

[8] Mitchell Kachun, s.v. "Afro-American Council," in Nina Mjagkij, ed., *Organizing Black America: An Encyclopedia of African American Associations* (New York: Garland Publishing, 2001), 17; Shawn Leigh Alexander, ed., *T. Thomas Fortune, The Afro-American Agitator: A Collection of Writings, 1880–1928* (Gainesville: University Press

of Florida, 2008), 134–144. Journalist T. Thomas Fortune had been advocating for the creation of a national civil rights organization like this since 1884. In his speech at the 1890 Afro-American League convention, he listed the issues the organization should address, noted above. These would be the same issues addressed in the twentieth century by the Niagara Movement and the NAACP. Alexander, *Fortune*, 134–144. The League was formally disbanded in 1893. Mjagkij, *Organizing Black America*, 17–18.

[9] August Meier, *Negro Thought in America, 1880–1915: Racial Ideologies in the Age of Booker T. Washington* (Ann Arbor: University of Michigan Press, 1963), 70.

[10] W. E. B. Du Bois, "The Ruling Passion: An Estimate of Joseph C. Price," *The Crisis* 22/23 (March 1922): 225.

[11] Davis, "History of Livingstone College," 40.

[12] Paula J. Giddings, *Ida: A Sword among Lions* (New York: HarperCollins, 2008), 135.

[13] Robert J. Norrell, *Up from History: The Life of Booker T. Washington* (Cambridge, MA: Harvard University Press, 2009), 130.

[14] Walls, *Joseph Charles Price*, 92–93.

[15] Davis, "History of Livingstone College," 39; Du Bois, "Ruling Passion," 224–225.

[16] Paul R. Griffin, "Black Founders of Reconstruction Era Methodist Colleges: Daniel A. Payne, Joseph C. Price, and Isaac Lane, 1863–1890" (Ph.D. diss., Emory University, 1983), 16.

[17] Griffin, "Black Founders," 206–207.

[18] W. J. Trent, untitled review of the biography *Joseph Charles Price*, by Walls, *AME Zion Quarterly Review* (October 1943): 80.

[19] Davis, "History of Livingstone College," 52–53.

[20] Fonvielle, *Reminiscences*, 107.

[21] W. J. Trent, "The Fiftieth Anniversary of Livingstone College," *AME Zion Quarterly Review* 12, no. 3 (1932): 1.

[22] Davis, "History of Livingstone College," 69.

[23] Fonvielle, *Reminiscences*, 112–114.

[24] Davis, "History of Livingstone College," 87.

[25] Walls, *Joseph Charles Price*, 505. The fourth was Rev. Cicero R. Harris. Harris left Livingstone in 1889, before Trent arrived at the school, when Harris became a bishop of the AME Zion Church. Constance E. H. Daniel, "Two North Carolina Families: The Harrises and the Richardsons," *The Negro History Bulletin* 13, no.1 (October 1949): 6. But he retained his ties to the school. The *1887–1888 Catalogue* lists him as both a trustee and an officer of the board of trustees. Livingstone College, *1887–1888 Catalogue*.

[26] Fonvielle, *Reminiscences*, 114–116.

[27] Davis, "History of Livingstone College," 89.

[28] Fonvielle, *Reminiscences*, 119, 122. "Lady Principal" apparently did not mean head of the Preparatory Department. The 1911–1912 Livingstone catalog listed Victoria Richardson in that position. Tucker was listed in the faculty section, but she was listed after instructors in the Preparatory Department, and just before the resident physician and registrar, suggesting that her position was not related to teaching. Livingstone College, *Catalogue of Livingstone College, Salisbury N.C., 1911–1912* (Lynchburg, VA: J. P. Bell Company, 1911) (hereafter *1911–1912 Catalogue*), 4.

[29] The *1911–1912 Catalogue* states that the "Lady Principal" supervised housekeeping in the girls' dormitory and throughout the campus. It also states that Tucker had an M.A. degree and was teaching history and English in the normal school. Livingstone College, *1911–1912 Catalogue*, 11, 25. It is not clear whether she had this degree or was teaching these courses when Trent was a student.

[30] Norrell, *Up from History*, 99.

[31] William Jacob Walls, *The Romance of a College: An Evolution of the Auditorium* (New York: Vantage Press, 1963), 31.

[32] Fonvielle, *Reminiscences*, 119, 121.

[33] Ida Houston Jackson, "In Memory of the Late Mrs. A. C. V. Tucker," *Star of Zion*, March 13, 1924.

[34] Faculty member Goler was a minister and also had an M.A. degree. Fonvielle, *Reminiscenses*, 36. In the Industrial Department, men taught printing, "practical gardening" and farming; and women taught "fancy needle work," as well as dressmaking and cooking. Fonvielle, *Reminiscenses*, 36; William Johnson Campbell, "The Origin and Development of Livingstone College and Hood Theological Seminary of the African Methodist Episcopal Zion Church and the Progressive Administration of President William Johnson Trent" (B.D. thesis, Bachelor Hood Theological Seminary, Livingstone College, 1950), 18.

[35] Livingstone College, *1887–1888 Catalogue*, 11–15.

[36] Fonvielle, *Reminiscences*, 27–28, 39, 41, 43–44, 48–50, 59, 81.

[37] Mary Kaplan, *Solomon Carter Fuller: Where My Caravan Has Rested* (Lanham, MD: University Press of America, 2005), 10–13.

[38] Fonvielle, *Reminiscences,* 73.

[39] Walls, *Joseph Charles Price*, 292.

[40] Davis, "History of Livingstone College," 123.

[41] Fonvielle, *Reminiscences*, 69.

[42] Ibid., 74; Walls, *Joseph Charles Price*, 290.

[43] Livingstone College, *1887–1888 Catalogue*, 7.

[44] Ibid., 40.

[45] Fonvielle, *Reminiscences*, 17; "250 Years of Rowan County," *Salisbury Post*, April 6, 2003 (special magazine insert), 28.

[46] Fonvielle, *Reminiscences*, 20.

[47] Ibid., 21.

[48] Livingstone College, *1887–1888 Catalogue*, 6–7.

[49] Ibid., 7, 9. In this regard they were not unlike other black schools of the day. For example, there were similar rules at other black Methodist colleges, like Wilberforce College and Lane College. Griffin, "Black Founders," 218–220.

[50] Fonvielle, *Reminiscences*, 92.

[51] Nariye Purifoy Larke, "Student Traditions at Livingstone College," 55 (paper prepared as year-long project for honors course in sociology, under Livingstone sociology professor R. Clyde Minor). Larke wrote the paper some time between 1926 and 1934: Minor came to Livingstone as a professor of sociology in 1926, and Larke graduated from Livingstone in 1934. For the project, she interviewed, among others, President Price's widow, President Emeritus Goler, and President Trent. Ibid., i–ii.

[52] Fonvielle, *Reminiscences*, 62.

[53] Ibid., 23–29, 61–68.

[54] Heath Thomas, "Appointment to School Board Tribute to Trent," *Salisbury Evening Post*, July 22, 1951.

[55] Thomas, "Appointment to School Board."

[56] Benjamin Mays, *Born to Rebel* (New York: Charles Scribner's Sons, 1971), 38. This took place in 1911, an indication of how little had changed with respect to financing the education of black youth in the intervening twenty years.

[57] According to his son, W. J. Trent Jr., Trent Sr. told this story often, with a laugh.

[58] Fonvielle, *Reminiscences*, 61.

[59] Thomas, "Appointment to School Board."

[60] Livingstone College, *1887–1888 Catalogue*, 31.

[61] Ibid., 18–21.

[62] Joseph C. Price, "Has the Progress of the Negro Been Commensurate with His Opportunities?," address reported in Livingstone College, *Southland*, 1891, 127.

[63] Livingstone College, *1887–1888 Catalogue*, 18–19. I am assuming that students studied the same subjects and used the same textbooks when Trent was in the B class, in 1890. I am also assuming that if they had different subjects and texts, the differences were not great.

[64] M. F. Maury, *Manual of Geography: A Treatise on Mathematical, Physical and Political Geography* (New York: University Publishing Co., 1892), 16.

[65] Ibid., 116.

[66] William Swinton, *First Lessons in Our Country's History: Bringing Out Its Salient Points, and Aiming to Combine Simplicity with Sense* (New York: Ivison, Blakeman, Taylor, and Co., 1879).

[67] Ibid., 27.

[68] Ibid., 42.

[69] Ibid., 105.

[70] Ibid.

[71] Ibid., 106.

[72] Ibid., 107.

[73] As a slave owner, Washington separated families, sold children, authorized his overseers to use violent means of control, and sent troublesome slaves to the West Indies, where they were likely to die at hard labor. He also bought teenaged girls so they would have many years to bear children, thus increasing the number of his slaves. Six months before his death he wrote in his will that his 123 slaves should be freed upon the death of his wife. Henry Wiencek, *An Imperfect God: George Washington, His Slaves, and the Creation of America* (New York: Farrar, Straus and Giroux, 2003), 111, 120–123, 131–132, 179–181, 353–354.

[74] William T. Harris, Andrew J. Rickoff, Mark Bailey, *The Fourth Reader* (New York: American Book Company, 1878), 28–33.

[75] Ibid., 90–95. There are two additional excerpts written by a woman. They include two poems by Felicia Heman, one about spring, and the other, about a boy. Ibid., 26, 120.

[76] Ibid., 44–47 (Lewis Carroll, "What Alice Said to the Kitten"), 180–182 (John Byrom, "The Three Black Crows").

[77] Fonvielle, *Reminiscences*, 61.

[78] Thomas, "Appointment to School Board."

[79] Fonvielle, *Reminiscences*, 81.

[80] Ibid., 89–90.

[81] Trent, review of *Joseph Charles Price*, 80.

[82] Livingstone College, *Southland*, 1891, cover; N. C. Newbold, *Five North Carolina Negro Educators* (Chapel Hill: University of North Carolina Press, 1939), 6–7.

[83] *Southland*, 1891, 1.

[84] Livingstone College, *The Southland* 1, no.3 (May 1890) (hereafter *Southland*, 1890), 159.

[85] Leona C. Gabel, *From Slavery to the Sorbonne and Beyond: The Life and Writings of Anna J. Cooper* (Northampton, MA: Department of History of Smith College, 1982), 7–25.

[86] Newbold, *Five North Carolina Negro Educators*, 5. Cooper had also taught Atkins when he was much younger, at a school in Chatham County, North Carolina. Ibid.

[87] Cooper, *Southland*, 1890, 159.

[88] Ibid., 159–162.

[89] Eric Foner, *Reconstruction: America's Unfinished Revolution, 1863–1877* (New York: HarperCollins, 2002), 590.

[90] W. H. Goler, *Southland*, 1890, 223, 229.

[91] http://history.house.gov/people/Detail/17259?ret=True.

[92] John R. Lynch "Should the Colored Vote Divide?," *Southland*, 1890, 238.

[93] John Mitchell Jr., "Will a Division of the Negro Vote Help toward the Solution of the Race Problem?," *Southland*, 1890, 243.

[94] Thomas, "Appointment to School Board."

[95] Richard H. Brodhead, ed., *The Journals of Charles W. Chesnutt* (Durham, NC: Duke University Press, 1993), 42. The following month Chesnutt walked twenty-three miles in one day, still looking for a teaching job. Ibid., 43. Apparently, at that time, Chesnutt didn't have a spare dollar either.

[96] Thomas, "Appointment to School Board."

[97] Leroy Davis, *A Clashing of the Soul: John Hope and the Dilemma of African American Leadership and Black Higher Education in the Early Twentieth Century* (Athens: University of Georgia Press, 1998), 198, 224. Hope became president of the Atlanta Baptist College (later renamed Morehouse College) in 1906. Ibid., 162. But it is very likely that presidents of black colleges were performing this service much earlier, indeed, as soon as their schools opened.

[98] Davis, "History of Livingstone College," 125.

[99] Benjamin Mays, who later became president of Morehouse College, also supported himself during his school years in part by working as a Pullman porter. Mays, *Born to Rebel*, 61.

[100] Thomas, "Appointment to School Board."

[101] W. J. Trent, "Emancipation Address" (Asheville, NC, n.d.).

[102] Thomas, "Appointment to School Board."

[103] D. A. Tompkins, *History of Mecklenburg County and the City of Charlotte from 1740–1903,* vol. 2, Appendix (Charlotte, NC: Observer Printing House, 1903), 198.

[104] See: http://www.census.gov/population/www/documentation/twps0027/tab12.txt.

[105] Edwin G. Burrows and Mike Wallace, *Gotham: A History of New York City to 1898* (New York: Oxford University Press, 1999), 1050, 1055, 1063–1066.

[106] Ibid., 1057, 1071, 1074.

[107] Ibid., 1112.

[108] Ibid., 483.

[109] Marcy S. Sacks, *Before Harlem: The Black Experience in New York City before World War I* (Philadelphia: University of Pennsylvania Press, 2006), 48.

[110] Ibid., 16.

[111] Ibid., 34–35, 111–112, 124–125.

[112] Ibid., 89.

[113] Ibid., 42.

[114] Ibid., 138.

[115] Thomas, "Appointment to School Board."

[116] Larry Tye, *Rising from the Rails: Pullman Porters and the Making of the Black Middle Class* (New York: Henry Holt and Company, 2004), 28.

[117] Ibid., 86.

[118] Ibid., 48–51.

[119] Ibid., 56, 59–60.

[120] Ibid., 88.

[121] Ibid., 92.

[122] Ibid., 45–47.

[123] Ibid., 88–89.

[124] Ibid., 25.

[125] Ibid., 34. Perhaps the company representative meant "all white women traveling on the train" when he said "our wives."

[126] Ibid., 62.

[127] Ibid., 61.

[128] Thomas, "Appointment to School Board."

[129] William Sanders Scarborough, *The Autobiography of William Sanders Scarborough: An American Journey from Slavery to Scholarship* (Michele Valerie Ronnick, Introduction) (Detroit, MI: Wayne State University Press, 2005), 6–7.

[130] The Tennessee Encyclopedia of History and Culture, "George Whipple Hubbard," http://tennesseeencyclopedia.net/entry.php?rec=666. Accessed May 23, 2014.

[131] George A. Towns, "Phylon Profile, XVI: Horace Bumstead, Atlanta University President (1888–1907)," *Phylon* 9, no. 2 (2nd Qtr., 1948): 109–114.

[132] "Dr. Lucy Moten Praised as Great Miner Teacher," *The Afro-American*, February 9, 1952.

[133] Blackpast.org, "Frances Grimké, 1850–1937," Blackpast.org: An Online Reference Guide to African American History, http://www.blackpast.org/aah/grimke-francis-1850-1937. Accessed May 23, 2014; *Southland*, 1891, 4 (names of officers and directors).

[134] "Address to the Public," *Southland*, 1891, 8–11.

[135] "Night Session: Second Day," ibid., 127–128. Punctuation and emphasis added.

[136] Address to the Public," *Southland*, 1891, 11.

[137] H. N. Payne, "The Presbyterian Church (North)," *Southland*, 1981, 49–51.

[138] J. C. Hartzell, "Educational Work of the Methodist Episcopal Church in the Southern States," *Southland*, 1891, 65–68. "Collegiate schools" included normal schools, colleges, and schools of theology. A. F. Beard, "Resume of the Work of the AMA," *Southland*, 1891, 59–60.

---

[139] Beard, "Resume of the Work of the AMA," *Southland*, 1891, 56–61.

[140] Morning Session: Second Day, *Southland*, 1891, 123–124.

[141] Night Session: Second Day, *Southland*, 1891, 130.

[142] Walls, *Joseph Charles Price*, 429.

[143] Alfred Moss, "Alexander Crummell: Black Nationalist and Apostle of Western Civilization," in Leon Litwack and August Meier, eds., *Black Leaders of the Nineteenth Century* (Urbana: University of Illinois Press, 1988), 237–247. Crummell would later be the central figure in the creation of the American Negro Academy (ANA), a national organization of black intellectuals, who, he hoped, "would take the lead in 'shaping and directing' the opinions and habits of the crude masses.'" Moss, "Alexander Crummell," 246. One of his admirers, W. E. B. Du Bois, would use Crummell's understanding of the role of black intellectuals to develop his concept of the "talented tenth." J. R. Oldfield, ed., *Civilization and Black Progress: Selected Writings of Alexander Crummell on the South* (Charlottesville: University Press of Virginia, 1995), 20. It is a sign of the small size of the black intellectual elite at this time to note that Anna Julia Cooper stayed with Crummell and his wife when she first moved to Washington, DC, to take up her position at the M Street High School. Her most cherished friendship there was with Charlotte Forten Grimké, wife of Rev. Francis Grimké, who was on the board of directors of the American Association of Educators of Colored Youth with Price and Atkins. Gabel, *From Slavery*, 33–34; Livingstone College, *Southland*, 1891, 4.

[144] Joseph C. Price, "Intellectual Culture: A Necessity" (speech given in James City, NC, 1879), 9. The papers of Joseph C. Price are located in the Andrew Carnegie Library, Livingstone College, Salisbury, North Carolina.

[145] Unfortunately, we do not have a copy of that address. But we do have speeches Crummell made at other schools during this period, from which we can see themes he might well have put forward at Livingstone.

[146] Alexander Crummell, "Excellence, an End of the Trained Intellect," in Oldfield, *Civilization and Black Progress*, 116–118 (speech presented to the graduating class of a woman's high school in Washington, DC, June 6, 1884).

[147] Alexander Crummell, "Right-Mindedness: An Address before the Garnet Lyceum of Lincoln University," in Oldfield, *Civilization and Black Progress*, 144 (address delivered c. 1886).

[148] Ibid., 145.

[149] Alexander Crummell, "The Need of New Ideas and New Aims for a New Era," in Oldfield, *Civilization and Black Progress*, 129–130 (speech delivered to graduating class of Storer College, Harpers Ferry, WV, in May 1885).

[150] Crummell, "Excellence, an End of the Trained Intellect," 118.

[151] Walls, *Joseph Charles Price*, 283.

[152] Davis, "History of Livingstone College," 40.

[153] W. E. B. Du Bois, "Ruling Passion," 224.

[154] William J. Walls, *The African Methodist Episcopal Church: Reality of the Black Church* (hereafter *AME Zion*) (Charlotte, NC: AME Publishing House, 1974), 283. By the time he arrived at Livingstone Langston already had a distinguished and varied career—as an attorney; president of the National Equal Rights League; professor and then dean of the law school at Howard University; minister to the court of Port-au-Prince; president of Virginia Normal and Collegiate Institute in Petersburg, Virginia; and

Congressman from Virginia. William Cheek and Aimee Lee Cheek, "John Mercer Langston: Principle and Politics," in Leon Litwack and August Meier, eds., *Black Leaders of the Nineteenth Century* (Urbana and Chicago: University of Illinois Press, 1988), 113, 118, 122–123. Du Bois was commencement speaker at Livingstone several times. Walls, *Joseph Charles Price*, 282–283. Frederick Douglass, noted abolitionist and a prominent member of the AME Zion Church, had accepted the invitation to give the commencement speech at Livingstone in 1895, but died before then. Walls, *AME Zion*, 149–152; Walls, *Joseph Charles Price*, 284.

[155] Walls, *Joseph Charles Price*, 283–284.

[156] Sharon Harley, "Mary Church Terrell: Genteel Militant," in Litwack and Meier, eds., *Black Leaders*, 311.

[157] Walls, *Joseph Charles Price*, 283–284.

[158] Walls, *AME Zion*, 186.

[159] Other than Crummell, it is not clear which of the speakers listed above made presentations at Livingstone during Trent's student years. John Mercer Langston died in 1897; Frances Willard, 1898; and Booker T. Washington, 1901. Mary Church Terrell lived until 1954, and W. E. B. Du Bois lived until 1963. Although these speakers could have made their presentation at Livingstone between 1890 and 1898 (Trent's student years), they could also have come before or later.

[160] Gabel, *From Slavery to the Sorbonne*, 31.

[161] Anna Julia Cooper, *A Voice from the South by a Black Woman of the South* (Xenia, OH: Aldine Printing House, 1891; reprint, New York and Oxford: Oxford University Press, 1988), 74. The two women graduates of Livingstone College were Esther Carthey, noted earlier as the first graduate of the college, and Ellen Dade, Livingstone's music teacher. Livingstone College, *1911–1912 Catalogue*, 61.

[162] Cooper, *Voice from the South*, 70–71.

[163] Ibid., 95–96.

[164] Ibid., 134.

[165] Ibid., 142. The selection taken from *The Southland* essay reappears in Cooper's essay "The Status of Women in America," in *Voice from the South*, at pages 142–145. In her book, the date given for this essay is 1892.

[166] In *Anna Julia Cooper, Visionary Black Feminist: A Critical Introduction* (New York: Routledge, 2007), Vivian M. May gives 1891 as the date of Cooper's first publication. Ibid., 8. But since *The Southland* essay was published in May 1890, this is not correct.

[167] "Testimonial Dinner for Doctor William Johnson Trent."

[168] "250 Years of Rowan County," 28; "Black Colleges Celebrate Centennial," *Hendersonville Times-News*, October 17, 1992; Davis, "History of Livingstone College," 117.

[169] Davis, "History of Livingstone College," 117.

[170] "250 Years of Rowan County," 28. Biddle University is now Johnson C. Smith University. One hundred years later—on October 16, 1992—10,217 people jammed the 7,000 seats in Livingstone's Alumni Stadium to watch Livingstone play Johnson C. Smith again. Brian Tomlin, "Thousands Celebrate a Centennial Season," *News and Record* (Greensboro, NC), October 18, 1992.

[171] "250 Years of Rowan County," 28.

[172] "Bull Pen Football," *Johnson C. Smith University Archives,* http://archives.jcsu.edu/echo/Bull%20Pen/Football_main. Accessed May 17, 2011.

[173] "Black Colleges Celebrate Centennial."

[174] "First Black College Football Game Played!" *The African American Registry,* www.aaregistry.com/african_american_history/1812/First_Black_college_football_game. Accessed April 4, 2008.

[175] "75-Year-Old Educator Recalls 1897 Shaw-St. Augustine Feud" (clipping does not contain name of newspaper or date).

[176] Campbell, "Origin and Development," 39.

[177] Brian Holloway, offensive lineman for the New England Patriots, 1981–1988 and five-time NFL All-Pro, e-mail message to author, March 17, 2010. One of these players is Santonio Holmes, Most Valuable Player in Super Bowl 2009. Lindsay H. Jones, "The Favorite Sons of Muck City" *Denver Post,* January 28, 2009 ("There was never denying Holmes' speed. He developed it by chasing rabbits in the sugar cane fields with the other boys."), www.denverpost.com/portlet/article/html/gragments/print_article.jsp?articleId=1156. Accessed March 17, 2010.

[178] Holloway, e-mail message to author, March 17, 2010.

[179] Addie W. Hunton, *William Alphaeus Hunton: A Pioneer Prophet of Young Men* (New York: Association Press, 1938), 62.

[180] Nina Mjagkij, *Light in the Darkness: African Americans and the YMCA, 1852–1946* (Lexington: University Press of Kentucky, 1994), 34.

[181] Mjagkij, *Light in the Darkness,* 34. By 1911, more than a third of all young men in the black colleges were members of YMCA organizations on campus. Hunton, *William Alphaeus Hunton,* 62.

[182] John Jamison Moore, *History of the AME Zion Church in America* (York, PA: Teachers' Journal Office, 1884), www.docsouth.unc.edu/church/...moore.html., 340–341.

[183] YMCA, *The Colored Men's Department of the Young Men's Christian Association* (New York: The International Committee of Young Men's Christian Associations, 1894), 11–12, 25. The seven schools represented at the 1892 conference included colleges, universities, seminaries, normal and industrial schools, and theological institutions. Ibid.

[184] YMCA, "Seventh Annual Conference," *The Messenger* 1, no. 2 (December 1896): 1.

[185] W. A. Hunton, "The Association Movement among the Colored Colleges," *The Intercollegian* 21, no. 5 (February 1899): 110.

[186] "News from the Associations," *Association Men,* December 1899, 104.

[187] YMCA, *College Bulletin* 1, no. 4 (February 1879): 1.

[188] YMCA, *Colored Men's Department,* 21–22.

[189] YMCA, *College Bulletin* 8, no. 4 (January 1886): 15.

[190] YMCA, *Colored Men's Department,* 6–7.

[191] Fonvielle, *Reminiscences,* 66–67.

[192] Ibid., 61.

[193] Walls, *Joseph Charles Price,* 261; YMCA, *Colored Men's Department,* 7. Livingstone also sponsored a branch of the Young Women's Christian Temperance Union (YWCTU). Women in this organization made annual visits to the poorhouse, carrying boxes of lunch, books, hymnals, and Bibles. They also held prayer meetings, Bible classes, and oratorical contests. Fonvielle, *Reminiscences,* 121.

194 "Conversion" in this context does not mean being converted from, for example, Judaism to Christianity. It means being born anew by repenting for one's sins, believing in "the Lord Jesus Christ," and experiencing the presence of the Holy Spirit. Walls, *AME Zion*, 98.

195 Joseph Charles Price, "Address Delivered at the Anniversary of the Boston YMCA, Sunday Evening, May 25, 1884," 1.

196 Mjagkij, *Light in the Darkness*, 33.

197 Ibid., 38.

198 Fonvielle, *Reminiscences,* 45.

199 Ibid., 64–65.

200 Larke, "Student Traditions," 52–53. Apparently the best "Examiner" was an African student, who would appear for the interrogation in African dress and ask the questions in his native language. Ibid.

201 Fonvielle, *Reminiscences*, 64–65.

202 Scott E. Giltner, e-mail message to author, May 19, 2010.

203 Thomas, "Appointment to School Board."

204 Fonvielle, *Reminiscences*, 100–101.

205 Walls, *AME Zion*, 506.

206 Walls, *Joseph Charles Price*, 70–71.

207 Ibid., 64.

208 Ibid., 70–71. Price suffered from Bright's disease. Ibid.

209 Walls, *Joseph Charles Price*, 70–76.

210 John W. Cromwell, *The Negro in American History: Men and Women Eminent in the Evolution of the American of African Descent* (1914; repr., New York: Johnson,1968), 178.

211 Walls, *Joseph Charles Price*, 70–76.

212 Ibid., 292–293. Livingstone College had invited Trent to make a speech for Founder's Day in 1902, a signal honor for a young man who had graduated from that school only four years earlier. Ibid.

213 W. J. Trent, "Founder's Day," in Walter L. Yates, *He Spoke Now They Speak: A Collection of Speeches and Writings of and on the Life and Works of J. C. Price* (Salisbury, NC: Hood Theological Seminary, 1952), iii, v; "Testimonial Dinner."

214 "Testimonial Dinner."

215 David Henry Bradley Sr., *A History of the AME Zion Church, Part II, 1872–1968* (Nashville, TN: Parthenon Press, 1970), 409.

216 The goal of the mission was to train young men to study in America, then to return for service in Africa. Edwin W. Smith, *Aggrey of Africa: A Study in Black and White* (Freeport, NY: Books for Libraries Press, 1971), 57.

217 Ibid., 39–52.

218 Ibid., 101–105 (letter from Aggrey to Trent, dated August 26, 1914: "Pray for me, Zeus, that I may be always humble and allow God to use me," quote at 105).

219 Judith Nina Kerr, "God-Given Work: The Life and Times of Sculptor Meta Vaux Warrick Fuller: 1877–1968" (Ph.D. diss., University of Massachusetts, 1986), 157. Fuller's paternal grandfather, born a slave in Virginia, purchased his freedom, bought the indenture of his future wife, and immigrated to Liberia in 1852. His maternal grandparents both went to Liberia in 1829 as missionary doctors. Ibid., 391.

[220] Walls funeral program; "William J. Walls, AME Zion Bishop," *New York Times*, April 24, 1975, 38.

[221] Davis, "History of Livingstone College," 135.

[222] William J. Walls to W. J. Trent, March 4, 1950. They met in Asheville. W. J. Trent to W. J. Walls, July 20, 1956. This was perhaps when Trent was working there during his college years.

[223] Walls, *Joseph Charles Price*, 455.

[224] Livingstone College, *1887–1888 Catalogue*, 19–23. The courses offered by the college expanded fairly rapidly. A student in the college between 1898 and 1902 also studied German, Shakespeare, Restoration poetry, comparative literature, ancient and modern history, and zoology. Smith, *Aggrey of Africa*, 59–60.

[225] Rufus E. Clement, "A History of Negro Education in North Carolina 1865–1928" (Ph.D. diss., Northwestern University, 1930), 145.

[226] Livingstone College, *1887–1888 Catalogue*, 23; Joseph Butler, *The Analogy of Religion, Natural and Revealed, to the Constitution and Course of Nature* (London: H.G. Bohn, 1852). Butler's *Analogy* was originally published in 1736 and had a reputation for being particularly difficult to understand. The 1852 edition of Butler's *Analogy* that the library found for me included an eighty-two-page outline of the book, written in the early nineteenth century by a professor who noted "the difficulties encountered by students in grasping the subtle, and not always happily expressed, argument of the Analogy." Ibid., iv. In that same copy, a student had written inside the front cover, on January 26, 1867: "Let those who enter here leave hope behind!"

[227] Mjagkij, *Light in the Darkness*, 37–38.

[228] Ibid., 54.

[229] Ibid.

[230] Ibid.

[231] Ibid., 56–57.

[232] Although the United States called this a war of "neutral intervention," entered into solely to stop the fighting between Spain and Cuba, in reality the United States had long wanted to own Cuba and saw the struggle of the Cuban people for independence as its opportunity to gain control of the island. Louis A. Pérez Jr., *The War of 1898: The United States and Cuba in History and Historiography* (Chapel Hill: University of North Carolina Press, 1998), 4–5, 18–19.

[233] C. Howard Hopkins, *History of the YMCA in North America* (New York: Association Press, 1951), 453–454.

[234] Hunton, *William Alphaeus Hunton*, 45.

[235] Ibid., 45–46.

[236] Mjagkij, *Light in the Darkness*, 47–48.

[237] Hunton, *William Alphaeus Hunton*, 46.

[238] YMCA, *Colored Men's Department*, 10–13, 14, 25; Colored Men's Department of Young Men's Christian Association of North America, "Seventh Annual Conference (Eastern Section) of Colored Young Men's Christian Associations, November 26–29, 1896: Association Topics," *The Messenger* 1, no. 2 (December 1896): 1.

[239] Fonvielle, *Reminiscences*, 61.

[240] Ibid.; Thomas, "Appointment to School Board."

[241] Glenda Elizabeth Gilmore, *Gender and Jim Crow: Women and the Politics of White Supremacy in North Carolina, 1896–1920* (Chapel Hill: University of North Carolina Press, 1996), 63.

[242] Livingstone College, "The Sixteenth Annual Commencement of Livingstone College, Salisbury, N.C., May 18–25, 1898," cover.

[243] Thomas, "Appointment to School Board."

[244] George Alexander Brooks Sr., *Peerless Laymen in the African Methodist Episcopal Zion Church* (State College, PA: Himes Printing Company, Inc., 1974), 1:140.

[245] Trent, Walker, and Clement were three of the four graduates in his class. The fourth was W.A. Peggans. Livingstone College, "Sixteenth Annual Commencement of Livingstone College" (n.p.).

[246] Brooks, *Peerless Laymen*, 1:32, 140; Livingstone College, *1911–1912 Catalogue*, 68.

[247] Livingstone College, *1911–1912 Catalogue*, 61–62.

[248] Walls, *Joseph C. Price*, 53–54.

[249] Gilmore, *Gender and Jim Crow*, 11.

[250] Josephine Price Sherrill, "Joseph Charles Price: Impressions of a Daughter," *The Living Stone* (Founder's Day Edition, February 1957), 4.

Chapter 3

[1] Joseph C. Price, "The Race Problem Stated," in Carter G. Woodson, ed., *Negro Orators and Their Orations* (New York: Russell and Russell, 1969), 490.

[2] Frenise A. Logan, *The Negro in North Carolina, 1876–1894* (Chapel Hill: University of North Carolina Press, 1964), 180.

[3] *Plessy v. Ferguson*, 163 U.S. 537 (1896).

[4] Rufus E. Clement, "A History of Negro Education in North Carolina, 1865–1928" (Ph.D. diss., Northwestern University, 1930), 129, 136.

[5] Glenda Elizabeth Gilmore, *Gender and Jim Crow: Women and the Politics of White Supremacy in North Carolina, 1896–1920* (Chapel Hill: University of North Carolina Press, 1996), 82–89.

[6] Louis A. Pérez Jr., *The War of 1898: The United States and Cuba in History and Historiography* (Chapel Hill: University of North Carolina Press, 1998), 4–5, 11–12.

[7] Ibid., 18–19.

[8] Ibid., 21. This congressional resolution also "disclaim[ed] any [...] intention to exercise sovereignty, jurisdiction, or control over said island, except for the pacification thereof, and assert[ed] its determination, when that [was] accomplished, to leave the government and control of the island to its people." Ibid. This would not happen. In January 1899, the United States began the military occupation of Cuba. In 1901, under United States congressional authority, the new Cuban government was denied the right to enter into agreements with foreign powers and was forced to both cede land to the United States for a military base and to grant the United States the right to intervene in order to maintain a government that was "adequate" to protect life, liberty, and property in Cuba. Ibid., 32–33.

[9] Marvin Fletcher, "The Black Volunteers in the Spanish-American War," *Military Affairs* 38, no. 2 (April 1974): 48.

[10] Jack D. Foner, *Blacks and the Military in American History: A New Perspective* (New York: Praeger Publishers, 1974), 86.

[11] This was an astonishingly high number of black soldiers: in the entire regular army, there were only 3,339 men in 4 Colored Regiments. War Department Adjutant General's Office to Mr. James Howard, memorandum, August 3, 1916, in Morris J. MacGregor and Bernard C. Nalty, eds., *Freedom and Jim Crow, 1865–1917,* vol. 3 of *Blacks in the United States Armed Forces: Basic Documents* (Wilmington, DE: Scholarly Resources, 1977), 159.

[12] Willard B. Gatewood Jr., "North Carolina's Negro Regiment in the Spanish-American War," *The North Carolina Historical Review* 48, no. 4 (October 1971): 373, 375.

[13] Ibid., 375 (battalion expanded); Captain Thomas L. Leatherwood, "The Military and Historical Portrait Group of the Officers of the Third North Carolina U.S.V. Infantry in the War with Spain," undated poster, Asheville, NC (hereafter Leatherwood poster). The poster has 36 photographs and thumbnail sketches of 34 of the 40 officers of the Third North Carolina.

[14] Gatewood, "North Carolina's Negro Regiment," 377.

[15] There were four all-black regiments in the regular army in 1898, but they had white officers. Joseph F. Steelman, *North Carolina's Role in the Spanish-American War* (Raleigh: Division of Archives and History, North Carolina Department of Cultural Resources, 1975), 23.

[16] Gatewood, "North Carolina's Negro Regiment," 372–373.

[17] Edward A. Johnson, *History of Negro Soldiers in the Spanish-American War and Other Items of Interest* (Raleigh: Capital Printing, 1899), 92.

[18] Foner, *Blacks and the Military*, 72–73.

[19] Philip S. Foner, *From the Era of Annexationism to the Outbreak of the Second War for Independence (1845–1895)*, vol. 2 of *A History of Cuba and Its Relation with the United States* (New York: International Publishers, 1962), 342–345.

[20] The resolution also requested that some of the bishops convey the resolution to the president in person. *Record of the Doings of the Board of Bishops of the AME Zion Connection*, bk. 2 (1898), 132–133.

[21] Philip S. Foner and J. Syme-Hastings, "A Tribute to Antonio Maceo," *Journal of Negro History* 55, no. 1 (January 1970): 65.

[22] Leatherwood poster.

[23] Steelman, *North Carolina's Role*, 24.

[24] Ibid., 25.

[25] Johnson, *History of Negro Soldiers*, 109–110. While this is a description of Camp Haskell, in Georgia, where the Third North Carolina would later be assigned, all military camps of the day were laid out in the same basic way. Marvin E. Fletcher, *The Black Soldier and Officer in the United States Army, 1891–1917* (Columbia: University of Missouri Press, 1974), 79.

[26] Fletcher, "Black Volunteers," 50; Fletcher, *Black Soldier*, 80.

[27] "Third North Carolina," *The Journal and Tribune* (Knoxville, TN), October 3, 1898; October 5; October 9; October 12.

[28] Fletcher, "Black Volunteers," 50.

[29] "Third North Carolina," October 3, 1898, and October 10, 1898.

[30] Young Men's Christian Association (YMCA), "YMCA Tents in the Army," *Christian Observer*, 1898.

[31] YMCA, "At the Front with the Boys in Blue," Army Edition, Secretarial Newsletter 2, no. 1 (July 1898, Cleveland): 1–2.

[32] Ibid., 1.

[33] Fletcher, *Black Soldier*, 10.

[34] Ibid., 77.

[35] MacGregor and Nalty, *Freedom and Jim Crow*, 160–161.

[36] YMCA, "At the Front."

[37] Leatherwood poster.

[38] W. F. Fonvieille, *Reminiscences of College Days* (Raleigh, NC: Edwards and Broughton, 1904), 137.

[39] "Third North Carolina," October 6, 1898.

[40] YMCA, "Army and Navy Christian Commission of the Young Men's Christian Associations" (1898), 2.

[41] YMCA, "At the Front," 2.

[42] YMCA, "Army and Navy Christian Commission," 2.

[43] Ibid.

[44] All four of the doctors in the regiment were graduates of Shaw's medical school. Leatherwood poster.

[45] Ibid.

[46] Frank Hollowell White, "The Economic and Social Development of Negroes in North Carolina since 1900" (Ph.D. diss., New York University, 1960), 10.

[47] Leatherwood poster.

[48] Ibid.

[49] *Year-Book of All Souls' Church, 1898*, Year-Books of All Souls' Parish, 1897–1907 (Biltmore, NC: Missionary Jurisdiction of Asheville, 1907), 26 (September).

[50] Leatherwood poster; "Harrison B. Brown," http://toto.lib.unca.edu/findingaids/mss/blackhigh/biography/brown_h_b. html. Brown's law office was right in the middle of the city, on Court Square, now Pack Square.

[51] Fletcher, "Black Volunteers," 51.

[52] John Jacob Beck, "Development in the Piedmont South: Rowan County, North Carolina, 1850–1900" (Ph.D. diss., University of North Carolina, 1984), 235.

[53] H. Leon Prather Sr., "We Have Taken a City," in David S. Cecelski and Timothy B. Tyson, eds., *Democracy Betrayed: The Wilmington Race Riot of 1898 and Its Legacy* (Chapel Hill: University of North Carolina Press, 1998), 31–33; Gilmore, *Gender and Jim Crow*, 111,114.

[54] Prather, "We Have Taken a City," 35–36; Gilmore, *Gender and Jim Crow*, 114.

[55] Gatewood, "North Carolina's Negro Regiment," 372; Leatherwood poster.

[56] Gilmore, *Gender and Jim Crow*, 113.

[57] 1898 Wilmington Race Riot Commission, *1898 Wilmington Race Riot Report* (North Carolina Department of Cultural Resources, Office of Archives and History, May 31, 2006), 57.

[58] The percentage of black soldiers in the Third North Carolina who were arrested during this period was not greater than the percentage in any other regiment. Johnson, *History of*

Negro Soldiers, 112. This suggests that there was not a higher rate of desertion among the black soldiers in the Third North Carolina after the Wilmington massacre.

[59] Gatewood, "North Carolina's Negro Regiment," 383 n.41.

[60] "Third North Carolina," October 5, 1898.

[61] Johnson, *History of Negro Soldiers*, 108–111. Meserve stated that it was the presence of so many former Shaw students in the Third North Carolina that led him to investigate the regiment. Ibid., 109.

[62] Foner, *Blacks and the Military*, 87–88.

[63] Gatewood, "North Carolina's Negro Regiment," 385.

[64] Fletcher, "Black Volunteers," 52.

[65] Foner, *Blacks and the Military*, 88.

[66] Janette Thomas Greenwood, *Bittersweet Legacy: The Black and White "Better Classes" in Charlotte, 1850–1910* (Chapel Hill: University of North Carolina Press, 1994), 200, 205.

[67] Steelman, *North Carolina's Role*, 27; W. J. Trent to Charles McNamee, February 17, 1900, Superintendent's Office Incoming Correspondence Collection (hereafter Incoming), Box (B) 77, Folder (F) 11, Biltmore Estate Archive, Asheville, North Carolina (BEA).

[68] Robert J. Norrell, *Up from History: The Life of Booker T. Washington* (Cambridge, MA: Harvard University Press, 2009), 72–73.

[69] Thomas, "Appointment to School Board."

[70] William Jacob Walls, *The African Methodist Episcopal Zion Church: Reality of the Black Church* (Charlotte: AME Zion Publishing House, 1974) (hereafter *AME Zion*), 325; C. R. Harris, "The Educational Work of the AME Zion Church," *The Southland* (January 1891), 80–81.

[71] Walls, *AME Zion*, 602. It is not clear what kind of school it was when Trent was there. W. J. Trent to C. McNamee, February 17, 1900; W. J. Trent to C. McNamee, April 24, 1900, Incoming, B77F11, BEA. The church leased the building and grounds to the city in 1932, and subsequently sold it. Walls, *AME Zion*, 325.

[72] William J. Trent, speech at Young Men's Institute, Asheville, March 25, 1945 (hereafter YMI speech).

[73] Trent, YMI speech.

[74] George Washington Vanderbilt was one of the grandsons of wealthy businessman Cornelius "Commodore" Vanderbilt.

[75] John M. Bryan, *Biltmore Estate: The Most Distinguished Private Place* (New York: Rizzoli, 1994), 10, 87–88.

[76] Bryan, *Biltmore Estate*, 110–111; Nan K. Chase, *Asheville: A History* (Jefferson, NC: McFarland and Company, 2007), 65, 69.

[77] Chase, *Asheville*, 69.

[78] Bryan, *Biltmore Estate*, 94.

[79] Chase, *Asheville*, 42.

[80] "Colored YMCA," *Asheville Daily Citizen*, September 1, 1890.

[81] "The Christian Institute," *Asheville Daily Citizen*, April 20, 1892.

[82] "For the Colored People," *Asheville Daily Citizen*, September 10, 1891.

[83] "The Christian Institute."

[84] Fenton H. Harris, *Short History and Report of Young Men's Institute, Incorporated* (Asheville, 1937), 3.

[85] W. J. Trent to Edward Harding, November 1, 1900, Incoming, B77F11, BEA; W. J. Trent to E. Harding, January 7, 1901, Incoming, B77F12, BEA.

[86] Harris, *Short History*, 3.

[87] "Young Men's Institute," *Asheville Daily Citizen*, February 13, 1893.

[88] The other trustee was Rev. W. J. Erdman. Harris, *Short History*, 3.

[89] Marie Louise Boyer, *Early Days: All Souls' Church and Biltmore Village* (privately printed in Biltmore, NC, for the Women's Guild of All Souls' Church, 1933), 19–20.

[90] W. J. Trent to C. McNamee, February 17, 1900.

[91] W. J. Trent to Rodney Rush Swope, April 24, 1900, Incoming, B77F11, BEA; Leatherwood poster.

[92] W. B. Fenderson to R. R. Swope, March 20, 1900, Incoming, B26F45, BEA. The black leadership class in North Carolina was so small in 1890 that we shouldn't be surprised to learn that Fenderson was a graduate of both Livingstone's normal school and college. Fonvieille, *Reminiscences*, 135–136. In 1900 he was pastor at Hopkins Chapel AME Church in Asheville, where Thomas Leatherwood was a parishioner. Hopkins Chapel AME Church, *The Hopkins Chapel African Methodist Episcopal Church Centennial Journal* (Asheville, NC, 1968), 11–12.

[93] Carrons Robinson to C. McNamee, March 18, 1900, Incoming, B67F34, BEA.

[94] C. McNamee to W. J. Trent, May 14, 1900, Superintendent's Office Outgoing Correspondence Collection (hereafter Outgoing), 27:443, BEA.

[95] C. McNamee to W. J. Trent, May 22, 1900, Outgoing, 27:516, BEA.

[96] W. J. Trent to C. McNamee, May 26, 1900, Incoming, B9F11, BEA.

[97] Chase, *Asheville*, 29–30.

[98] U.S. Department of the Interior, National Park Service, *Historic Resources of Downtown Asheville, National Register of Historic Places—Inventory Nomination Form*, signed by David R. Black, John W. Clauser, and Jim Sumner (September 14, 1978), item 7, page 1, and item 8, page 6.

[99] I visited the Young Men's Institute May 17, 2011.

[100] U.S. Department of the Interior, National Park Service, *National Register of Historic Places Inventory, Nomination Form: Young Men's Institute*, Catherine W. Bishir et al. (nomination certified by State Historic Preservation Officer May 12, 1977). The building was designated as historic property May 7, 1981. City Ordinance 1212 (*An Ordinance Designating a Building and Property Known as "YMI Building" Located on Market and Eagle Streets in Buncombe County as Historic Property)*; National Park Service, "Young Men's Institute Building," National Register of Historic Places Travel Itinerary: Asheville, NC, www.nps.gov/nr/travel/asheville/you.htm.

[101] William J. Walls, introduction, *Centennial Journal*.

[102] C. McNamee to W. J. Trent, May 22, 1900; Asheville City Directory, 1900–1901.

[103] Harris, *Short History*, 3.

[104] E. Harding to R. R. Swope, November 7, 1904, Outgoing, 38:610, BEA.

[105] Chase, *Asheville*, 64.

[106] Trent, YMI speech.

[107] *Year-Book of All Souls' Church, 1900*, 52.

[108] *Year-Book of All Souls' Church, 1898*, 26–27; *Year-Book of All Souls' Church, 1899*, 44.

[109] *Year-Book of All Souls' Church, 1900*, 52–53.

[110] W. J. Trent to C. McNamee, Incoming, B77F11, BEA (monthly reports dated June 1, August 1, and September 1, 1900; July report missing).

[111] Bryan, *Biltmore Estate*, 88. Because of this meticulous system, over a hundred years later, in 2011, Biltmore archivist Jill Hawkins was able to retrieve all correspondence involving Trent for me within only a few days.

[112] *Year-Book of All Souls' Church,1901*, 56–60; W. J. Trent to E. Harding, November 10, 1900, Incoming, B77F11, BEA.

[113] C. McNamee to W. J. Trent, May 7, 1901, Outgoing, 30:307, BEA (unsigned, but on same page as signed letter from McNamee to Trent).

[114] E. Harding to W. J. Trent, February 10, 1902, Outgoing, 32:261, BEA.

[115] W. J. Trent to E. Harding, February 11, 1902, Incoming, B77F13, BEA.

[116] W. J. Trent, *Annual Report*, Young Men's Institute (June 1, 1902), 56.

[117] Angela M. Hornsby, "'The Boy Problem': North Carolina Race Men Groom the Next Generation, 1900–1930," *Journal of Negro History* 86, no. 3 (Summer 2001): 293.

[118] W. J. Trent, *Annual Report*, Young Men's Institute (June 1, 1905), 39–40.

[119] W. J. Trent, *Monthly Report*, Young Men's Institute (April 30, 1904); W. J. Trent to E. Harding, November 1, 1900, Incoming, B77F11, BEA.

[120] "Colored Women Swell YMI Fund," n.d., newspaper name not given, but included with 1910 articles at Pack Memorial Library in Asheville.

[121] W. J. Trent to C. McNamee, November 22, 1900, Incoming, B77F11, BEA; W. J. Trent to E. Harding, November 24, 1903, Incoming, B93F2, BEA; "City News," *Asheville Gazette-News*, May 20, 1904.

[122] William Jacob Walls, *Joseph Charles Price: Educator and Race Leader* (Boston: Christopher Publishing House, 1943), 292–293.

[123] William Johnson Trent, "What Improvements Should Be Made in Our Churches," in I. Garland Penn and J. W. E. Bowen, eds., *The United Negro: His Problems and His Progress* (Atlanta: D. E. Luther Publishing Co., 1902), iii, v.

[124] Ibid., 159–160.

[125] "And Jesus went into the temple of God, and cast out all them that sold and bought in the temple, and overthrew the tables of the moneychangers, and the seats of them that sold doves, And said unto them, It is written, My house shall be called the house of prayer; but ye have made it a den of thieves." Matthew 21:12–13 (King James Version).

[126] Trent, "What Improvements," 150–151.

[127] Bob Terrell, *Historic Asheville* (Alexander, NC: WorldComm Press, 1997), 170. The white library was so well developed that in 1904 the executive committee of the Asheville Library Association decided to improve the third floor of the building, and learned that the library had just purchased 250 new books. "City News," *Asheville Gazette-News*, May 11, 1904. Black residents would not get a public library until 1927. Lenwood Davis, *The Black Heritage of Western North Carolina* (Asheville, 1983), 34.

[128] Lucy Mae Harrison, Oral History Register, Black Highlander Collection, Ramsey Library, University of North Carolina–Asheville, audiocassette 2, side 2, II/2/36, OH-VOA H372 Lu; electronic record issued July 5, 2001.

[129] W. J. Trent to C. McNamee, *Monthly Report*, September 30, 1902, Incoming, B77F13, BEA.

[130] W. J. Trent to C. McNamee, March 21, 1903, Incoming, B93F2, BEA. The novel *The Marrow of Tradition* is about the 1898 Wilmington massacre.

[131] We can also see that Trent paid attention to what new books by black Americans were being published: three of the books on this list had been published in either the year he bought them or the previous year. It might well be a sign of the popularity of the institute's library that Trent eventually had to buy a bookcase with locks to solve the problem of books' disappearing. W. J. Trent to C. McNamee, March 21, 1903, Incoming, B93F2, BEA.

[132] Charles Blackburn Jr., "Making History," in *Our State: Down Home in North Carolina*, September 2006, 4, http://shaw.edu/assets/Making_History.pdf; Freeman Irby Stephens, MD, "Medicine in Asheville: 1800–2000,"n.d., n.p., unpublished manuscript; W. J. Trent to C. McNamee, *Monthly Report*, October 31, 1902, Incoming, B77F13, BEA; W. J. Trent to C. McNamee, *Monthly Report*, December 31, 1902, Incoming, B77F13, BEA.

[133] Hopkins Chapel, *Centennial Journal*, 11.

[134] Livingstone College, *Catalogue of Livingstone College, Salisbury, N.C., 1911–1912* (Lynchburg, VA: J. P. Bell Company, 1911), 21.

[135] Angela Hornsby-Gutting, *Black Manhood and Community Building in North Carolina, 1900-1930* (Gainesville: University Press of Florida, 2009), 89–90.

[136] Indenture (Buncombe County, NC, June 18, 1902), bk.123:430.

[137] Altona Malinda Trent Johns, "Some Recollections" (undated), 1, 4 (Johns was the only child of W. J. Trent and Anna Belle Trent); Altona Anderson Mitchell, Ancestry.com. *North Carolina, Death Certificates, 1909–1976*. Provo, UT: Ancestry.com Operations Inc., 2007; William Mitchell, Ancestry.com. *North Carolina, Death Certificates, 1909–1975*. Provo, UT: Ancestry.com Operations Inc., 2007.

[138] "W. J. Trent Welcome," *Star of Zion*, June 4, 1925.

[139] White, "Economic and Social Development," 8, 10.

[140] Johns, "Some Recollections." Both Anna Belle and Eleanora played piano for the YMI. W. J. Trent to E. Harding, *Monthly Reports*, February 2, 1905, and June 30, 1905, Incoming, B93F2, BEA.

[141] W. J. Trent, "The Celebration of Emancipation Day," *Asheville Citizen*, January 4, 1904; Julius (surname illegible), "Grand Celebration of the Emancipation of the Negro," *Asheville Citizen*, January 2, 1904.

[142] W. J. Trent, "Service at the YMI," *Asheville Gazette-News*, January 6, 1904. See also the following articles by Trent in the same newspaper: "At the YMI," January 5, 1904; "Good meeting at YMI," January 9, 1904.

[143] "Sumptuous Feast," *Asheville Citizen*, February 16, 1904.

[144] W. J. Trent to C. McNamee, March 4, 1904, Incoming, B93F2, BEA.

[145] Edwin W. Smith, *Aggrey of Africa: A Study in Black and White* (Freeport, NY: Libraries Press, 1971), 67; Johns, "Some Recollections," 4; George Alexander Brooks Sr., *Peerless Laymen in the African Methodist Episcopal Zion Church* (State College, PA: Himes Printing Company, 1974), 1:1.

[146] "North Carolina, Marriages, 1759–1979," index, Family Search, https://familysearch.org/ark:/61903/1:1:F8H8-23X, Wm Johnson Trent and Annie B.

Mitchell, 06 Apr 1904; citing Wake, North Carolina, reference p25a; FHL: microfilm 236,325.

[147] Indenture (Buncombe County, NC, July 1, 1904), bk.133:444; *Asheville City Directory, 1906–1907*, 240.

[148] Johns, "Some Recollections," 4.

[149] Ibid., 4–5. Eleanora also played for the AME Zion church in town; Anna Belle, who played the organ as well as the piano, gave private piano lessons at home after her marriage. Ibid.

[150] Smith, *Aggrey of Africa*, 62, 71.

[151] W. J. Trent to E. Harding, June 30, 1904, Incoming, B93F2, BEA.

[152] E. Harding to W. J. Trent, July 1, 1904, Outgoing, 38: n.p., BEA.

[153] E. Harding to W. J. Trent, August 26, 1904, Outgoing, 38:194, BEA.

[154] W. J. Trent to E. Harding, August 29, 1904, Incoming, B93F2, BEA.

[155] E. Harding to W. J. Trent, August 30, 1904, Outgoing, vol. 38: 328, BEA.

[156] W. J. Trent to E. Harding, October 4, 1904, Incoming, B93F2, BEA.

[157] See YMCA of Western North Carolina, "Our History," www.ymcawnc.org/about-us/our-history.

[158] Chase, *Asheville*, 80–81; Arthur T. Vanderbilt II, *Fortune's Children: The Fall of the House of Vanderbilt* (New York: William Morrow, 1989), 278. When the debts were paid after Vanderbilt's death in 1914, there was less than $1 million dollars in his net estate. His wife inherited the homes at Bar Harbor, Washington, DC, and Asheville, but not enough money to run them. Ibid., 278.

[159] W. J. Trent to E. Harding, *Monthly Report*, October 31, 1903, Incoming, B93F2, BEA.

[160] W. J. Trent to E. Harding, October 21, 1904, Incoming, B93F2, BEA.

[161] E. Harding to W. J. Trent, October 22, 1904, Outgoing, 38: 561, BEA.

[162] E. Harding to W. J. Trent, November 3, 1904, Outgoing, 38: 561, BEA.

[163] E. Harding to R. R. Swope, November 7, 1904, Outgoing, 38: 602, BEA. Trent paid for small repairs out of YMI income. Ibid.

[164] Bryan, *Biltmore Estate*, 147; Trent, YMI speech; Trent, *Annual Report* (June 1905), 41.

[165] W. J. Trent to E. Harding, *Monthly Report*, October 4, 1905, Incoming, B93F2, BEA; Indenture (Buncombe County, NC, September 5, 1905), bk. 136:581.

[166] *Year-Book of All Souls' Church, 1906*, 42.

[167] Trent, YMI speech.

[168] Ibid. Trent wrote that he was sure that if it hadn't been Walker who spoke for the group, they would not have been able to reach this positive result. In this brief history he also stated that the black community raised only $2,500 and borrowed $6,500 from Kelley. Ibid. However, that only yields $9,000, not $10,000. It is not clear where the error lies. There is also some confusion as to the name of the white lender. Cf. Trent, YMI speech (Mike Kelley), and Hornsby, "'The Boy Problem,'" 293 (Kelly Miller).

[169] Vanderbilt, *Fortune's Children*, 81, 271, 277.

[170] Ibid., 135.

[171] Bob Terrell, *Historic Asheville* (Alexander, NC: Land of the Sky Books, 2001), 171, 178.

[172] Articles of Incorporation of the Young Men's Institute (Asheville, NC, May 8, 1906). Handwritten notes on the document list the profession of the signatories.

[173] Unpaginated copy of newspaper article.

[174] *Year-Book of All Souls' Church, 1904,* 44.

[175] William Alphaeus Hunton, "The Colored Men's Department of the Young Men's Christian Association," *The Voice of the Negro* 2, no. 6 (June 1905): 394. We have already seen the role of the Y's Colored Men's Department in black colleges and universities, and in cities. In addition to these two major divisions in the black YMCA, college/university associations, and city associations, there was also at this time a railroad association in West Virginia, an industrial association among coal miners in Iowa, and several associations in the black infantry. Ibid., 391.

[176] Flyer, conference announcement, n.d.

[177] Historically, Hunton had worked with the black colleges and universities, and Moorland focused on the city associations. As a rule, then, it was Moorland who put together the secretarial letters.

[178] Jerold M. Packard, *American Nightmare: The History of Jim Crow* (New York: St. Martin's Press, 2002), 67–73, 90–92.

[179] "250 Years of Rowan County" (insert to the *Salisbury Post,* April 6, 2003), 36; Gilmore, *Gender and Jim Crow,* 144.

[180] Leroy Davis, *A Clashing of the Soul: John Hope and the Dilemma of African American Leadership and Black High Education in the Early Twentieth Century* (Athens: University of Georgia Press, 1998), 165–167.

[181] YMCA, Colored Men's Department, Secretarial Letter (hereafter SL), October 1906.

[182] Addie Waite Hunton, *William Alphaeus Hunton: A Pioneer Prophet of Young Men* (New York: Association Press, 1938), 132.

[183] David Fort Godshalk, *Veiled Visions: The 1906 Atlanta Race Riot and the Reshaping of American Race Relations* (Chapel Hill: University of North Carolina Press, 2005), 106–107.

[184] Gilmore, *Gender and Jim Crow,* 131.

[185] YMCA, SL, March 1907.

[186] YMCA, SL, April 1907.

[187] Anna Belle Trent died from a burst appendix. Jeanne Johns Adkins, e-mail message to author, January 11, 2010. Adkins is the youngest child of Altona Trent Johns.

[188] *Asheville City Directory, 1907–1908,* 309, 315; Adkins, e-mail to author, May 10, 2011.

[189] YMCA, SL, April 1908.

[190] Nina Mjagkij, *Light in the Darkness: African Americans and the YMCA, 1852–1946* (Lexington: University Press of Kentucky, 1994), 63. These summer training sessions would be held in Asheville again in 1909 and 1910, after which they moved to a campsite on Chesapeake Bay, Maryland. Ibid.

[191] YMCA, SL, April 1908.

[192] Thomas W. Hanchett, *Sorting Out the New South City: Race, Class, and Urban Development in Charlotte, 1875–1975* (Chapel Hill: University of North Carolina Press, 1998), 126.

[193] Greenwood, *Bittersweet Legacy,* 139, 278 n.65; Hanchett, *Sorting Out the New South City,* 133–134, 139–141.

[194] Hanchett, *Sorting Out the New South City,* 130; charmeck.org/mecklenburg/county/ParkandRec/TrailofHistory.

[195] "Mrs. W. J. Trent Passes," *Star of Zion*, June 14, 1934; Maye Beze Jackson, notes from Tate family Bible (in Jackson's possession). Jackson is a grandchild of Thaddeus L. Tate.

[196] Built in 1886, this was the only graded school for black children in the county for many years. Black families used to move into town so their children could attend school there. Hanchett, *Sorting Out the New South City*, 129–130.

[197] J. E. Kwegyir Aggrey, "Trent-Tate Wedding," *Charlotte Observer*, July 1, 1909.

[198] Ibid.

[199] Ibid.

[200] YMCA, SL, June 1909.

[201] YMCA, SL, November 1909.

[202] "Annual Conference of the Colored Y.M.C.A." (unnamed newspaper, December 2, 1909).

[203] Mjagkij, *Light in the Darkness*, 3.

[204] In 1908, Watson replaced George E. Haynes, who served as third international secretary between 1905 and 1908. Ibid., 62, 154 n.40.

[205] "Banner Session for the Uplift of the Colored Race," unnamed newspaper, December 5, 1909.

[206] *Asheville City Directory, 1911*, 326.

[207] Maggie Tate Trent, notes in baby book, 1910.

[208] Louise Marie Rountree, *Administrative Profiles for the Centennial Celebration, February 6, 1980* (Salisbury, NC: Livingstone College, 1980), n.p.

[209] *Asheville City Directory, 1911*, 326. I have been unable to find information about this publication.

[210] Smith, *Aggrey of Africa*, 85, 100.

[211] Walls, *AME Zion*, 596.

[212] Ibid., 343. Thad Tate, who had loaned the church money to help build the publishing house, was also a member of this committee. Ibid.

[213] W. J. Walls to W. J. Trent, March 4, 1950.

[214] Trent, *Monthly Report*, October 31, 1903, Incoming, B93F2, BEA.

[215] Walls, *AME Zion*, 599–600.

[216] Stephens, "Medicine in Asheville."

[217] Judith Nina Kerr, "God-Given Work: The Life and Times of Sculptor Meta Vaux Warrick Fuller, 1877–1968" (Ph.D. diss., University of Massachusetts, 1986), 157, 159.

[218] Theresa Leininger-Miller, *New Negro Artists in Paris: African American Painters and Sculptors in the City of Light, 1922–1934* (New Brunswick, NJ: Rutgers University Press, 2001), 8–10.

[219] YMCA, SL, June 1909.

[220] YMCA, SL, June 1910.

[221] YMCA, SL, December 1910.

[222] The schools were Atlanta University, Clark College, Spelman College, Morris Brown College, Gammon Theological Seminary, Turner Seminary, and Johnson C. Smith Theological Seminary.

[223] In the Bible, this is an image of safety and peace. The phrase appears, for example, at Micah 4:3–4 (King James Version): "And they shall beat their swords into plowshares, and their spears into pruning hooks: nation shall not lift up a sword against nation, neither

shall they learn war any more. But they shall sit every man under his vine and under his fig tree; and none shall make them afraid: for the mouth of the LORD of hosts hath spoken it."

[224] W. J. Trent to Mr. and Mrs. Kwegyir Aggrey, June 3, 1911. By the time this letter was written, the Aggreys had three children, and would later have a fourth. Smith, *Aggrey of Africa*, 72.

[225] Indenture (Buncombe County, NC, July 3, 1911), bk.176:321.

[226] Trent, YMI speech.

Chapter 4

[1] John Dittmer, *Black Georgia in the Progressive Era, 1900–1920* (Urbana: University of Illinois Press, 1977), 12.

[2] Ronald H. Baylor, *Race and the Shaping of Twentieth-Century Atlanta* (Chapel Hill: University of North Carolina Press, 2000), 7.

[3] By 1904, there were 2,000 students in Atlanta's private black high schools and colleges. David Fort Godshalk, *Veiled Visions: The 1906 Atlanta Riot and the Reshaping of American Race Relations* (Chapel Hill: University of North Carolina Press, 2005), 61.

[4] W. J. Trent, autobiographical sketch, 1935. The papers of William Johnson Trent are located in Heritage Hall and the Andrew Carnegie Library, Livingstone College, Salisbury, North Carolina.

[5] Jacqueline Ann Rouse, *Lugenia Burns Hope: Black Southern Reformer* (Athens: University of Georgia Press, 1989), 57.

[6] Ibid., 57–58; Benjamin E. Mays, *Born to Rebel* (New York: Charles Scribner's Sons, 1971), 79–87; Gary M. Pomerantz, *Where Peachtree Meets Sweet Auburn: A Saga of Race and Family* (New York: Penguin Books, 1996), 78–79.

[7] Clifford M. Kuhn, Harlon E. Joye, and E. Bernard West, *Living Atlanta: An Oral History of the City, 1914–1948* (Athens: University of Georgia Press, in conjunction with the Atlanta Historical Society, 1990), 82.

[8] Pomerantz, *Where Peachtree Meets Sweet Auburn*, 73–75.

[9] Douglas A. Blackmon, *Slavery by Another Name: The Re-Enslavement of Black Americans from the Civil War to World War II* (New York: Random House, 2009), 351; Alex Lichtenstein, "Good Roads and Chain Gangs in the Progressive South: 'The Negro Convict Is a Slave,'" *The Journal of Southern History* 59, no.1 (February 1993): 91–93, 100, 102. By 1930 Georgia had more forced labor slaves than ever before: more than 8,000—almost all black—worked on chain gangs in 116 counties. It was not until the attack on Pearl Harbor in December 1941 that U.S. attorney general Biddle ordered federal prosecutors to start building cases attacking involuntary servitude and slavery. And it was not until 1951 that Congress passed a law making any form of slavery a crime. Blackmon, *Slavery by Another Name*, 371, 377–379, 381.

[10] Dittmer, *Black Georgia*, 94–103. In 1908 the Georgia state constitution was amended to list as electors those men who could meet any one of the five following qualifications: (1) served in the Confederate or U.S. armed forces; (2) descended from one who served in the Confederate or U.S. armed forces; (3) was of "good character" and understood "the duties and obligations of citizenship under a Republican form of government"; (4) could read the Constitution, and write any portion of it read to him; (5) owned a certain amount

of property. Ga. Const. Art. 1, sec. 1, par. 4 (amended 1908). It is easy to see how black citizens would lose the right to vote with these limitations in place.

[11] Rouse, *Lugenia Burns Hope*, 58, 60, 62.

[12] *Atlanta City Directory* for 1913, 1914, 1916, 1919, and 1921.

[13] Rouse, *Lugenia Burns Hope*, 58, 63.

[14] Dittmer, *Black Georgia*, 13.

[15] W. E. B. Du Bois, ed., *The Negro American Family* (Atlanta: Atlanta University Press, 1908), 65.

[16] Kuhn, Joye, and West, *Living Atlanta*, 21.

[17] W. J. Trent Jr., notes, 1975.

[18] Jeanne Johns Adkins, e-mail message to author, May 28, 2011; Lawrence Otis Graham, *Our Kind of People: Inside America's Black Upper Class* (New York: HarperCollins, 1999), 345; August Meier and David Lewis, "History of the Negro Upper Class in Atlanta, Georgia, 1890–1958," *The Journal of Negro Education* 28, no. 2 (Spring 1959): 130.

[19] Meier and Lewis, "History of the Negro Upper Class in Atlanta," 131.

[20] Note, however, that in Asheville the Trents had attended Hopkins AME Chapel AME Church, not an AME Zion church, thus already making a break in family tradition.

[21] Pomerantz, *Where Peachtree Meets Sweet Auburn*, 71.

[22] Proctor was an 1894 graduate of the Yale University School of Divinity. Pomerantz, *Where Peachtree Meets Sweet Auburn*, 71; Godshalk, *Veiled Visions*, 77–78.

[23] Allison Dorsey, *To Build Our Lives Together: Community Formation in Black Atlanta, 1875–1906* (Athens: University of Georgia Press, 2004), 60, 66.

[24] Altona Trent Johns, "Henry Hugh Proctor," *The Black Perspective in Music* 3, no. 1 (Spring 1975): 26. The author, Trent's daughter, was in her seventies when she penned this recollection of her childhood church.

[25] Henry Hugh Proctor, quoted in Michael Leroy Porter, "Black Atlanta: An Interdisciplinary Study of Blacks on the East Side of Atlanta, 1890–1930" (Ph.D. diss., Emory University, 1974), 70–71.

[26] Henry H. Proctor, *Between Black and White: Autobiographical Sketches* (Boston: Pilgrim Press, 1925), 107.

[27] Ralph E. Luker, *The Social Gospel in Black and White: American Racial Reform, 1885–1912* (Chapel Hill: University of North Carolina Press, 1991), 190.

[28] Johns, "Henry Hugh Proctor," 27.

[29] Luker, *Social Gospel*, 190.

[30] Adkins, e-mail message to author, May 8, 2011; Clarence A. Bacote, *The Story of Atlanta University: A Century of Service, 1865–1965* (Atlanta: Atlanta University, 1969), 34–35.

[31] Adkins, e-mail message to author, July 5, 2011. There was no public high school for black youth in Atlanta until 1924. Indeed, in 1913 the Atlanta Board of Education tried to abolish the seventh and eighth grades in black schools. Kuhn, Joye, and West, *Living Atlanta*, 130–131.

[32] Nina Mjagkij, *Light in the Darkness: African Americans and the YMCA, 1852–1946* (Lexington: University Press of Kentucky, 1994), 136; YMCA, Colored Men's Department, Secretarial Letter (hereafter SL), November 1909.

[33] Leroy Davis, *A Clashing of the Soul: John Hope and the Dilemma of African American Leadership and Black Higher Education in the Early Twentieth Century* (Athens: University of Georgia Press, 1998), 162. The school name was changed to Morehouse College in 1913. Ibid., 197.

[34] Davis, *Clashing of the Soul*, 185–186 (1908); W. J. Trent to Dr. and Mrs. Torrence, February 14, 1915 (hereafter Torrence letter) (1915); Mjagkij, *Light in the Darkness*, 92 (1917); "Atlanta's New YMCA," *Atlanta Independent*, May 15, 1920.

[35] Davis, *Clashing of the Soul*, 124, 200.

[36] Porter, "Black Atlanta," 126; Dan Moore Sr., *Sweet Auburn: Street of Pride* (Atlanta: APEX Museum, 1986), 50–51. For purposes of clarity and continuity, I will refer to the Wheat Street Y as the "Auburn Avenue Y."

[37] Davis, *Clashing of the Soul*, 186.

[38] Porter, "Black Atlanta," 126–130.

[39] Kuhn, Joye, and West, *Living Atlanta*, 10.

[40] Mjagkij, *Light in the Darkness*, 73.

[41] Ibid., 74, 77.

[42] It was initially contemplated that the building would cost $100,000. YMCA, Colored Men's Department, John B. Watson, *Report of Service at Conference of Secretaries, Colored Men's Department* (January 1, 1913) (hereafter *Watson Report*), 1. Not surprisingly, it ended up costing more.

[43] YMCA, SL, March 1913; YMCA, *Watson Report*, 6–7.

[44] YMCA, *Watson Report*, 6–7.

[45] Ibid., 8.

[46] Ibid., 7–9.

[47] Ibid., 9.

[48] YMCA, Colored Men's Department, Statement, January 1912.

[49] YMCA, SL, February 1912.

[50] YMCA, *Watson Report*, 1.

[51] YMCA, SL, November 1912.

[52] "The City Pastors Organize," *Atlanta Independent*, December 27, 1912.

[53] YMCA, SL, December 1912.

[54] YMCA, *Watson Report*, 9–10. There is no further information describing the complaints of the white men who helped with this campaign.

[55] YMCA, SL, March 1913.

[56] YMCA, SL, November 1913.

[57] "Our Next Issue Will Begin to Print the Names of the Subscribers to the Y.M.C.A. New Building, and the Amount Paid Up to Date. It Will Take Several Issues to Get Them All In. But Watch for the List. Paid in Full Will be Printed First," *Atlanta Independent*, January 17, 1914 (banner headline).

[58] "The Y.M.C.A. Fund Grows," *Atlanta Independent*, February 21, 1914.

[59] "Subscribers That Have Paid Part on Their Pledges," *Atlanta Independent*, January 31, 1914.

[60] "Some Interesting Facts about the Standing of the Churches," *Atlanta Independent*, February 28, 1914.

[61] "The Y.M.C.A. Meeting at Wheat Street Church," *Atlanta Independent*, February 21, 1914.

[62] YMCA, J. E. Moorland, SL, June 1909.

[63] YMCA, J. E. Moorland, SL, November 1912.

[64] W. J. Trent Jr., notes, 1975; Adkins, e-mail message to author, May 25, 2012.

[65] YMCA, SL, September 1914.

[66] John Daniels, *In Freedom's Birthplace: A Study of the Boston Negroes* (Boston: Houghton Mifflin, 1914).

[67] Ibid., 159, 214.

[68] Ibid., 219, 221.

[69] *Addresses of John Hay* (New York: The Century Co., 1906); H. G. Wells, *The World Set Free* (London: Macmillan and Company, 1914).

[70] Frances Hodgson Burnett, *The Dawn of a To-Morrow* (New York: Charles Scribner, 1905); Pendennis (only name given), "Mrs. Frances Hodgson Finds a New Field for Her Pen," *New York Times,* May 20, 1906 .

[71] John Fox, *Little Shepherd of Kingdom Come* (New York: Charles Scribner's Sons, 1903); John Fox, *The Trail of the Lonesome Pine* (New York: Charles Scribner's Sons, 1908).

[72] W. J. Trent, speech at Young Men's Institute, March 25, 1945 (hereafter YMI speech); "Dr. Trent to Speak at YMI," *Asheville Citizen-Times*, March 25, 1945.

[73] Torrence letter.

[74] Edwin W. Smith, *Aggrey of Africa: A Study in Black and White* (Freeport, NY: Libraries Press, 1971), 101–105.

[75] W. J. Trent, "Life Sketch of President W. J. Trent of Livingstone College," 1935.

[76] Rouse, *Lugenia Burns Hope*, 26.

[77] Truman K. Gibson Jr. and Steve Huntley, *Knocking Down Barriers: My Fight for Black America* (Evanston, IL: Northwestern University Press, 2005), 80.

[78] Torrence letter.

[79] Gibson and Huntley, *Knocking Down Barriers*, 26.

[80] Carole Merritt, *The Herndons: An Atlanta Family* (Athens: University of Georgia Press, 2002), 143.

[81] Pomerantz, *Where Peachtree Meets Sweet Auburn*, 108.

[82] By 1927, when he died, Herndon had three barbershops, commercial buildings in Atlanta, and over a hundred houses between Georgia and Florida. Godshalk, *Veiled Visions*, 20.

[83] Dittmer, *Black Georgia*, 37–38, 48–49, 101–102; Rouse, *Lugenia Burns Hope*, 29. Herndon participated in the inaugural meeting of the Niagara movement in Niagara Falls, Canada, in July 1906, and helped guide the movement during its first year. Godshalk, *Veiled Visions*, 70.

[84] YMCA, SL, September 1914.

[85] Mjagkij, *Light in the Darkness*, 79.

[86] W. J. Trent Jr., notes, 1983.

[87] Dorsey, *To Build Our Lives Together*, 92–94. Not surprisingly, the black teachers were also underpaid: they earned $200 a year less than similarly situated white teachers. Ibid., 94.

[88] Since there was no public secondary school for black youth in Atlanta until 1924, black colleges and universities often provided secondary school education. Morehouse College

had the Morehouse Academy for secondary school students; Atlanta University also had a secondary school.

[89] Chad L. Williams, *Torchbearers for Democracy: African American Soldiers in the World War I Era* (Chapel Hill: University of North Carolina Press, 2010), 14–15.

[90] Ibid., 52–53.

[91] Kuhn, Joye, and West, *Living Atlanta*, 20–25; Pomerantz, *Where Peachtree Meets Sweet Auburn*, 84–85.

[92] The *Atlanta City Directory* for 1910 and for 1920 show the Trents living at the same address both years. Also, had they lost their home to a fire, it is likely that this story would have come down in family history, and there is no hint of such a story.

[93] Williams, *Torchbearers for Democracy*, 55.

[94] Adriane Lentz-Smith, *Freedom Struggles: African Americans and World War I* (Cambridge, MA: Harvard University Press, 2009), 83.

[95] Lentz-Smith, *Freedom Struggles*, 81.

[96] Williams, *Torchbearers for Democracy*, 106–109, 119; Davis, *Clashing of the Soul*, 242.

[97] Lentz-Smith, *Freedom Struggles*, 94.

[98] Williams, *Torchbearers for Democracy*, 119–120.

[99] Lentz-Smith, *Freedom Struggles*, 109–110.

[100] Williams, *Torchbearers for Democracy*, 160–161.

[101] Ibid., 163–166. It is not true, however, that France had no color line. That line existed, but it was mainly to keep white French separate from their black and brown colonial subjects. Lentz-Smith, *Freedom Struggles*, 108.

[102] Davis, *Clashing of the Soul*, 236–239, 243, 253.

[103] Local Board for Division No. 4, City of Atlanta, State of Georgia (FHL Roll Number: 1556952); World War I Selective Service System Draft Registration Cards, http://www.archives.gov/research/military/ww1/draft-registration/index.html.

[104] Williams, *Torchbearers for Democracy*, 187.

[105] George Alexander Brooks Sr., *Peerless Laymen in the African Methodist Episcopal Zion Church* (State College, PA: Himes Printing Company, 1974), 1:33.

[106] Lisa Pertillar Brevard, *A Biography of E. Azalia Smith Hackley, 1867–1922, African-American Singer and Social Activist* (Lewiston, NY: Edwin Mellen Press, 2001), 108–109. Twenty-eight Atlanta church choirs joined in one chorus for this event. Trent was one of the soloists. "Music and Art," *The Crisis* 14, no. 6 (October 1917): 310.

[107] YMCA, Colored Men's Department, J. B. Watson, *Report of J.B. Watson on Work Done in Year 1918, with Some Recommendations for Consideration in 1919* (January 3, 1918), 2.

[108] Ira Berlin, *The Making of African America: The Four Great Migrations* (New York: Penguin Books, 2010), 157–158.

[109] Nina Mjagkij, *Loyalty in Time of Trial: The African American Experience during World War I* (Lanham, MD: Rowman & Littlefield, 2011), 23.

[110] W. E. B. Du Bois, "Returning Soldiers," in David Levering Lewis, ed., *Harlem Renaissance Reader* (New York: Viking Press, 1994), 5.

[111] Williams, *Torchbearers for Democracy*, 215–217.

[112] Ibid., 249–253.

[113] Ibid., 223, 225, 232–234, 246, 258–260. The riot in Tulsa, Oklahoma, was perhaps the most destructive and the most deadly. White rioters killed between 75 and 150 black people and set fire to over 35 blocks, leaving over 1,000 black families homeless and destroying Greenwood, the relatively prosperous black section of Tulsa. Alfred L. Brophy, *Reconstructing the Dreamland: The Tulsa Riot of 1921; Race, Reparations, and Reconciliation* (Oxford: Oxford University Press, 2002), 1, 60.

[114] Cameron McWhirter, *Red Summer* (New York: Henry Holt, 2011), n.p. This information is from the map opposite page 1. The map also shows that the next closest state in terms of lynching was Mississippi, with three such incidents, then Arkansas, with two. In sixteen other states, there was one major riot or lynching during that period.

[115] Davis, *Clashing of the Soul*, 235.

[116] NAACP, *Thirty Years of Lynching in the United States, 1889–1918* (New York: Negro Universities Press, 1969), 41.

[117] Hugh M. Dorsey, "A Statement from Governor Hugh M. Dorsey as to the Negro in Georgia" (speech, Atlanta, April 22, 1921), 1–2. This document is in the Kautz Family YMCA Archives, E. L. Andersen Library, University of Minnesota at Minneapolis.

[118] McWhirter, *Red Summer*, 53.

[119] Rouse, *Lugenia Burns Hope*, 3; Davis, *Clashing of the Soul*, 262; W. J. Trent, "Life Sketch of President W. J. Trent of Livingstone College" (1935). In one of the peculiarities of Southern life at this time, neither Trent nor the Hopes would have been able to join this "interracial" organization when it was founded in 1919, because the white membership did not allow black members until 1920. Davis, *Clashing of the Soul*, 261.

[120] Glenda Elizabeth Gilmore, *Defying Dixie: The Radical Roots of Civil Rights, 1919–1950* (New York: W. W. Norton, 2008), 19. Meetings in Atlanta were often held at the Butler Street Y. Davis, *Clashing of the Soul*, 294.

[121] Kimberly E. Nichols, "Commission on Interracial Cooperation," in Nina Mjagkij, ed., *Organizing Black America: An Encyclopedia of African American Associations* (New York: Garland Publishing, 2001), 175–176.

[122] Kuhn, Joye, and West, *Living Atlanta*, 204, 339; Dittmer, *Black Georgia*, 208; YMCA, "The Work of the Inter-Racial Committee," 1920, 8–10.

[123] Davis, *Clashing of the Soul*, 260.

[124] Andre D. Vann, "Trent, William Johnson Sr.," in Faustine Childress Jones-Wilson, ed., *Encyclopedia of African-American Education* (Westport, CT: Greenwood Press, 1996), 477. Trent was also a founding member of the Atlanta Urban League. Lenwood G. Davis, "A History of Livingstone College, 1879–1957" (Ph.D. diss., Carnegie-Mellon University, 1979), 142.

[125] "Atlanta's New YMCA Which Will Be Opened Sunday at 3:30 with Strong Program," *Atlanta Independent*, May 15, 1920.

[126] "Grand Opening of Colored YMCA," *Atlanta Independent*, May 16, 1920.

[127] "YMCA Opening Tomorrow," *Atlanta Independent*, May 15, 1920.

[128] "Secretary Trent Given Big Send-Off by Y.M.C.A.," *Star of Zion*, July 2, 1925 (reprinted from *Atlanta Independent*).

[129] "Grand Opening."

[130] "Atlanta's New YMCA."

[131] U.S. Department of the Interior, National Park Service, *National Register of Historic Places Inventory, Nomination Form for Sweet Auburn Historic District*, 47, Lynne Gomez-Graves, nps.gov/docs/NHLS/Text/76000631.pdf.

[132] This version of the story of Paul on the road to Damascus comes from Acts 9:3–9 (King James Version).

[133] Judith Nina Kerr, "God-Given Work: The Life and Times of Sculptor Meta Vaux Warrick Fuller, 1877–1968" (Ph.D. diss., University of Massachusetts, 1986), 288.

[134] Author's notes from tour of Butler Street YMCA, May 4, 2012, with Butler Street Y executive secretary Rhonda Copenny.

[135] YMCA of the USA, *YMCA in America, 1851–2001* (2000), 20.

[136] Porter, "Black Atlanta," 133–136.

[137] W. J. Trent Jr. to editor, *Greensboro Daily News*, November 30, 1979. As Trent Jr. continued in this letter: "We had books in our house sometimes if we didn't have meat!"

[138] Porter, "Black Atlanta," 131.

[139] U.S. Federal Census: Year: *1920*; Census Place: *Atlanta Ward 4, Fulton, Georgia*; Roll: *T625_250*; Page: *10B*; Image: *689*; Enumeration District: *85*; Rouse, *Lugenia Burns Hope*, 58–59.

[140] Renie Dobbs, of the well-respected family of John Wesley Dobbs, played the piano for tea parties as a teenager. Pomerantz, *Where Peachtree Meets Sweet Auburn*, 108.

[141] W. J. Trent Jr., notes, 1975.

[142] Gibson Jr. later recalled seeing a photo of Trent Jr. and himself together when they were babies. Gibson and Huntley, *Knocking Down Barriers*, 80.

[143] Rouse, *Lugenia Burns Hope*, 33–34.

[144] Ibid., 44–48. Other college presidents' wives taught classes, directed programs, and were deans at the school. Ibid., 55.

[145] Ibid., 1–6.

[146] John Donald Gustav-Wrathall, *Take the Young Stranger by the Hand: Same-Sex Relations and the YMCA* (Chicago: University of Chicago Press, 2000), 96–98, 101–104.

[147] The Nineteenth Amendment, which provides that American citizens may not be denied the right to vote because of sex, was ratified August 18, 1920.

[148] W. J. Trent Jr., notes, 1983.

[149] Kuhn, Joye, and West, *Living Atlanta*, 159–161, 170–171.

[150] Johns, "Henry Hugh Proctor," 27–31. Johns had records of the concerts only up to August 1915 and was not sure when the concerts stopped. We know, however, that Proctor left Atlanta in 1919. Ibid., 32.

[151] Edna Ethel Heyliger, "A Study of the Development of the Atlanta University School of Social Work, 1920–1942" (M.A. thesis, Atlanta University, 1943), 14–15. The school, initially called Atlanta School of Social Service, officially opened in the fall of 1920. In April 1924 the school was incorporated under its new name. Ibid., 10.

[152] Graham, *Our Kind of People*, 129. The group chose the name based on ancient Greek organizations: "Boulé" meant "council of noblemen" or "senate." Ibid., 131.

[153] Ibid., 129–130.

[154] Charles H. Wesley, *History of Sigma Pi Phi: First of the Negro-American Greek-Letter Fraternities* (Washington, DC: Association for the Study of Negro Life and History, 1954), 25.

[155] Graham, *Our Kind of People*, 136. In 1999 there were about 3,700 Boulé members organized in 105 chapters. Ibid., 134.

[156] Wesley, *History of Sigma Pi Phi*, 77, 134–137. The first black women's Greek-letter organization, Alpha Kappa Alpha, was founded on the campus of Howard University during academic year 1907–1908. In 1913 it became the first such group to be incorporated. Marjorie H. Parker, *Alpha Kappa Alpha through the Years* (Chicago: Mobium Press, 1990), 1, 9–10, 37.

[157] Wesley, *History of Sigma Pi Phi*, 135–136.

[158] Skip Mason, "History of Kappa Boulé," Sigma Pi Phi Fraternity, Inc., http://kappaboule1920.org/kappaboulehistory.html. The Kappa Boulé membership later included Benjamin Mays, W. E. B. Du Bois, Martin Luther King Jr., Maynard Jackson, Julian Bond, and Whitney Young. Ibid.

[159] Mjagkij, *Light in the Darkness*, 66.

[160] Meier and Lewis, "History of the Negro Upper Class," 132–133.

[161] "William Johnson Trent [...] As We Know Him," http:toto.lib.unca.edu/findingaids/mss/blackhigh/blackhigh/Biographies/trent_will; Livingstone College, publicity release, January 20, 1952.

[162] Pomerantz, *Where Peachtree Meets Sweet Auburn*, 81–82.

[163] Dittmer, *Black Georgia*, 57.

[164] David M. Fahey, "Grand United Order of Odd Fellows" and Robert E. Weir, "Prince Hall Masons," in Mjagkij, ed., *Organizing Black America*, 252, 593.

[165] Dorsey, *To Build Our Lives Together*, 101–106.

[166] David G. Hackett, "The Prince Hall Masons and the African American Church: The Labors of Grand Master and Bishop James Walker Hood, 1831–1918," in Peter P. Hinks and Stephen Kantrowitz, eds., *All Men Free and Brethren: Essays on the History of African American Freemasonry* (Ithaca, NY: Cornell University Press, 2013), 133.

[167] Hackett, "Prince Hall Masons," 134–135.

[168] Smith, *Aggrey of Africa*, xi, 143.

[169] William J. Walls, *The African Methodist Episcopal Zion Church: Reality of the Black Church* (Charlotte, NC: AME Zion Publishing House, 1974) (hereafter *AME Zion*), 599–600.

[170] George Clinton became editor of the *Star of Zion* in 1892 and bishop in 1896; John W. Smith became editor in 1896 and bishop in 1904; George Clement was named editor in 1904 and bishop in 1916. Ibid., 350–351.

[171] Livingstone College, Board of Trustees, minutes (hereafter minutes), September 7, 1920.

[172] Livingstone College, minutes, September 7, 1920.

[173] YMCA, J. E. Moorland, "Work of Colored Men's Department for 1922–1923," 1.

[174] Mell Plumbing Company to John Hope, October 14, 1920; John Hope to Mell Plumbing Company, October 18, 1920.

[175] John Hope to J. E. Moorland, December 18, 1920.

[176] YMCA, *Report of Visits Made by J. H. McGrew in Company with Dr. J. E. Moorland and Mr. C. H. Tobias, Atlanta GA,* March 17, 1922, 4. McGrew became an international secretary for African-American Y work in 1921. Mjagkij, *Light in the Darkness*, 136.

[177] W. J. Trent to John Hope, April 8, 1922.

[178] Mjagkij, *Light in the Darkness*, 58.

[179] J. B. Watson, letter to the editor, *Star of Zion*, July 30, 1925.

[180] Livingstone College, minutes, August 5, 1921, and December 6, 1921.

[181] Reginald W. Brown, *Oakdale/Union Hill Cemetery, Salisbury, North Carolina: A History and Study of a Twentieth Century African American Cemetery*, 2nd. ed. (Westminster, MD: Heritage Books, 2008), 21. According to Brown, the Oakdale/Union Hill Cemetery "is like the Rosetta Stone for studying the Livingstone College Historic District." Ibid., 19.

[182] *Salisbury City Directory 1919–1920*, 242; *Salisbury City Directory 1922–1923*, 281; *Greensboro City Directory 1924*, 772.

[183] Livingstone College, minutes, April 25, 1923.

[184] William J. Walls, "Alumni Recommendations," attached to Livingstone College, minutes, May 29, 1923.

[185] The next minutes in the college archives are for the board's May 26, 1925, meeting. Those minutes note the absence of board member Trent, and the presence of board member Higgins, the second alumnus recommended by the Alumni Association.

[186] Mjagkij, *Light in the Darkness*, 131–132.

[187] YMCA, J. E. Moorland, "Work of Colored Men's Department for 1922–1923," 1.

[188] YMCA, Channing Tobias, Secretarial Newsletter (hereafter SNL), December 1923.

[189] YMCA, "Capital Investment, Source of Funds, and Property Debt of YMCA's for Colored Men and Boys in 25 Cities," n.d., 1. When it was built, it was only the third Rosenwald YMCA in the South, where 90 percent of black Americans lived. The other two buildings were in Washington, DC; and Baltimore. Mjagkij, *Light in the Darkness*, 81.

[190] YMCA, "Colored People Who Have Made Large Individual Gifts to Young Men's Christian Association Buildings," n.d., 3.

[191] W. J. Trent Jr., notes, 1975.

[192] Eileen Southern, *The Music of Black Americans: A History* (New York: W. W. Norton, 1971; 2nd edition, 1983), 169–170 (page reference is to the 1971 edition).

[193] "Dr. W. J. Walls Addresses Atlanta Y.M.C.A.," *Star of Zion*, January 3, 1924 (reprinted from *The Atlanta Independent*).

[194] "An Emergency Fund for Livingstone," *Star of Zion*, January 31, 1924.

[195] Louise Marie Rountree, *Administrative Profiles for the Centennial Celebration, February 6, 1980* (Salisbury: Livingstone College, 1980). When Trent was applying for the position at the Young Men's Institute in 1900, he listed Suggs as a reference. W. J. Trent to Rodney Rush Swope, 24 April 1900, Superintendent's Office Incoming Correspondence Collection, Box 77, Folder 11, Biltmore Estate Archives.

[196] Walls, *AME Zion*, 315.

[197] Davis, "History of Livingstone College," 73, 128.

[198] Walls, *AME Zion*, 599–600; "Bishops," *Star of Zion*, May 29, 1924.

[199] *Star of Zion*, April 17, 1924.

[200] "Mr. John J. Eagan Passes Away," *Star of Zion*, April 10, 1924; and "Just a Word— But as to Candidates," Star of Zion, April 17, 1924.

[201] Livingstone College, minutes, May 27, 1924.

[202] Smith, *Aggrey of Africa*, 81–95.

[203] Ibid., xii.

[204] Ibid., 65–66; E. D. W. Jones, "Shaking the Plum Tree: A Tribute to Dr. Aggrey," *Star of Zion*, August 11, 1927.

[205] Livingstone College, minutes, May 27, 1924.

[206] Walls, *AME Zion*, 351; YMCA, *The Colored Men's Department of the Young Men's Christian Association* (New York: The International Committee of Young Men's Christian Associations, 1894), 6–7.

[207] W. J. Trent, "Zion's Representatives at the Federal Council of Churches in Atlanta," *Star of Zion*, January 1, 1925.

[208] J. Francis Lee, "Reply to Letter," *Star of Zion*, January 8, 1925.

[209] Livingstone College, minutes, January 15, 1925.

[210] W. H. Davenport, "General Conference Proceedings: Bishops Meet in Charlotte," *Star of Zion*, January 22, 1925.

[211] I have been unable to determine who Innes was.

[212] Livingstone College, minutes, May 27, 1925.

[213] "Commencement at Livingstone," *Star of Zion*, June 4, 1925. Other black Y leaders soon followed in his footsteps. In 1926 David D. Jones became president of Bennett College and Mordecai W. Johnson became president of Howard University. J. B. Watson became president of Arkansas State College in 1929, and Benjamin E. Mays became president of Morehouse College in 1940. Mjagkij, *Light in the Darkness*, 131.

[214] Livingstone College, *The Living Stone*, October 1926, 6.

[215] W. J. Trent to W. J. Walls, December 10, 1936.

[216] W. H. Davenport, "W. J. Trent Welcome," *Star of Zion*, June 4, 1925.

[217] "W. J. Trent," *Star of Zion*, July 2, 1925 (editorial reprinted from *Atlanta Independent*).

[218] YMCA, SNL, July 1925.

[219] YMCA of the USA, *YMCA in America*, 19.

[220] *Star of Zion*, July 30, 1925.

[221] Ibid.

[222] "President Trent's Visits," *Star of Zion*, July 28, 1925.

[223] Heath Thomas, "Appointment to School Board Tribute to Trent," *Salisbury Evening Post*, July 22, 1951.

[224] Davenport, "W. J. Trent Welcome."

[225] Morehouse College, *Annual Catalogue, 1924–1925*, 81.

[226] Morehouse College, *Annual Catalogue, 1923–1924*, 17.

[227] "The Opening of Livingstone," *Star of Zion*, September 24, 1925; Smith, *Aggrey of Africa*, 230.

Chapter 5

[1] Rowan County Convention and Visitors' Bureau, *African-American Heritage Trail*, pamphlet (n.d.), 14; William J. Walls, *The African Methodist Episcopal Zion Church: Reality of the Black Church* (Charlotte: AME Zion Publishing House, 1974) (hereafter *AME Zion*), 312. Booker T. Washington had helped Livingstone get money from Andrew Carnegie for the library. Livingstone College, "The Price Memorial Campaign for Livingstone College," flyer (1926), 7.

[2] Victoria Richardson and Josephine C. Price, *Carnegie Library Report, Livingstone College, October 1, 1925, to July 1, 1926*, n.p.

[3] U.S. Department of the Interior, Bureau of Education, *Survey of Negro Colleges and Universities*, bulletin, 1928, no. 7 (Washington, DC: United States Government Printing House, 1929), 552.

[4] Walls, *AME Zion*, 308; W. F. Fonvielle, *Reminiscences of College Days* (Raleigh: Edwards and Broughton, 1904), 119; *Salisbury City Directory, 1924–1925*; *Salisbury City Directory, 1926–1927*.

[5] *Sketch Book of Livingstone College and East Tennessee Industrial School, Salisbury, North Carolina* (East Tennessee Industrial School Print, 1903), 4, 34.

[6] The 1911 catalog did, however, list twelve courses in its Industrial Department, and four in its Domestic Arts Department. Livingstone College, *Catalogue of Livingstone College, Salisbury, N. C., 1911–1912* (Lynchburg, VA: J. P. Bell Company, 1911), 46–53.

[7] Walls, *AME Zion*, 318.

[8] Lenwood G. Davis, "A History of Livingstone College, 1879–1957" (Ph.D. diss., Carnegie-Mellon University, 1979), 182.

[9] Ibid., 176.

[10] Livingstone College, *Annual Catalog, 1926–1927*, 6.

[11] Edwin W. Smith, *Aggrey of Africa: A Study in Black and White* (Freeport, NY: Libraries Press, 1971), 226–227, 236–243. Novelist Chinua Achebe wrote about the "[g]reat African nationalist [...] James Kwegyir Aggrey, Dr. Aggrey of the Gold Coast. The colonial service accepted him into Achimota College, not as principal, which he deserved, but as an assistant to a nice but colorless English cleric. So Aggrey was co-opted and contained by colonial rule." Chinua Achebe, *The Education of a British-Protected Child* (New York: Alfred A. Knopf, 2009), 29.

[12] Smith, *Aggrey of Africa*, 248.

[13] Davis, "History of Livingstone College," 57–58.

[14] Ibid., 76–78.

[15] "Livingstone Gets New Rating," *Star of Zion*, April 8, 1926.

[16] "Livingstone College Finals Speaker Sees Bright Future," *Salisbury Post,* May 26, 1943 (statement by associate director of GEB). AME Zion historian William J. Walls also stated that the debt the school carried was for $150,000. William J. Walls, *The Romance of a College: An Evolution of the Auditorium* (New York: Vantage Press, 1963), 25. Articles in two AME Zion publications, however, stated that the school owed $300,000 when Trent became president. "Bishop Walls Leads in Founder's Day Campaign," *The Seminarian* 1, no. 2 (May 1943): 1; AME Zion Church, Philadelphia and Baltimore Conference, *Livingstone College Campaign, November 8, 1939 to January 30, 1940*, pamphlet, n.d. I am using the lower amount because it is the amount quoted by both an officer of the GEB, which donated money to the school, and William J. Walls, a bishop in the church for forty-four years, who was elected historian of the AME Zion Church upon his retirement in 1968. Walls, *AME Zion*, 600. He was also president of the board of trustees for Livingstone College for thirty-three years, including the year Trent became president. Louise Marie Rountree, *Administrative Profiles for the Centennial Celebration, February 6, 1980*.

[17] E. L. Madison, "An Open Letter," *Star of Zion*, March 18, 1926.

[18] William Johnson Campbell, "The Origin and Development of Livingstone College and Hood Theological Seminary of the African Methodist Episcopal Zion Church and the Progressive Administration of President William Johnson Trent" (thesis, B.D. degree, Hood Theological Seminary, 1950), 43–44.

[19] Ibid., 80.

[20] Davis, "History of Livingstone College," 75.

[21] Campbell, "Origin and Development," 46; Madison, "Open Letter."

[22] Campbell, "Origin and Development," 43–44.

[23] Livingstone College, "Price Memorial Campaign," 2.

[24] This was a personal gift, and not related to the J. B. Duke Foundation. "B. N. Duke Gives Money to Two Local Colleges," *Star of Zion*, June 24, 1926.

[25] "Board Promised $75,000 to Livingstone," *Star of Zion*, March 10, 1927.

[26] "Livingstone President Reviews College History in Address to Rotary Club: City and County Being Asked for $25,000 Help" (name of newspaper unknown), March 29, 1938.

[27] Davis, "History of Livingstone College," 156.

[28] "The Price Memorial Campaign a Live Issue," *Star of Zion*, May 19, 1927.

[29] W. J. Trent, "The Price Memorial Campaign for Livingstone College," *Star of Zion*, May 6, 1926.

[30] James D. Anderson, *The Education of Blacks in the South, 1860–1935* (Chapel Hill: University of North Carolina Press, 1988), 247.

[31] Livingstone College, "Price Memorial Campaign," 2–10.

[32] Livingstone College, *Souvenir of Livingstone College: A Few Views and Facts Relative to the $250,000 Price Memorial Campaign and the Industrial Department*, pamphlet (1927), n.p.

[33] Campbell, "Origin and Development," 46.

[34] Ibid., 44. Clement received his M.A. degree in history from Northwestern in 1922. He attended graduate school there during the summer of 1923, but didn't return until the summer of 1926, thus showing Trent's influence. Livingstone College, *Annual Catalog, 1926–1927*, 6.

[35] Livingstone College, *The Living Stone* 32, no. 2 (October 1926): 5, 12.

[36] U.S. Department of the Interior, *Survey of Negro Colleges*, 549.

[37] Ibid., 552.

[38] On April 28, 2010, I participated in a roundtable discussion about Trent and Livingstone, with men and women who had been students and teachers at Livingstone in the 1940s and 1950s. Raemi Lancaster Evans, a granddaughter of Kweygir Aggrey, arranged the meeting, which took place in the Andrew Carnegie Library on Livingstone's campus. Even though these respondents were not at Livingstone when Trent became president in 1925, I am assuming that Trent's style of interacting with students and teachers was formed many years before—perhaps when he was Y director for the Third North Carolina Volunteer Infantry, in the Spanish-American War—and had not greatly changed.

[39] Rev. J. A. Armstrong, e-mail message to author, March 11, 2010.

[40] This fictional statement is from a pageant written by Abna Aggrey Lancaster, eldest child of Kwegyir Aggrey. Abna Aggrey Lancaster, "Links in the Legacy of Zion and Livingstone" (self-published, c. 1971), 22–23. Lancaster was a professor of English at Livingstone for many years. George Alexander Brooks Sr., *Peerless Laymen in the*

African Methodist Episcopal Zion Church (State College, PA: Himes Printing Company, 1974), 1:4.

[41] Brooks, *Peerless Laymen*, 1:142–43.

[42] W. J. Trent, "Heralds of a New Day," 1945. The story about Hector is from Homer, *The Iliad*, bk. 6, lines 478-485.

[43] Vernon Jones, "The Student Life of Livingstone," *Star of Zion*, February 25, 1926.

[44] Bishop W. J. Walls, "Newbold Says 'Livingstone Improves,'" *Star of Zion*, March 11, 1926.

[45] "Livingstone Gets New Rating."

[46] "Livingstone College Commencement," *Star of Zion*, May 20, 1926.

[47] "Commencement at Livingstone: The Inauguration of President Trent," *Star of Zion*, June 3, 1926.

[48] Fannie C. Clay, "An Address Delivered at the Inauguration of President Trent," *The Living Stone* 32, no. 2 (October 1926): 4–5.

[49] "Livingstone College Commencement."

[50] Richardson and Price, *Carnegie Library Report*, n.p.

[51] Livingstone College, *Annual Catalog, 1926–1927*, 6–8.

[52] University of Chicago, Office of the University Registrar, Transcript of William Johnson Trent, Summer 1926. Trent spent three summers studying at the University of Chicago. Livingstone College, "Livingstone College Publicity Release" (January 20, 1952), 2.

[53] Editorials, *The Living Stone* 32, no. 2 (October 1926): 3.

[54] "Livingstone College," *Star of Zion*, October 22, 1925.

[55] *The Living Stone*, 32, no. 2 (October 1926): 12–13.

[56] W. J. Trent Jr., journal, 1926.

[57] *Commencement, Morehouse College, Wednesday, June 2, 10 A.M., 1926* (program). The college program included the graduating class of the Morehouse Academy.

[58] W. E. B. Du Bois, *Writings* (New York: The Library of America, 1986), 1286.

[59] Morehouse College, *The Torch* (1923), 22.

[60] W. J. Trent Jr., journal, 1926.

[61] Morehouse College, *The Morehouse Tiger* 1 (Atlanta: Forte and Davies Co., 1925), n.p.; Morehouse College, *Torch*, 76; Samuel G. Freedman, "Generational Shift in Black Christianity Comes to Harvard," *New York Times*, November 11, 2012.

[62] Rowan County, *African-American Heritage Trail*, 10.

[63] Ibid.

[64] "Musician Altona Johns Dies at 73," *N.Y. Amsterdam News*, July 30, 1977. According to Jeanne Adkins, youngest child of Altona Trent Johns, Johns taught Latin at Bennett, as well as music. Jeanne Adkins, e-mail message to author, February 28, 2012.

[65] It was later renamed the Monroe Street School. Rowan County, *African-American Heritage Trail*, 15.

[66] See photograph of wedding party of Sallie Butler and John Rattley, who were wed at Clinton Chapel in Charlotte on June 6, 1881: http://cmhpf.org/Pictures/photographsrattley2.htm. The photograph includes Sallie's sister, the young Mary Butler (bottom, left), who would become Maggie Tate's mother. The photograph also shows nine people who are not family members. Included in that group are Mary Lynch and Victoria Richardson (standing, second and fourth from left).

Another point of connection between Maggie Tate and Lynch was Grace AME Zion Church in Charlotte, the home church of Maggie's family. It was also the home church of Mary Lynch. Janette Thomas Greenwood, *Bittersweet Legacy: The Black and White "Better Classes" in Charlotte, 1850–1910* (Chapel Hill: University of North Carolina Press, 1994), 229, 242.

[67] Glenda Elizabeth Gilmore, *Gender and Jim Crow: Women and the Politics of White Supremacy in North Carolina, 1896–1920* (Chapel Hill: University of North Carolina Press, 1966), 165–174.

[68] Ibid., 155, 162.

[69] Ibid., 156.

[70] Ibid., 162, 190.

[71] "Mrs. W. J. Trent Passes," *Star of Zion*, June 14, 1934.

[72] Livingstone College, *1930 Blue Bear Yearbook* (Benton Review Shop, Fowler, IN), 53.

[73] The church, founded in 1965, was named Soldiers Memorial to honor those Union soldiers who fought to liberate the slaves. Rowan County, *African-American Heritage Trail*, 5.

[74] "A History of Soldiers Memorial African Methodist Episcopal Zion Church," 3–7. George Alexander Brooks Sr. maintains that Trent joined Moore's Chapel AME Zion Church, which was very close to Livingstone's campus and very popular with the faculty. Brooks, *Peerless Laymen*, 1:141. It may be that Trent attended both churches at different times during his many years in Salisbury.

[75] Livingstone College, *Annual Catalog, 1926–1927*, 5–8; "Livingstone College Has Record Breaking Enrollment," *Star of Zion*, October 21, 1926; Smith, *Aggrey of Africa*, 250. Rose Aggrey's husband, Kwegyir Aggrey, remained in Africa to continue his work. Smith, *Aggrey of Africa*, 250.

[76] Livingstone College, *Annual Catalog, 1926–1927*, 18–20, 40, 45, 49. Interestingly, at this time the high school still required two years of Latin. Ibid., 45.

[77] Reginald W. Brown, e-mail message to author, July 27, 2010.

[78] "Marian Anderson Will Sing at Livingstone College Wednesday Evening," *Salisbury Sunday Post*, December 2, 1928.

[79] "Prof. W. J. Trent Succeeding," *Star of Zion*, April 7, 1927 (republished from *The Crisis*).

[80] "Commencement Exercises at Livingstone," *Star of Zion*, May 26, 1927.

[81] "Let Us Rejoice," *Star of Zion*, December 15, 1927. Davenport wrote "three short years," but Trent did not become president until 1925.

Many years later, a Livingstone document stated that the A rating came from the Southern Association of Colleges and Secondary Schools. Livingstone College, "Testimonial Dinner for Doctor William Johnson Trent," 1952. However, according to a 1926 report published in the *Star of Zion*, letter evaluations were made by the North Carolina State Department of Education. "Livingstone Gets New Rating." The relationship between these two organizations is not clear.

[82] U.S. Department of the Interior, *Survey of Negro Colleges*, 545.

[83] Davis, "History of Livingstone College," 150.

[84] Smith, *Aggrey of Africa*, 274–281.

[85] W. J. Trent, "A Man of Great and Lasting Good," *Star of Zion*, August 11, 1927.

[86] Altona Trent Johns, "Foreword: As I Remember," in Samuel Lucius Gandy, ed., *Human Possibilities: A Vernon Johns Reader* (Washington, DC: Hoffman Press, 1977), ix.

[87] Taylor Branch, *Parting the Waters: America in the King Years, 1954–1963* (New York: Simon and Schuster, 1988), 8–9.

[88] Ibid., 6.

[89] Patrick L. Cooney and Henry W. Powell, *The Life and Times of the Prophet Vernon Johns: Father of the Civil Rights Movement*, under chapter 13: "Vernon Johns in Charleston, West Virginia, 1927–1928," Vernon Johns Society, www.vernonjohns.org/tca1001/vjtofc.html; Johns, "Foreword," x. Jeanne Johns Adkins confirmed that the dates and places in the Cooney and Powell document are correct. Jeanne Johns Adkins, e-mail message to author, March 30, 2013.

[90] Altona and Vernon Johns would have five more children.

[91] U.S. Department of the Interior, *Survey of Negro Colleges*, 553–554.

[92] Ibid., 551.

[93] Wendell E. Pritchett, *Robert Clifton Weaver and the American City: The Life and Times of an Urban Reformer* (Chicago: University of Chicago Press, 2008), 14.

[94] U.S. Department of the Interior, *Survey of Negro Colleges*, 550–551.

[95] Livingstone College, Board of Trustees, minutes, July 12, 1929 (hereafter minutes).

[96] Livingstone College, minutes, March 6, 1928.

[97] Davis, "History of Livingstone College," 152.

[98] Walls, *AME Zion*, 318.

[99] This sequence was offered between 1928 and 1931. Davis, "History of Livingstone College,"183.

[100] Ibid., 183–184.

[101] David Levering Lewis, ed., *The Portable Harlem Renaissance Reader* (New York: Viking, 1994), 751.

[102] Alain Locke, ed., *The New Negro: Voices of the Harlem Renaissance* (New York: Simon and Schuster, 1925). David Levering Lewis calls this book a "catalytic anthology." Lewis, *Harlem Renaissance Reader*, 751.

[103] Lewis, *Harlem Renaissance Reader*, xv.

[104] Davis, "History of Livingstone College," 201–202.

[105] Ibid., 176, 182, 202.

[106] Ibid., 202.

[107] Livingstone College, *Annual Catalog, 1931–1932*, 33–36.

[108] Alain Locke, "The New Negro," in *New Negro*, 4, 11.

[109] Davis, "History of Livingstone College," 155.

[110] "Ground Breaking at Livingstone," *Star of Zion*, February 20, 1930.

[111] Livingstone College, minutes, June 3, 1930.

[112] Davis, "History of Livingstone College," 155.

[113] Pritchett, *Robert Clifton Weaver*, 32.

[114] David M. Kennedy, *Freedom from Fear: The American People in Depression and War, 1919–1945* (New York: Oxford University Press, 1999), 69–71.

[115] Harley E. Jolley, *"That Magnificent Army of Youth and Peace": The Civilian Conservation Corps in North Carolina, 1933–1942* (Raleigh: Office of Archives and History, North Carolina Department of Cultural Resources, 2007), 2.

[116] Pritchett, *Robert Clifton Weaver*, 32–33.

[117] Jolley, *"That Magnificent Army,"* 2.

[118] Kennedy, *Freedom from Fear*, 163.

[119] Thomas C. Parramore, "Express Lanes and Country Roads: North Carolina 1920–2001," in Joe A. Mobley, ed., *The Way We Lived in North Carolina* (Chapel Hill: University of North Carolina Press, 2003), 477.

[120] Ibid., 479.

[121] Ibid., 480.

[122] Jolley, *"That Magnificent Army,"* 2.

[123] Davis, "History of Livingstone College," 158.

[124] Marybeth Gasman, *Envisioning Black Colleges: A History of the United Negro College Fund* (Baltimore: Johns Hopkins University Press, 2007), 17–18.

[125] Walls, *AME Zion*, 315.

[126] Livingstone College, minutes, January 15, 1932.

[127] Livingstone College, minutes, May 16, 1932.

[128] Ibid.

[129] Livingstone College, minutes, January 11, 1933.

[130] Livingstone College, minutes, June 6, 1933.

[131] AME Zion Church, Philadelphia and Baltimore Conference, *Livingstone College Campaign, November 8, 1939, to January 30, 1940*, pamphlet, n.d.

[132] Davis, "History of Livingstone College," 194.

[133] Fred McCuistion to W. J. Trent, December 8, 1936 (attached to W. J. Trent letter to W. J. Walls, December 10, 1936). The letter came from the Committee on Approval of Negro Schools, a division of the association.

[134] "Livingstone Is Seeking Funds to Complete Bldgs.," *Salisbury Sunday Post*, December 6, 1936.

[135] W. J. Trent to W. J. Walls, August 10, 1937.

[136] W. J. Walls to W. J. Trent, August 23, 1937.

[137] W. J. Trent to W. J. Walls, September 8, 1937.

[138] W. J. Trent to W. J. Walls, September 9, 1937.

[139] W. J. Walls to W. J. Trent, September 3, 1937.

[140] AME Zion Church, *Livingstone College Campaign.*

[141] Notes on material found in Andrew Carnegie Library, Livingstone College, file drawer with Trent papers and memorabilia (last seen by author in November 1998). The North Carolina Public Service sold gas and electricity. *Salisbury City Directory, 1922–1923*, 238.

[142] Minutes, January 13, 1928, and March 6, 1928. The following year, Trent told the board that he had had the house built and needed the assistance of the trustees. Minutes, June 4, 1929. The small white frame house Trent had built across the street from Livingstone's campus still stands today.

[143] Livingstone College, "Forty-Eighth Annual Commencement of Livingstone College," program, June 4, 1930.

[144] "57 Receive Awards from the U. of P.," *New York Times*, May 11, 1931.

[145] "Dr. Rufus E. Clement, Dean of Louisville Municipal College is Chosen President of Atlanta University," *Atlanta U. Bulletin*, July 1937, 3.

[146] North Carolina State Board of Health, Bureau of Vital Statistics, Standard Certificate of Death, Buncombe County, Registration District Number 11-2065, Certificate No. 207.

[147] Lucy Mae Harrison, Oral History Register, Black Highlander Collection, D. H. Ramsey Library, University of North Carolina at Asheville, audiocassette 1, side 1, OH-VOA H372Lu; electronic record issued July 5, 2001; interview granted March 12, 1994.

[148] North Carolina State Board of Health, Bureau of Vital Statistics, Standard Certificate of Death, Rowan County, Registration District Number 80-2576, Certificate No. 15.

[149] "Mrs. W. J. Trent Passes"; North Carolina State Board of Health, Bureau of Vital Statistics, Standard Certificate of Death, Rowan County, Registration District Number 80-80, Certificate No. 118.

[150] "Funeral Services of Mrs. Margaret Hazel Tate-Trent," funeral program, June 4, 1933.

[151] "Mrs. W. J. Trent Passes."

[152] Walls, *AME Zion*, 596.

[153] Reginald W. Brown, interview with author, September 17, 2008.

[154] Livingstone College, *Catalogue of Livingstone College, 1919–1920*, 65; Rowan County, *African-American Heritage Trail*, 10.

[155] Rowan County, *African-American Heritage Trail*, 10.

[156] Adrienne Lash-Jones, telephone interview with author, January 15, 2013. Lash-Jones is a granddaughter of Wiley H. and Mayzonetta Lash.

[157] "Funeral Services for Mrs. Hattie Covington Trent," funeral program, April 15, 1952.

[158] "Horticulturist: First Lady's Philosophy Works," *The Living-Stone* 1, no.1 (February 14, 1940): n.p.

[159] Brown, interview with author, September 17, 2008; Livingstone College, publicity release (1952), 3.

[160] Julia B. Duncan to W. J. Walls, June 15, 1937.

[161] W. J. Trent to W. J. Walls, July 13, 1937.

[162] W. J. Walls to W. J. Trent, July 30, 1937.

[163] "President Trent Resumes Duties," *The Living Stone*, December 1938.

[164] "We Salute Livingstone College and President William Johnson Trent," *Star of Zion*, February 3, 1944.

[165] "Socialite Marries the Dean of Livingstone: White-Purifoy Nuptials Unite Popular Pair," *The Pittsburgh Courier*, June 29, 1935.

[166] "Graduates," *Journal and Guide*, n.d.

[167] "Mary Trent Now in USA," *The New York Age*, November 27, 1948; Livingstone College, "Heart of Gold," *Livingstone College Bulletin* 7, no. 2 (March 1951): 1.

[168] Johns, "Foreword," viii; Cooney and Powell, *Life and Times*, under chapters 13–17.

[169] Johns, "Foreword," viii.

[170] Greenwood, *Bittersweet Legacy*, 77.

[171] Altona Trent-Johns, *Play Songs of the Deep South* (Washington, DC: Associated Publishers, 1944).

[172] Jeanne Johns Adkins, e-mail message to author, February 15, 2013.

[173] Cooney and Powell, *Life and Times*, under chapter 16, "Vagabond, 1933–1937."

[174] Department of English, North Carolina A&T State University, *Piedmont Afro-American Humanists on Review* (Greensboro), 46.

[175] "The Reminiscences of Dr. William J. Trent Jr." (October 14, 1980), 1–2, in the Columbia Center for Oral History Collection (CCOHC). In CCOHC pagination, the first number refers to the volume, and the subsequent numbers refer to the page(s).

[176] H. Crosby, dean, Graduate School, University of Pennsylvania, language examination certificates (1937); "W. J. Trent Jr. Gets New Job under Federal Works Agency," *Journal and Guide* (1939).

[177] Pritchett, *Robert Clifton Weaver*, 29–30, 41, 75–76.

[178] Ibid., 45–46.

[179] Kennedy, *Freedom from Fear*, 98.

[180] Ibid., 144.

[181] Ibid., 151–152.

[182] Pritchett, *Robert Clifton Weaver*, 54; W. J. Trent Jr., "Address to the Eastern Regional Conference of the National Negro Congress" (speech, Baltimore, October 9, 1938), 3.

[183] Pritchett, *Robert Clifton Weaver*, 55.

[184] Ibid., 44–45.

[185] Ibid., 49.

[186] Rita Liberti, "'We Were Ladies, We Just Played Basketball Like Boys': African American Womanhood and Competitive Basketball at Bennett College, 1928–1942," *Journal of Sport History* 26, no. 3 (Fall 1999): 572, 577.

[187] Federal Emergency Administration of Public Works, Release No. 3405 (July 28, 1938).

[188] Trent Jr. was not the only faculty member at Livingstone who received no salary. At times, none of them received a salary. "Reminiscences of Dr. William J. Trent Jr.," CCOHC, 1–7.

[189] Lenwood G. Davis, William J. Rice, and James H. McLaughlin, *African Americans in Winston-Salem/Forsyth County: A Pictorial History* (Virginia Beach: Donning Company Publishers, 1999), 66–69, 70–71, 142; Bertha Hampton Miller, "Blacks in Winston-Salem, North Carolina, 1895–1920: Community Development in an Era of Benevolent Paternalism" (Ph.D. diss., Duke University, 1981), 97, 99, 103, 122; "The Flamboyant Will Scales," *The Chronicle*, February 24, 1979, n.p. Mary and William Scales would eventually have close to a quarter of a million dollars. Miller, "Blacks in Winston-Salem," 97.

[190] Pritchett, *Robert Clifton Weaver*, 75.

[191] Federal Emergency Administration of Public Works, Press Release No. 3405.

[192] Pritchett, *Robert Clifton Weaver*, 79.

[193] J. J. Madigan to W. J. Trent Jr., postal telegraph, July 19, 1938; "Bennett Professor Gets Federal Post" (1938) (name and date of newspaper not available).

[194] W. J. Trent Sr. to W. J. Trent Jr., July 31, 1938.

[195] W. J. Trent Jr. to Mary McLeod Bethune, December 21, 1938.

[196] "Reminiscences of Dr. William J. Trent Jr.," CCOHC, 1-6.

[197] W. J. Trent Jr., "Statement of Travel 7/38 to 7/39."

[198] Terence Young, "'A Contradiction in Democratic Government': W. J. Trent Jr. and the Struggle to Desegregate the National Park Campgrounds," *Environmental History* 14, no.4 (October 2009): 651.

[199] Ibid., 671.

[200] Robert C. Weaver, "The Black Cabinet," in Katie Louchheim, ed., *The Making of the New Deal: the Insiders Speak* (Cambridge, MA: Harvard University Press, 1983), 262; Nancy J. Weiss, *Farewell to the Party of Lincoln: Black Politics in the Age of FDR* (Princeton, NJ: Princeton University Press, 1983), 136–137. When he entered the federal government, Hastie was assistant solicitor in the Department of the Interior, and he later became a civilian aide to Secretary of War Stimson. Phillip McGuire, *He, Too, Spoke for Democracy: Judge Hastie, World War II, and the Black Soldier* (New York: Greenwood Press, 1988), xiii.

[201] Weiss, *Farewell to the Party of Lincoln*, 138.

[202] W. J. Trent Jr. to Ruth Logan, June 20, 1974.

[203] Weiss, *Farewell to the Party of Lincoln*, 154–155.

[204] W. J. Trent, untitled speech, North Carolina A&T University, Greensboro, 1935.

[205] A. J. Sarré, director of personnel, FWA, to W. J. Trent Jr., April 1, 1940; "Reminiscences of Dr. William J. Trent Jr.," CCOHC, 1–2.

[206] "W. J. Trent, Jr., Gets New Job under Federal Works Agency," *Norfolk Journal and Guide* (only date provided: 1939).

[207] Truman K. Gibson Jr. and Steve Huntley, *Knocking Down Barriers: My Fight for Black America* (Evanston, IL: Northwestern University Press, 2005), 80. At the time they met in Chicago, Gibson, an attorney, was representing, among others, champion heavyweight boxer Joe Louis. Ibid., 75.

[208] Ibid., 80–82. According to Gibson, Trent and Weaver were the two "chief recruiters" in finding new black advisors for federal agencies. Ibid.

[209] Jeanne Johns Adkins, e-mail message to author, April 1, 2013.

[210] In December 1941 Trent Jr. was thirty-one years old.

[211] Livingstone College, "Heart of Gold," *Livingstone College Bulletin* 7, no. 2 (March 1951): 4. Paris was liberated from Nazi control in August 1945, so it is likely that Estelle Trent worked in Paris with the Red Cross between August and December 1945. The only information I was able to obtain from the Red Cross stated that she was in "Club Service" during World War II, in the European and Far Eastern Theater of Operations, including Korea. Patrick R. Bruyere, e-mail message to Nicky Fox, September 7, 2010. Bruyere noted that he could not provide more detail about her work with the Red Cross because many of the older records had been purged. Ibid. According to a 1948 newspaper article, Estelle Trent served in France and Scotland, not France and England. "Mary Trent Now in USA," *The New York Age*, November 27, 1948. It is not clear where the error lies.

[212] James J. Madison, *Slinging Doughnuts for the Boys: An American Woman in World War II* (Bloomington: Indiana University Press, 2007), 11.

[213] Ibid., 23–25.

[214] Ibid., 25.

[215] While undergoing six weeks of training in Washington, DC, the white and black trainees were assigned to segregated housing. Ibid., 141, 276; Kathryn Richardson Tyler with Jesse O. Thomas, *American Red Cross Negro Personnel in World War II, 1942–1946*, vol. 32 in *The History of the American National Red Cross* (Washington, DC: The American National Red Cross, 1950), 41–44.

[216] Madison, *Slinging Doughnuts*, 141–142.

[217] Tyler, *American Red Cross Negro Personnel*, 17.

[218] Ibid., 41.

[219] Madison, *Slinging Doughnuts*, 141.

[220] Brenda L. Moore, *To Serve My Country, To Serve My Race: The Story of the Only African American WACs Stationed Overseas during World War II* (New York: New York University Press, 1996), 121–122, 141.

[221] Ibid., 141.

[222] Ibid., 136.

[223] Kennedy, *Freedom from Fear*, 710.

[224] Leslie Stokes, phone interview with author, April 12, 2012. Stokes is from Farmville, Virginia, home of the Vernon Johns family, and is an alumnus of Livingstone College.

[225] Tyler, *American Red Cross Negro Personnel*, 54–56.

[226] Madison, *Slinging Doughnuts*, 10–11.

[227] Ibid., 20–21.

[228] Ibid., 39.

[229] Ibid., 21.

[230] Ibid., 161, 193.

[231] Ibid., 244–245.

[232] *State of Missouri ex rel. Gaines v. Canada*, 305 U.S. 337, 342–343 (1938).

[233] 305 U.S. 342.

[234] 305 U.S. 345, 350–352.

[235] W. J. Trent Jr., "Private Negro Colleges Since the *Gaines* Decision," *Journal of Educational Sociology* 32, no. 6 (February 1959): 268.

[236] W. J. Walls to W. J. Trent, October 27, 1941.

[237] "Broughton Addresses National Negro Church Convention Here," *Salisbury Evening Post*, August 13, 1942.

[238] H. A. I. Clement, "Dr. Mary McLeod Bethune Speaks Here," *Salisbury Evening Post*, August 13, 1942.

[239] Valerie Nicholson, "First Lady Gives Salisbury a Day from One of World's Busiest Lives," *Salisbury Evening Post*, August 13, 1942; "Mrs. Roosevelt Is Greeted at Station Here," *Salisbury Evening Post*, August 13, 1942.

[240] "Mrs. Roosevelt Breaks Bread with Local Group Delegates," *Salisbury Evening Post*, August 13, 1942.

[241] "First Lady Outlines Ideals of Equal Opportunities in Panel Discussion Here Today," *Salisbury Evening Post*, August 13, 1942.

[242] "Eleanor Roosevelt Speaks Here on Freedoms for Which We Struggle," *Salisbury Evening Post*, August 14, 1942.

[243] Bill Snider, "Governor Extols Cooperation of Races in N.C.," *Salisbury Evening Post*, August 13, 1942.

[244] Rufus E. Clement, "The Student in the College for Negroes," *The Journal of Educational Sociology* 19, no. 8 (April 1946): 503. The author includes in this number all two- and four-year black institutions, whether accredited or not. Ibid.

[245] Livingstone College, *Annual Catalog, 1942–1943*, 84.

[246] Ibid., 40–71.

[247] W. J. Trent, "An Address by W. J. Trent, President of Livingstone College, Salisbury, North Carolina, at the United Negro College Fund Campaign Meeting, Hotel Waldorf-Astoria, New York City, Wednesday, May 3, 1944," 2–3.

[248] Kennedy, *Freedom from Fear*, 476–477.

[249] "Livingstone College Founder's Day in the Offing," *Star of Zion*, January 4, 1945.

[250] Brooks, *Peerless Laymen*, 1:142.

[251] Campbell, "Origin and Development," 91–92.

[252] AME Zion Church, "Livingstone College Campaign," 1939.

[253] "Bishop Walls Leads in Founder's Day Campaign," *The Seminarian* 1, no.2 (May 1943): 1.

[254] Davis, "History of Livingstone College," 145.

[255] "Livingstone College Finals Speaker."

[256] W. W. Brierly to W. J. Trent, May 15, 1942.

[257] Campbell, "Origin and Development," 89.

[258] "Livingstone Dedicates Price Memorial Building," *The Seminarian* 1, no. 2 (May 1943):1.

[259] "Livingstone College Finals Speaker."

[260] Gasman, *Envisioning Black Colleges*, 204.

[261] John D. Rockefeller Jr.'s financial gifts led to his control of the United Negro College Fund during its early years. Gasman, *Envisioning Black Colleges*, 33, 39–40, 57–58.

[262] Shauna K. Tucker, "The Early Years of the United Negro College Fund," *The Journal of African American History* 87, New Perspectives on African American Educational History (Autumn 2002): 417. There would be twenty-seven member colleges in the UNCF when it was created, schools that represented the strongest black colleges, in both an academic and financial sense. Henry N. Drewry and Humphrey Doermann, *Stand and Prosper: Private Black Colleges and Their Students* (Princeton, NJ: Princeton University Press, 2001), 93.

[263] "Reminiscences of Dr. W. J. Trent Jr.," CCOHC, 1–7.

[264] Tucker, "Early Years," 417.

[265] "Reminiscences of Dr. W. J. Trent Jr.," CCOHC, 1–10.

[266] Ibid., 1–5.

[267] In 1943, W. J. Trent Jr., at thirty-three years of age, was draft eligible. For that reason, he hesitated to accept the position as executive director of the Fund. Dr. Frederick D. Patterson requested and obtained a draft deferral for him. Goodson, ed., *Chronicles of Faith*, 129–130.

[268] Michael L. Gillette, *Lady Bird Johnson: An Oral History* (Oxford: Oxford University Press, 2012), 77.

[269] W. J. Trent, "Life-Sketch of President W. J. Trent," 1.

[270] "Reminiscences of Dr. W. J. Trent Jr.," CCOHC, 1–7, 1–8.

[271] "One Agency's Loss Is Another's Gain," *Norfolk Journal and Guide*, March 25, 1944.

[272] P. B. Young to W. J. Trent Jr., February 14, 1944.

[273] "We Salute Livingstone College and President William Johnson Trent," *Star of Zion*, February 3, 1944.

[274] W. J. Trent, *Quadrennial Report*, March 1944, 2–4.

[275] "President Trent's Letter to Alumni," *The Livingstone College Bulletin* 1, no.1 (April 1944).

[276] "27 Negro Colleges in $1,500,000 Drive," *New York Times*, May 4, 1944.

Chapter 6

[1] Frederick D. Patterson to W. J. Trent Jr., November 14, 1963.

[2] Peregrine Whittlesey, e-mail messages to author, May 27 and 29, 2014; "The Reminiscences of Dr. William J. Trent Jr." (October 14, 1980), 1-9, in the Columbia Center for Oral History Collection (CCOHC); "The Reminiscences of Dr. William J. Trent Jr." (August 14, 1981), 2-127. In CCOHC pagination, the first number refers to the volume, and the subsequent numbers refer to the page(s).

[3] Martia Graham Goodson, ed., *Chronicles of Faith: The Autobiography of Frederick D. Patterson* (Tuscaloosa: University of Alabama Press, 1991), 130.

[4] "Reminiscences of Dr. William J. Trent Jr."(October 14, 1980), 1-22–23.

[5] Ibid., 1-14, 1-25.

[6] William J. Trent Jr., "The Problems of Financing Private Negro Colleges," *Journal of Negro Education* 18, no. 2 (Spring 1949): 118.

[7] William J. Trent Jr., *Interim Report of Executive Secretary at the Meeting of United Negro College Fund, Inc., Atlanta, Georgia, June 27, 1944*, 1–2, 6. Those thirteen cities were Boston, Chicago, Cleveland, Dallas, Detroit, Houston, Memphis, New York City, Philadelphia, Pittsburgh, Richmond, Rochester, and Washington, DC. Ibid., 7–10.

[8] David M. Kennedy, *Freedom from Fear: The American People in Depression and War, 1929–1945* (New York: Oxford University Press, 1999), 574–575, 591, 718–720.

[9] Ibid., 721–722.

[10] Ibid., 703.

[11] Ibid., 732, 739–742.

[12] Ibid., 809.

[13] Ibid., 815, 824.

[14] Ibid., 845–847.

[15] Ibid., 849–851.

[16] William J. Trent, untitled speech, North Carolina A&T University, Greensboro, 1935.

[17] William J. Trent, "Broadcast WSTP, December 17, 1946." WSTP is a radio station in Salisbury, NC.

[18] William J. Trent Jr., "Cooperative Fund-Raising for Higher Education," *Journal of Negro Education* 24, no. 1 (Winter 1955):11.

[19] Trent Jr., "Problems of Financing Private Negro Colleges," 118.

[20] Marybeth Gasman, *Envisioning Black Colleges: A History of the United Negro College Fund* (Baltimore, MD: Johns Hopkins University Press, 2007), 29–30; William J. Trent Jr., "The Relative Adequacy of Sources of Income of Negro Church-Related Colleges," *Journal of Negro Education* 29, no. 3 (Summer 1960): 359; Trent Jr., "Cooperative Fund Raising, 8. The member schools located in the North had to be accredited by the relevant accreditation association. Trent Jr., "Problems of Financing Private Negro Colleges," 117.

[21] Trent Jr., "Cooperative Fund Raising," 9.

[22] Ibid., 9–10.

[23] W. J. Trent Jr. to Turner C. Battle III, July 20, 1976.

[24] "Reminiscences of Dr. William J. Trent Jr." (October 14, 1980), 1-35.

[25] Charles S. Johnson, "The Control and Administration of the Negro College," *The Journal of Educational Sociology* 19, no. 8 (April 1946): 494. Johnson was a professor at

Fisk University and later became that school's first black president. BlackPast.org, "Johnson, Charles S. (1893–1956)," BlackPast.org: An Online Reference Guide to African American History, http://www.blackpast.org/aah/johnson-charles-s-1893-1956. Between 1914 and 1929 there were approximately a dozen strikes at historically black colleges and universities, as students protested both their lack of access to governing the schools and the schools' rigid rules. Martin Summers, *Manliness and Its Discontents: The Black Middle Class and the Transformation of Masculinity, 1900–1930* (Chapel Hill: University of North Carolina Press, 2004), 242.

[26] "Reminiscences of Dr. William J. Trent Jr." (August 14, 1981), 2-132–133.

[27] Gasman, *Envisioning Black Colleges*, 39. Kimball was at various times executive vice-president of the Rockefeller Foundation, associate of the Rockefeller Brothers Fund, trustee and treasurer of Rockefeller University, and an assistant to John D. Rockefeller Jr. Bruce Lambert, "Lindsley F. Kimball, 97, is Dead; Founded New York Blood Center," *New York Times*, August 21, 1992.

[28] Gasman, *Envisioning Black Colleges*, 40–42.

[29] "Reminiscences of Dr. William J. Trent Jr. (October 14, 1980), 1-57.

[30] Ibid., 1-26–27.

[31] Trent Jr., "Relative Adequacy," 363.

[32] Shauna K. Tucker, "The Early Years of the United Negro College Fund, 1943–1960," *Journal of African American History* 87 (Autumn 2002): 421.

[33] Trent Jr., "Relative Adequacy," 363.

[34] William J. Trent, *Annual Report to Board of Trustees of Livingstone College, 1944–1945*, 1.

[35] W. J. Trent to W. J. Walls, October 8, 1944.

[36] Trent, *Annual Report, 1944–1945*, 3.

[37] W. J. Trent to W. J. Walls, June 22, 1949.

[38] William J. Trent, *Annual Report to Board of Trustees of Livingstone College, 1952–1953*, June 1, 1953, 2.

[39] William J. Trent, untitled speech, 1950. Those five black North Carolina schools in the Fund were Livingstone College, Bennett College, Johnson C. Smith University, St. Augustine's College, and Shaw University. Ibid.

[40] William J. Trent, *Annual Report to Board of Trustees of Livingstone College, 1950–1951*, June 5, 1951, 2.

[41] Trent Jr., "Cooperative Fund Raising," 11.

[42] William J. Trent, *President's Quadrennial Report of Livingstone College, Salisbury NC, Beginning April 1, 1952, and Ending March 31, 1956*, May 1956, 5, 11.

[43] Lenwood G. Davis, "A History of Livingstone College, 1879–1957" (Ph.D. diss., Carnegie-Mellon University, 1979), 162.

[44] Henry N. Drewry and Humphrey Doermann, *Stand and Prosper: Private Black Colleges and Their Students* (Princeton: Princeton University Press, 2001), 79.

[45] Davis, "History of Livingstone College," 207.

[46] Ibid.

[47] Ibid., 162–163.

[48] "3 Livingstone College Pre-Med Students Make Straight A's," *Star of Zion*, February 16, 1950.

[49] The Selective Service Readjustment Act ("G.I. Bill of Rights") was enacted in June 1944, a few days after the United States invaded France. Its goal was to facilitate the integration of 16 million World War II veterans into America, by helping them attend college, buy homes, start businesses, and find jobs. Ira Katznelson, *When Affirmative Action Was White: An Untold History of Racial Inequality in Twentieth-Century America* (New York: Norton, 2005), 113–114.

[50] Ibid., 130–132.

[51] Marybeth Gasman et al., *Unearthing Promise and Potential: Our Nation's Historically Black Colleges and Universities* 35, no.5, ASHE Higher Education Report (San Francisco: Jossey-Bass, 2010), 64.

[52] Katznelson, *When Affirmative Action Was White*, 134. Black veterans were also cut out of vocational education, on-the-job training, and help finding jobs, all funded by the G.I. Bill. Ibid., 134–140.

[53] Summers, *Manliness and Its Discontents*, 242.

[54] William J. Trent Sr., "Notice to All Parents of Students Attending Livingstone College," January 25, 1946.

[55] "Livingstone Has Student Strike," *Salisbury Evening Post*, January 30, 1946.

[56] "Livingstone Student Group Goes to Court," *Salisbury Evening Post*, February 1, 1946.

[57] "Livingstone Has Student Strike."

[58] "Livingstone Student Group Goes to Court."

[59] "Livingstone Students Will Have To Re-Apply for Admission," *Salisbury Sunday Post*, February 3, 1946.

[60] Livingstone College, board of trustees, minutes, February 13, 1946, 2–3 (hereafter minutes). Professor Harold Clement was fired because he opened a post office box for correspondence about the strike, presumably a box used by the strikers. Professor Charles A. Benjamin was fired for failure to support the administration during the strike. Ibid.

[61] Ibid., 4–7. The board also decided during this meeting not to rehire the two faculty members Trent dismissed for facilitating the student strike. Ibid., 8.

[62] Ibid., 4.

[63] Davis, "History of Livingstone College," 206.

[64] Minutes, February 13, 1946, 4.

[65] William J. Trent, *Annual Report to Board of Trustees of Livingstone College, 1945–1946*, June 30, 1946, 2.

[66] "Bishop Signer in College Suit," *Salisbury Evening Post*, February 4, 1946.

[67] Alice Horton, "Negro News and Activity," *Salisbury Evening Post*, October 4, 1944. The open house continued all weekend. Ibid.

[68] W. J. Trent to William J. Walls, September 10, 1944.

[69] William J. Walls to W. J. Trent, September 30, 1944.

[70] Ibid.

[71] W. J. Trent to William J. Walls, October 8, 1944.

[72] "Dr. Trent to Speak at YMI," *Asheville Citizen*, March 25, 1945.

[73] Hattie Covington Trent, *My Memory Gems* (Salisbury, NC: Livingstone College, 1948).

[74] J. Van Catledge Jr., "Foreword," in Trent, *My Memory Gems*, vii.

[75] "Livingstone College in Stirring Commencement," *Star of Zion*, June 7, 1945.

[76] Rev. A. H. Hatwood and Edgar Lubin Hatwood Sr., *The Story of Zion's Sesquicentennial*, 1946, cover; William J. Walls, *The African Methodist Episcopal Zion Church: Reality of the Black Church* (Charlotte, NC: AME Zion Publishing House, 1974) (hereafter *AME Zion*), 563.

[77] "AMEZ's Told to Work for One World," *Amsterdam News*, September 14, 1946.

[78] Hatwood and Hatwood, *Zion's Sesquicentennial*, 44.

[79] The local YMCA and YWCA also hosted sesquicentennial events and housed out-of-town visitors who were attending the celebration. Ibid., 42, 56.

[80] Ibid., 35.

[81] Ibid., 35–37, 41.

[82] Walls, *AME Zion*, 563.

[83] Hatwood and Hatwood, *Zion's Sesquicentennial*, 42–43, 48; Walls, *AME Zion*, 563.

[84] Walls, *AME Zion*, 560.

[85] Hatwood and Hatwood, *Zion's Sesquicentennial*, 44–45.

[86] Ibid., 39, 48.

[87] Ibid., 37; Walls, *AME Zion*, 596; George Alexander Brooks Sr., *Peerless Laymen in the African Methodist Episcopal Zion Church* (State College, PA: Himes Printing Company, 1974), 1:35–36.

[88] Hatwood and Hatwood, *Zion's Sesquicentennial*, 40.

[89] "Negroes' Self-Aid in U.S. Commended," *New York Times*, September 21, 1946.

[90] Ibid.

[91] Hatwood and Hatwood, *Zion's Sesquicentennial*, 40; "Negroes' Self-Aid in U.S."

[92] Hatwood and Hatwood, *Zion's Sesquicentennial*, 40, 50.

[93] Livingstone College, minutes, June 3, 1947.

[94] "Founder's Day at Livingstone College," *Star of Zion*, February 16, 1950.

[95] "Livingstone College Observes Trent Day: Silver Anniversary," *Star of Zion*, May 4, 1950; "College Pays Tribute to President Trent on 25th Year at Livingstone," *Livingstone College Bulletin* 6, no. 3 (May 1950): 1.

[96] The plaque is in the possession of the author.

[97] William J. Trent, *Annual Report to Board of Trustees of Livingstone College, 1949–1950*, June 5–6, 1950, 4.

[98] "Trent Collection, Books Received to Date, June 23, 1950." This one-page document is located in the Andrew Carnegie Library, Livingstone College. When Langston Hughes visited Livingstone later that year for a poetry reading, a photographer took a picture of Hughes and Trent standing in front of the "Trent Collection" plaque and book collection, with Hughes inscribing a volume of his poetry. "Library Presents Langston Hughes," *The Living Stone* (December 1950). Because no hotel rooms were available for black people in Salisbury, black speakers and artists stayed with Livingstone faculty and administrators. Hughes stayed with the Aggrey family. Raemi Lancaster Evans, group interview. Similarly, when Marian Anderson came to Salisbury to perform at Livingstone in 1926 and 1928, she stayed with the Trents. "Reminiscences of Dr. William J. Trent Jr."(August 14, 1981), 2-153. In this situation, then, segregation provided a rich artistic and intellectual environment for Livingstone's faculty, administrators, and their families.

[99] *Livingstone College Bulletin* 6, no. 3 (May 1950): 1.

[100] William J. Walls, *The Romance of a College: An Evolution of the Auditorium* (New York: Vantage Press, 1963), 25.

[101] Indeed, the following year, the Committee on Approval of Negro Schools of the Southern Association of Colleges and Secondary Schools sent Trent a letter warning that Livingstone needed to correct several deficiencies, including low faculty salaries, inadequate faculty training, and high administrative expenses, before the following meeting of the Association. J. Henry Highsmith to W. J. Trent, December 20, 1951.

[102] Heath Thomas, "Appointment to School Board Tribute to Trent," *Salisbury Evening Post*, July 22, 1951.

[103] "Dr. W. J. Trent Is First Negro Member of City School Board," *Salisbury Evening Post*, July 18, 1951.

[104] Taylor Branch, *Parting the Waters: America in the King Years, 1954–1963* (New York: Simon and Schuster, 1988), 13, 66.

[105] *Smith v. Allwright*, 321 U.S. 649 (1944) (white primaries); *Morgan v. Virginia*, 328 U.S. 373 (1946) (interstate transport); *Shelley v. Kraemer*, 334 U.S. 1 (1948) (racial covenants); *Henderson v. US*, 339 U.S. 816 (1950) (railway dining cars).

[106] Jeffrey J. Crow, Paul D. Escott, and Flora J. Hatley, *A History of African Americans in North Carolina*, rev. ed. (Raleigh: North Carolina Department of Cultural Resources, 2002), 163. McKissick entered the law school only after the NAACP won a court order to admit him. He became an activist in the civil rights movement and was head of the Congress of Racial Equality (CORE) in the 1960s. Glenn Fowler, "Floyd McKissick, Civil Rights Maverick, Dies at 69," *New York Times*, April 30, 1991.

[107] The U.S. Congress never passed antilynching legislation. Sheryl Gay Stolberg, "Senate Issues Apology over Failure on Lynching Law," *New York Times*, June 14, 2005.

[108] "Brief Biography of Dr. Trent," *Star of Zion*, January 31, 1952.

[109] "Heart of Gold," *Livingstone College Bulletin* 7, no. 2 (March 1951): 1–2; *Livingstone College Bulletin* (August 1948): 2. While in Japan she served as program director at Army Service Clubs in Yokohama, Kobo, and Gifu. "Mary Trent Now in USA," *New York Age*, November 27, 1948.

[110] "Heart of Gold," 1–2.

[111] "Funeral Services for Mrs. Hattie Covington Trent" (program).

[112] Patrick L. Cooney and Henry W. Powell, *The Life and Times of the Prophet Vernon Johns: Father of the Civil Rights Movement*, under chapter 23: "Vernon Johns at Dexter Avenue Baptist Church: 1948–1952," Vernon Johns Society, www.vernonjohns.org/tcal001/vjtofc.html; Cooney and Powell, *Life and Times*, under chapter 25: "Montgomery, Later Years, 1950–1952."

[113] Branch, *Parting the Waters*, 6–26. A year and a half later, Dexter Avenue Baptist Church hired Martin Luther King Jr. as pastor. Because of Vernon John's activism while he was minister at Dexter, he has been considered a "forerunner" of King's work both at Dexter Baptist and in the larger civil rights movement. Ibid.

[114] Jeanne Johns Adkins, e-mail message to author, July 5, 2013.

[115] Minutes, February 10, 1954; Stephen Gill Spottswood to W. J. Trent Jr., July 1, 1971.

[116] W. J. Trent to W. J. Trent Jr., December 4, 1943; Lester B. Johnson Jr. to author, July 30, 2012.

[117] "Beloved Educator Will Tour Europe as Reward for Long Years' Service," *Salisbury Evening Post*, July 11, 1952.

[118] "Funeral Services for Mrs. Hattie Covington Trent."

[119] "President Trent Reports on Trip Abroad," *The Alumni Bulletin*, September 1952, 1.

[120] "President Reports on European Trip," *The Living Stone* (October 1952), 1.

[121] *Jet*, July 2, 1953, n.p.

[122] Eileen Southern, *Biographical Dictionary of Afro-American and African Musicians* (Westport, CT: Greenwood Press, 1982), 79.

[123] Allan Keiler, *Marian Anderson: A Singer's Journey* (New York: Scribner, 2000), 44.

[124] Penman Lovinggood, *Famous Modern Negro Musicians* (New York: DaCapo Press, 1978), 34. This text was originally published in 1921. Other artists on his select list include such notables as Roland Hayes, Samuel Coleridge-Taylor, and Nathaniel E. Dett. He also noted that Collins was on the editorial staff of the art journal *Music and Poetry*. Ibid., 37.

[125] Southern, *Biographical Dictionary*, 79.

[126] Ibid.

[127] *A History of Soldiers Memorial AME Zion Church*, 9; Raemi Lancaster Evans, group interview with author, Livingstone College, April 28, 2010.

[128] Jeanne Johns Adkins, e-mail message to author, July 5, 2011.

[129] Reginald W. Brown, interview with author, Salisbury, NC, September 17, 2008.

[130] *Brown v. Board of Education*, 347 U.S. 483, 495 (1954).

[131] William J. Trent Jr., "A Statement from the United Negro College Fund," *Journal of Negro Education* 24, no. 4 (Autumn 1955): 498–499 (Patterson statement on *Brown*).

[132] *Brown v. Board of Education of Topeka*, 349 U.S. 294, 300 (1955).

[133] Mark Newman, *The Civil Rights Movement* (Edinburgh, Scot.: Edinburgh University Press, 2004), 52–53.

[134] Crow, Escott, and Hatley, *History of African Americans*, 169–172.

[135] Trent Jr., "Relative Adequacy," 363.

[136] William J. Trent Jr. and Frederick D. Patterson, "Financial Support of the Private Negro College," *Journal of Negro Education* 27, no. 3 (Summer 1958): 404. Enrollment in the black colleges also increased during this period, from 22,000 students in 1953–1954 to 24,000 in 1958–1959. Gasman, *Envisioning Black Colleges*, 96–98.

[137] Trent, *Annual Report, 1950–1951*, 4.

[138] William J. Trent Jr., "Private Negro Colleges since the *Gaines* Decision," in *Journal of Educational Sociology* 32, no. 6, special issue, Southern Higher Education since the *Gaines* Decision: A Twenty Year Review (February 1959): 271. After Congress enacted Title VII of the 1964 Civil Rights Act, prohibiting employment discrimination, black colleges and universities had to compete for black faculty with the better-provisioned public and private white schools. 42 U.S.C. sec. 2000e et seq., as amended.

[139] William J. Trent, unpublished speech, 1955.

[140] AME Zion Church, "Livingstone College," *The Missionary Seer*, February 1956, 4–5; Trent, *Quadrennial Report, 1952–1956*, 7.

[141] References to these events are in Lyceum programs from 1949 and 1951, and are, as well, in back copies of *The Living Stone* between 1948 and 1957 (author's notes). Julia Bell Duncan served as registrar and treasurer of Livingstone College for fifty years. Rowan County Convention and Visitors' Bureau, *African American Heritage Trail*, pamphlet (n.d.), 10. Robert McFerrin Sr. was the first African American man to sing in the Metropolitan Opera in New York City. His son, Bobby McFerrin, is a jazz vocalist and composer. "Showcasing an Eclectic Musical Biography and Some, Not All of That Jazz: Bobby McFerrin and the Jazz at Lincoln Center Orchestra," *New York Times*,

September 14, 2012; "'Porgy' and Music's Racial Politics," *New York Times*, December 13, 1998.

[142] George L. P. Weaver was director of the Civil Rights Committee of the Congress of Industrial Organizations (CIO). After the 1955 CIO merger with the American Federation of Labor, he became head of that union's Civil Rights Committee. "George L. P. Weaver, Assistant Secretary of Labor," *Washington Post*, July 18, 1995.

[143] Trent, *Quadrennial Report,1952–1956*, 1–3.

[144] Livingstone College, *Diamond Jubilee Bulletin*, June 1957, n.p.

[145] Donald C. Agnew to W. J. Trent, September 13, 1956.

[146] Newman, *Civil Rights Movement*, 54–58; *Browder v. Gayle*, 352 U.S. 903 (1956).

[147] "W. J. Trent Resigns as Livingstone Head," *The Afro-American*, June 15, 1957; Jeanne Johns Adkins, two e-mail messages to author, April 16, 2013.

[148] William J. Walls to W. J. Trent, March 24, 1956; W. J. Trent to William J. Walls, March 27, 1956.

[149] William J. Walls to W. J. Trent, March 30, 1956; W. J. Trent to William J. Walls, April 13, 1956.

[150] W. J. Trent to William J. Walls, July 20, 1956.

[151] Minutes, February 10, 1954.

[152] Minutes, June 5, 1956. The minutes quoted this statement by Clement. This was a sign of its importance, as quotes rarely appeared in the board minutes.

[153] Minutes, June 5, 1956.

[154] Livingstone College, "Re-elected," *The Alumni Bulletin*, June 1956, 4.

[155] Livingstone College, "William Johnson Trent: Milestone after Milestone," *The Alumni Bulletin*, June 1956, 2.

[156] "Trent President Emeritus July 1st," *The Alumni Bulletin*, June 1957, 1.

[157] Lindsley F. Kimball to W. J. Trent, June 14, 1957.

[158] Brooks, *Peerless Laymen*, 1:48–50.

[159] Branch, *Parting the Waters*, 222–224.

[160] Louise Marie Rountree, *Administrative Profiles for the Centennial Celebration, February 6, 1980* (Salisbury, NC: Livingstone College, 1980), n.p.

[161] "Testimonial for Dr. W. J. Trent, '98, President Emeritus, Set for June 1st," *The Alumni Bulletin*, May 1959, 1.

[162] *Livingstone College*, photo and text (1958); Minutes, September 11, 1959.

[163] Samuel E. Duncan, *President's Quadrennial Report of Livingstone College, Salisbury NC, Beginning April 1, 1956, and Ending March 31, 1960*, March 1960, 16.

[164] In a letter dated May 15, 1957, Rev. M. L. King Jr. thanked Altona Trent Johns for giving a concert at Dexter Avenue Baptist Church. The papers of Martin Luther King Jr., "To Altona Trent Johns," The Martin Luther King Jr. Research and Education Institute at Stanford University, http://mlk-kpp01.stanford.edu/kingweb/publications/papers/vol4/570515A-007%20To%20Altona%20Trent%20Johns.htm.

[165] Cooney and Powell, *Life and Times of the Prophet Vernon Johns*, under chapter 27: "Vernon Johns' Final Years."

[166] William J. Trent Jr., "The United Negro College Fund's African Scholarship Program," *Journal of Negro Education* 31, no. 2 (Spring 1962): 205–208.

[167] Gasman, *Envisioning Black Colleges*, 139–140. A photograph taken at this meeting appears on these same pages.

[168] President John F. Kennedy to William J. Trent Jr., telegram, June 15, 1963.

[169] Wendell E. Pritchett, *Robert Clifton Weaver and the American City: The Life and Times of an Urban Reformer* (Chicago: University of Chicago Press, 2008), 220. Weaver was sworn in on February 11, 1961. In 1965, when President Lyndon B. Johnson appointed him head of the newly created Department of Housing and Urban Development, Weaver became this country's first black cabinet member. Ibid., 2, 220.

[170] William J. Trent Jr. to "a very special group," January 6, 1961. In Kathleen A. Hauke's biography of Ted Poston, the author referred to Trent's invitation and included a photograph of the assembled group. Kathleen A. Hauke, *Ted Poston: Pioneer American Journalist* (Athens: University of Georgia Press, 1998), 154–155; see photo of assembled group following page 140. Frederick D. Patterson was president of Tuskegee Institute and the founder of the United Negro College Fund. In 1987 President Ronald Reagan awarded him the Presidential Medal of Freedom. Goodson, *Chronicles of Faith*, 43, 123–124, 183. Ralph Bunche created the Political Science Department at Howard University, where he taught for many years; he worked in the federal government during World War II as a senior social science analyst; and he was actively involved in the creation of the United Nations. In 1950 Bunche received the Nobel Peace Prize for achieving an armistice agreement between Palestine and the Arab states. Brian Urquhart, *Ralph Bunche: An American Life* (New York: W. W. Norton, 1993), 44, 102–103, 110, 112–122; Gunnar Jahn, Nobel Award ceremony speech, http://www.nobelprize.org/nobel_prizes/peace/laureates/1950/press.html. Thurgood Marshall, an attorney in private practice in Baltimore, became chief counsel to the NAACP in 1940 and represented that organization in many civil rights cases before the U.S. Supreme Court. In 1967 President Lyndon B. Johnson nominated Marshall to a position on the Supreme Court and the Senate confirmed the nomination. Marshall was the first black person to serve on the Court. Juan Williams, *Thurgood Marshall: American Revolutionary* (New York: Random House, 1998), xv–xvi, 11–13, 61–62, 99–101.

[171] William J. Trent Jr., note in diary for 1954; "Slews of News," *The Pittsburgh Courier*, August 15, 1953; Altona Adelaide Johns Anderson, eldest daughter of Altona Trent Johns, e-mail message to author, June 30, 2013.

[172] Altona Adelaide Johns Anderson, e-mail message to author, June 30, 2013. Estelle Trent Stewart was still alive when Trent retired in 1957. "Dr. Trent Resigns from Livingstone" (June 1957) (name of newspaper not available).

[173] Samuel E. Duncan, Livingstone College, *Quadrennial Report, 1956–1960; Livingstone College Bulletin* 16, no. 4 (Spring 1968), 1. In 1968, the tenth year of Duncan's presidency, as he was preparing to attend a committee meeting about the construction of the tenth new college building, he died. "College Leader, Dr. Duncan, Dies," *Salisbury Evening Post*, July 11, 1968.

[174] Branch, *Parting the Waters*, 271, 273; Glenda Elizabeth Gilmore, *Gender and Jim Crow: Women and the Politics of White Supremacy in North Carolina, 1896–1920* (Chapel Hill: University of North Carolina Press, 1996), 225; Peniel E. Joseph, *Stokely: A Life* (New York: Basic Civitas, 2014), 19.

[175] Branch, *Parting the Waters*, 272–273. There had also been earlier sit-ins in the North. For example, as early as the 1840s, black parents in Buffalo, New York, sent their children to the white schools to protest the bad conditions in the city's "African" school. The black children were soon removed from those schools. Arthur O. White, "The Black Movement against Jim Crow Education in Buffalo, New York, 1800–1900," *Phylon* 30:380 (1969).

[176] Branch, *Parting the Waters*, 274.

[177] Ibid., 275.

[178] Ibid., 283.

[179] Newman, *Civil Rights Movement*, 70.

[180] Joseph, *Stokely*, 46.

[181] Branch, *Parting the Waters*, 276.

[182] Presidents of the black state schools also had to be aware of possible pressure from the state. In Montgomery, Alabama, soon after the Greensboro sit-in, 35 black students from Alabama State University walked into the white cafeteria in the state capitol, asked to be served, then left when they were refused. Governor Patterson ordered the president of Alabama State, H. Councill Trenholm, a state employee, to expel all 35 students, and he did. This led to a rally of over 4,000 the next day, a prayer vigil at the capitol, and the expulsion of even more black students by the state board of education. Branch, *Parting the Waters*, 280–282. Thousands of students were expelled from state schools during the civil rights movement. Newman, *Civil Rights Movement*, 72.

[183] Newman, *Civil Rights Movement*, 72; Branch, *Parting the Waters*, 323–324.

[184] Capus M. Waynick, John C. Brooks, and Elsie W. Pitts, eds., *North Carolina and the Negro* (Raleigh: State College Print Shop, 1964), 152–153.

[185] Rowan County, *African-American Heritage Trail*, 6.

[186] "The Old Order Changed," *Salisbury Post*, August 29, 1962. It was not until 1966 that a federal court held that North Carolina's constitutional amendments designed to evade the requirements of *Brown v. Board* violated U.S. Supreme Court doctrine about school segregation and were therefore unconstitutional. *Hawkins* v. *North Carolina State Board of Education*, 11 *Race Relations Law Reporter* 745 (1966).

[187] "Educator Has Birthday," *Salisbury Post*, January 1, 1962.

[188] "Trent Funeral Services Set," *Salisbury Evening Post*, June 15, 1963.

[189] Micah 6:6–8 (New Revised Standard Version).

[190] 1 Corinthians 13:1–8.

[191] "Dr. Trent's Funeral," n.d.; "Dr. W. J. Trent Guided Livingstone 33 Years," *Norfolk Journal and Guide*, June 29, 1963.

[192] "Trent Funeral Services Set."

[193] These words come from 2 Timothy 4:7 (King James Version).

[194] "Dr. William J. Trent," *Salisbury Sunday Post*, June 16, 1963.

[195] "Fund Established in Memory of President Trent," *The Alumni Bulletin*, July 1963, 5. Six months after his father's death, William Johnson Trent Jr. left the UNCF after twenty years of service. By then, he had put the organization on a sound footing, where it had grown in influence and prestige. By the time he left, it had received over $93 million in donations and was in a position to grow even more in the coming years. United Negro College Fund and Time Inc., joint press release, November 11, 1963; James P. Brawley to W. J. Trent Jr., February 15, 1964.

INDEX

Notes:

WJT refers to William Johnson Trent

Trent Jr. refers to William Johnson Trent, Jr.

Names enclosed in quotation marks are nicknames and may have been used in the text to refer to the individual

Page numbers in *italics* refer to pages containing photographs.

A

African Methodist Episcopal (AME) Zion Church: creation, iii, 13; liturgical style, 152; expansion to the South, 13–14; creating schools, iv, 16; financial support of Livingstone College, 32, 194, 216, 217; missionary society of, 295n62; connection to Masons, 177–178; publications of, 44, 134, 178, 184–185, 203, 330n170; supporting liberty for people of Cuba, 94; Quadrennial Christian Education Convention, 235–236; sesquicentennial celebration, 259–261, 347n79; China Grove church, 25–26; Clinton Chapel, 5, 38–39; Grace AME Zion church, 38–39, 131, 152, 301n205, 336n66; Soldiers Memorial AME Zion Church, 207, 336n73

Aggrey, Kwegyir, *140*; arrival at Livingstone College, 81–82; friendship with WJT, 132, 135–136, 161, 240; at wedding of WJT and Anna Belle, 121–122; marriage, 121; writing about wedding of WJT and Maggie, 132; children, 204, 209, 323n224; credentials, 81–82; pastoral appointments, 207; career advancement, 134, 209; considered for Livingstone College presidency, 185; at announcement of WJT as Livingstone College president, 190; on Phelps-Stokes Commission, 178, 185; return to Gold Coast as vice-principal of Achimota School, 193; death, 209

Aggrey, Rose "Rosebud" Rudolf (formerly Douglass), 121, 135, 193, 205, 206–207, 209, 323n224

Alston, Primus, 38, 53

AME Zion Church. *See* African Methodist Episcopal (AME) Zion Church

American Association of Educators of Colored Youth, 67–69, 308n143

American Negro Exposition, 230

Anderson, J. B., 188

Anderson, Marian, 208, 270, 347n98

Andrew Carnegie Library, *144*, 191–192, 199, 203, 208, 210, 263–264, 274, 280, 332n1, 347n98

antilynching legislation, 265, 266, 348n107. *See also* lynching

Armstrong, Samuel Chapman, 33

Asheville, North Carolina, 108–109, 117, 318n127

Association of Colored Women's Clubs, 207

Atkins, Simon, 59, 60, 67, 68, 79, 107, 306n86

Atlanta, GA: black troops returning after Spanish American War, 103; at beginning of 20th century, 149–151; creation of black middle class in, 150–151; known as "black Athens", 135; commercial black Atlanta, 172–173; primary and secondary education in, 152, 162, 182, 324n31, 326nn87–88; segregation in, 149–150; racial violence in, 128–129, 150, 169

Atlanta Colored Music Festival Association, 176

Atlanta Cotton States and International Exposition, 81

Atlanta fire (1917), 163–164

Atlanta Mutual Life Insurance Company, 161–162

Atlanta riot (1906), 128–129, 150

Atlanta School of Social Work, 176, 329n151

Atlanta University, 151, 152, 162, 219